# SUMMER JOB BRITAIN 2003

# SUMMER JOBS BRITAIN 2003

## Including Vacation Traineeships & Internships

EDITORS

**Andrew James
David Woodworth**

Assisted by Katie Lydon

Distributed in the USA by
The Globe Pequot Press, Guilford, Connecticut

**Published annually by
Vacation Work, 9 Park End Street, Oxford**
www.vacationwork.co.uk

Thirty fourth edition

SUMMER JOBS IN BRITAIN

Copyright © Vacation Work 2003

No part of this publication may be reproduced or transmitted in any form or by any means without the prior written permission of the publisher.

ISBN 1-85458-270-4 (hardback)
ISBN 1-85458-269-0 (softback)

ISSN 0143 3490

Statement for the purposes of
The Employment Agencies Act 1973:
The price of **Summer Jobs in Britain**
is £15.95 (hardback) or £9.99 (softback) and is for the book and
the information contained therein; it is not refundable.

Cover design by Miller Craig & Cocking Design Partnership

Maps by Andrea Pullen

Typeset by Brendan Cole

Printed and bound in Italy by Legoprint SpA, Trento

# Preface

For the past few years every edition of **Summer Jobs in Britain** has contained more jobs than its predecessor, and this edition for 2003 is no exception. Whether you are looking for a job to occupy mind or body and whether your aim is to improve your bank balance, enhance your CV or to help others, we hope that you will find what you are looking for in these pages.

The summer has always been a period when employers in Britain look for large numbers of additional staff. Even when the recession of the last decade was at its worst people still, for example, ate fruit and vegetables and went on holiday, so agriculture and tourism continued to provide a reliable source of short-term work. **Summer Jobs in Britain** is designed to help you in your search for a job, whether you wish to work near home or further afield. Alongside the many vacancies in tourism and agriculture the book features a growing **Vacation Traineeships & Internships** section, as well as other more varied work ranging from archaeological digs to providing sports tuition.

In this book we have collected details of job vacancies supplied to us by employers in England, Scotland, Wales and Northern Ireland. The jobs have been arranged in regional chapters under the following headings: Business & Industry, Children, Holiday Centres & Amusements, Hotels & Catering, Language Schools, Medical, Outdoor, Sport, Voluntary Work and Vacation Traineeships & Internships, the latter providing on-the-job work experience for students in business and industry.

Many employers in the book express a willingness to take on overseas applicants. While nationals of EU and EEA countries, young nationals of Commonwealth countries and American students can seek work in the UK without too much difficulty, it can be hard for most other foreign citizens. Nevertheless, there are a number of special schemes recognised by the Home Office which give non-EU nationals the opportunity to work for a limited period in this country. Detailed information is given about all such programmes in the introduction.

The companies and individuals listed in **Summer Jobs in Britain** are for job-seekers to apply to directly; the publishers cannot undertake to contact individual employers or to offer assistance in arranging specific jobs.

The Directory is an annual publication and is VALID FOR 2003 ONLY. A thoroughly revised edition for 2004 will be published in November 2003.

Andrew James<br>
David Woodworth<br>
Oxford, October 2002

# Contents

|   | Page |
|---|---|
| **Preface** | 5 |

**Working this Summer** Overview –
Business and Industry – Children – Holiday Centres and Amusements – Hotels and Catering – Language Schools – Medical – Outdoor – Sport – Voluntary Work – Vacation Traineeships & Internships – Au Pairs, Home Helps and Paying Guest Agencies – Further Sources of Information and Employment ..................................................................... 8

**Tax and the Minimum Wage** ........................................................................ 22

**Creating Your Own Job** ................................................................................ 23

**Tips on Applying for a Job** ........................................................................... 24

**Work Permits and Special Schemes**
   *For EEA Citizens*
   *For Non-EEA Citizens*: Citizens of Commonwealth Countries – Students from North America – Seasonal Agricultural Work Scheme – Voluntary Work – Traineeships & Internships – Non EEA Students Studying in the UK – Au Pairs ........................................ 26

**Abbreviations and Glossary of Qualifications** ........................................... 29

## The Directory

| | | |
|---|---|---|
| **Nationwide** – | Organisations which have branches in numerous parts of Britain ........................................ | 30 |
| **1. London and the Home Counties** | – Berkshire, Buckinghamshire Hertfordshire, London, Middlesex, Surrey ............ | 65 |
| **2. The West Country** | – Cornwall, Devon, Dorset, Gloucestershire, Somerset, Wiltshire .................. | 109 |
| **3. The South Coast** | – Channel Islands, Hampshire, Isle of Wight, Kent, West Sussex, East Sussex .......................... | 138 |
| **4. East Anglia** | – Cambridgeshire, Essex, Norfolk, Suffolk .......... | 170 |
| **5. The Midlands** | – Bedfordshire, Cheshire, Derbyshire, Herefordshire, Leicestershire, Lincolnshire, Northamptonshire, Nottinghamshire, Oxfordshire, Shropshire, Staffordshire, Warwickshire, West Midlands, Worcestershire ........................................................ | 188 |
| **6. The North** | – Cumbria, County Durham, Greater Manchester, Isle of Man, Lancashire, Merseyside, Northumberland, Tyne & Wear, Yorkshire ...................................... | 221 |

**7. Scotland** ..................................................................................................... 245
**8. Wales and Northern Ireland** .................................................................... 272
**Au Pairs, Home Helps and Paying Guest Agencies** .................................. 287
**Useful Publications** ...................................................................................... 297

# Working this Summer

## Overview

This book goes to the printers in the midst of some economic uncertainty and confusion. Recent events have precipitated national and international close shaves with recession. However, while the stock market has suffered and some industries, notably manufacturing (down 5.3% in June 2002, to a 23-year low) and telecoms have contracted, consumer confidence has remained buoyant, held up by low interest rates. Unemployment figures have fluctuated slightly but by August 2002 they were at a 27-year low (5.2%), and the prospects for finding summer work in 2003 are favourable. Recent surveys have estimated that up to 80% of organisations need temporary workers just to cover staff summer holidays – this indicates huge potential without even considering the numbers of seasonal vacancies the summer brings.

With the advent of tuition fees and scrapping of grants for students in Britain, finding a holiday job to keep finances ticking over is increasingly important for undergraduates – a recent Barclays survey found that 77% of students work in the summer. The National Union of Students recently estimated that the average student will now leave university with accumulated debts of £12,500. As this book proves, however, there are plenty of jobs around to help ease the burden.

## CATEGORIES OF WORK

To make this book easier to use we have divided the jobs listed into the following categories.

### Business and Industry

This category includes working as *Drivers, Temps, Office Workers, Labourers and Cashiers*, amongst others.

**Temping.** Britain has the largest temporary workforce in Europe, with over 1 million agency workers, and it is widely expected to continue to grow. Work as a 'temp' involves providing short term cover for staff away on holiday, sick leave etc., and is usually arranged by an agency. Jobs are available in virtually all corners of business and industry, though the majority are clerical/office-based and favour those with secretarial or computer skills, or experience of an office environment.

Temping work is attractive as it is available at any time of the year (though much more in popular holiday periods), can offer flexible hours, and can be found at short notice. Length of placements is immensely variable and so you can often decide which weeks you would like to work, as opposed to committing to a full summer of work. Using temporary staff is increasingly popular with employers, especially small companies who need to easily pick up and discard skilled staff to cope with peaks and troughs in business. Current economic uncertainty can also be a bonus for temps - companies are more likely to bolster themselves against recession by avoiding commitment to new permanent staff.

Another bonus is that temping can be extremely lucrative, particularly for those with relevant qualifications or skills in word processing, the use of popular software packages and switchboard. The average temping pay in London is £10 per hour before tax, but some office-based jobs pay hourly rates well into the teens. However, be prepared for anything as low as £4.50 depending on skill level and location. Temping can also be valuable to those looking for more vocational experience as well as cash over the summer. You could secure a placement in a sector where internship schemes are rare, such as marketing or media, giving you vital insight and also an edge over other candidates if you eventually apply for permanent jobs in that sector. Even if you later target a different sector, having demonstrated and practised transferable skills as a temp will help secure employment.

In addition to the agencies listed in this book, most towns have several agencies specialising in temporary work. If you are looking for more than financial reward, it pays to be choosy, as different agencies specialise in different areas – for example, Judy Fisher Associates (☎020-7437 2277) carries only media placements. To find agencies in your area, look under *Employment Agencies* in the *Yellow Pages* or try the employment agencies' association at www.rec.uk.com.

**Shop Work.** Recent developments in retail mean that there is sizeable demand for extra staff in the summer. The explosion of out-of-town retail parks with huge stores, and the new concept of the super or 'extra' store, demonstrated in Walmart's ASDA take-over and the new B&Q Warehouse stores has created large numbers of casual vacancies. The trend for late-night and 24-hour shopping has prompted similar vacancies in supermarkets. Those willing to work antisocial hours are in demand, and working the night shift generally ensures a significantly bigger pay packet. Most jobs are part-time, but if a full-time summer job becomes available, already working there makes you more likely to be chosen as a replacement.

If you are applying for a full time job, then be aware that more upmarket stores like Marks & Spencer will favour applicants with an interest in eventually working there permanently. Other stores with less emphasis on continuous customer service are less picky. Seasonal demand is also raised by tourism and permanent staff going on holiday.

**Sales.** The idea of employment as a sales person conjures up outdated images of traipsing from house to house trying to sell dusters or encyclopaedias. While this type of work still exists, telesales (which involves selling a product over the telephone) is a more popular method nowadays, often operating from large purpose built call centres. *The Times* newspaper recently referred to the industry as 'mushrooming', and as internet shopping becomes more popular and retail space becomes more expensive, the number of centres is expected to grow. Call centre staff tend to be young, and staff turnover high, as there is sometimes a burn-out problem when staff may be continuously monitored to assess their performance. In view of the long term future of the industry, though, effort is now being made to enhance the working environment. Pay is often fairly good – Recruitment UK estimates £6-8+ per hour. Hours can be flexible as many firms open well into the evening to cater for customers who are at work all day.

A good telephone manner may be all you need to get a sales job with a holiday tour operator, though the ability to speak a European language will give you the edge over monolinguists; work with holiday companies needs to be arranged early, in the spring. Some companies may offer pay solely on a commission basis; it is wise to check whether you will be dealing with customers looking to buy, as with holiday companies, or making unsolicited 'cold calls', for which you may need to be a bit more thick-skinned and may earn less commission. Make sure you know the exact conditions before you sign a contract.

**Cleaning.** Office and industrial cleaning is another area that offers temporary vacancies. Most cleaning companies prefer to employ staff for long periods, but they will occasionally take people on temporarily for jobs such as cleaning newly-built or refurbished office blocks, or for the annual deep-clean of those factories which still shut down for a couple of weeks each summer. Local councils are sometimes a good source of such jobs, as they tend to implement big clean-ups of local schools and facilities once term finishes.

**Factory Work.** Spending the summer on a production line may not be your idea of fun, but the potential for work in this field is good. The factories most likely to require extra staff are those preparing for the Christmas rush, as they begin to increase production in August, or those that deal with the packaging and processing of seasonal food. Huge quantities of fruit and vegetables are harvested between late spring and early autumn and must be preserved by canning or freezing. The main vacancies in this business are for line workers, packers and delivery drivers.

Be prepared for early mornings, shift work and high levels of boredom. Pay is not outstanding, but starts at around £4.50, and shift work can be much more lucrative.

## Children

This category includes opportunities as *Leaders, Playworkers, Instructors* and even *Managers*.

In response to the desperation of parents trying to occupy their children in the long summer holidays, recent years have seen a boom in American style holiday centres, camps and playschemes for the younger generation. These have become increasingly important as more parents go out to work and private child-care costs rocket. Playschemes and centres vary in size and content; some are run by big operating chains, like PGL, and some by local councils. Work for the latter may be on a voluntary basis as budgets are tight. The long term potential for work in this area is high – PGL reports that it has bookings until 2008.

For these jobs, applicants will often not require qualifications. New UK legislation, however, means that many employers will require successful applicants intending to work with children to undergo a police check. Where employers have mentioned it, it is listed in the book, but be aware that it may be expected even if not mentioned in the advert. Some centres no longer offer more dangerous sports, such as rifle-shooting or even climbing, in response to parental fears, and those that do will require solid qualifications from teaching staff. Preference is likely to be given to those with experience of working with children. Trainee primary school teachers are particularly well suited.

Jobs on holiday camps can vary from teaching sports to organising discos. Since much of the work is similar to that in camps geared towards children and/or adults, more details are given below under *Holiday Centres*.

## Holiday Centres and Amusements

**Tourism.** Although the annual summer congestion around Britain's airports testifies to the fact that most families now prefer to holiday abroad rather than here, the British tourist industry remains huge. The trend for short breaks and long weekends away within the UK is increasing, with the West Country the most popular destination area. This pattern looks set to continue, as no-frills airlines offer internal flights that work out cheaper (and much quicker) than taking the train; Easyjet now flies from London to Newquay, making the south-west a viable weekend destination for many more people. New attractions such as the Eden Project in Cornwall and the Imperial War Museum in Manchester are boosting regional tourism, while events like the Commonwealth Games 2002 have encouraged international interest in Britain.

All of this is working to counter the effects of the foot and mouth outbreak of 2001, which cost the tourist industry over £5 billion when footpaths and swathes of countryside were left closed for over six months. However, at the time of writing Britain had been declared free of foot and mouth for nine months and the tourist industry was recovering, and was in some places better than before, having used the devastation of the disease as a good incentive for change. Global tourism also suffered a blow in September 2001 with the attacks on the World Trade Center, but initial fear of international travel boosted domestic tourism. Recent figures suggest that Britain's £14 billion inbound tourist industry has not been too badly affected – April 2002 showed a 10% increase in foreign visitors on the previous year.

Television and films are a major force in marketing different regions as more and more tourists want to retrace the steps of film stars and see for themselves the setting of their favourite film. The British film industry's recent international successes, including *Notting Hill* and *Bridget Jones' Diary*, have increased tourist interest in London and the UK as a whole. Glen Nevis in Scotland annually attracted over a million *Braveheart* fans, while Whitby, the setting for TV's *Heartbeat* series, continues to attract hordes of nostalgic viewers.

**Holiday Centres.** One of the greatest recent trends in UK tourism has been the growth of holiday camps, activity centres and theme parks. These centres are some of the largest seasonal employers in the country. Not only do they take on thousands of staff between them - the largest can take on hundreds each - but they also offer a diverse range of jobs, both unskilled and skilled. Many chains of holiday centres, such as Butlins Skyline, have been refurbished and updated, distancing themselves from the 'Hi-De-Hi' image, and may require receptionists, lifeguards, car park attendants, entertainers, shop assistants and so on. Chains of leisure resorts like CenterParcs and Oasis have sprung up to capitalise on the demand for short fitness-enhancing breaks, and so are likely to want specialised sports instructors as well as offering unskilled employment. As a result of the number and type of posts offered, they are often popular and competitive - the opportunity to spend a summer working with many other young people in a holiday environment can prove quite attractive. It is essential to apply as soon as possible because many of the big employers start recruitment early in the year. Although extra people are hired later in the season, to cover bank holidays and busy weeks, these are frequently contacted from a reserve list complied from the surplus of earlier applications.

If you fail to find employment with one of the centres listed in the book, try a speculative, personal approach. The British Tourist Authority (☎020-8846 9000; www.travelengland.org.uk) can provide information on the major theme and leisure parks throughout England. Visit Scotland (☎0131-332 2433; www.visitscotland.com) and the Wales Tourist Board (☎029-2049 9909; www.visitwales.com) provide the same information for Scotland and Wales. The book *Explorer Britain* (AA Publishing, £14.99) also provides a comprehensive directory of attractions that you might write to.

# Hotels and Catering

Hotels and catering establishments offer a range of jobs including work as *Waiting, Bar and Chamber Staff, Receptionists, Chefs and Kitchen Assistants.*

Many of the temporary hotel and restaurant jobs during the summer season are to be found in the country's main tourist resorts and beauty spots. Big hotel chains may provide the best opportunities for those based in or near cities, as they employ large numbers of staff and have a relatively fast turnover, meaning short term vacancies can be available at any time of the year. Several chains have also increased their trade and therefore employment needs by offering weekend package breaks – the Hilton Group is doing this and reported a 15% increase in sales. The appearance of hotels at most large service stations around the country provides another source of potential work. The disadvantage is that major chains are less likely to provide accommodation and more likely to want, and be able to get, experienced and trained staff for certain duties.

Working in a large and impersonal hotel in a city is likely to be more regimented and formal than spending the summer in an independent, family-run guest house on the coast, and so perhaps less friendly and enjoyable (unless you end up working for Basil Fawlty). If you choose a remote area with a lower cost of living and/or fewer opportunities to spend, such as the Scottish Highlands or the Black Mountains, you will find it easier to save the money you earn. Many hotels start advertising for summer staff before Easter, and generally applicants who can work for the entire season are preferred.

Hotel work can be hard and tiring, and you are usually expected to work shifts, sometimes at unsociable hours. Hotel and restaurant kitchens are particularly hot and frantic, with chefs notorious for their short tempers. On good days, however, hotel work is lively, varied and can be exciting. Before taking up a job offer, though, always ask for precise details about your duties. Many job titles do not provide a clear definition of the work and may vary in meaning between different establishments: 'kitchen porter', for example, may translate as 'general dogsbody' in one place, and refer to a specific role in another. Small hotels tend to employ general assistants for a range of duties as diverse as cleaning toilets to working on reception.

Fast food restaurants generally have a high turnover of staff at any time of the year; the main chains, including McDonalds and Pizza Hut, employ large numbers of people throughout the country. Motorway service stations and roadside restaurants like Little Chef also need extra workers in the summer.

Unless you are applying to be a chef, you will seldom require qualifications to work in a hotel or restaurant; while experience is often preferred, it is by no means always essential. A neat appearance and resilient nature may be enough, though increasingly language skills can be an advantage.

**Wages.** Standard pay in bars and restaurants tends to be around £4.50-£5 an hour, but higher for silver service and in London, and usually lower for fast food restaurants. Hotels usually offer a similar rate, but often offer added perks like use of their leisure facilities. Tips can be an often substantial bonus to waiting and bar staff, but be aware that centrally pooled and divided tips may be included in the National Minimum Wage.

**Youth Hostels.** The YHA employs Seasonal Assistant Wardens to help run its 230 Youth Hostels in England and Wales. Work is available for varying periods between February and October. Contact details for further information about working in a Youth Hostel can be found in the entry in the Nationwide chapter.

# Language Schools

The staff needs of language schools are principally for *EFL Teachers and Social Organisers*.

Teaching English as a foreign language (TEFL) is perhaps no longer the major growth industry it was a decade ago, but it still offers a large number of summer jobs that often pay better than average. Starting from around June, people of all nationalities and ages, though usually teenagers and students, come to Britain to learn or improve their English and absorb some British culture. The schools that cater for them proliferate along the south coast and in major university/tourist cities like Oxford, Cambridge, Edinburgh and London.

Most British language schools require their teachers to have a TEFL qualification, though some will take on graduates with an English or languages degree, or PGCE students; a few employ undergraduates in those disciplines. There are a vast number of TEFL courses and qualifications on offer, varying widely in length, location and cost. Check the advertisements for those that seem most respected before committing to a course. One of the most widely recognised and required certificate is the Cambridge CELTA. Courses take place in a variety of national and international locations, and usually take four weeks (contact University of Cambridge Local Examinations Syndicate, Syndicate Buildings, 1 Hills Road, Cambridge CB1 2EU; ☎01223-553355; e-mail efl@ucles.org.uk; www.cambridge-efl.org.uk).

The other major certificate is awarded by Trinity College London (Trinity College London, 89 Albert Embankment, London SE1 7TP; ☎020-7820 6100; fax 020-7820 6161; e-mail tesol@trinitycollege.co.uk), which stipulates a minimum of 130 hours of teaching over a 4 week period (or part-time over a longer period). Many of the courses advertised cost between £750 and £1,000, for some of which exam and accommodation costs are included. For a full guide to TEFL courses, see the *ELT International Careers Guide* (price £12.95 plus £2 postage, distributed by Book Systems Plus, BSP House, Station Road, Linton, Cambridgeshire CB1 6NW; ☎01223-894870; fax 01223-894871) which includes tables comparing costs, duration, dates and locations.

The majority of residential language schools often take on staff to work as social supervisors and organisers, both at the school outside of teaching time and on day trips. The bigger ones may also require sports and activity instructors. These positions frequently require no qualifications other than interest and an ability to work with young people.

# Medical

This category consists largely of opportunities for *Nurses and Care and Support Workers*.

Britain's care industry is currently suffering both from a shortage of health professionals and the pressure of an ageing population. Much of the work available is with the elderly, though some is available with the sick and disabled (applicants in these areas should be aware that new UK legislation may require police checks on those intending to work with vulnerable adults). This year has seen a massive increase in the number of nursing agencies looking for staff – often stating a need for unlimited numbers of workers all year round. Recent figures listed at www.doh.gov.uk indicated a sharp increase in vacancies in almost all areas of the health industry; 3.2% of all general nursing posts are vacant for more than 3 months. In 2002 REC ranked the medical sector first in terms of need for temporary staff – for the second year.

Overall, then, there should be little difficulty in finding work in this field. Often agencies do not even require experienced applicants as on-the-job training is given. Generally, though, applicants must be over 18 and having your own transport can be an advantage. In addition to the vacancies in this book, specialist nursing agencies can be found in the Yellow Pages or at www.rec.co.uk.

# Outdoor

The majority of vacancies in this category are for *Fruit Pickers, Farm Staff and Marquee Erectors*.

**Agriculture.** While increased mechanisation has reduced the number of pickers required at harvest time, agriculture remains the second largest source of seasonal work after tourism. Soft fruit is still hand-picked, and since some other crops don't necessarily ripen at the same time machines can't always be used for them. Furthermore, fruit sold in supermarkets must comply with increasingly precise European legislation on size and shape, and so extra staff are needed to help with selection. However, the rise in numbers of pick-your-own farms has affected the number of picking jobs in some places.

Food processing factories cannot pick their own, and so pickers and packers will always be required. In recent years tons of fruit has gone unpicked because of a shortage of seasonal workers to pick them. In February 2002 the government answered the calls of farmers to alter employment and immigration laws to supply them with enough willing foreign workers; the Seasonal Workers Agricultural Scheme and Working Holidays Scheme will now be extended, and applicants from Eastern European EU candidate countries will be eligible.

The best areas for summer fruit and vegetable picking work in the summer are from the Vale of Evesham over to the River Wye (in the Midlands), Kent, Lincolnshire, East Anglia (especially the Fens) and north of the Tay in Scotland (especially Perthshire). Harvest types and times vary between regions, so raspberries may ripen two weeks later in Scotland than in the south of England. Strawberries and gooseberries are among the first fruits to ripen in southern Britain, usually in June. Processing and packing work is generally available in the Vale of Evesham after the main harvest season. Work involving harvesting outdoor salad crops is also available in the Hampshire and West Sussex area.

Kent and Herefordshire are the centres of hop picking, and the harvest is in September. A high degree of mechanisation is now used, but people are still needed to drive tractors, strip hop flowers from vines and so on. Women can be automatically allocated the indoor work, so make it clear if you are looking for an outdoor job.

The apple harvest runs from August until mid-October and offers traditionally more lucrative work. The industry is currently threatened by an increasing number of cheap foreign imports, but recent moves attempting to commit supermarkets to certain quotas of home produce may shore it up.

The easy accessibility of French hypermarkets with their cheap wine, and the scores of less expensive New World brands appearing in supermarkets have similarly destabilised the fledgling British wine industry. However, some vineyards, mainly on the South Coast, may still require workers, though the grape harvest is less predictable as the sugar content depends on the often elusive sun. There are 400 vineyards in the UK – 60 commercial and the rest private hobbies. For more information, contact the UK Vineyard Association (☎01728-638080).

Over the last two decades the number of areas of farmland devoted to cherry growing has shrunk from over 4,000 acres to under 800. However, a new variety of dwarf tree recently developed by the supermarket chain Tesco may begin to rejuvenate the industry, not least because workers will not have to climb ladders to reach the fruit, as previously.

While fruit picking is generally short term, it is possible to string several jobs together by following ripening crops around the country, or by choosing a farm with several crops that will ripen in sequence. On the spot applications are often productive, with no interview required, and it is sometimes possible to secure employment at very short notice (note that most farmers prefer the first approach to be via telephone). Jobs available may be increased by later or better harvests, by the farmer underestimating the number of pickers required, or by workers with other commitments leaving before the harvest is over. Conversely, even if you have secured a position, bad weather may mean no work on a particular day, and lost income.

Picking fruit can be exhausting and backbreaking – it is wise to watch more experienced workers to pick up any good techniques – although some farms have tried to make things easier for pickers, for example by growing strawberries on tables so they can be picked comfortably from a standing position. Due to the economy and temporary nature of much accommodation offered by farmers, a comfortable night's sleep may not always follow a tiring day's work. Some provide comfortable bunkhouses and meals, but others require you to bring your own tent and cater for yourself. Some provide communal cooking facilities, but these can sometimes be in a poor state of cleanliness as upkeep is no-one's direct responsibility. The Food and Farming Information Service also advises workers to take out insurance to cover personal belongings, and to visit farms in advance if possible.

The new website Fruitfuljobs.com can help people find jobs with accommodation on UK farms and although the main season runs from March to October work is available throughout the year. For further details see their entry under *Websites* in the *Worldwide* chapter.

Farmers can recruit students from any part of the EU. In addition, some farms take part in the Seasonal Agricultural Workers scheme, which enables them to recruit student pickers from outside the EU. This is done through the organisations Concordia (YSV) Ltd (Heversham House, 2nd Floor, 20/22 Boundary Road, Hove, East Sussex BN3 4ET; ☎01273-422293; fax 01273-422443) and HOPS(GB) (YFC Centre, NAC, Stoneleigh Park, Kenilworth, Warwickshire CV8 2LG (☎02476-857206; fax 02476-857229). These organisations accept only overseas applicants for fruit and vegetable harvesting and all participants must pay a registration fee. In return Concordia and HOPS(GB) exercise control over participating farms and expect certain standards. The farms take from one up to as many as several hundred workers at one time, of many different nationalities, often largely from southern and eastern Europe. Further information about the Seasonal Agricultural Workers scheme is given under *Work Permits and Special Schemes*.

In addition to harvesting work, there are also opportunities for other types of farm work, as a general assistant on a family farm or as a groom, for example. Both these and picking jobs are listed in the Outdoor sections of the regional chapters in the book. Some organic farms take on volunteers: for details of one scheme see the entry for WWOOF in the Voluntary Work section in the *Nationwide* chapter.

*Wages.* Pay varies according to the fruit and the difficulty involved in the picking process. Many farmers pay piecework rates, which means that you are paid according to the quantity you pick. This method can be very satisfactory when a harvest is at its peak but when fruit is scarce earning more than the minimum can be much more difficult. However, even if you are paid on a piece work basis the amount you earn for each hour worked must average the rates set out in the Agricultural Wages Order. Before starting work, you should obtain a copy of the current order from the Agricultural Wages Board. If you have any queries about the rate you are being paid, the Agricultural Wages Board Regional Office staff should be able to advise you. Be prepared to cope with frustration when three days of rain means no picking and therefore no wages.

The Agricultural Wages Board (Nobel House, 17 Smith Square, London SW1P 3JR) sets minimum weekly and hourly rates for agricultural workers in England and

Wales. At the time of writing, for standard workers aged 19 and over in England and Wales (different rates apply in Scotland and Northern Ireland) the minimum wage was £4.77 an hour and £7.16 for overtime. For casual workers who are engaged by the hour or the day the minimum rate for workers aged 19 was £4.10 (£6.15 for overtime). The rates for younger workers are lower. It is anticipated that a new Wages Order will have come into force on October 1 2002.

Many farmers calculate wages by a combination of piecework and hourly rates of pay. Remember that the farmer is legally obliged to pay you at least the appropriate minimum rate for your age for the hours worked. Ask exactly how much you will be paid before accepting a job: some people have been paid as little as 12p for picking a pound of strawberries. The Department for Environment, Food and Rural Affairs (DEFRA) has a helpline for both employers and employees who want to know more about the Agricultural Wages Order: the number for England and Wales is 0845-0000134.

*Gangmasters.* Gangmasters can be involved in the recruitment of seasonal summer staff on farms. While most gangmasters treat their workers fairly, a significant minority could exploit their workers in some way. Exploitation can take different forms and might involve underpayment of wages, unsafe working conditions, use of illegal workers, and illegal deductions from pay for transport and accommodation. If you have any concerns about your rights, you should ask for a copy of the leaflet *Planting, Picking or Packing Agricultural Produce? Your Rights Explained* from DEFRA Publications (☎0645-556000; Website www.defra.gov.uk) or ring their Helpline on 0645-335577.

*Useful Addresses.* Many farmers have entries in this book, but you may find a local farm which is too small to need to advertise nationally. Economic pressures have forced farmers to diversify, and an increasing number of farms are being opened to the public, sometimes generating extra jobs for guides, cleaners and so on. Temporary jobs are sometimes advertised in *Farmers Weekly*, though prospective employers are likely to require some experience.

Organic farms often rely on voluntary assistance too. EU volunteers should send a s.a.e. to WWOOF (World Wide Opportunities on Organic Farms), PO Box 2675, Lewes, Sussex BN7 1RB for details of membership and the opportunities available on organic farms in the UK and worldwide throughout the year. In return for hard work, workers receive free meals, accommodation, the opportunity to learn and transport to and from the local station.

**Removals and Marquee Work.** While manual jobs with removal firms are available at any time of year, the summer is a real boom time for marquee erectors. During the sunny season there is a never-ending round of agricultural shows, festivals, wedding receptions and so on. And while a village fair may require just one marquee, a music festival will require a whole range of tents plus large amounts of furniture and equipment. All this has to be loaded and unloaded from lorries, as well as driven to and from a depot; for this and other driving work possession of an HGV driving licence would be a useful advantage. Overtime is often available, so marquee work can be lucrative. The disadvantage for women is that most employers specify a minimum height for loading work and take on only men.

# Sport

The range of jobs under this category includes, amongst others, *Instructors, Coaches, Boat Crew, Stable Staff, and Walk Leaders*.

Sports holiday centres often specialise in sea, river or mountain activities and as such are often found in remote and beautiful places such as Scotland and the Lake District. They almost always need to recruit live-in workers. While there are opportunities for unskilled staff, most vacancies are for sports instructors, teachers and camp managers. Applicants will normally require governing-body qualifications and a reasonable amount of experience; growing concern about insufficient supervision and instruction at activity centres in the past has resulted in tougher new controls.

Sources of information for anyone choosing to approach an outdoor activity centre independently, on the off-chance of finding a vacancy, include *The Action Guide to Britain* (Harvill Press, £12.99).

Recent sporting events and successes have increased interest in certain areas of sport, and if you have qualifications in these areas then your chances of finding work could be increased. *Watersports*, for example, are increasingly popular as advances in wetsuit and equipment technology mean participants no longer have to freeze in British coastal waters and lakes, and that beginners can experience relative success very early. Teaching centres along the south and west coasts particularly are keen to recruit windsurfing, sailing and canoeing instructors in ever-increasing numbers. Several lake centres also advertise in this book.

Anyone with life-saving qualifications could consider working as a lifeguard at a leisure centre. Several local authorities advertise such vacancies in this book.

*Riding:* Riding schools and trekking centres (which are particularly common in Wales) take on experienced riders. Since a lot of the work is dealing with groups, the ability to get on well with people is also important.

There might be a riding school or holiday centre in your area where you could ask about the possibility of a temporary job. The British Horse Society (☎ 0870-120 2244; fax 01926-707800; e-mail enquiry@bhs.org.uk; www.bhs.org.uk) publishes a register of 700+ approved riding centres called *Where to Ride and Train*, price £2. This is available by mail order from the BHS Bookshop, Stoneleigh Deer Park, Kenilworth, Warwickshire CV8 2XZ (☎ 01926-707700); the list is also available on the above website.

The Association of British Riding Schools (Queen's Chambers, Office No. 2, 38-40 Queen Street, Penzance, Cornwall TR18 4BH) lists a directory of its members on its website, www.abrs.org. You should also contact them for information about trekking holidays and centres. Employment can also be found with racing stables, which sometimes require the stable staff they recruit to ride their horses.

If you are looking for employment as a sports coach, it is advisable to check the listings for children's camps as they often also require qualified instructors.

# Voluntary Work

The category of voluntary work encompasses a large range of activities including *Archaeology, Children, Conservation and the Environment, Heritage, Physically/ Mentally Disabled, Social and Community Schemes and Workcamps.*

Many organisations throughout the UK need volunteers to help with a host of different types of work, from caring for people with disabilities or the elderly to taking part in conservation and archaeological projects.

Voluntary experience can provide the dual benefit of giving you an insight into a particular area of work and boosting your CV. Recent newspaper features have suggested that employers look favourably on candidates with voluntary work on their CVs, since this indicates skill acquisition and development. Some organisations represent sectors, such as arts administration, that are particularly difficult to get into as a graduate – experience with them could give you an edge over other candidates in the future. Most of the voluntary organisations in this book do not require specific skills; willingness and enthusiasm are the most important attributes.

Working with people with special needs is both physically and emotionally demanding. However, many volunteers find the challenge to be both a rewarding and maturing experience. Most organisations provide free board and lodging, and sometimes a small amount of pocket money and help with travel expenses. Many social or community projects need volunteers all year round, but there is always a demand in the summer for extra staff to help with outings and holidays.

Conservation and archaeological projects are increasingly popular. They do tend, however, to be short term and often require a contribution from the volunteer. The level of contribution depends on what it is for; some placements simply need a donation to cover board, lodging and travel, while others are arranged by agencies that will require a fee.

Museums, stately homes and gardens frequently operate on a very tight budget and may be pleased to receive offers of voluntary help; some may even pay a small wage. They will often offer accommodation and flexible working hours, to allow you to see some of the local area. *Historic Houses, Castles and Gardens (incorporating Museums & Galleries*, price £7.95, is published by Johansens and is crammed full of addresses. *The National Trust Handbook*, which lists all the UK properties open to the public, is free with membership or available from all good bookshops for £4.50. The Trust also produces a variety of free leaflets about properties in certain areas.

Festivals and events are a good source of temporary voluntary work, though very short term. Cheltenham Festival of Literature and Birmingham Film and TV Festival are among the larger advertisers here – you can apply personally to smaller local events, particularly in university or historical towns. You might be paid travel and other expenses and will usually get free entrance to all the events of the festival.

Sources of Information. *The International Directory of Voluntary Work* (£11.95, published by Vacation Work, 9 Park End Street, Oxford OX1 1HJ) has been fully revised and includes information on both short and long-term opportunities. The National Council for Voluntary Organisations (Hamilton House Mailings, Earlstrees Court, Earlstrees Road, Corby NN17 4AX; ☎01536-399016; fax 01536-399012) publishes the *Voluntary Agencies Directory*, price £30 plus £6 postage and packing, which lists over 2,500 organisations countrywide.

The National Centre for Volunteering (☎020-7520 8900; www.volunteering.org.uk; e-mail Volunteering@thecentre.org.uk) is a national database of local volunteering opportunities that is updated annually, and is an excellent source of contact names and addresses of organisations requiring help in your area. It also provides details of Volunteer Bureaux which are found in most big towns and dispense information about, and do some of the recruiting for, local voluntary organisations.

Information on voluntary work in Wales can be obtained from The Wales Council for Voluntary Action: Baltic House, Mount Stuart Square, Cardiff Bay CF10 5FH (☎0870-607 1666; fax 029-2043 1701; e-mail help@wcva.org.uk; www.wcva.org.uk). Offices also in Colwyn Bay (☎01492-539800) and Newtown (☎01938-552379).

# Vacation Traineeships & Internships

This heading covers placements and schemes which aim to provide young people with an opportunity to gain on-the-job training during their holidays. They are variously referred to by firms as 'work placements', 'internships', 'vacation placements', 'training schemes' and a myriad of other names. 'Internships' is originally an American term formerly used only by US-based or international firms, but rapidly gaining currency in the UK. They are generally short-term placements for students lasting from 2 weeks to the whole summer holiday.

Traineeships and internships may not appeal to those wanting a summer job just to have fun or to earn enough money for a holiday or to repay an overdraft. While some employers offer fantastic renumeration, others see the reward as the experience itself and just pay expenses. In the long run, a work placement can prove to have been the most valuable investment of your vacations.

The content and style of traineeships and internships varies from one firm to another. Some, especially large banks, accountants and consultancies, will put you into a position of real responsibility so you can learn the ropes of the business from its centre. Others operate more of a 'work-shadow' scheme where you are expected to follow and observe a member of staff, and perhaps help them with their work. Companies in such areas as computer programming will only recruit applicants who already have particular skills, say C++ programming, and therefore focus on helping you to apply those skills in a business environment, rather than teaching you new skills.

Advertised traineeships and internships tend to be most numerous in areas of Science, Technology and Engineering, since these industries have seen a serious decrease in numbers of students coming into them. In other areas, like finance and law, competition is likely to be strong. Traineeships and internships in oversubscribed areas tend to be the unpaid ones; media and marketing among others. If you are looking for a traineeship in a large blue-chip organisation it is wise to consult their website for details, since they often don't feel it necessary to advertise or to recruit beyond major universities.

**The Advantages of Vacation Training & Internships.** Since the introduction of tuition fees and abolition of grants, the financial rewards of doing a traineeship/internship have become increasingly alluring: many schemes pay impressive salaries. Even so, for many the value of the experience gained far outweighs that of the salary. Traineeships/internships can give you a valuable insight into potential careers, especially as you are likely to be given a meaningful role rather than simple menial tasks. It is an incredible advantage, when looking for permanent jobs, to have had a taste of various industries without having had to make a commitment to any, and perhaps more importantly to have it listed on your CV.

In addition, employers are more likely to value a candidate who spent a summer gaining experience and skills, and probably cultivating a more mature approach to work, than one who worked sporadically at a local pub. When it comes round to interview time for graduate jobs, you will have already been able to practice and will be better prepared as a result. Having done a traineeship/internship will also provide a good source of interview conversation. Employers frequently say that they are looking for work experience, practical business skills, personality and initiative, and if you are able to demonstrate these on your CV a minimum degree requirement for the job may be waived.

Many companies also treat their schemes as extended assessment periods, where while you are getting an insight into them, they can assess your suitability for a permanent position. Some interns leave with a permanent job offer in the bag and even sponsorship for their final year. Even if the company does not make you a job offer, a good reference from them can help you find work elsewhere. Experience in sectors where placements are rare, like media or the arts, can enable you to build up a bank of contacts that would help enormously in future job hunts.

**Experience and Qualifications.** Most employers specify a preferred field of study relevant to the job. Unsurprisingly, arts undergraduates are not generally targetted by engineering or computing firms. The internship schemes of larger companies are geared towards university students, with many specifying further that they must be in their penultimate year of study. Some, however, particularly unpaid and work shadow schemes, will offer work to pre-university students. Others may operate special or informal schemes for those trying to get experience during a gap year or after A-Levels – here a personal approach sometimes pays.

More generally, employers are looking for self-motivated students with a positive attitude, the ability to work well in a team and an aptitude to analyse and solve problems quickly and effectively. If you give the impression that you really want just a holiday job, you are unlikely to be considered for a post.

## Au Pair, Home Help and Paying Guest Agencies

Amongst the types of job to be found in this category are positions for *Au Pairs, Mother's Helps, Playscheme Leaders and Paying Guests*.

**Playschemes.** Most local authorities organise playschemes for children during the summer holidays, as a cheaper alternative to private childcare. Throughout the country dozens of playleaders and assistants are needed to run activities for children of all ages. Cash limits mean that some councils ask specifically for volunteers. Councils will usually advertise in local newspapers a few months before the end of the school term, or you can contact their education or leisure departments to find out what they will be offering.

Domestic Work. Anyone preferring closer contact with children should consider working in a family as a mother's help or (for applicants from overseas) as an Au Pair. This work usually requires some experience and involves light housework and looking after children. Mother's helps and au pairs work to assist the mother, not replace her as a nanny might, and therefore qualifications are not usually necessary.

There are many agencies in the UK which specialise in placing home helps. Details of these and other au pair opportunities are listed in the Au Pair, Home Help and Paying Guest chapter towards the end of the book. If you prefer to find work independently, job advertisements appear in *The Lady* magazine and occasionally in *Horse and Hound*, both available from newsagents.

## Further Sources of Information and Employment

**Jobcentres.** Jobcentre Plus, part of the Government Department for Work and Pensions, runs the Jobcentre Network where a full range of temporary vacancies can be found by searching on touch-screen terminals known as Jobpoints. In London the Hotel & Catering Jobcentre, in Denmark Street, runs a Temporary Desk for those seeking work in the catering and hospitality sectors. At other Jobcentres, such as Fountain Street in Manchester, you can ask to join a Temporary Jobs Register covering a range of employment sectors. Jobcentre Plus, the Government Executive Agency responsible for the network of over 1,000 Jobcentres in Great Britain, advertises all of its vacancies at www.worktrain.gov.uk and on its own website: www.jobcentreplus.gov.uk.

To find the address of your nearest Jobcentre either look in the telephone directory under 'Jobcentre' or look at the website www.jobcentreplus.gov.uk/. Jobcentre vacancies can be accessed by telephone through Employment Service Direct on 0845 6060 234.

Jobseeker Direct (0845-6060-234) is a phone service designed to help you find a full or part-time job. Telephone advisors have access to jobs nationwide and can help match your particular skills and requirements to vacant positions. Anyone without a job can use the service whether or not they are claiming Jobseeker's Allowance. In addition, the self-service Jobpoint terminals located in every Jobcentre give access to a database of over 400,000 vacancies and are available for use by anyone looking for work.

The Jobcentre Plus website www.jobcentreplus.gov.uk also advertises nationwide vacancies, particularly those in more specialised fields: it has access to all the jobs currently available to Jobseeker Direct.

Big companies such as Butlins Skyline like to recruit early and advertise vacancies through their local Jobcentre in the spring. In the summer, many jobs are available on the spot too. The organisers of big local events and farmers, for example, sometimes use Jobcentres to recruit staff.

**Employment Agencies.** While the number of agencies dealing with temporary work in London can be positively daunting, outside the capital the range is much more narrow. It is worth registering with as many agencies as possible in order to enhance your chances of finding work. The jobs offered are frequently office based, though increasingly agencies specialise in different industry sectors. Brook Street Bureau and Reed, which have branches all over the UK, both tend to concentrate on clerical work. Manpower, also with offices nationwide, has information on labouring and warehouse jobs. You can find their addresses under 'Employment Agencies' in the Yellow Pages.

Under the Employment Agencies Act it is illegal for an agency to charge a fee for finding someone a job: agencies make their money by charging the employers.

**The Internet.** The Internet can be an invaluable aid to the jobseeker. Details of new vacancies are posted on www.vacationwork.co.uk, which also has links to other relevant sites.

**National Institutes.** One way of finding out more about Vacation Training opportunities within a specific field is to contact the relevant national professional body or institute. Institutes do not themselves offer traineeships, but may be able to offer general advice and/or give names and addresses of companies within their field. Here are a few – others can be found under *ASSOCIATIONS-TRADE* at www.yell.com.

*Hotel & Catering International Management Association:* 191 Trinity Road, London SW17 7HN (☎020-8772 7400, fax 020-8772 7500).

*Institute of Chartered Accountants in England and Wales:* Gloucester House, 399 Silbury Boulevard, Central Milton Keynes MK9 2HL (Student Recruitment Section: ☎01908-248108; www.icaew.co.uk/careers).

*Institute of Chartered Accountants of Scotland:* Head Office: CA House, 21 Haymarket Yards, Edinburgh EH12 5BH (☎0131-347 0100; fax 0131-347 0105; Website www.icas.org.uk).

*Institute of Public Relations:* 15 Old Trading House, Northburgh Street, London EC1V OPR.

*International Federation of the Periodical Press:* Queen's House 55-56, Lincoln's Inn Fields, London WC21 3NB.

*Royal Institute of British Architects:* 66 Portland Place, London W1N 4AD

*Royal Town Planning Institute:* 41 Botolph Lane, London EC3R 8DL (☎020-7929 9494; fax 020-7929 9490; www.rtpi.org.uk). This organisation runs a Vacation Employment Register which is designed to put prospective employers in touch with planning students on RTPI accredited courses who are looking for work over the summer vacation.

*Society of Financial Advisers.:* 20 Aldermanbury, London EC2V 7HY (☎020-8989 8464; fax 020-7726 0131; e-mail info@sofa.org; www.sofa.org).

## TAX AND NATIONAL INSURANCE

**Income Tax.** Single people are entitled to a personal tax allowance, which means that you don't pay income tax until your yearly earnings exceed £4,615 (2002/3 figure). Few people are likely to earn this much over the vacation. Earnings above the personal allowance attract a tax rate of 10% until they reach £6,535, after which point the rate is 22%.

To avoid paying tax you need to fill out the right form; if your employer uses the PAYE system, new employees will usually be taxed under an 'emergency code' until the Tax Office receives this form from your employer. Students in higher education should fill in form P38(S), and school and college leavers a P46. If you pay any tax before you are put on the correct tax code, then you can claim a rebate during the year if your estimated yearly earnings do not exceed the personal allowance. If you have not been put on the right tax code by the time you leave your job, send a tax rebate claims form to the Tax Office together with your P45, which you will get when you finish work. If you are being paid by cash or cheque, not PAYE, then worrying about codes and rebates should not be necessary. Further information and figures for 2003/4, when available, can be found at www.inlandrevenue.gov.uk.

**National Insurance.** National Insurance contributions are compulsory for employees over 16 years of age if they earn over a certain limit. The rate you pay is calculated according to your wages. Currently, anyone who earns less than £89 a week pays nothing and then 10% of earnings above that figure.

If you require information in addition to that given above, contact the Contributions Agency or the Tax Office (as relevant), www.inlandrevenue.gov.uk or else your local Citizens Advice Bureau.

## The National Minimum Wage

The UK has a national minimum wage which as of October 2002 will be £4.20 per hour for those aged 22 and over and £3.60 per hour for those aged 18-21. However, there are a small number of cases in which the minimum wage does not apply, notably if a worker is aged under 18 but also in other cases such as, for example, for people living with and working for a family business or if a worker is aged under 26 and in the first year of an apprenticeship; in addition if an employer provides accommodation he can also deduct up to £22.75 of a worker's pay for the cost of providing it. So, a low wage that appears to be breaking the law may in fact be legal.

This is a complicated subject. Those wanting more detailed information, leaflets or to register a complaint should call the National Minimum Wage Helpline on 0845-6000 678, write to NMW Enquiries, Freepost PHQ1, Newcastle-upon-Tyne NE98 1ZH, or visit www.tiger.gov.uk.

# Creating Your Own Job

You might not want to spend time sending off speculative letters or phoning around potential employers chasing a job vacancy that might not exist or may already have been filled. The alternative is to make a job for yourself, by creating a service that people in your area might be willing to pay for. A company called Shell LiveWire produces a free essential business and advice kit for anyone aged 16-30 wishing to start up a business (Hawthorn House, Forth Banks, Newcastle-upon-Tyne NE1 3SG; 0845-757 3253; www.shell-livewire.org).

Window cleaning, car-washing, housework and babysitting are a few of the most obvious odd-jobs you could offer to do, and there are many more. Before turning self-employed you should ask yourself some questions:

**1. What do people want?** Do a little market research among neighbours and friends, read local papers and look at adverts placed in local shops. Try to identify particular needs in the area.

**2. What can I offer?** It is surprising how easily existing skills or hobbies can be turned into financially rewarding enterprise. Some suggestions:
*academic qualifications:* private tuition, translation.
*carpentry:* simple woodwork, mending gates, making/putting up shelves.
*cooking:* lunch and dinner party catering or sandwich-making.
*cycling:* bicycle repairs (highly recommended), courier work (suitable for those with a mountain bike who live in a big city).
*gardening:* grass-cutting, weeding or pruning.
*knitting:* making jumpers, cardigans, etc. on commission.
*music:* busking, playing in pubs, DJ-ing or giving music lessons.
*sewing:* dressmaking, repairs and alterations, cushion-making.
*word-processing:* CV-typing, report and essay typing.
*walking:* dog exercising, tourist guiding or shopping for the elderly.

**3. Who wants me?** After you have identified a job you can do and for which you think there is local demand, you need to publicise your services. The best way to start it with advertisements in local shop windows and supermarket notice boards, which are either very cheap or free. It is worth thinking about your market as you do this – for example if you are offering music lessons it is probably more worthwhile to advertise in a music shop than a grocer's store. If you can afford it, you could place an ad in the local newspaper, and it will also be useful to deliver a handbill to your target area.

**4. Is it worth it?** Before getting too carried away imagining yourself as the next Richard Branson, stop and ask yourself how much money you are hoping to make and whether you will be able to do so using your particular idea. Work could be sporadic, unpredictable and even only occasional. If you need a regular income, think very carefully.

The principal feature of successfully creating a job for yourself is your reputation. If you impress someone with your hard work, promptness and efficiency, they will tell others.

# Tips on Applying for a Job

**1.** Most employers like to make their staff arrangements in good time, so apply early and according to the dates mentioned in the job details.

**2.** Before applying for a position, check that you fulfil all the requirements, such as age and qualifications. Employers usually have definite reasons for setting requirements and will stick to them, so you are wasting both your time and theirs if you apply for a job for which you are clearly not suitable.

*Period of work:* employers generally prefer to take on one person for the whole season. If you are able to work for longer than the minimum period quoted, you are more likely to get the job.

*Accommodation:* it is particularly important to note whether or not lodging is provided, especially for those who are coming from abroad. In areas which attract many tourists over the summer, temporary rented accommodation can be either difficult to find or prohibitively expensive. Some employers can recommend lodgings in the area or be of more positive help, but often they are reluctant to recruit those without pre-arranged accommodation.

**3.** Prepare an application. This will normally be in the form of a covering letter and a *curriculum vitae* (CV). The point of the application is to show (i) that you want the job, (ii) that you want to work for that organisation, and that (iii) you have had the appropriate experiences and demonstrated the relevant skills and qualities so that the employer wants you.

In order to achieve these three objectives you must first consider why the specific job interests you and secondly what are the key qualities and skills needed - typically these may include social/interpersonal skills, organisational abilities, leadership, verbal and written communication skills, numeracy, intelligence, diligence, conscientiousness, thoroughness, work processing, etc. Once these factors have been worked out, it is time to write a complementary CV and covering letter to show that you are the best person for the job.

*Curriculum Vitae:* This should be typed on one A4 sheet in note form and include the following details, ordered in titled groups of information:
(a) Personal details (name, address, telephone number, nationality, age, marital status);
(b) Educational qualifications and current place and subject of study if you are a student, otherwise your present occupation;
(c) Relevant Experience which may include work experience, organising social events, captaining a football team or activity in school or university societies;
(d) Skills such as computing, word processing, other languages, driving licence;
(e) Interests and Hobbies;
(f) Referees - preferably one from work and one personal.

*Covering Letter:* this should be fairly short (again one side of A4) and tidy, preferably typed. This is your chance to explain why the job must be given to you in terms of points (i), (ii) and (iii) above, using the information on the CV to support your argument. Use positive, enthusiastic language and include the following information, possibly in separate paragraphs:
(a) Which exact position you have chosen and why it appeals to you (and also make it clear which geographical region you have chosen if there are several to

choose from);
(b) Why you have chosen that particular organisation - here it is worth being extremely complimentary towards them – making it clear you have researched their business where possible;
(c) Why they should employ you - and use your CV to prove that your claims are true.

**4.** Address the letter to the person specified in the entry, whether this gives an actual name or merely the title, e.g. Personnel Manager, Student Training Officer, etc.

**5.** Always enclose a stamped addressed envelope (s.a.e.) or, if you are applying from abroad, an International Reply Coupon (IRC). IRCs are available from any post office. It can be both expensive and inconvenient for employers to reply to a large number of applicants, especially once the positions have been filled. Some employers simply won't respond to applications without a s.a.e. or IRC.

**6.** When an interview is necessary, and this applies in particular to firms offering vacation traineeships, you should be able to show a basic knowledge of, and interest in, the activities of the company in question, as well as demonstrate that you are seriously considering a career in that particular field. In other words, you must demonstrate premeditated enthusiasm for the employment sector, the work and the organisation. It is also essential to realise that how you say it is as important as what you say - be positive, friendly and enthusiastic.

**7.** If you receive a job offer, check all the relevant information: the job details given in this Directory are supplied by the employer, but it is wise confirm them before accepting the position. Things to check include wages, board and lodging, hours and the conditions of work. Some staff have ended up working unpaid overtime, others have been sacked without warning, so clarify **all** terms and conditions in advance.
Ask your employer to put the relevant details in writing (though for these to become legally binding, both parties must sign a contract).

**8.** If you are offered more than one job, decide quickly which you prefer and inform all employers of your decision as soon as possible, especially for jobs where vacancies advertised were limited.

**9.** Many young people regard their summer job as a holiday, but this is seldom the attitude taken by the employer. If the job details indicate that a hotel needs an assistant to serve three meals a day six days a week, or a hop farmer needs pickers to work seven days a week in all weathers, then you should be warned that there will be far more work than holiday.

**10.** Finally, ask for a reference when you leave your job, since this should enhance your chances of finding work in the future. In some fields, such as retail and childcare, the ability to produce a reference is considered important.

# Work Permits and Special Schemes

The primary route for entry into the UK for the purpose of employment is the work permit system. Work permits are issued only where a genuine vacancy exists and where particular qualifications or skills are required that are in short supply from the resident and EEA labour force.
Before writing letters to prospective employers, overseas applicants should clarify the terms under which they may visit and work in Britain. Anyone arriving at UK Immigration without the necessary visa, letter of invitation or other required documentation, could be sent back home on the next available flight. An outline of the regulations is given below. For further information, contact the nearest British Consulate or High Commission.

## Visa Requirements

You may need a visa to enter the UK irrespective of the reason for your visit. Citizens of Western Europe, most Commonwealth countries and of the USA do not need a tourist visa to enter Britain. Since the fall of communism in the Eastern Bloc, many Eastern Europeans – including Poles, Czechs and Hungarians – no longer need visas either.

Nationals of the former Soviet Union and most Asian and African countries are required to obtain a visa. Exceptions include Israel, Japan, South Africa and Zimbabwe. It is advisable to check visa requirements at the nearest UK Diplomatic Post.

## Work Permits

Wherever relevant, entries in this book specify if the company or organisation in question welcomes applications from overseas. Unfortunately, this does not mean that all foreigners can legally work for them in this country. It is an offence under the Immigration Act of 1971 to take employment in breach of conditions of stay, and a person found to be working illegally may be fined and may also be liable to deportation. An employer employing overseas nationals whom he or she knows to be working in breach of their landing conditions may also be liable to prosecution and a fine of up to £5,000.

Having studied the section below carefully, if you believe you are eligible for some kind of permit, make enquiries with the consulate or relevant organisation as soon as possible: preparing the necessary documentation may take some months.

**EEA Citizens** Nationals of the European Economic Area are free to enter the United Kingdom to seek employment without a work permit. At present this applies to citizens of EU countries and Norway, Iceland and Liechtenstein. However EEA nationals still require a permit for the Channel Islands and the Isle of Man.

EEA nationals intending to stay longer than six months may apply for a residence permit, although there is no obligation on them to do so.

**Non-EEA Citizens.** The general position under the Immigration Rules is that overseas nationals (other than EEA nationals) coming to work in Britain must have work permits before setting out. The employer (**not** the employee) has to apply to the Department of Education and Employment, which administers the scheme. Permits are issued only for specific jobs requiring a high level of skill and experience for which resident or EEA labour is not available. In other words, a UK employer will not receive a work permit for a non-EEA citizen unless it is a job for which there is no EEA National available.

There are, however, a number of labour routes that do not require a work permit:

*Citizens of Commonwealth Countries:* nationals of Commonwealth countries (including Australia, New Zealand, Canada and South Africa) between the ages of 17 and 27 are permitted to visit the UK as a 'Working Holiday Maker'. This allows them to take up casual employment which will be incidental to their holiday, but not to engage in business or to pursue a career. The period which can be spent in the UK is two years.

Prior entry clearance is mandatory and must be obtained from the British High Commissions or Embassy in your home country.

Commonwealth citizens with at least one British-born grandparent may wish to apply for 'UK Ancestry employment entry clearance' from the British High Commission: this eliminates altogether the need for a work permit. Married couples must apply for separate entry clearance before travelling.

*Students from North America:* US students seeking temporary work in the UK can benefit from the 'Work in Britain Program'. This allows full-time college students and recent graduates over the age of 18 to look for work in Britain, finding jobs through programme listings or through personal contacts. Jobs may be pre-arranged, though most participants wait until arrival in Britain to job hunt. They must first obtain a 'British Universities North America Club (BUNAC) Card', which is recognised by the British Home Office as a valid substitute for a work permit ; this 'BUNAC Card' must be obtained before leaving the US for Britain, as it acts as an entry document. It allows the holder to work for a maximum of six months at any time of year: extensions are never granted. The BUNAC card is available for a fee of approx. $225 from the Council on International Educational Exchange (Council) at 205 East 42nd Street, New York, NY 10025, USA (toll free ☎ 1-888-GO BUNAC).

A similar programme, called the Student Work Abroad Programme (SWAP), is organised for Canadian students, graduates and young people, with varying age restrictions applying. It is administered by the Canadian Universities Travel Service, which has over 40 offices in Canada. For details see www.swap.ca.

*Seasonal Agricultural Work Scheme*: farm camps under this scheme are authorised by the Home Office and are the main hope for non-EEA and non-Commonwealth nationals wishing to work in this country. Special 'entrance authorisation cards' are issued to a certain number of non-EEA nationals each year.

The recruitment for these farms is handled by seven agencies, including the Harvesting Opportunity Permit Scheme, or HOPS, and Concordia (for address see *Agriculture* above). Between them they recruit pickers for over 160 farms between March and November. While you can contact the farmers directly, you are advised to apply through the above-mentioned agencies. Prospective participants should be aged 18 to 25 and should be full-time students in their own country.

*Voluntary Work.* Overseas nationals may be admitted for up to 12 months for the purpose of voluntary work without requiring a permit, providing he or she will be working for a registered charitable organisation and receiving no remuneration other than pocket money, board and accommodation. The work which they do must be closely related to the aims of the charity i.e. working with people, and they must not be engaged in purely clerical, administrative or maintenance work (for which a work permit is required). Volunteers are expected to leave the United Kingdom at the end of their visit.

*Vacation Traineeships & Internships.* Permission can be given for overseas nationals with pre-arranged work placements to obtain permits for professional training or managerial level work experience for a limited amount of time. The UK employer offering the placement has to apply for a permit to Work Permits (UK) at the address below.

Practical training places in the UK for US nationals are available through the Career Development Programme administered by the Association for International Practical Training (AIPT), 10400 Little Patuxent Parkway, Suite 250, Columbia, Maryland 21044-3510 (410-997-2200; aipt@aipt.org/ www.aipt.org). To be eligible you must be aged 18-35 with relevant qualifications and/or at least one year of work experience in a career field. A good starting place is AIPT's online placement system (www.pinpointtraining.org).

While many companies in the book are happy to employ overseas students as trainees, since most of them run their schemes in order to try out potential employees, they may not be keen to take on anyone who cannot return to them after their studies.

The Department for Education and Employment issues permits under its Training and Work Experience Scheme for limited periods of pre-arranged on-the-job training to gain a professional qualification, or for short periods of managerial level work experience. This can include students on recognised exchange placements through AIESEC, or the International Farm Experience Programme.

*Non EEA Students Studying in the UK.* Overseas students studying in Britain who wish to take up vacation work no longer have to obtain permission to do so. As long as they do not pursue a career by filling a full-time vacancy or work for more than 20 hours per week during term time, except where the placement is a necessary part of their studies with the agreement of the educational institution.

*Au Pairs.* For details of regulations affecting au pairs see the chapter *Au Pair, Home Help and Paying Guest* at the end of the book.

## Further Information

Once in the UK, general information about who needs work permits and other immigration matters can be obtained from the Home Office Immigration and Nationality Directorate, Block C, Whitgift Centre, Croydon CR9 1AT (☎0870-6067766; www.ind.homeoffice.gov.uk): be prepared to wait in line for your call to be answered, it will be eventually. Guidance leaflets are also available from the Correspondence Unit of UK Visas, 89 Albert Embankment, London SE1 7TP ( www.fco.gov.uk). The Department for Education and Employment, Overseas Labour Service, W5, Moorfoot, Sheffield S1 4PQ (☎0114-2594074; www.dfee.gov.uk/ols) can advise employers on the rules of the work permit scheme.

# ABBREVIATIONS

| | | | |
|---|---|---|---|
| approx. | approximately | max. | maximum |
| a.s.a.p. | as soon as possible | min. | minimum |
| B & L | board and lodging | p.a. | per annum |
| CV | curriculum vitae | s.a.e. | stamped addressed envelope |
| IRC | International Reply Coupon | w.p.m. | words per minute |

## Glossary of Qualifications

The following list of qualifications (often the name of the institute or association which issues them) are listed in alphabetical order.

ACA/ACCA – (Chartered) Association of Certified Accountants
BASI – British Association of Ski Institutes
BCU – British Canoe Union
BHSIC – British Horse Society Instructor's Certificate
BTEC – Business and Technology Education Certificate
CIMA – Chartered Institute of Management Accountants
City and Guilds 706/1, 706/2 – catering qualifications
GCSE – General Certificate of Secondary Education
GNAS – Grand National Archery Society
HGV – Heavy Goods Vehicle driving licence
HND – Higher National Diploma
LGV – Light Goods Vehicle driving licence
LTA – Lawn Tennis Association
MLTB – Mountaineering Leadership Training Board
NAMCW – National Association for Maternal and Child Welfare
NNEB – National Nursery Examination Board
OND – Ordinary National Diploma
PCV – Passenger Carrying Vehicle
PLG – Pool Life Guard
RGN – Registered General Nurse
RLS (S) – Royal Life Saving (Society)
RSA – Royal Society of Arts (Examinations Board)
RYA – Royal Yachting Association
SEN – Senior Enrolled Nurse
TEFL/EFL – (Teaching) English as a Foreign Language

**N.B.** The author and publishers have every reason to believe in the accuracy of the information given in this book and the authenticity and correct practices of all organisations, companies, agencies etc. mentioned; however, situations may change and telephone numbers can alter, and readers are strongly advised to check facts and credentials for themselves.

Readers are invited to write to Andrew James and David Woodworth, Vacation Work, 9 Park End Street, Oxford OX1 1HJ with any comments, corrections and first hand information. Those whose contributions are used will be sent a free copy of the next edition or any other Vacation Work publication of their choice.

# NATIONWIDE

Organisations which have branches in various parts of Britain

## Business and Industry

**BETTERWARE:** Head Office, Stanley House, Park Lane, Castle Vale, Birmingham B35 6LJ.
**Distributors** to deliver and collect Betterware's Household Products brochure. Expected earnings £40-£200 per week, dependent on hours available. To work full or part time, at least 8 hours per week. Vacancies exist in all parts of the UK at all times of the year. Full-time career opportunities in sales management also exist for the right candidates.

For more details or to make an *application* please call Betterware Recruitment on 0845 125 5000 (local rate).

**BLUE ARROW LIMITED:** 800 the Boulevard, Capability Green, Luton, Bedford LU1 3BA (☎0800-0855 777; www.bluearrow.co.uk).
**Temporary/Permanent Staff (500,000 per year)** to work in offices, catering, industry and construction around the UK. Contracts may be of any length of time from a day onwards. Relevant previous experience may or may not be required. Minimum age 16.

Those interested should *contact* the above freephone number or can visit one of Blue Arrow's 250 branches around the country.

**HORIZON HPL:** Signet House, 49-51 Farringdon Road, London EC1M 3JB (☎020-7404 9192-3; fax 020-7404 9194; e-mail horizonhpl.London@btinternet.com). A training centre established in 1991 which organises paid work placements in hotels, shops and companies in the UK and in France for EU citizens, including English and French tuition and preparation to sit British and French examinations.
**Company Staff.** Placements are available all year round (in a variety of fields) from 3 months to 1 year. They receive a trainee wage and accommodation if working in a hotel. Applicants from 17-50 years. An interview is necessary.

*Applicants* should contact the agency 2 months in advance of intended work date.

**MAJESTIC WINE WAREHOUSES:** Majestic House, Otterspool Way, Watford WD25 8WW (☎01923-298200; fax 01923-819105; www.majestic.co.uk). Majestic is the UK's foremost by-the-case retailer of wines, beers and spirits. There are over 100 stores throughout England, Scotland and Wales and expansion plans for another 8-10 stores a year.
**Temporary Drivers** to help with delivery driving, merchandising and dealing with customers. Wages vary according to location (£4.45-£4.75 per hour). Vacancies available in most holiday periods, particularly at Christmas and during the summer. Applicants should enjoy working with the public, must have held a driving licence for at least a year and be over 19. The job is physically demanding. No accommodation is provided.

*Application forms* can be obtained by phoning 01923-298210 or by writing to the Recruitment Manager at the above address.

**PROMOTIONAL SUPPORT LTD:** 276 Chase Road, Southgate, London N14 6HA (☎020-8886 7009; fax 020-8886 0078). Organises roadshows, exhibitions and events and supplies promotional staff for clients such as Walkers, Robinsons, Pepsi and other blue chip clients.
**Temporary Promotional Contracts** available. Wages from £40-£60 per day. To work 8-10 hours a day. Min. period of work 1 day at any time of year. No accommodation available.

Applicants should have bubbly, outgoing, attractive personalities. Overseas applicants considered. Interview preferred, but not necessary.

*Applications* at any time to Louise at the above address. E-mail louise@promotionalsupport.co.uk or post a CV and photograph with sae.

# Children

**ARDMORE LANGUAGE SCHOOLS:** Hall Place, Berkshire College, Burchetts Green, Maidenhead, Berkshire SL6 6QR (☎01628-826699; fax 01628-829977; e-mail mailbox@ardmore.org.uk; www.ardmore.org.uk). Ardmore Language Schools offers summer junior vacation courses in English to overseas juniors. Residential centres located throughout Britain.
**Centre Directors, Assistant Centre Directors, Centre Administrators, Head Teachers, EFL Teachers, Senior Sports Leaders, Sports Leaders** at residential colleges in the South East. Those aged 20+ preferred. Period of work 2-8 weeks during June, July and August.

Further details from and *applications* to Ardmore Language Schools at the above address.

**BARRACUDAS SUMMER ACTIVITY CAMPS:** Bridge House, Bridge Street, St.Ives, Cambridgeshire PE27 5EH (☎01480-497533; fax 01480-492715; e-mail info@barracudas.co.uk; www.barracudas.co.uk). Barracudas runs summer day camps for 5-14 year olds.
**Camp Managers (16).** Wages on application. Experience in teaching or management required.
**Assistant Camp Managers (16).** Wages on application. Experience in teaching or management required.
**Senior Group Leaders (16).** Wages on application. Experience in teaching or management required.
**Group Co-ordinators (100).** Wages from £145 per week. Experience with children/sports necessary.
**Group Assistants (100).** Wages from £145 per week. Experience with children/sports necessary.
**Football Coaches (50).** Wages from £145 per week. Experience in football coaching and excellent knowledge of the game needed.
**Arts and Crafts Instructors (50).** Wages from £145 per week. Experience in arts and crafts needed.
**Dance and Drama Instructors (50).** Wages from £145 per week. Drama and dance experience necessary.
**Lifeguards (50).** Wages from £180 per week. Should be NPLQ/RLSS qualified.

All staff to work 37½-42½ per week. Minimum period of work of 2 weeks. Staff required from mid-July to end of August. Minimum age 18. Foreign applicants with fluent English are welcome. No accommodation available.

*Applications* should be made from November onwards to Sarah Price or Rachel Fabb at the above address. Interview required.

**EAC ACTIVITY CAMPS:** First Floor, 59 George Street, Edinburgh EH2 2LQ (☎0131-477 7574; fax 0131-477 7571; e-mail afisher@activitycamps.com; www.activitycamps.com). Multi activity day and residential camps in Edinburgh, Glasgow, Oxford, Canterbury, York, Manchester, London and Taunton. For children aged 5-16.
**Camp Directors (7).** Wages £230-£250 per week with accommodation available; must be over 21.
**Assistant Camp Directors (7).** Wages £180 per week; must be over 21. **Qualified Instructors** required for canoeing, wall climbing/abseiling, archery and swimming. Wages £150 per week. Relevant qualifications essential: BCU Instructor, EFL, MLTB/SPSA, GNAS, or Bronze Medallion/PLG.
**Group Captains (8).** £150 per week.
**Group Monitors (16).** £140 per week.
**Activity Leaders (40).** Wages £135 per week; must be at least 18.
**Senior Activity Leaders (12).** Wages £220 per week; must be over 21.
Accommodation and food provided. Must have all round sporting ability and be enthusiastic. Sporting qualifications and coaching awards preferred.
All staff to work 40 hours per week. Min. period of work 5 weeks between June and September. The work is hard but good fun. Overseas applicants welcome. All applicants must be available for interview.
*Applications* from January to Andrew Fisher, EAC Activity Camps.

**EF INTERNATIONAL LANGUAGE SCHOOLS:** 74 Roupell Street, London, SE1 8SS (☎020-7401 8399; fax 020-7401 3717; www.ef.com).
**EFL Teachers** required for July and August to work full-time. Wages vary according to location and experience. Candidates should have at least a first degree and CTEFLA.
*Applications* with CVs should be sent to the Director of Studies at the above address. Vacancies are also available at schools in Brighton, Bournemouth and Cambridge.

**EF LANGUAGE TRAVEL:** EF House, 36-38 St Aubyn's, Hove, Sussex BN3 2PD (☎01273-822777; fax 01273-729561). Language courses with free time programmes for international students in locations in the UK and Ireland.
**Group Leaders and Teachers (650 nationwide).** Salary varies depending on region and experience. Min. age 20 years. Teaching or leadership experience preferred. Applicants must have a standard of English as high as that of a native speaker. Both residential and non-residential staff required, accommodation available for residential appointments only.
**Activity Organisers (40 nationwide)** to plan an activity programme for all students in one particular town or residential centre. Salary varies depending on region and experience. Min. age 20 years. Previous organisational experience essential. All staff to work flexible hours, 6 days a week. Min. period of work 3 weeks between late May and late August. All applicants must be available for interview.
*Applications* as soon as possible to the Recruitment Officer at the above address.

**ISIS EDUCATIONAL PROGRAMMES:** 259 Greenwich High Road, Greenwich, London SE10 8NB (☎0208-293 1188; fax 0208-293 1199; e-mail recruitment@isis group.co.uk). ISIS runs Language/Activity Centres in summer at 15 locations around the UK including Oxford, Bath, Cambridge, Winchester, York and Edinburgh.
**EFL Teachers (150)** to teach mainly teenagers on courses from 18 June to 27

August. Wages £180 per week. To work 3 hours teaching mornings and 3 hours of repeat lessons in the afternoon (i.e. 30+ hours a week but lesson preparation for only 15 hours). Teaching qualification needed.
**Activity Leaders (100+)** Wages start from £140 per week. To lead thirteen sessions (mornings and afternoons) per week. Period of work 18 June to 27 August. Hours are guaranteed. No special qualifications. Appointments are personality based.

The above wages include full board and lodging, but non-residential arrangements also possible with higher wages.

*Applications* to the H.R. Manager, at the above address

**PGL TRAVEL:** Alton Court, Penyard Lane (874), Ross-on-Wye, Herefordshire HR9 5GL (☎01989-767833; e-mail pglpeople@pgl.co.uk; www.pgl.co.uk/people). With 25 activity centres located in the UK, France and Spain, PGL Travel provides adventure holidays and courses for children. Each year 2,500 people are needed to help run these adventure centres.
**Group Leaders** required to take responsibility for groups of children, helping them to get the most out of their holiday. Minimum age 18. Previous experience of working with children is essential.
**General positions available** in catering, administration, driving (car, PCV or LGV), stores, site cleaning and nurses (RGN or SEN) etc.

From £50-85 per week plus full B & L. Vacancies available for short or long periods between February and October. Overseas applicants eligible to work in the UK welcome. *Applications* can be made online or a form obtained from the above address.

**SUPER CAMPS LTD:** 2a Newbury Street, Wantage, Oxon OX12 8BU (☎01235-772173; fax 01235-772179; e-mail info@supercamps.co.uk). Runs multi-activity Christmas, Easter and summer day camps for children aged 4-13 in centres in Oxfordshire, Berkshire, Buckinghamshire and Hertfordshire. Super Camps is committed to providing safe and fun-packed activities (including art/craft and sports) for all children attending its camps.
**Site Leaders (8).** £250+ per week. Qualified teachers with camp experience.
**Second In Charge (8).** £200 per week. Qualified/trainee teachers or individuals with substantial children's camp experience.
**Swimming Pool Lifeguards (8).** £150 per week. Must have experience and hold a recognised and up-to-date life saving/coaching qualification (RLSS, Bronze Medallion etc).
**Activity Instructors (8).** £150 per week. To teach a range of activities to children aged 4-13 years. First aid and relevant childcare qualifications/camp experience are an advantage. Training is provided, therefore enthusiastic individuals with an interest in sports or arts and crafts and a genuine interest in working with children are welcome to apply.

Staff needed for April, from the end of July and August and at Christmas. Free B & L provided at some sites. Good experience for those wishing to go into a teaching, childcare or recreation/leisure profession. Overseas applicants considered subject to language ability and relevant qualifications. *Applications* all year round to Personnel at the above address.

**3D EDUCATION AND ADVENTURE LTD:** Business Support, Osmington Bay, Weymouth, Dorset DT3 6EG (☎01305-836226; fax 01305-834070; e-mail darren@3d-education.co.uk; www.3d-jobs.co.uk). 3D is a specialist provider of activity and educational experiences for young people. Owned by Center Parcs, 3D

has been operating since 1991 and gone from strength to strength year on year.
ACTIVITY INSTRUCTORS (500) Employed and trained as either multi-activity instructor, field studies instructor, specialist watersports instructor or IT instructor, staff will work with children at specialist holiday centres across the south of England as well as across the UK and Europe with Pontins and Center Parcs.

Field studies instructors must hold or at least be gaining a relevant degree. IT instructors need to have a broad range of IT skills. Any sports coaching awards or national governing body awards are advantageous, if applying for Activity instructor and Watersports instructor positions, although those with relevant experience will be considered. Training courses are held from late January through to July, so there is plenty of opportunity to develop your skills and qualifications.

Most important is an applicant's enthusiasm, personality and energy, coupled with a true desire to work in the outdoor leisure industry. Excellent accommodation and catering packages are offered with payment and working hours as covered by minimum wage and working time legislation. Minimum period of work 14 weeks.

*Applicants* should telephone 01305-836226 for a recruitment pack or visit http://www.3d-jobs.uk between September and June. Before employment all applicants must complete a residential training programme in the UK.

## Holiday Centres and Amusements

**BOURNE LEISURE LIMITED:** Park Lane, Hemel Hempstead, Hertfordshire HP2 4YL. Owns and operates 40 holiday parks in resorts throughout England, Scotland and Wales.
**Bar Team Members, Catering Team Members, Cooks and Shop Assistants.**

Competitive wages and full training given. Accommodation available at a small charge. Applicants must possess an outgoing personality, smart appearance and be willing to work flexible hours. Vacancies exist between the months of March and October for team members who are available to work for a minimum of 8 weeks.

For more information on Bourne Leisure's parks and details on how to *apply* see the advertisement above.

# BOURNE LEISURE
L I M I T E D

With 40 holiday parks situated in coastal locations throughout England, Scotland and Wales, we are looking to recruit team members who are available for a minimum period of 8 weeks, March - October, for the following positions:-

- ❖ BAR TEAM MEMBERS
- ❖ CATERING TEAM MEMBERS
- ❖ COOKS
- ❖ SHOP ASSISTANTS

Previous experience is not essential. Applicants must possess an outgoing personality, smart appearance and be willing to work flexible hours. Minimum age 18. Accommodation is available at a small charge. Competitive wages with incentives offered and full training given. In the first instance, visit our websites for further information on the Company and our locations. Either submit an on line application form including full details of position applied for, dates available, preferred location and references or contact the Complex Manager at the park of your choice to request an application form.

www.british-holidays.co.uk

www.havenholidays.co.uk

**OCTAGON MOTOR SPORTS LTD:** Fawkham, Longfield, Kent DA3 8NG (☎01474-872331; fax 01474-879259; e-mail recruitment@octagon.com; www.octagon.com). Operates several major British motor sport leisure venues. Seasonal staff are always needed to work venues around England, but especially at Brands Hatch and Silverstone.

**Marshals** To marshal track activities. Includes some weekend work. Must be flexible and able to work as part of a team.

**Bar Assistants** To work behind a busy bar. Variable hours to include evening work and weekends. Experience in cash handling and stock rotation an advantage. Must be flexible and able to work long hours.

**Catering Assistants** Duties will include some cooking, serving, cash handling, general hygiene and maintenance. Variable hours to include evening work and weekends. Cash handling and food production experience essential.

**General Assistants** Variable hours to include evening work and weekends. To assist the Catering Department and help ensure that all services are provided to the highest standard.

**Cleaning Operatives** To ensure that all areas are maintained in a clear, tidy safe and hygienic manner.

Wages available on application. Staff are required from March to November, to work as and when required on a fixed term contract. Overseas applicants must have a valid work permit.

*Applications* to the Human Resources Administrator, from March at the above address.

## Hotels and Catering

**ANGLO CONTINENTAL PLACEMENTS AGENCY:** Dial Post House, Dial Post, Nr Horsham, Sussex RH13 8NQ (☎01403-713344; fax 01403-713366; e-mail sharon@anglocontinental.fsnet.co.uk; www.anglocontinentalplacement.co.uk). A friendly agency established in 1988 who operate throughout the UK. The office is open from 8.30 to 5.30 Mon-Fri. Hotel and Catering staff placed all over the UK. They wish to work with new agencies abroad.

Chefs, Waiting Staff, Receptionists, Commis Chefs, Chefs de Parties, Porters, Etc Required. Positions available in all aspects of the hotel industry.

Live-in positions available. Staff wanted from New Zealand, Australia and South Africa and EEC. Previous work experience not essential. Min. period of work 6 months.

Applications including CV and references to Sharon Wolfe at the above address.

**CENTRE D'ECHANGES INTERNATIONAUX (CEI):** 164/168 Westminster Bridge Road, Devonshire House, London SE1 7RW (☎020-7960 2600; fax 020-7960 2601; e-mail info@cei-frenchcentre.com). The CEI helps European nationals to find a job and provides accommodation and English courses in London. It recruits for the following areas of work:

**Hotel and Restaurant Positions.** In London, Portsmouth and throughout Great Britain. Wages from £3.70 per hour dependent on level of English spoken and experience. Accommodation sometimes provided.

**Catering Assistants (40)** In summer camps; police check necessary. Accommodation provided; wages from £3.70 per hour for 40 hours per week.

For all positions, staff are required all year round. Minimum period of work of 8 weeks. Applicants from anywhere in the European community welcome; must be 18 or over.

*Applications* should be made at least 10 weeks before arrival in the UK, to the Employment Consultant at the above address. Interview sometimes required.

**CHEF CENTRE LTD:** 1 Kingly Street, London W1B 5PA (☎020-7439 0771; fax 020-7287 3576; e-mail info@chefcentre.com). A recruitment agency established 30 years ago with a long-standing client base and contacts.

**Temporary/Seasonal Chef Work.** Wages negotiable, often living-in; to work as required. Staff required from March to December. Must have a City and Guilds 706.II or equivalent NVQ and food hygiene certificate. Accommodation is frequently available as part of the package. Overseas applicants with relevant experience, qualifications and a work permit if from outside the EU are welcome.

*Applications* at least one month before intended work date to Alison, Suzi, Emily or Mike at the above address.

**CHOICE HOTELS EUROPE:** 112 Station Road, Edgware, Middlesex HA8 7BJ (☎020-8233 2001; fax 020-8233 2080; e-mail FBernardon@ChoiceHotelsEurope.com). Owns, manages and franchises over 400 hotels in 13 European countries.

Guidance can be offered with finding jobs in Europe, but posts are primarily for the UK and Ireland.
**Receptionists, Chefs, Waiting Staff, Bar Staff.** Salary in accordance with Minimum Wages Regulation.Minimum period of work of 6 months; 1 year in Front Office. 39 h/week spread over 5 days. Applicants are considered all year round and in all parts of the UK.

Applicants must be over 18, customer orientated, smart and pleasant. Priority given to those with hotel qualifications and/or experience of the business. Good working knowledge of English essential (must be fluent for Receptionist positions).

*Applications* in writing to Françoise Bernardon, Human Resources Officer, at the address above.

**CIP RECRUITMENT:** 195 Victoria Street, London SW1E 5NE (☎ 020-7630 9993/0123; fax 020-7630 0170).
Agency specialising in **Catering Recruitment** throughout the UK. Short-term assignments are available, particularly during the summer months, for all grades of qualified chefs, catering managers, front-of-house staff, catering assistants, kitchen porters, housekeepers and chamber staff. Assignments and wages vary but for example a castle in Scotland providing five star catering for shooting-parties from June to November will offer full board for the period of employment. Salaries offered range from £200-£500 per week, depending on the grade of chef.

*Contact* CIP on the above number, overseas applicants should wait until they are in the UK to call.

**DE VERE & VILLAGE HOTELS:** 2100 Daresbury Park, Warrington WA4 4BP (☎ 01928-756154; fax 01928-756341; www.deveregroupplc.co.uk.). De Vere Group Plc is a highly focused Company concentrating on two growth markets – hotels and health and fitness.The Company has two distinctive hotel brands; De Vere Hotels and Village Leisure Hotels.
**Waiting Staff, Room Attendants, Porters, Bar Staff, Commis Chefs and Casual Banqueting Staff.** Must be over 18 and available to work for a minimum of 4 weeks between May and October. Accommodation may be available, although it is not guaranteed. Overseas applicants who speak fluent English and are eligible to work in the UK may apply.

*Applications* should be forwarded directly to the Human Resources Manager at the desired location. Addresses of individual hotels can be obtained from our website www.deveregroupplc.co.uk.

**GREAT ADVENTURES:** Grafham Water Centre, Perry, Huntingdon, Cambridgeshire PE18 0BX (☎ 01480-810521; fax 01480-812739; e-mail grafham.water@education.cambridgeshire.gov.uk; www.grafham-water-centre.co.uk). Provides activity and special interest holidays with centres in Cambridgeshire and Derbyshire.
**Catering Assistants (10).** £184 per week plus food and accommodation. To work 40 hours per week from May to July; min. period of work 2 months. Work also available for 10 months. Food hygiene certificate preferred. Overseas applicants welcome.

*Applications* from January to Mr Ian Downing at the above address.

**HATTON HOTELS GROUP:** Hatton Court, Upton Hill, Upton St Leonards, Gloucester GL4 8DE (☎ 01452-617412; fax 01452-612945; e-mail res@hatton-court.co.uk; www.hatton-hotels.co.uk). A privately owned collection of character hotels in Gloucestershire, Wiltshire, Somerset and Jersey. Accredited Investors in

People who operate high quality service-orientated hotels.
**Bar Staff, Restaurant Staff, Housekeeping Staff.** Good rates of pay plus B & L and tips. 5 day working week on rota. Excellent training and incentives provided.
*Applications* should be sent to Personnel at the above address.

**HORIZON HPL:** Signet House, 49-51 Farringdon Road, London EC1M 3JB (☎020-7404 9192-3; fax 020-7404 9194; e-mail horizonhpl.london@btinternet.com). A training centre established in 1991 which organises paid work placements in hotels and companies in the UK and France for EU citizens, including English and French tuition and preparation to sit British and French examinations.
**Hotel Work.** Placements are available all year round (in a variety of fields) from 3 months up to 1 year. They receive a trainee wage and free accommodation. Applicants from 17-50 years. An interview is necessary.
*Applicants* should contact the agency 2 months in advance of intended work date.

**HOSPITALITY DIRECT RECRUITMENT:** 1 North Pallant, Chichester, West Sussex PO19 1TL (☎01243-787003; fax 01243-787694; e-mail aminto@hdrecruit.com; www.hdrecruit.com). A recruitment agency in direct contact with top hotels and restaurants throughout the UK and Channel islands.
**All Chefs and Front-of-House Management Personnel** positions. Wages on application. Variable hours; permanent and temporary positions available. Minimum period of work of 4 months. Staff required from March-December. Accommodation available.
*Applications* from November to Andrew Minto at the above address.

**MILL HOUSE INNS LTD:** Barclay House, Falcon Close, Quedgeley, Gloucester GL2 4LY (☎01452-887222; e-mail info@millhouseinns.co.uk; www.millhouseinns.co.uk). Owns a current estate of 50 managed houses all over the UK. Most are located in wonderful countryside settings with a focus on casual family dining.
**Bar Staff (20), Waiting/Table Service Staff (20), Kitchen Porters (10), Chefs (20), Receptionists/Administration Staff (5).** Wages depend on site location. Flexible working hours.
Accommodation available, but not always at places of work, at a cost already deducted from pay. Full training is provided. Min. period of work 8 weeks between March and October. Overseas applicants are considered, but must be proficient in written and spoken English and have necessary work authorisation. Applicants should have a neat appearance and a pleasant personality.
*Applications* from March to Personnel at the above address; they will provide further information on positions available at individual establishments.

**MONTPELIER EMPLOYMENT AGENCY:** 34 Montpelier Road, Brighton, Sussex BN1 2LQ (☎01273-778686; fax 01273-220359; e-mail info@themontpelieremploymentagency.co.uk). Specialises in positions away from Brighton, and runs a full countrywide service. The agency has been established for 38 years and particularly seeks experienced hotel staff such as chefs and restaurant and reception staff.
**All Types Of Catering Staff** required for positions in hotels and restaurants throughout Britain. Wages negotiable. Usually 5 days per week. Min. period of work 12 weeks from May/June to September/October. Previous hotel and catering experience essential. Overseas applicants must already be resident in the UK with valid work authorisation.
*Applications* from April/May to the Montpelier Employment Agency.

**SHEARINGS HOLIDAY HOTELS:** Miry Lane, Wigan, Lancashire, WN3 4AG (www.shearingsholidays.com). Shearings Hotels is one of the UK's largest hotel groups, with nearly 40 hotels in the UK. Most hotels operate 48 weeks of the year with a season which extends from February to December, including Christmas and the New Year.
**Housekeeping, Restaurant and Kitchen Staff.** Wages typically £4.10 per hour or £3.60 if live-in; to work 39 hours per week. Minimum period of work 3 months. Experience in hotel work valuable but not essential. Live-in accommodation is available. Foreign applicants need to have English of at least an intermediate standard.
*Applications* to the Personnel and Training Manager at the above address, or visit their website.

**TOWNGATE PERSONNEL LTD:** 3 Alum Chine Road, Westbourne, Bournemouth, Dorset BH4 8DT (☎01202-752955; fax 01202-752954; e-mail enquiries@towngate-personnel.co.uk; www.towngate-personnel.co.uk). A recruitment agency specialising in the hospitality industry. Also recruits permanent management staff and experienced operational staff for seasonal positions (March-October).
**Short-term live-in assignments** in hotels throughout England.
**Silver Service Waiting Staff (50).** £180-£200 per week.
**Chefs: All Grades (50).** £200-£400 per week.
To work in various hotels throughout the UK mainland, the Channel Islands and the Isle of Man. To work a 5 to 6 day week. Previous experience essential.
**Hotel Receptionists (20)** for hotels on the Channel Islands. £150-£220 per week. To work 5 to 6 day week. Hotel reception experience a must.
All staff required for a minimum of 6 months between April and September. Accommodation included. Overseas applicants welcome.
*Applications* from March to James Tucker, Operations Manager, at the above address.

**YHA:** National Recruitment Department (Hostel Staff) PO Box 11, Matlock, Derbyshire DE4 2XA (www.yha.org.uk). The YHA, a registered charity, is the largest budget accommodation provider in Britain with 240 youth hostels in diverse locations throughout England and Wales.
**General Assistants** needed to help run the YHA's youth hostels throughout England and Wales. Work is available for varying periods, between February and October each year. Preferred min. age 18 years. Assistants undertake a variety of tasks including catering, cleaning, reception and general maintenance. Experience in one or more of the above areas is desirable, customer service experience and enthusiasm are essential. Non-EU nationals require a valid work permit.
All posts are subject to an interview, usually at the hostel where the vacancy is. For an *application* form call the YHA National Recruitment line on 07626-939216 between November and June or send a large s.a.e. to the above address. Alternatively visit the YHA website at www.yha.org.uk

# Language Schools

**ANGLO EUROPEAN STUDY TOURS LTD.:** 8 Celbridge Mews, London W2 6EU (☎020-7229 4435; fax 020-7792 8717; e-mail c.woollam@aest.co.uk). Runs summer courses for 10-18 year olds all over the UK, offering general English plus sports, entertainments and excursions.

**EFL Teachers** Wages £190-£220 per week. To work 22 hours a week, Monday to Friday, at centres all over the UK. Staff required June-August. Applicants must have a TEFL qualification (RSA or Trinity) and a degree. Mainly non-residential posts available.
*Applications* to Claire Woollam, Director of Studies, at the above address.

**ARDMORE LANGUAGE SCHOOLS:** Hall Place, Berkshire College, Burchetts Green, Maidenhead, Berkshire SL6 6QR (☎01628-826699; fax 01628-829977; e-mail mailbox@ardmore.org.uk; www.ardmore.org.uk). Ardmore Language Schools offers summer junior vacation courses in English to overseas juniors. Residential centres located throughout Britain.
**Centre Directors, Assistant Centre Directors, Centre Administrators, Head Teachers, EFL Teachers, Senior Sports Leaders, Sports Leaders** at residential colleges in the South East.
**EFL Teachers** also required for International Homestay in Weybridge.
Those aged 20+ preferred. Period of work 2-8 weeks during June, July and August. Further details from and *applications* to Ardmore Language Schools at the above address.

**EMBASSY CES:** Lorna House, 103 Lorna Road, Hove, East Sussex BN3 3EL (☎01273-322353; fax 01273-322381; e-mail vacjobsuk@embassyces.com; www.embassyces.com). Organises summer schools for international students, combining English lessons and an activity/excursion programme at schools and universities around the UK.
**Activity Leaders (200)** to organise a variety of daytime, evening and weekend activities. Experience of working with children or in the leisure or tourism industry is desirable but full training will be given. All applicants must speak fluent English, have enthusiasm and initiative and be hardworking.
**EFL Teachers (300)** Applicants must be 18+ and have RSA CELTA or Trinity cert. TESOL. Previous experience is desirable.
Wages dependent on experience. 6 days work per week. Positions are available from June to September. Full board accommodation is available at residential centres.
*Apply* from February onwards either online (click on the UK Summer Jobs' link) or contact the Recruitment Department for an application pack. Interview necessary, usually by telephone.

**INTERNATIONAL QUEST CENTRES:** Idun House, 9 Stradbroke Road, Southwold, Suffolk IP18 6LL (tel/fax 01502-722648). Work available in language centres in Edinburgh, Hertford, London, Medway, Oxford, Portsmouth, Winchester and Loughborough. The agency has been established for 23 years, and only offers work if vacancies actually exist.
**EFL Teachers (200).** Wages in 2002 were £10.80 per hour for certificate holders and £9.60 for undergraduates. 18 hours per week. Min. period of employment 2 weeks. Undergraduates studying modern languages or primary school teachers welcome; EFL an advantage but not essential. Applicants must speak English to a native standard.
*Applications* from April to Anna Maria McCarthy, Quest Recruitment Manager, at the above address. Interviews take place in Edinburgh, London, Loughborough and Winchester. Successful candidates must attend an induction session for which they are paid.

**ISIS EDUCATIONAL PROGRAMMES:** 259 Greenwich High Road, Greenwich, London SE10 8NB (☎0208-293 1188; fax 0208-293 1199; e-mail recruitment@isisgroup.co.uk). ISIS runs Language/Activity Centres in summer at 15 locations around England including Oxford, Bath, London, Cambridge, Winchester, York and Edinburgh.
**EFL Teachers (150+)** to teach mainly teenagers. Wages from £180 p.w.
3 hours teaching mornings and 3 hours of repeat lessons in the afternoon (i.e. 30 hours a week but lesson preparation for only 15 hours). Teaching qualification needed.
**Activity Leaders (100+)** Wages start from £140 p.w. To lead thirteen two and a half hour sessions (mornings and afternoons) over six days. Hours are guaranteed. No special qualifications needed. Appointments are personality based.
The above wages include full board and lodging, but non-residential arrangements also possible with slightly higher wages. Available from June to August. *Applications* to the H.R. Manager, at the above address

**PGL TRAVEL:** Alton Court, Penyard Lane (874), Ross-on-Wye, Herefordshire HR9 5GL (☎01989-767833; e-mail pglpeople@pgl.co.uk; www.pgl.co.uk/people). With 25 activity centres located in the UK, France and Spain, PGL Travel provides adventure holidays and courses for children. Each year 2,500 people are needed to help run these adventure centres.
**EFL Teachers** £100 per week plus board and accommodation. Required to work between March and August in the UK.
Full *details and application forms* from the above address; applications can also be made online.

**STAFFORD HOUSE STUDY HOLIDAYS:** 19 New Dover Road, Canterbury, Kent CT1 3AH (☎01227-811506; fax 01227-787740; e-mail recruitment@staffordhouse.com). British Council accredited language school that has been running EFL summer schools for several years.
**Management Staff, EFL Teachers, Activity Leaders** required to work at centres throughout the UK. Good rates of pay and excellent working conditions.
For *further information* please e-mail the above address.

**TWIN GROUP:** 24 Clarendon Rise, Lewisham, London SE13 SEY (☎020-8297 1132; fax 020-8297 0984; e-mail m.borley@twinschool.co.uk; www.twinschool.co.uk).
**EFL Teachers.** Wages from £210 to £275 per week. Involves both teaching and running activities, with groups of up to 15 students. Must hold at least Cert. TEFL qualifications.
**Activity Organisers, Administration Officers and Welfare Officers.** Wages of £250 per week.
Work is available in July and August in schools mainly in the south of England with a few in the Midlands and East Anglia. Some centres require applicants to be residential and some do not.
*Applications* to Marcus Borley at the above address as soon as possible.

**WELS GROUP OF INTERNATIONAL HOUSE SCHOOLS:** International House, Castle Road, Torquay TQ1 3BB (☎01803-299691; fax 01803-291946; e-mail info@ih-westengland.co.uk; www.ih-westengland.co.uk). English language programmes at three centres (formerly run by ELCO) in Hertfordshire, Buckinghamshire, and Sussex; also two year-round schools running summer English programmes for juniors in Bath and Torquay. Part of a group with over 120 affiliated schools in 40 countries.

**EFL Teachers (20-30).** Salary £250-£350 per week. Min. period of work three weeks. Staff required 1 July to 29 August. Must have a university degree and either a PGCE or UCLES DIP TEFL or UCLES Cert TEFL or Trinity Cert. Accommodation provided free of charge at Buckinghamshire and Sussex centres.
*Contact* Richard Gubbin at the above address from February 2003. Interview required.

**YES EDUCATION CENTRE:** 12 Eversfield Road, Eastbourne, East Sussex BN21 2AS (☎01323-644830; fax 01323-726260; e-mail dos@yeseducation.co.uk). A friendly, independent school commmitted to high academic and professional standards.
**EFL Teachers.** Wages £175-£400 per week for adult and junior schools in Eastbourne, and junior schools in Abingdon, Brighton, Hastings, Oxford and Seaford. Staff required in July and August. No accommodation provided. Relevant teaching qualifications required.
*Applications* to the Director of Studies for Eastbourne, or Mrs Brigid Simcox, Course Director External Centres, for the other towns.

# Medical

**ACTIVE ASSISTANCE:** Lime Tree House, 15 Lime Tree Walk, Sevenoaks, Kent TN13 1YH (☎01732-746672; fax 01732-746674; enquiries@activeassistance.com ; www.activeassistance.com). Active Assistance provides live-in carers to physically disabled clients in their own homes.
**Care Assistants** required for live-in positions. Wages from £47.50 per day worked. Minimum period of work 3 months at any time of year. Must be 21 or over and have a driving licence. Suitably qualified foreign applicants with good spoken English are welcome.
*Applications* at any time to the Personnel Department at the above address or please complete the on-line form on the above Website address.

**ALL CARE SOUTH WALES:** 228 Holton Road, Barry CF63 4HS (☎01446-701020; fax 01446-722788).
**Home Care Workers (6)** needed between July-September to work various hours and days for wages of £4.50 per hour. Applicants must be over 21.
*Applications* to Anne Payne at the above address.

**CHRISTIES CARE LTD:** The Old Post Office, High Street, Saxmundham, Suffolk IP17 1AB (☎01728-605000; fax 01728-605026; e-mail recruit@christiescare.com; www.christiescare.com). Founded in 1987, the company provides live-in care to dependent adults in their own homes nationwide.
**Carers (50)** for live-in positions with clients in their own homes. Clients are all dependent adults with many different ailments who need varying degrees of care such as incontinence management, hoist work for paraplegics, experience with dealing with dementia and the bedridden; all need home help with cooking, shopping and housekeeping. Salary up to £400 per 7 days. Staff required all year round; minimum period of work 7 full days. Applicants with experience preferred but training provided. Minimum age 18. Must be able to work legally in the UK.
*Applications* to the Recruitment Department at the above address.

**CONSULTUS:** 17 London Road, Tonbridge, Kent (☎01732-355231; fax 01732-360693; e-mail info@consultuscarers.co.uk; www.consultuscarers.co.uk). Founded

in 1962 by the present Managing Director, Consultus is now one of the major providers of live-in care in Britain. Their aim is to help the elderly remain in their own homes for as long as possible.
**Live-in Carers (20)** needed nationwide to perform domestic duties and some personal care for elderly private clients. Duties may include cooking, cleaning, housekeeping, shopping and a varying degree of personal care of the client. Wages from £45+ per day, with own room in client's house. To work on two-week live-in assignments. Positions are available all year. Over 21 only. Some experience of care of the elderly/disabled necessary. Foreign applicants with relevant permits and clear English welcome.
*Applications* should be made at any time to the Residential Care Department at the above address. Interview necessary.

**CURA DOMI-CARE AT HOME:** Guardian House, Borough Road, Godalming, Surrey GU7 2AE (☎01483-302275; fax 01483-304302).
**Carers** required to care for elderly and disabled people in their own homes. Wages vary according to the position being offered but are typically £330-£420 a week, plus accommodation and travel expenses, as relevant, and paid annual leave. Period of work by arrangement. Positions are either residential (nationwide) or non-residential (local to Guildford, Surrey). Applicants are given an interview and training session. Qualified Handling and Moving courses available free to all carers plus 24 hour office support. Overseas applicants with fluent English and the necessary documents to work in the UK welcome.
*Applications* to the above address.

**NURSES DIRECT:** 26 Harmer St, Gravesend, Kent DA12 2AX (☎0800-376 6154; fax 0870-124 8146; e-mail k.may@nursesdirect.co.uk). Has 14 offices serving South London, Kent, Surrey, Sussex, Hampshire, South Devon and Dorset. They employ trained nurses and experienced carers to work for various organisations.
**Trained Nurses (50); Care Assistants (75) Learning Disability Support Workers (35).** Wages are competitive. To work weekdays or weekends. No min. period of work. Positions are available all year. Minimum age 18. Required qualifications depend on the position sought. Foreign applicants are welcome if they are authorised to work in the UK and have a good standard of English.
*Applications* should be made as early as possible to Kevin May at the above address. A local interview will be necessary.

**PGL TRAVEL** Alton Court, Penyard Lane (874), Ross-on-Wye, Herefordshire HR9 5GL (☎01989-767833; e-mail pglpeople@pgl.co.uk; www.pgl.co.uk/people). With 25 activity centres located in the UK, France and Spain, PGL Travel provides adventure holidays and courses for children. Each year 2,500 people are needed to help run these adventure centres.
**Nurses** (RGN, EGN. or equivalent) needed to work in the UK. Vacancies available for short or long periods between February and October. Full board and accommodation provided plus £100 per week. Suitably qualified overseas applicants who are eligible to work in the UK welcome.
Full *details* and an application form can be obtained from the above address; applications can also be made online.

# Outdoor

**CENTRE D'ECHANGES INTERNATIONAUX (CEI):** 164/168 Westminster Bridge Road, Devonshire House, London SE1 7RW (☎020-7960 2600; fax 020-

## Come and Get Fruity With Us!

jobs on UK farms – ideal for backpackers
accommodation provided – short and long term placements

check out:

**www.fruitfuljobs.com**

**Fruitful Ltd.**

---

7960 2601; e-mail info@cei-frenchcentre.com). The CEI helps European nationals to find a job and provides accommodation and English courses in London. It recruits for the following areas of work:
**Farm Work (50)** Wages from £4 per hour; minimum of 40 hours per week, depending on season.
**Activity Instructors (20)** In summer camps; police check necessary. Accommodation provided; wages from £3.70 per hour for 39 hours per week. Experience working with children necessary; good level of English required.

For all positions, staff are required all year round. Minimum period of work of 8 weeks. Applicants from anywhere in the European community welcome; must be 18 or over.

*Applications* should be made at least 10 weeks before arrival in the UK, to the Employment Consultant at the above address. Interview not always required.

**EVENTS STAFF LTD:** 25 York Road, Northampton NN1 5QA (01604-627775; fax 01604-627004). A recruitment company that supplies staff to events such as the British Grand Prix, large scale outdoor events and shows, and various horse racing fixtures across the country.
**Stewards, Programme Sellers, Ticket Sellers, Car Park Attendants, Waiting and Bar Staff (1000+ at peak of summer).**

*Applications* welcome any time. Applicants must be over 16, and willing to work long hours outdoors. Call the above number for an information pack.

**FIELD AND LAWN (MARQUEES) LTD:** Southlands, Leeds Road, Thorpe Willoughby, North Yorkshire YO8 9PZ (☎01757-210444; e-mail allen@fieldandlawn.com). A young and enthusiastic company which takes a pride in its product and employees. Work hard, play hard atmosphere.
**MARQUEE ERECTORS** required to work long hours erecting marquees throughout England and Wales. Wages starting at £5 per hour. The work is very strenuous so fitness is essential. Overseas applicants, particularly from New Zealand, South Africa and Australia, welcome.
Positions are available from May to November.

*Applications* from 1 April through to end of September to the Operations Manager at the above address or telephone number or e-mail allen@fieldandlawn.com.

**LEAPFROG INTERNATIONAL LTD:** Riding Court Farm, Datchet, Berkshire SL3 9JU (☎01753-589300; fax 01753-580881; e-mail emt@leapfrog-int.co.uk).

**Events Crew (Up To 100)** Ages 18-40, needed to help set up and run outdoor activities such as team-building challenges, family fun days and 'Its a knockout' tournaments. Wages are a set figure per event; hours of work vary from day to day. Period of work between June and September. Events take place all around the UK. Travel to events is organised by Leapfrog International from their headquarters in Datchet. Applicants should be enthusiastic, outgoing, enjoy working with people and like to travel. A clean driving licence is an advantage; previous experience not essential as full training will be given.

Please call The Event Management Team for an *applications* pack.

# Sport

**GREAT ADVENTURES:** Grafham Water Centre, Perry, Huntingdon, Cambridgeshire PE18 0BX (☎01480-810521; fax 01480-812739; e-mail grafham.water@education.cambridgeshire.gov.uk; www.grafham-water-centre.co.uk). Run special interest and activity holidays and courses with centres in Cambridgeshire and Derbyshire.

**Activity Instructors (20)** wanted for canoeing, windsurfing, sailing, archery, climbing and mountain biking. Wages £184 per week plus food and accommodation. To work 40 hours per week from May to July; min. period of work 2 months. Positions also available for 10 months. Must have N.G.B. qualifications. Overseas applicants welcome.

*Applications* from January to Mr Ian Downing at the above address. Interview required.

**HF HOLIDAYS LIMITED:** Imperial House, Edgware Rd, London NW9 5AL (☎020-8905 9556 quoting LEA1). The UK's leading walking holiday company (founded 1913) is a non-profit seeking organisation which owns 19 Country House Hotels based in some of the most scenic parts of Britain.

**Walk Leaders** are required to lead walks catering for all levels of walker. Applicants may choose where, how often and when they want to lead the walking holidays (from 2-30 weeks per year). Full board and accommodation, travel expenses and training opportunities will be provided. This is an excellent opportunity to improve leadership skills and for ML logbook experience.

Applicants should be experienced walkers with leadership potential, fully competent in the use of map and compass, considerate and tactful. Residential assessment courses are held during the winter and spring(difficult for applicants living abroad) so application by February is essential.

For *applications* or an information pack contact the Walking Department at the above address.

**PGL TRAVEL:** Alton Court, Penyard Lane (874), Ross-on-Wye, Herefordshire HR9 5GL (☎01989-767833; e-mail pglpeople@pgl.co.uk; www.pgl.co.uk/people). PGL provides adventure holidays and courses for children. It has 25 activity centres located in the UK, France and Spain. Each year 2,500 people are needed to help run these adenture centres.

**Experienced Activity Instructors** in canoeing, sailing, windsurfing, pony trekking, multi-activites, drama, arts and crafts and English language. From £50-85 per week plus free B & L. Vacancies available for short or long periods between February and October. Qualifications not essential as full training will be provided. Minimum age 18.

*Applications* can be made online, or request a form from the above address.

## Websites

**anyworkanywhere.com:** e-mail anyworkanywhere.com; www.anyworkanywhere.com
This organisation provides a free source of information to people looking for casual, seasonal and temporary work in the UK and wide through the site www.anyworkanywhere.com. It lists a variety of employment including work in 16th century pubs, forestry conservation in the Caledonian mountains, hotel work, fruit and vegetable picking, jobs in activity centres, care work and childcare.
The site also provides other useful information on work and travel such as directories of hostels, cyber cafés and embassies and links to other useful and relevant sites. For those who are a little more adventurous and just want to turn up and see what jobs are available further afield it includes a guide to the main locations and times of ski seasons and harvests worldwide.

*Advertising Casual, Seasonal, Temporary & Even Long-Term Job Opportunities Worldwide!*
**AnyworkAnywhere.com**

**Fruitfuljobs.com:** email info@fruitfuljobs.com  www.fruitfuljobs.com
Fruitful Ltd provides jobs with accommodation on UK farms. The work offered can range from just a few weeks casual work to a full time career. Types of jobs include field, packhouse and camp supervisors, quality controllers, drivers, pickers and packers and although the main season runs from March to October work is available throughout the year.
The majority of jobs are on fruit farms and are ideal for backpackers as they offer work in the countryside providing the opportunity to get out of London and save some money! The workforces are multi-national which is great for the social side of things and also means that the growers have plenty of experience employing overseas travellers.
Please see www.fruitfuljobs.com for more information

# Voluntary Work

## Archaeology

**COUNCIL FOR BRITISH ARCHAEOLOGY:** Bowes Morrell House, 111 Walmgate, York YO1 9WA (☎ 01904-671417; fax 01904-671384; e-mail info@britarch.ac.uk; www.britarch.ac.uk).
The CBA works to promote the study and safeguarding of Britain's historic environment, to provide a forum for archaeological opinion, and to improve public

interest in, and knowledge of, Britain's past.
Details of **Excavations** and other fieldwork projects are given on the Council's website and in the Council's publication *British Archaeology*. The magazine appears six times a year. An annual subscription costs £23; however, it also forms part of an individual membership package which is available for £26 per year and brings extra benefits.

Having studied the magazine you should make *applications* to the Director of the projects which interest you.

## Children

**NATIONAL ASTHMA CAMPAIGN:** Providence House, Providence Place, London N1 ONT (☎0207-704 5892; fax 020-7704 0740; pladbury@asthma.org.uk). Runs PEAK (Project for Eczema and Asthma Kids).
**Volunteer Helpers, Doctors and Nurses** to work with children and young people with asthma and eczema on one-week adventure and activity holidays in July and August. The young people are aged 6-17 and the camps take place in locations throughout the UK.

Board and accommodation are provided; those accepted must take part in a training weekend, with travel and board paid. Applicants must be aged at least 17 and are expected to stay for the duration of a camp; relevant medical or sporting and childcare experience desirable. Volunteers will also be needed for family weekends throughout the winter.

For *further information* please contact the Peak Manager at the above address.

**SCRIPTURE UNION:** 207-209 Queensway, Bletchley, Milton Keynes, Bucks MK2 2EB (☎01908-856177; fax 01908-856012; e-mail holidays@scriptureunion.org.uk; www.scriptureunion.org.uk).
An International non-denominational Christian movement that has been running residential holidays for children and young people throughout England and Wales for over 100 years
**Volunteers** to help as team members on Scripture Union residential 7-10 day holidays around the UK for young people aged from 8-18+. Volunteers are expected to be on site 24 hours a day to help organise activities during the holiday as part of a team; training is given before the beginning of the holiday.

Volunteers pay for their own accommodation and meals, but a Volunteer Grant Fund may assist with some of the costs. Minimum period of work one week. Applicants must be committed Christians in sympathy with the aims of Scripture Union and aged 18 or over; there are particular needs for people with qualifications in catering, first aid, life-saving, sports, mountaineering and working with disabled people.

*Applications* should be sent to the Holidays Administrator at the above address.

## Conservation and the Environment

**BTCV:** 36 St. Mary's Street, Wallingford, Oxfordshire OX10 0EU (☎01491-821600; e-mail information@btcv.org.uk; www.btcv.org).
BTCV is the UK's leading practical conservation charity. Every year it involves over 130,000 volunteers in projects to protect and enhance our environment.

BTCV offers a programme of over **500 Conservation Working Holidays** each year in the UK and overseas. These last from 3 to 10 days, and include wetland management in the Norfolk Broads, dry stone walling in Cumbria and wolf tracking

in Slovakia.
No experience is required, just plenty of enthusiasm and energy. Prices start at £25 for a weekend and £50 for a week to cover food, accommodation and training in conservation skills (£200 plus for international holidays). Volunteers typically work from 9am-5pm with evenings free and a day off during the week. Accommodation ranges from village halls to youth hostels and field centres.
For further information *contact* the above address or visit the BTCV website.

**CATHEDRAL CAMPS:** 16 Glebe Avenue, Flitwick, Bedfordshire MK45 1HS (☎01525-716237; e-mail admin@cathedalcamps.org.uk; www.cathedralcamps.org.uk). Registered Charity No. 286248.
**Volunteers** required to work in groups of 15-25 people undertaking maintenance, conservation and restoration of cathedrals and their surroundings all over the country. Hours normally 8.30am-5.30pm, 4½ days a week. The one-week camps take place from July to September. A contribution of approx. £60 is asked to go towards the cost of the camp and board and lodging. Min. age 16; most are aged 17-25.
For further details and an *applications* form contact Shelley Bent at the above address.

**EARTHWATCH:** 267 Banbury Road, Oxford OX2 7HT (☎01865-318831; fax 01865-311383; e-mail info@earthwatch.org.uk; www.earthwatch.org/europe). An international charity that promotes the sustainable conservation of our natural and cultural heritage through conservation, research and education, creating partnerships between scientists, the public, educators and businesses.
Earthwatch recruits **Paying Volunteers** to help research scientists on environmental projects worldwide. Around 4,000 volunteers take part each year, on projects lasting from three to eighteen days. They currently offer around 130 projects in 45 countries, including 10 in the UK. You could work as part of a team helping to conduct a study of Britain's Basking sharks, tracking dinosaurs on the Yorkshire coast, or monitoring mammals in Oxfordshire's ancient Wytham Woods.
No special skills are required since any training that is required is given in the field. All English speaking volunteers over 16 are welcome. Volunteers pay a share of the project costs, which range from £120 to £1265, with reductions for members. Most prices include food and accommodation, but travel is extra.
For *further details* and availability contact Earthwatch at the address above.

**THE NATIONAL TRUST:** 33 Sheep Street, Cirencester, Gloucestershire GL7 1RQ (☎01285-651818; fax 01285-657935; volunteers@nationaltrust.org.uk; www.nationaltrust.org.uk/volunteers).
Leading conservation and environmental charity.
The National Trust has a range of **Volunteering Opportunities** if you are looking to fill a gap year, change career or gain work experience. Roles range from assisting with wardening, gardening, housekeeping and interpretation to events and conservation. All located at beautiful Trust sites. Training is provided and accommodation may be available; some placements are available through the New Deal scheme; out-of-pocket expenses covered. Minimum length of commitment generally 6 months.
For an *information pack* call 0870-609 5383, e-mail or visit their website.

**WWOOFUK (World Wide Opportunities on Organic Farms):** PO Box 2675, Lewes, Sussex BN7 1RB. (tel/fax 01273-476286; e-mail hello@wwoof.org; www.wwoof.org).
An opportunity to help the organic growers, get into the countryside (UK and

worldwide) and meet like-minded people to learn and share in an atmosphere of mutual trust.
**Volunteers** are needed to spend time working on organic farms, gardens and smallholdings around the UK: organic farming avoids the use of artificial fertilisers and pest killers, and can be labour intensive. Simple accommodation and food are provided. Short and long stays available. Applicants must have a genuine interest in furthering the organic movement. *Applications* welcomed from students/individuals of any nationality all year round. EU applicants do not need work permits, Australians, New Zealanders and Canadians need vacation work permits, all others need work permits.

For further information and *applications* send a s.a.e. to the above address or go to their website.

## Heritage

**WATERWAY RECOVERY GROUP:** PO BOX 114, Rickmansworth, Herts WD3 1ZY (☎01923-711114; fax 01923-897000; e-mail enquiries@wrg.org.uk; www.wrg.org.uk).
The National co-ordinating body for voluntary labour on the inland waterways of Great Britain.
**Volunteers** needed to restore Britain's derelict canals: work may involve restoring industrial archaeology, demolishing old brickwork, driving a dumper truck, clearing mud and vegetation and helping at a National Waterways festival. To work either on weekends or weeklong canal camps. Work is available year round; minimum period of work 1 day. No experience or qualifications are necessary but applicants should be at least 17 years old.
Accommodation and food provided; accomodation in a village hall or similar for £35 per week/£5 per day. Overseas applicants welcome.
*Apply* to The Enquiries Officer at the above address.

## Physically/Mentally Disabled

**THE CAMPHILL VILLAGE TRUST:** Delrow House, Hilfield Lane, Aldenham, Watford, Herts WD25 8DJ (☎01923-856006).
The Association of Camphill Communities runs working communities for mentally handicapped adults and children throughout Britain. They are based on anthroposophy, as founded by Rudolf Steiner.
**Voluntary Helpers** are required for the household, workshop or on the land. Free B & L and a small personal allowance are provided.There are a limited number of summer jobs available, otherwise the min. period of work is 12 months. Min. age 20. Overseas applicants welcome.

For a list of the addresses of Camphill Village Trust centres, *apply* in writing to the Secretary at Delrow House.

**LEONARD CHESHIRE:** Central Office, 30 Millbank, London SW1P 4QD (☎020-7802 8200; fax 020-7802 8250; e-mail u.salmon@london.leonard-cheshire.org.uk).
Leonard Cheshire is the UK's leading charity providing support services for people with physical and learning disabilities. Many of the 80 residential homes offer **Opportunities For Volunteers**, who assist with the day-to-day care and social activities of physically disabled residents.

Board, lodging and pocket money is provided. Period of work from 6 to 12 months. Volunteers must be able to speak good English. *Enquiries* to Head of Volunteer Support c/o the above address.

**RADAR (Royal Association for Disability and Rehabilitation):** 12 City Forum, 250 City Road, London EC1V 8AF (☎020-7250 3222; fax 020-7250 0212; minicom 020-7250 4119; e-mail radar@radar.org.uk; www.radar.org.uk).
A national organisation run by and working with disabled people to remove architectural, economic and attitudinal barriers. Provides information and advice about a variety of subjects affecting the daily life of disabled people, including civil rights, holidays, mobility, employment and social services.
   Has a comprehensive list of appropriate contacts organisations to which it can refer **Volunteers**.
   For further details and *applications* contact RADAR at the above address.

**RIDING FOR THE DISABLED ASSOCIATION:** Lavinia Norfolk House, Avenue R, Stoneleigh Park, Warwickshire CV8 2LY (☎024-7669 6510; fax 024-7669 6532; e-mail rdahq@riding-for-disabled.org.uk; http://www.riding-for-disabled.org.uk).
The RDA is a registered charity consisting of some 600 member groups throughout the UK. Providing holidays for disabled people is one of the many services it offers to its members.
**Volunteer Helpers** required to help on RDA holidays throughout the summer months, providing 24 hour care and supervision for between 3 and 7 days. Living expenses are provided along with free accommodation at some venues. Volunteers are needed for a minimum of 3 days between May and September. A knowledge of horse riding is preferable along with a First Aid/medical qualification and work experience with disabled people. Suitably qualified foreign applicants are welcome. Minimum age 16.
   Applicants should contact the above address from January for details of the holidays being run and to make *applications*.

**THE 3H FUND:** 147a Camden Road, Tunbridge Wells, Kent TN1 2RA (☎01892-547474; fax 01892 524703).
**Carers (around 100)** required to assist with one-to-one care for physically disabled people on holiday. Holidays are usually for one week to 10 days and take place between May and September.
   B & L are provided, but a contribution of £175 is requested for the overseas holidays: advice can be given on raising this by sponsorship. Applicants should have a sense of humour, a strong back, great patience and a sense of responsibility. Experience is an advantage but not essential. Volunteers can enjoy a working holiday with much fun and laughter whilst enabling the people with disabilities to also enjoy a holiday. Applicants should be aged between 18 and 60.
   *Applications* to the Holidays and Grants Administrator, from November to the above address.

**WINGED FELLOWSHIP TRUST:** Angel House, 20-32 Pentonville Road, London N1 9XD (☎020-7833 2594; fax 020-7278 0370; e-mail admin@wft.org.uk; www.wft.org.uk).
WFT provides holidays for disabled people and breaks for carers. **Volunteers** needed for one or two weeks at a time, to help trained staff enhance the holiday atmosphere for the guests. Holidays are available at purpose-built centres in Essex, Nottingham, Cornwall, Merseyside and Southampton, where guests can enjoy a break with or

without their regular carer. Volunteers are provided with free accommodation and meals in exchange for their time. Overseas applicants with good English welcome.

For an *application form* please contact Flavia at the above address.

## Social and Community Schemes

**L'ARCHE:** 10 Briggate Silsden, Keighley, West Yorkshire BD20 9JT (☎01535-656186; fax 01535-656426; e-mail info@larche.org.uk; www/larche.org.uk).
Seeks to reveal the particular gifts of people with learning disabilities who belong at the very heart of their communities, and who call others to share their lives. There are L'Arche communities in Kent, Inverness, Liverpool, Lambeth, Bognor, Brecon, Edinburgh and Preston where people with and without learning disabilities share life in ordinary houses.
**Volunteer Assistants** aged 18-65 required to share life and work with people with learning disabilities in an ecumenical Christian-based community. Volunteers receive upwards of £25 per week and free B & L. Staff required all year round for a minimum of three months. After completing the application form candidates are invited to visit the community and interviews are held. Overseas applicants in possession of the necessary work visas are welcome.

*Applications* by Easter to the above address.

**CSV (COMMUNITY SERVICE VOLUNTEERS):** 237 Pentonville Road, London N1 9NJ (freephone 0800-374991; fax 020-7837 9318; e-mail volunteer@csv.org.uk; www.csv.org.uk).
**Volunteers** go away from home for 4-12 months and volunteer on a range of social care and community projects in Britain. You could support children with special needs, homeless people or enable someone with a disability to lead an independent life. You gain valuable work experience by volunteering with CSV.
  All volunteers receive free accommodation and food (or a food allowance of £33.50 per week), all expenses and a living allowance of £27 per week. You can start a placement at any time of the year. Support is provided to all volunteers. No qualifications are required and volunteering with CSV is available to everyone aged 16 and over.
  Further details from the above address or from freephone number.
*Applications* are welcome at any time.

**COTTAGE & RURAL ENTERPRISES LTD.:** 36D Newgate Street, Morpeth, Northumberland NE61 1BA (☎01670-511157; fax 01670-511080; e-mail carefun d.north@freeuk.com).
CARE provides support to people with a learning disability through the provision of residential accommodation work and other daycare facilities which offer each person the opportunity to live a full and purposeful life.
**Volunteers** work alongside staff in assisting people with learning disbilities in CARE's communities around England. Around 40 hours work a week; volunteers receive an allowance and board and lodgings. A minimum commitment of 4 weeks is expected at any time of the year. Minimum age 18; must have good communication skills.
  *Applications* to Mr Gary Richardson, Assistant Director of Fundraising, at the above address.

**THE PRINCE'S TRUST VOLUNTEERS:** 18 Park Square East, London NW1 4LH (☎020-7543 1234; fax 020-7543 1367; www.princes-trust.org.uk).

The Prince's Trust Volunteers is a programme for 16-25 year olds which builds confidence, motivation and skills through teamwork in the community. It has been running successfully throughout the UK since 1990 and some 10,000 people now take part each year.

**Personal Development Programme.** Everyone who takes part joins a team of about 15 people, led by a trained team leader. The programme involves team-building activities, an outdoor residential week away and work experience and projects in the community. The community work involves tasks that help the environment and people in need. Most tasks are local so accommodation is not provided. The usual period of commitment is approx. 12 weeks. Placements available all year round.

Anyone interested should *call* freephone 0800-842 842 for the contact details of their nearest programme.

**TOC H:** 1 Forest Close, Wendover, Aylesbury, Buckinghamshire HP22 6BT (☎01296-623911; fax 01296-696137; e-mail info@toch.org.uk; www.toch.org.uk).

Toc H offers short residential volunteering opportunities throughout the year in Britain and Europe, lasting usually from a weekend up to two weeks. **Project Work** undertaken can include: work with people with different disabilities; work with children in need; playschemes and camps; conservation and manual work; study and/or discussion sessions. These projects provide those who take part with opportunities to learn more about themselves and the world we live in.

Minimum age 16, but there is no upper age limit. The Toc H events programme is published yearly and can be viewed on their website. There is no closing date for *applications*, but you are advised to apply early. Annual recruitment is over 500.

## Workcamps

**ATD FOURTH WORLD:** 48 Addington Square, London SE5 7LB.

ATD Fourth World is an international voluntary organisation which adopts a human rights approach to overcome extreme poverty. It supports the effort of very disadvantaged and excluded families in fighting poverty and taking an active role in the community. Founded in a shanty town on the outskirts of Paris in 1957, it now works in 27 countries on 5 continents.

ATD Fourth World organises workcamps, street workshops and Family Stays in London and Surrey in the UK and other European countries. The workcamps are a combination of **Manual Work** in and around ATD's buildings, conversation and reflection on the lives and hopes of families living in extreme poverty and on the aims and objectives of the organisation.

The street workshops bring a festival atmosphere to underprivileged areas. **Voluntary Artists, Craftsmen Etc** share their skills with the children and their parents. These street workshops for painting, crafts, computing and books etc. take place in the streets of deprived areas and make it possible to break down barriers allowing freedom of expression and building confidence.

The family stays allow families split up by poverty, perhaps with children in care, to come together for a break. The volunteers assist ATD Fourth World workers to give the families a holiday to grow together and learn new skills. The camps, Street Workshops and Family stays take place from July to September. Most last two weeks. Participants pay their own travel costs plus a contribution to the cost of food and accommodation. ATD is willing to take on foreign applicants.

For further information volunteers should *contact* ATD Fourth World at the above address enclosing a s.a.e.

**CONCORDIA:** Heversham House, 20-22 Boundary Road, Hove BN3 4ET (tel/fax 01273-422218; e-mail info@concordia-iye.org.uk; www concordia-iye.org.uk). Concordia is a small not-for-profit charity committed to international youth exchange. Its International Volunteer Programme offers young people the opportunity to join an international team of **Volunteers Working On Community-Based Projects** ranging from nature conservation, restoration and construction to more socially based schemes; they last for 2-3 weeks with a main season running June-September, although there are some spring projects.

In general no special skills or experience are required but real motivation and commitment are essential. Volunteers pay a registration fee of approx. £60 for UK projects and must fund their own travel. Board and accommodation available free of charge.

Volunteers aged 20 or over are also required to act as group co-ordinators, for which training is required and expenses are paid.

Details of projects will be available from March/April; for further information send an s.a.e. to the Volunteer Programme Manager or consult the above Website. Please note that foreign applicants must apply through a voluntary organisation in their own country; if necessary Concordia can pass on details of partner organisations.

*Applications* should normally be made to the above address.

**INTERNATIONAL VOLUNTARY SERVICE (IVS):** IVS-GB South, Old Hall, East Bergholt, Colchester CO7 6TQ (☎01206-298215; fax 01206-299043); IVS-GB North, Castlehill House, 21 Otley Road, Leeds LS6 3AA (☎0113-2304 600); IVS-Scotland, 7 Upper Bow, Edinburgh EH1 2JN (☎0131-226 6722).
IVS is the British branch of Service Civil International (SCI). It organises about 40 workcamps in Britain each year as well as sending volunteers to workcamps in over 35 countries overseas.
**Volunteers** work for two to four weeks in an international team of 10-20 people, sharing domestic and social life as well as the work. The projects include work with children, work with people with physical or mental disabilities and manual work, often connected with ecology or conservation. The projects are not holidays: the work can be hard and demands commitment.

Most workcamps are between June and September. Volunteers pay membership plus a registration fee (£35-£115) and their own travel costs, and must be 16 or over (or 18 for workcamps overseas). Free B & L is provided on the project. IVS is working toward equal opportunities and welcomes applications from women, black people, people with disabilities, people from ethnic minorities, gay men and lesbians. Applicants from overseas should apply for IVS Schemes through partner voluntary organisations in their own country. Americans should contact SCI, Innisfree Village, Route 2, Box 506, Crozet, Virginia 22932, USA.

*Write for* more information to one of the regional addresses above, enclosing £4 for the listing of summer workcamps (available from April). Enquiries from January will be put on a mailing list to receive the listing when it is ready.

**NATIONAL TRUST WORKING HOLIDAYS:** c/o OpenContact Direct Marketing, Sapphire House, Roundtree Way, Norwich NR7 8SQ (☎0870 429 2428; e-mail workingholidays@nationaltrust.org.uk; www.nationaltrust.org.uk/volunteering).
A charity dependent on volunteers which cares for more than 248,000 hectares of outstanding countryside, almost 600 miles of unspoilt coastline, and over 200 historic houses and gardens.
The National Trust organises over **400 Working Holidays** in outdoor conservation work, biological surveying, archaeology, construction and various other interests.

These take place on National Trust properties in England, Wales and Northern Ireland throughout the year. Each project involves 12 or so volunteers and lasts for 1 week to 10 days. There are also some weekend projects.

Volunteers pay from £54 per week to help cover the cost of board and lodging, and are responsible for their own travel expenses. Accommodation varies from purpose-built hostels to converted barns; volunteers supply bedding or sleeping bags. Min. age 17. Overseas applicants welcome but must be over 18 and have good conversational English.

For a brochure, please telephone, e-mail or write using the above contact details.

**PILGRIM ADVENTURE:** 27 Oldbury Court Road, Fishponds, Bristol BS16 6JJ (☎0117-957 3997; www.pilgrim-adventure.org.uk). An ecumenical Christian organisation founded in 1987. Provides an annual programme of 'Pilgrim Journeys' on foot and by boat through Celtic Britain and Ireland.

**Volunteer Team Members** to help lead all age groups of 10-25 people taking part in Pilgrim Adventure's annual programme of Pilgrim Journeys within the UK and Ireland. Staying in hostels, monasteries, tents and small hotels. Team members should be able to co-lead at least one Pilgrim Journey of about 7 days each year, and take an active part in the planning of Pilgrim Journeys throughout the year. Training will be provided.

Applicants must have a sense of adventure and Christian commitment. *Applications* to Mr David Gleed at the above address.

**QUAKER VOLUNTARY ACTION:** Friends Meeting House, 6 Mount Street, Manchester M2 5NS (tel/fax 0161-819 1634; e-mail qva@quakervolaction.freeserve.co.uk; www.qva.org.uk).

QVA runs short-term (2-3 weeks) volunteer projects in Britain and Northern Ireland each year which mainly take place in the summer. Some medium-term and long-term **Opportunities** are now being developed. Please phone or e-mail for details. The topics include manual projects, work with adults or children who have mental or physical disabilities, playschemes, youth work or community art events. All projects meet a particular need in a local community which could not be met without the help of QVA volunteers.

Food and accommodation (usually basic) is provided free of charge. Volunteers pay for their own travel to the project and their own pocket money, and a small registration fee is also charged.

Special experience is not required. Volunteers with disabilities are welcome to apply. Foreign applicants should apply through an organisation in their own country; QVA can only deal with *Applications* from UK residents. There are opportunities to go on projects in other countries (Western and Eastern Europe, USA and Japan). Min. age 18. The new Summer Programme is available in April; to obtain a copy please send a large s.a.e. with a 33 pence stamp to the above address.

# Vacation Traineeships & Internships

## Accountancy, Banking and Insurance

**BARCLAYS BANK PLC:** Graduate Recruitment, 1st Floor, 155 Bishopgate, London, EC2M 3XA (www.graduatecareers.barclays.com).

Barclays is much more than just high street banking for personal customers. The

Group is also a leading provider of financial services to high net worth clients, small and medium businesses, multinational corporations and financial institutions.
**Barclays'Summer Business Placements** are designed to give penultimate year students quality work experience and provide a taste of what it is like to work for Barclays on our graduate programme. Students will have the opportunity to gain practical commerical experience and to develop skills at the heart of an international organisation.

Placements last for 8 weeks, commencing in July with a short induction course. This includes presentations from senior people, team activities and social events. After induction, placement students will join their team for the summer within their chosen business area. Placements exist in Barclays Corporate or Retail banking businesses or within a specialist function such as Marketing, Human Resources, Finance or Technology Solutions. Additionally placements can be a foundation for a career with one of the top 12 employers of choice (Times Top 100 Survey). If students perform well during their placement and show the potential to make a valuable contribution to the business, they will be offered a place on the graduate programme for September 2004.

Applicants must be penultimate year students expecting a 2:1 degree and holding a minimum of 22 UCAS points. *Applications* are on-line only and the closing date is 12 noon on 3 January 2003.

**DELOITTE AND TOUCHE:** Hill House, 1 Little New Street, London EC4A 3TR (☎0800-323333; e-mail gradrec.uk@deloitte.co.uk; www.graduates.deloitte.co.uk). Professional services firm with offices in Aberdeen, Belfast, Birmingham, Bristol, Cambridge, Cardiff, Crawley, Edinburgh, Glasgow, Isle of Man, Guernsey, Jersey, Leeds, Liverpool, London, Manchester, Newcastle, Nottingham, Southampton and St Albans.

Deloitte and Touche offer **100 Vacation Trainee Placements** each year throughout the UK primarily for work within Chartered Accountancy areas, though experience within other service lines may be possible. Placements are open to penultimate year students with 24 UCAS points and grade B at Maths and English Language GCSE, and the expectation of a 2:2 from any degree discipline. Placements are offered during Christmas, Easter and Summer vacations with a competitive salary paid. Overseas applicants are welcome but must have a valid work permit.

You can *apply* online at www.graduates.deloitte.co.uk.

**ERNST & YOUNG:** Graduate Recruitment, Becket House, 1 Lambeth Palace Road, London SE1 7EU (freephone 0800-289208; www.ey.com/uk/graduate).
Ernst & Young is one of the world's largest professional services firms dedicated to helping their clients identify and capitalise on business opportunities throughout the world. They serve clients from 675 offices in over 130 countries. From most of their 21 offices in the UK the firm offers **Students** in their penultimate year at university the opportunity to work for a period of up to eight weeks in the summer vacation. The scheme consists of a one week induction course followed by around eight weeks practical work experience in specific business unit/office for the remainder of the programme. The programme provides a real-life experience of working within Ernst & Young and their culture, enabling you to obtain a better understanding of what a career with them would involve.

Applicants should have a minimum of 22 UCAS points, excluding general studies, and possess the determination to build a successful business career. For further information and an application form contact your careers service or ring the above freephone number.

**KPMG:** 8 Salisbury Square, Blackfriars, London EC4Y 8BB (☎freephone 0500-664655; www.kpmgcareers.co.uk).
KPMG is one of the world's big four firms of business advisers, providing solutions to clients' business problems right across the globe. They have offices in 159 different countries staffed by over 110,000 people worldwide.
KPMG runs **Vacation Programmes** offering an insight into the workings of a leading business advisory firm; it shows both the opportunities available to graduates and how a major international firm operates. KPMG offers on a national basis vacation experience to students of any degree discipline in their penultimate year at university. The length of the programmes vary and they may include workshadowing partners, managers and both qualified and trainee business advisers.

KPMG also offer a *Leading Edge* programme for those in their first year of study which involves a two day residential course aiming to provide a series of both personal and professional skills to aid career development; these are run at a variety of universities from late September.

For further details contact the Graduate Recruitment department at the above address or apply online.

**PRICEWATERHOUSECOOPERS:** No. 1 London Bridge Street, London SE1 9QL (☎0808-100 1500; fax 020-7804 3030; www.pwcglobal.com).
PricewaterhouseCoopers is the world's largest professional services organisation, providing a full range of business advisory services including auditing, business advisory, tax and actuarial services.

The **Summer Vacation Programme** gives students an insight into what the company does, the way it works and its company culture. The programme runs in London and regional offices, in a range of business areas – Assurance and Business Advisory Services, Tax and Legal Services, Actuarial, Corporate Finance and Recovery, and Management Consulting Services. Students are given a combination of business training and work experience similar to that of a graduate. Working with teams, students are able to make a direct contribution to the work of the firm while developing their own personal skills.

Pricewaterhousecoopers are looking for outstanding penultimate year undergraduates of any degree discipline. As competition for places is fierce you will need a strong academic record, expecting at least a 2:1, and should be able to demonstrate excellent communication and interpersonal skills.

For more information call into your careers service, telephone Freephone 0808-100 1500, or visit the Website at www.pwcglobal.com/uk/bridges. Apply before Easter.

**SAINSBURYS SUPERMARKETS:** 169 Union Street, London.
For **Finance Positions** see Sainsburys under *Business and Management* below.

**WATSON WYATT WORLDWIDE:** Terra Firma, 86 Station Road, Redhill, Surrey (☎01737-241144; fax 01737-274312; e-mail graduate.recruitment@en.watsonwyatt.com; www.watsonwyatt.com/graduate). A global consulting firm focused on human capital and financial management.
**Actuarial, Investment and HR Consulting Summer Scheme (approx. 20).**
Wages of approx. £250 per week. Placements last for 6 weeks. Applicants should be penultimate year students, expecting a 2:1 degree or have 24 UCAS points. No accommodation is available but assistance may be given in finding some.

*Applications* should be made by 31 March on line using the above website address.

## Business and Management

**BELAF STUDY HOLIDAYS:** Banner Lodge, Cherhill, Calne, Wiltshire SN11 8XR (☎01249-812551; fax 01249-821533; e-mail belaf@aol.com). An agency founded in 1975 that organises work traineeship placements in Southern England, London and the surrounding regions, Wiltshire, Dorset, Hampshire, Gloucestershire and Somerset.

**Work Placements (40).** Mainly unpaid. Placements last from 4-8 weeks and are available throughout the year, except in July and August. Placements available in sectors including tourism, catering, engineering and education. Minimum age 17 years; applicants must have a reasonable standard of English.

*Applications* from January-May to Carole Browne at the above address.

**DIALOGUE DIRECT LTD:** www.funkyjobs.co.uk; email: jobs@dialoguedirect.co.uk; tel:08454-583 901. A successful international fundraising agency working on behalf of charities and NPOs (non-profit organisations). Raising donations *face to face* for well-known charities all over the UK, in mobile teams. Work available year-round with main campaign in the summer months.

**Dialoguers.** OTE £180-£450 per week. (avg £250/ wk for those without previous training/ experience). Accommodation and team car hire paid for. All candidates start as face-to-face fundraisers, communicating directly with the public. Flexible contracts. Work is in small, live-in, UK mobile teams. Must have a positive and flexible attitude towards work and team-life, excellent communication skills and an energy and passion to succeed and represent good causes. Must be able to work and live successfully in a small team.

**Team Guides**: Fast progression for the right candidate to Team Guide. DialogueDirect has in-house training with a yearly seminar for Team Guides from across DD Europe.

All candidates must be over 18yrs and available to work away from home, minimum five week contract. No maximum age limit. Overseas applicants with fluent English and a working visa welcome, particularly those from New Zealand, Australia, America and South Africa.

Call the local number above for immediate interview.

---

**Travel, work, play...**

Dynamic fundraising agency looking for hardworking, self-motivated individuals, 18 yrs+ with excellent communication skills. Work away from home in a small travelling team, raising funds for well-known charities and NPOs (non-profit organisations).

Travel and accommodation paid. Good earnings - OTE £200-£450/wk
(avg. £250/wk for those without previous training/experience).
Minimum 5 weeks/ Long term prospects (Team Guide positions after experience)/ Training provided

T: 08454 583901    E: jobs@dialoguedirect.co.uk    www.funkyjobs.co.uk

*DialogueDirect*

---

**HEWLETT-PACKARD**: Caine Road, Bracknell, Berks RG12 1HN (☎01344-362335; fax 01344-362771; e-mail lister@hp.com). Internationally renowned company providing high technology hardware and professional business and IT services and consultancy.

**1 Year Undergraduate Placements (80)** in Sales, Marketing, HR, Finance, IT, and Services and Support. Students studying science and business-related disciplines are especially welcome.

*Applications* should be made to Tom Lister, Fresh Talent Acquisition Manager, Human Resources, at the above address.

**JOHN LEWIS PARTNERSHIP:** 171 Victoria Street, London SW1E 5NN (☎020-7592 6339; fax 020-7592 6301; e-mail careers@johnlewis.co.uk; www.johnlewis.co.uk).

The John Lewis Partnership offers around **8 Placements**, lasting 6 weeks, to penultimate year university students of any discipline. Successful candidates gain an overall view of trading in a department store. They gain experience of the different presentation, stock control and selling techniques applicable to a wide assortment of products. This is backed up by attachments in selling support departments and a project on a commercial aspect of the business. Trainees receive £220-£240 per week; no accommodation is provided.

You should have good written and verbal communication skills as you will be working with senior management, colleagues on the shop floor and customers and you will also make a presentation based on your project.

*Applications* should be sent to the Recruitment Manager by 5 April 2002.

**SAINSBURYS SUPERMARKETS:** 169 Union Street, Southwark, London SE1 0NL (☎020-7695 7944; fax 020-7695 2927; e-mail wjcetau.sainsburys.co.uk; www.sainsburys.co.uk/fresherthinking).

**Summer Placements** are available in Finance, Quality or Buying. The positions are open to university students only. Wage was £13,495 per annum pro rata in 2002. The placements last for 6 weeks during the summer months and are based at the Head Office, Holborn, London. Suitably qualified foreign applicants may apply if they plan to work in the UK after graduation.

*Applications* should be made online via the above website.

**THISTLE TOWER HOTEL:** St Katharine's Way, London E1 1LD (☎020-7481 3745; fax 020-7680 0256; e-mail hrtower@thistle.co.uk; www.thistlehotels.com)
**Student Vacation Traineeships** are offered in the following areas;
Human Resources Trainee; work will involve recruiting, selecting and interviewing. Kitchen Staff; to work with a team of chefs preparing food. Housekeeping; work will involve supervising, cleaning and the maintaining of bedrooms to hotel standard. Receptionist/Cashier; a customer service position, checking guests in and out of the hotel.

The placements are paid or unpaid depending on the department worked in and last from 3 months to 1 year. Experience is not always necessary as training is provided. Applicants from overseas with proper work documents are welcome.

*Applications* should be sent to Claire Porter, Deputy Human Resources Manager at the above address.

# The Law

**BEVAN ASHFORD SOLICITORS:** 35 Colston Avenue, Bristol BS1 4TT(☎0117-9751690; fax 0117-9291865; e-mail HRtraining@bevanashford.co.uk; www.bevan-ashford.com).

Bevan Ashford solicitors offer student **Vacation Traineeships** to 2nd year law students or 3rd year non-law students who are applying for training contracts with the firm after graduation. The placements consist of 1 week unpaid work experience with a day spent in a different department work shadowing and some case study work to test ability and aptitude. The placements are based in Bristol, Exeter, Taunton, Tiverton, Plymouth, Birmingham and London

*Applications* should be sent to HR and Training by 21 March, by *application* form only, available from the website or in hard copy.

**MASONS:** 30 Aylesbury Street, London EC1R OER (☎020-7490 4000; fax 020-7490 2545; e-mail graduate.recruitment@masons.com; www.masons.com, www.out-law.com). Masons is one of the most highly regarded specialist law firms in Europe and the Asia Pacific region. Offices in six prominent UK business regions in England & Scotland as well as elsewhere in Europe & Asia, operating on a 'one-firm' approach with each office offering a national service. Provides a complete legal service to clients operating in the Construction & Engineering, Information Technology, Energy and Infrastructure industries.

Their **Summer Vacation Scheme** placements run for two weeks each between mid-June and the end of August. They are looking for $2^{nd}$ year Law students and final year non-Law students who are expected to achieve at least a 2:1 final degree and hold 24 UCAS Points. There are approximately 18 places available in London and 5 in Manchester. Applicants should be law students in their 2nd year or non-law students in their final year. Placements last for 2 weeks and take place between June and August. Salary is £250 per week in London and £200 per week in Manchester. No accommodation is provided but Masons provide a list of hostels and student halls in London to assist students.

*Applications* should be made online by 21st February, and any enquiries directed to Julie Lester, Graduate Recruitment Assistant, at the above address.

**NABARRO NATHANSON:** Lacon House, 84 Theobalds Road, London. WC1X 8RW (☎020-7524 6000; fax 020-7524 6524; e-mail graduateinfo@nabarro.com; www.nabarro.com).
Nabarro Nathanson offer **60 Vacation Traineeship** placements each year to final year non-law students, penultimate year law students, CPE and LPC students seeking a training contract two years on. The placements last for three weeks between mid June and late August and trainees are paid £200 per week. Placements are available at their London, Sheffield and Reading offices. No accommodation is available. Suitable foreign applicants looking for a training contract in the UK who are authorised to work there are welcome.

*Applicants* should call the freephone number 0800-0564021 from November for a copy of their brochure and applications form.

# Media

**BBC:** Work Experience Team, Room 508, Henry Wood House, 3 & 6 Langham Place, London W1 1AA (e-mail work.experience@bbc.co.uk; www.bbc.co.uk/workexperience).
The world's largest public broadcaster.
Take a look at working life at the BBC. You can spend a few days or up to 4 weeks in an unpaid positions in one of many areas across the UK. Areas in which **work experience placements** are available include:
**Journalism:** Gain an insight into BBC News, Radio, TV, Online and World Service.
**Business Support:** Not everyone makes programmes – find out about roles in areas

like HR, Rights, Publishing and BBC Archives.
**Programme making:** See how programmes are put together – see what a runner really does.
**Specialist Craft & Technical:** Bringing programmes to life – opportunities to work with cameras, sound, lighting and costumes.

Competition for these places is understandably fierce. *Applications* should be made online via www.bbc.co.uk/workexperience.

## Public Sector

**THE ARMY:** Freepost, CV37 9GR (☎ 08457-300111 www.army.mod.uk).
Although the Army does not offer vacation training as such, it does run the Gap Year Commission, which is open to students who wish to take a year out after leaving school and before taking up a firm place at University. It is aimed at students of high academic ability who demonstrate a responsible and mature attitude and show leadership potential.

Successful candidates attend a 3 week course at Sandhurst and are commissioned into their chosen Corps or Regiments as 2nd Lieutenants, on a special rate of pay of £1000 per month. They serve for a minimum of four months and a maximum of 18 months. There is no subsequent obligation to serve in the Army.

As a first step, *applications* can be made online or by calling the above number.

**THE CIVIL SERVICE:**
Has 173 departments and agencies and employs nearly half a million people, making the Civil Service one of the largest employers in the UK.

**Offers one day visits** and paid and unpaid **work experience opportunities** across a range of departments. Further information on vacancies and application procedures can be found at www.civilservice.gov.uk.

Closing dates vary between departments but all *applications* should be made before the end of March 2003. Note that the closing date for Foreign and Commonwealth Office placements is mid-December.

**POST OFFICE:** The Assessment Centre, Coton House, Rugby, Warwickshire CV23 0AA.
The Post Office Finance Vacation Scheme offers 10 traineeships for 8 weeks over the summer. It gives penultimate-year undergraduates, who are hoping to pursue a career in **Accountancy**, an opportunity to gain career-related work experience and training, whilst completing a 'real-life' project.

**Vacancies** occur nationwide, and in all of the Post Office businesses. Students studying any degree subject will be considered, although good A level grades (24 UCAS points) or equivalent qualifications are asked for. Overseas applicants eligible to work in the UK will be considered. The salary is approximately £200 per week, plus London weighting if applicable.

Written enquiries should be made to the above address enclosing a current cv. *Applications* for any other vacation work in The Post Office should be made to the Personnel Manager at local Royal Mail or Post Office Counters offices.

## Science, Construction and Engineering

**CORUS:** Ashorne Hill Management College, Leamington Spa CV33 9PY (☎ 01926-488025; fax 01926-488024; e-mail recruitment@corusgroup.com; www.corusgroupcareers.com).

Corus is a customer-focused, innovative, solutions-driven company. Corus manufactures, processes and distributes metal products as well as providing design, technology and consultancy services.
Every year Corus offers **30 Summer Placements and 100 12-month Placements** around the UK in the following areas; engineering, manufacturing and operations management, metallurgical and technical services, research development and technology, commercial (sales and marketing), supplies, logistics, finance and human resources. These positions are suitable for students in their first or second year at university. Salary is based on £12,500 per year pro rata. Help can be given in finding accommodation.

*Applications* should be made on line only after consulting www.corusgroupcareers.com.

**ESSO & EXXON MOBIL GROUP:** Recruitment Centre, MPO2, ExxonMobil House, Ermyn Way, Leatherhead, Surrey KT22 8UX (☎0845-330 8878; www.exxonmobil.com/ukrecruitment).
ExxonMobil offer around **35 Eight-week Summer Placements** during July and August for degree students. **Production Department.** Aberdeen, London. Studying any Engineering discipline. **Manufacturing & Distribution.** Fawley. Studying Chemical Engineering. **Fuels Marketing.** Leatherhead. Any degree subject. **Finance.** London. Any numerate degree. **Information Technology.** Fawley, Leatherhead. IT or Business related degree.
The summer placements are open to penultimate year students and salaries will be a minimum of £14,250 (pro-rata). All students will be given a project to complete (based on a real business scenario), receive some skills training and attend a two day outward bound type course. At the end of the placement students will have the opportunity to go through the graduate recruitment process where hopefully Exxon Mobil can make a mutually informed decision as to whether they would be suitable for a graduate position.

Closing date is 7 March 2003. Please *apply* via www.exxonmobil.com/ukrecruitment or call 0845-330 8878 for an application form.

**FABERMAUNSELL:** Marlborough House, Upper Marlborough Road, St Albans AL1 3UT (☎0208-784 5736; fax 0208-784 5937; e-mail jacqui.brown@fabermaunsell.com; www.fabermaunsell.com).
An international multi-disciplinary consulting engineering firm. Offices throughout the UK.
**Work placements.** available in Civil/Transportation engineering. Open to students of electrical, mechanical, building services, transportation, civil or structural engineering. Competitive salary offered. Suitably qualified foreign applicants with fluent English considered. No accommodation available

*Applications*, comprising a CV and covering letter, should be made to Jacqui Brown at the above address. Interview required; applicants are advised to look at the company website www.fabermaunsell.com for more information.

**FORD MOTOR COMPANY LIMITED:** Head Office, Eagle Way, Warley, Brentwood, Essex CM13 3BN (☎01277-251467; fax 01277-251186; e-mail ahamil22@ford.com; www.ford.co.uk/recruitment).
**Positions** are available in most areas of the business, including HR, Finance, IT and Purchasing. The job descriptions for each of these roles will vary substantially. However, the student will play a large part in the day-to-day routine of the company and will undertake certain projects. They will have significant responsibility. Positions are open to undergraduates.

Wages are approx. £1,200 per month plus various benefits. Terms of employment

are for 8 weeks to 3 months and can be taken at any time of the year. What is specifically offered at different times can be seen more clearly on the company website.
The location of the traineeships will be decided by Ford. They will be either in Essex (Dagenham, Dunton, Warley, Trafford House), Southampton, Halewood, South Wales, Coventry or Daventry. Accommodation is not provided nor is help in finding lodgings, other than the provision of a list of letting agents in the local area. Foreign applicants who do not need a working visa to be arranged are welcome.
*Applications* will only be accepted if made online at www.Ford.co.uk/recruitment.

**IMI PLC:** PO Box 216, Witton, Birmingham B6 7BA (☎0121-356 4848; fax 0121-356 2877; e-mail grad.recruit@imi.plc.uk; www.imiplc.com).
IMI is a leading international engineering group. It is divided into companies representing different business areas:IMI Norgen is a leading world manufacturer of pneumatic solutions; IMI Cornelius is the world's largest producer of equipment for dispensing soft drinks and beer; and CCI is the world leader in severe service valves. It specialises in providing innovative engineering solutions in the most demanding and difficult environments. IMI has offices in over 60 countries worldwide but predominantly in the UK, USA and Germany.

Each year IMI offers a number of **Vacation Placements (approx 12)** to penultimate year students studying for a degree in Mechanical, Manufacturing or Electrical and Electronic Engineering. The salary for the placement is £770 per month. During their placement students are required to attend a 2 day management skills training course. On completion of a successful placement, students wil be offered sponsorship through their final year at university and a place on the IMI Graduate Engineering Training Scheme. Placements can be overseas depending on individual language skills and availability.
Successful candidates should be able to work for a period of 8-12 weeks.
*Application* forms available from above address and the company website. Closing date for applications 28 February 2003.

**LOGICA:** Freepost 21, London W1E 4JZ (☎020-7446 2333).
Logica is one of the leading IT companies in the FTSE 100, bringing together around 8,500 people from offices in 23 countries. They are in business to help leading organisations worldwide achieve their business objectives through the innovative use of information technology.and they develop and support many of the world's most complex IT projects.

Logica offer a number of **Summer Vacation Oportunities** across the UK and are interested in applicants in their penultimate year who are studying a computer science related degree. Accommodation is not provided.
Please apply online at www.logica.com/ukgraduates.

**MARS:** Dundeee Road, Slough, Berks SL1 4JX (☎01753-514999; fax 0173-215559; e-mail mars.graduate@eu.effem.com; www.mars.com/university).
Offices in Berkshire, Hampshire, Yorkshire, Anglia and Worcestershire.
**Student Placements** are offered in the following areas; Commercial; Engineering; Finance; IT; Logistics; Marketing; Personnel; Production Manufacturing; Research and Development; Sales and Software Engineering. Placments vary in length and location. More and regularly updated information available on the website. Wages from £250-300 per week. Overseas applicants are welcome and Mars assists in the finding of accommodation.
*Applications* should be made online or addressed to Mars Graduate Marketing

and received by 18 December 2002.

**MOTT MACDONALD:** St Anne House, Wellesley Road, Croydon CR9 2UL (☎0208-774 2176; fax 0208-681 5706; e-mail graduate.recruitment@mottmac.com; www.mottmac.com).
The firm is a multi-disciplinary engineering consultancy engaged in development touching many facets of everyday life from transport, energy, water and the environment to the building and communications industries.
Traineeships are offered in our offices throughout the UK.
**Placements** are offered within the design office for civil, mechanical and building services engineering students. There are approximately 50 vacancies per year and preference is given to penultimate year university students. Placements take place during the summer vacations and last for 8-12 weeks; trainees receive £190-£230 per week. Overseas applicants are welcome. Where possible they will try and place you in an office near your home.
*Applications* should be addressed to The Graduate Recruitment Team at the above address between January and February.

**NIAB:** Huntingdon Road, Cambridge CB3 0LE (☎01223-342234; fax 01223-342206; e-mail jobs@Niab.com; www.niab.com).
**Vacation Work** involving working in fields, laboratories, etc. is offered to about 30 applicants a year, at regional trial centres and the head office. £4.69 per hour for experienced applicants or those staying longer than 3 months; £4.18 per hour for other applicants. Accommodation not provided although lists of accommodation are available.
*Applications* from April/May for summer work to the Personnel Office at the above address.

**ROLLS-ROYCE PLC:** Recruitment Response Handling Unit, P.O. Box 31, Derby DE24 8BJ (☎01332-260390; fax 01332-513929; e-mail ecr@rolls-royce.com; www.rolls-royce.com/careers).
Rolls-Royce plc is a global company providing power on land, sea and air. The company has established leading positions in civil aerospace, defence aerospace, marine and energy markets. With the philosophy that only world-class people can deliver world-class service, they require staff not only to be skilled in their jobs, but also to understand the wider commercial implications of what they do and to be motivated to make the best possible contribution.
**Vacation Trainees.** Vacancies typically occur in commercial, engineering, procurement, human resources and logistics. The training period usually lasts for 10 weeks within one department that is of relevance to the course of study. Open to penultimate year undergraduates only. Students complete an individual project or contribute towards a major piece of work within the department.
**Industrial Trainees.** Usually takes place during the final training period of a sandwich course. The training programme will be influenced by business requirements. For example, twelve-month programmes in finance usually include 3 different attachments within the Company. Attachments in engineering or research may last 6 or 12 months and trainees may be required to undertake one major project in one department.
   Placements will be based in the Midlands, South West or Scotland. *Applications* online at www.rolls-royce.com/careers. There is no closing date. Selection will be via an Assessment Centre.

**SCOTT WILSON:** Scott House, Basing View, Basingstoke, Hampshire RG21 4JG (☎01256-461161).
A dynamic multi-disciplinary international consulting group involved in engineering, transportation planning and environmental planning projects throughout the UK, Europe, and world markets.

The company has a regular requirement for Civil Engineering students who have completed at least one year of their University course to undertake **Summer Vacation Work** based in their Basingstoke offices. Opportunities are available within their Maritime, Highways and Transportation sections.

Applicants should have a genuine interest in their subject, be adaptable, and show initiative. Duties and duration of placement may vary considerably depending on the workload at the time. *Applications* should be made in April to the Personnel Department at the above address.

**SKANSKA CONSTRUCTION:** Maple Cross House, Denham Way, Maple Cross, Richmansworth, Hertforshire WD3 9AS (☎01923-423571; fax 01923-423242; e-mail robert.dunn@skanska.co.uk; www.skanska.co.uk).
**Trainee Positions (30)** working in the positions of civil engineer, building engineer, quantity surveyor, land surveyor or in construction management. Placements are nationwide and site-based. Wages are subject to previous experience. Ideally to work over the summer vacation and for a min. period of 8 weeks. University or College degree students (HNC or HND) or pre-university gap year students considered. Some assistance with accommodation available.

*Applications* should be made before May to Mr R.W. Dunn at the above address. Interview required.

# London and Home Counties

**Prospects for Work.**
*London:* if you want to move to London to work during the summer season, think first about where you are going to live. While rented accommodation is not difficult to find the price is likely to be high and staying for only a short period may prove difficult. However, there are several youth hostels, as well as a seasonal 'hostel under canvas', Tent City (020-8743 5708), which charges £5 per night and is open from June to September. You may be able to find a cheap deal among the 'Accommodation to Rent' columns of the city's many newspapers and magazines. In addition to numerous local papers there are several publications which are not associated with any particular area. The main ones to look out for are: *TNT* and *Southern Cross* (both free), the *Evening Standard* (daily), *Time Out* and *Loot*. These publications also carry job advertisements. Vacancies arise most commonly in retail, secretarial, hotel, restaurant and domestic work. The chance of finding a job will be increased if you are flexible as to where you can work, so consult the local paper in several different districts.

Various Jobcentres in London have special Temporary Sections. The Hammersmith Jobcentre (Glen House, 22 Glenthorne Road, W6 0PP; ☎020-8210 8100; fax 020-8210 8181) offers a range of temporary work, including retail, administrative and construction jobs. Their vacancies are not just for Hammersmith, but also for W6, W14, SW13, SW14. They also keep lists of vacancies with the local Borough Council – these tend to be clerical and administrative posts.

There are also hundreds of private employment agencies, especially along Oxford Street. Drake International (branches at 20 Regent Street SW1, ☎020-7484 0800; 44 South Molton Street, W1Y; 43 Maiden Lane, WC2E) covers a range of fields, including secretarial, industrial, driving and catering, for both permanent and temporary positions. Many such agencies advertise in *TNT* magazine.

Prospects for finding vacation traineeships and internships are particularly good in London, as it is the location of many big companies' head offices. The diversity of business in London means that opportunities in virtually any area of industry could be available.

*Home Counties:* in the comparatively prosperous Home Counties job prospects can be fairly good over the summer. In particular, there is a demand for staff among marquee erectors and events organisers. The Jobcentre in Reading (0118-980 8200) displays jobs at Ascot and Windsor racecourses, Henley Regatta, music festivals and other events both in the city and elsewhere in the region through its new Jobpoint system. Epsom, Newbury and Sandown are the other main racecourses in the area; it is worth contacting these at any time of year.

Reading is a major source of longer-term summer employment in the Home Counties. Finding rented accommodation here is surprisingly easy too. Office, domestic, retail and packing work tend to be the most common, though it is worth approaching the local authority, which runs various summer programmes. Vacancies tend to be most numerous in the earliest months of the year. Try looking in the *Reading Evening Post* (daily), the *Reading Chronicle* (weekly) and the *Newbury and Thatcham Observer* (weekly).

Windsor is a busy tourist town all year round, but especially over the summer. Temporary work may be available at the Leisure Pool as well as at the local hotels and river boat companies. McDonalds is among the largest employers of temporary staff. The Jobcentre in Maidenhead (☎01628- 844900) has a wide range of vacancies, both full and part time, permanent and temporary, and in a variety of occupations. The weekly *Maidenhead Advertiser* (on Fridays) has job pages.

In Luton, north of London, there is some demand for factory workers, who may need forklifting qualifications. In addition, a large number of vacancies exist within the service centre, including retail work which is steadily increasing due to the expansion of the airport. Various other types of work are also available, including manual labour, caring, and catering.

# Business and Industry

**ADVENTURE BALLOONS:** Winchfield Park, London Road, Hartley Wintney, Hants RG27 8HY.
**Office Staff (1/2)** to work from 8.30am-5.30pm Monday-Friday. Wage £200 per week; no accommodation available. Period of work from March to October.

Applicants need computer experience and a good telephone manner.
*Applications* to the Manager at the above address.

**ANGEL HUMAN RESOURCES PLC:** Angel House, 4 Union Street, London Bridge, London SE1 1SZ (☎020-7940 2000; fax 020-7940 2018; e-mail hq@angelhr.org; www.angelhr.org). Angel was founded in 1965 and adheres strictly to the codes of practice laid down by its professional bodies. Open 7am-6pm Monday to Friday with branch offices throughout London and the South East.
**Chefs, Cooks, Waiting and General Catering and Kitchen Assistants;** work may be offered in **Catering Environments**, throughout the year. Work also available for **Administrators**. Work may also be offered to experienced **Office Staff**; to **Warehouse and Factory** staff; to experienced or qualified **Nurses and Carers**. Pay may vary between £4.10 and £16 per hour dependent on experience. Work may also be offered to experienced office staff with 50wpm typing; to warehouse and factory staff; and to experienced or qualified nurses and carers.
*Applicants* from abroad should note that placements can only be made after arrival in the UK; Angel cannot enter into correspondence prior to arrival in the UK. Work can usually be offered within 2-3 days of arrival. Angel cannot assist with accommodation. Apply to the office in person or by phone on arrival in London.

**BLUE ARROW:** Blue Arrow Construction, Refuge House, 2nd Floor, 9-10 Riverfront, Enfield EN1 3SZ (☎0208-367 9541; e-mail enfield148@bluearrow.co.uk).
**Shopfitters.** Minimum wage £10.50 per hour. Previous experience necessary.
**Labourers.** Minimum wage £5 per hour. Minimum age 18. Site experience required.
**Trade Mates.** Minimum wage £6.50 per hour. Minimum age 18. Site experience necessary.
**Electricians.** Minimum wage £10 per hour. JIB approved.
**Plumbers.** Minimum wage £10 per hour. Previous experience required.
   Hours vary for all positions. Staff required all year round to work in the Home Counties; minimum period of work 1 week. Overseas applicants with work permits welcome.
*Applications* can be made by phone at any time on 0800-328 6890.

**CARRON MARQUEES:** Holt Farm, Old Lane, Dockenfield, Farnham, Surrey GU10 4HG (☎01252-795252; fax 01252-794120). Marquee hire company catering for local parties and weddings.
**Drivers (2)** to drive a 7½ ton lorry. Wages £7 per hour, free accommodation. To work a minimum of 40 hours per week, including weekends. Min. period of work of 1 month. Position is available from May to September. Applicants should be strong and fit and aged over 25. Overseas applicants welcome.
*Applications* should be made to Richard from early May onwards. Interview necessary.
**CATAMARAN CRUISERS:** Embankment Pier, Victoria Embankment, London WC2N 6NU (☎020-7695 1824; fax 020-7839 1034; e-mail nicola.gilbert@bateauxlondon.com or sally.elsdon@bateauxlondon.com). London pleasure boat company operating between central London and Greenwich, providing river cruises with commentary and refreshments.
**Pier Supervisors (5).** Wages £4.66 per hour, 5 or 6 days per week.
**Retail Assistants(15)** to work on board boats. Wages £4.22 per hour, 5 or 6 days per week.
**Retail Assistants (5)** for the shop. Wages £4.66 per hour, 5 or 6 days per week.

**Ticket Agent (1).** Wages £35 per day, 5 days per week. Additional pay may include a 5% loyalty bonus at end of contract, supplementary pay of extra hours, and commission in retail jobs.

Applicants should be 18+, able to swim, have experience with dealing with the public in front line situation, a positive attitude and a happy smile. Second language an advantage. Min. period of work 2 months. Positions are available from April to October. Foreign applicants with reasonable English welcome. No accommodation available.

*Applications* to Nicola Gilbert or Sally Esldon at the above address from March onwards. Interview necessary.

**CATCH 22:** 199 Victoria Street, London SW1E 5NE (☎020-7821 1133; www.c22.co.uk). Employment agency covering the whole of the London area.
**General Industrial Staff** for temporary jobs such as furniture moving, driving, warehouse and message-running. Flexible hours but usually 8 hours a day and preferably 5 days a week. Possibility of overtime. Work available all year round. Min. period of work 3 months. No accommodation available. Min. age 18. Must be adaptable to different environments and have a good level of English.

*Apply* by phone when in the UK to the above number.

**FRED (UK) 2000 LIMITED:** Copthall House, Victoria Road, Aldershot, Hampshire (☎01252-315544; fax 01252-342727; e-mail freduk2000@hotmail.com). Specialised recruitment agency.
**Industrial and Technical Staff (10).** Wages from £5 per hour. To work Monday to Friday. Min. period of work of 1 week. Positions are available all year. Positions open depend on qualifications. Foreign applicants entitled to work in the UK and with acceptable spoken English welcome. Accommodation available for some positions.

*Applications* should be made at any time to a Recruitment Consultant at the above address. Interview necessary, by telephone is sufficient.

**HARRODS LTD:** Knightsbridge, London SW1X 7XL (☎020-7893 8793; www.harrods.com).
**Sales Staff, Clerical Staff, Selling Support Staff** to work in August and from October through to January to cover the Christmas and January Sale. Applicants must be a minimum of sixteen years old, be eligible to work in the UK. Fluent spoken English is essential.

Interested applicants should *visit* the Harrods Recruitment Centre, 11 Brompton Place, SW1. Opening hours Monday-Saturday 10am-7pm.

**MARGARET HILTON TRAVEL INN:** Oakley House, Oakley Road, Luton (☎01582-567972; fax 0870-2419000; e-mail margaret.hilton@whitbread.com). Part of the largest budget hotel brand in the UK.
**Call Centre Team Members.** Wages £6.14 per hour. To work within the hours of operation, 8am-8pm. Positions are available from August, based in Luton and Bedford. Prior experience helpful but not essential but communication and keyboard skills are necessary. Minimum age 16. Foreign applicants welcome. No accommodation available.

*Applications* should be made to Linda Thomasson, PA, from November 2002. Interview necessary.

**MONTHIND CLEAN:** 91 London Road, Copford, Colchester, Essex C06 1L9 (☎01206-215300; fax 01206-212126; e-mail info@monthindclean.co.uk;

www.monthind-clean.co.uk). The company provides contract cleaners for various businesses.
**Cleaners.** Wages to be arranged. To work mainly during evenings. Minimum age 18. No experience necessary. Work available during any vacation. Applicants must understand English and be able to comply with Health and Safety Rules. No accommodation available. Foreign applicants with work permits and acceptable spoken English welcome.

*Applications* can be made all year round to Penny Cander at the above address.

**POWDER BYRNE:** 250 Upper Richmond Road, Putney, London SW15 6TG (www.powderbyrne.com). Powder Byrne is an exclusive tour operator offering tailor-made holidays, using 4 and 5 star hotels in exotic Mediterranean destinations.
**Resort Managers.** required to manage a team of staff in resort, to provide a high calibre of service to clients and liase with head office. Pay is £110 per week. Clean driving licence, 21+ and customer service experience required.
**Drivers** to transport guests in company minibuses. Pay is £70 per week. Applicants should be 21+, good time-keepers, reliable and have a full clean driving licence and customer services experience.
**Nursery Nurses** to manage resort crèches for children aged 6 months to 4 years. Pay is £80 per week. Relevant experience and NNEB qualification or equivalent required. (Non-qualified assistants are also required, for a wage of £65 per week).
**Children's Club Co-ordinators** to organise and run kids clubs for 4 to 14 year olds. Pay is £80 per week. Child care experience and lots of energy required.
Accommodation, food, transport to resort, insurance and provided for all positions. Duration of contracts from 2 weeks to 6 months between April and October.

*Applications* can be made all year round on line or by post to Mike Aubrey at the above address. Interview necessary.

**VAUXHALL AFTERSALES:** Griffin House, Osborne Road, Luton LU1 3YT (☎ 01582-426477; fax 01582-426446).
**Warehouse Operatives (60);** duties include manual function shift work. Wages were £6.99 per hour in 2002, plus shift premium if applicable. To work 38 hours a week. Staff needed from July for 6-9 weeks. No accommodation is available. Applicants must be over 18.

*Applications* to the Personnel Dept. TW4 from October onwards.

**WETHERBY STUDIOS:** 23 Wetherby Mansions, Earls Court Square, London SW5 9BH (☎ 020-7373 1107).
**Male Photographic Models.** Wages £100 cash for 2-hour sessions. Dozens needed throughout the year. No accommodation available. Should be aged 18-40 years, but physique is more important than age. While more than half the models used are slim, it can be difficult to find men who have worked on their chest and arm definition, which is required if picture sessions promoting leisure wear are planned. Moustaches and beards permissible. No modelling experience necessary. Applicants must supply snapshots to show how they photograph facially and physically. Follow-ups are frequent, depending on the photographers' reactions to the first test shots. Overseas applicants and all colours more than welcome, but must speak fluent English.

*Applications* to Mr Mike Arlen, Director, Wetherby Studios.

**WILLIAM HILL ORGANIZATION LTD:** 1-5 Morris Place, Finsbury Park, London N4 3JG (☎ freephone 0800-917 8210; e-mail achandler@williamhill.co.uk). One

of the largest betting organisations in the country with over 1,500 branches; summer opportunities may lead to a career.
**Cashiers** to work various flexible hours in betting shops during the summer (days and evenings), including Saturdays. Positions in London only. Min. age 18. Training will be given. Period of work 10-16 weeks between April and August.
*Applications* between January to March to the Recruitment Office, William Hill Organisation.

# Children

**ADVENTURE & COMPUTER HOLIDAYS LTD:** PO Box 183, Dorking, Surrey RH5 6FA (☎01306-881299; www.holiday-adventure.com). A small, friendly company with 20 years experience in running activity holidays for children aged 4-13. Based in a school in Surrey.
**Camp Leaders, Teachers** required for day camps. £135-£175 per week. To work 9am-5pm. Min. period of work 1 week. Work available in half-terms and school holidays throughout the year (mostly July-August). Qualifications or experience with children preferred. Staff need to live in London or Surrey area. Minimum age 16.
*Applications* any time to Ms Sarah Bradley, Director, at the above address. Interview required.

**CAMP BEAUMONT:** Kingswood House, 11 Prince of Wales Road, Norwich NR1 1BD (☎01603-284284; E-mail adventures@kingswood.co.uk). Non-residential day camps are located around Greater London in Kent, Essex, Surrey etc. Residential camps are located in Surrey, Norfolk, Isle of Wight and Normandy.
**Group Leaders** for summer camps. Leaders instruct in non-specialist activities, assist activity instructors and help to run camps. Minimum age 18. Previous experience of working with children and interest in sports, arts & crafts, music and drama essential. Group leaders are responsible for the welfare of the children in their group at all times,
**Activity Instructors** to lead specialist activities for 3-7 sessions per day at camps. Appropriate recognised qualifications must be held e.g GNAS Instructor for Archery.
Period of employment July and August. Wages £144-£167 per week less £70 for food and accommodation.
To *apply* write to or e-mail the Recruitment Department at the above address.

**CROSS KEYS**: 48 Fitzalan Road, Finchley, London N3 3PE (☎020-8922 9686; fax 020-8343 0625; www.campsforkids.co.uk).
**Group Leaders and Group Assistants (20)** to work at a residential children's activity camp based near Diss in Norfolk. Duties involve being responsible for junior or senior children aged 6-17 and include the care of children and the planning and running of activities and supervising trips. Wages of £120-£180 per week plus accommodation, food and drink. Period of work July 13-August 16. Possession of a minibus licence would be an advantage.
Group Leaders, Group Assistants (20) to work in a daytime children's activity camp in north London. To work as part of a team of three adults per 24 children running games and activities within a school environment. Wages of £125-£200 per week depending on position and experience. Working hours generally 8.30am-3.30pm but may vary slightly. Should have an interest/background in childcare. Camps take place in all school holidays; summer camps will take place July 22-August 16.

Applicants for either camp must be enthusiastic team workers and aged at least 18. Full in-house training will be given. Possession of lifeguard/first aid qualifications would be an advantage.

*Applications* to Richard or Susan on 020-8371 9686 or go to 'staff zone' on the above website.

**CROYDON PLAY PLUS:** 2nd Floor, Day Lewis, 324-340 Bensham Lane, Thornton Heath CR7 7EQ (☎020-8239 7189; fax 020-8239 7196).
**Holiday Playworkers (10+)** needed for the summer. Wages £4.55 per hour. To work 5 hour shifts per day for 3-6 weeks in Croydon area. To assist with play activities and to accompany children on outings. The many duties include preparing play activities and clearing away, preparing and clearing snacks, helping with collection of children from school and generally participating in all the activities involving children and supervising safety. Children aged 4-11 years. Minimum age 18 with childcare experience.

For *applications* contact Jean Bellinfantie, Accounts Officer at the above address. Must be police checked, give two references and be able to attend interview in June.

**HORNIMANS ADVENTURE PLAYGROUND:** c/o 1 Bosworth Road, London, W10 5EG (☎020-8969 5740).
**Summer Playworkers (2)** to work from 23rd July to 31st August. Playworkers work from 11am-6pm, with some variations, to a total of 36 hours per week, for a wage of £245. Applicants should be over 18 and ideally have skills in drama, arts and crafts and sports.

*Applications* should be made to Jane Marshall, Joint Playleader at the above address.

**JIGSAW GROUP LTD:** 600 Thames Valley Park (☎0118-9266 277; fax 0118-9662 949; e-mail TVP@jigswaw.com). Jigsaw is a private nursery group providing childcare for children aged 3 months to 5 years. There are 30 units with vacancies for the childcare sector.
**Early Years Practitioners (Nursery Nurses).** Wages from £10,500-16,000 p.a. pro rata. To work 40 hours per week Monday to Friday.
**Early Years Support Worker (Assistant).** Wages from £7,500-9,500 p.a. pro rata. To work 40 hours per week or 1-6pm Monday to Friday.
Min. period of work of 1 week. Positions are available all year. Appropriate qualifications required (NNEB, NVQ3 or B-Tec equivalent). No accommodation available. Suitably qualified foreign applicants welcome.

*Applications* should be made as soon as possible to Ann Fitzpatrick at Jigsaw central office (☎020-8343 8008). Interview necessary.

**LONDON BOROUGH OF HAMMERSMITH AND FULHAM:** Education Department, The Town Hall, King Street, London, W6 9JU (☎0208-8748- 3020 ext 3641; fax 020-8576 5505).
**Part time Youth Workers** to work in evening youth clubs during term times. Wages approx £9.74 per hour to work Monday to Saturday. Child related qualification or experience of work with children helpful but not essential. Overseas applicants with a work permit welcome. All applicants will be subject to a check for criminal convictions.

*Applications* can be made at any time to Personnel at the above address.

**MRS J. MARBER:** 27 Ham Farm Road, Ham Common, Richmond, Surrey TW10 5NA (☎ 020-8546 9457).
**Au Pair** required for an adult family. Duties to include light housework, ironing, washing up and walking the dog. Own bedroom and bathroom provided. To work 5 hours a day/5 days a week. Minimum stay 3 months. Period of work May to October. Position most suitable for a female student: aged 17-25, non-smoker and with a good knowledge of English. Public transport is available in the area.
*Applications*, including a recent photograph and s.a.e. or IRC, to Mrs J. Marber at the above address.

**NORTH HERTFORDSHIRE DISTRICT COUNCIL:** Council Offices, Gernon Road, Letchworth, Hertfordshire SG6 3JF (☎ 01462-474333; fax 01462-474500).
**Playworkers** for summer playschemes. Duties include general supervision, health and safety, planning of activities and creating a fun and happy environment to play in. Wages from £145 to £200. All staff work 35 hours a week, Monday to Friday. To work 21 July-22 August, depending on summer holidays. Applicants must be over 18. Experience of working with children aged 5-11 is essential. Teacher/Nursery nurse training/qualifications are an advantage. Accommodation not provided.
*Applications* to Rebecca Coates.

**MRS PEREIRA:** 511 Activity Club, Tottenham Sports Centre, 701-703 Tottenham High Road NI7 8AD (☎ 020-8801 1400; fax 020-8801 9360). After school and school holidays programme for supervising and entertaining children; club caters for 45-52 children aged 3-11.
**Child Supervisors (9).** Duties include local school pick-up, art and craft activities, some cleaning, and child supervising.
Wages start from minimum national wage. To work Monday to Friday; 20-21 hours per week in term time and 25 to 30 hours in holidays. Min. period of work negotiable. Positions are available around the year. No accommodation available. Applicants need any childcare qualification or a first aid certificate; only those who are reliable, motivated and trustworthy need apply.
*Applications* to Miss Liz O'Brien at the above address from November. Interview necessary.

**PGL TRAVEL:** Alton Court, Penyard Lane (874), Ross-on-Wye, Herefordshire HR9 5GL (☎ 01989-767833; e-mail pglpeople@pgl.co.uk; www.pgl.co.uk/people). PGL Travel provides adventure holidays and courses for children. PGL has 25 activity centres located in the UK, France and Spain. Each year 2,500 people are needed to help run these adventure centres. Over 100 staff needed in Surrey.
**Experienced Activity Instructors** in canoeing, sailing, windsurfing, pony trekking, multi-activites, drama, arts and crafts and English language. Qualifications not essential as full training will be provided. Minimum age 18.
**Group Leaders** also needed to take responsibility for groups of children, helping them to get the most out of their holiday. Previous experience of working with children is essential. Minimum age 18.
Wages from £50-85 per week plus free B & L. Vacancies available for short or long periods between February and October.
*Applications* can be made online, or request a form from the above address.

**STONY STRATFORD CHILDRENS CENTRE:** London Road, Stony Stratford, Milton Keynes MK14 7AQ (tel/fax 01908-562485; e-mail stony.stratford.childrens. centre@milton-keynes.gov.uk).

**Playworkers (4-6)** to supervise and instigate play activities, perform domestic duties and participate in trips etc. Wages from £170-190 per week. To work 39 hours per week, Monday-Friday. Minimum period of work 6 weeks. Positions available mid-July to September. Must be keen and have sports/craft skills and interests. Must relate well to children. Suitable foreign applicants considered providing police check can be carried out. Fluent English essential. Minimum age 18. No accommodation available.
*Applications* should be made from May 2003 to Tammie Redman.

**WOKING LEISURE CENTRE AND POOL IN THE PARK:** Woking Park, Kingfield Road, Woking, Surrey GU22 9BA (☎01483-771122; fax 01483-776005)
**Children's Holiday Activity Staff (20)** Wages £4.75 to £5.77; to work from 8.30am to 4.30pm Monday to Friday. Staff needed from 27 July to 31 August. Must be over 18.
**Pool Lifeguards (10)** Wages £5.19 to £6.31 per hour; to work from 20 June to 10 September. Hours variable over a 7 day period. Must have a national pool lifeguard qualification.
*Applications* to Jacki Wikeley, Children's Activities Co-ordinator, or the Duty Manager, Pool in the Park.

# Holiday Centres and Amusements

**BEALE PARK:** Lower Basildon, Reading, Berkshire RG8 9NH (☎0118-9845172; fax 0118-9845171; e-mail bealepark@bun.com; www.bealepark.co.uk). A non profit-making charitable trust which offers many leisure activities and birdwatching, set in a Thames-side family park in an area of outstanding natural beauty.
**Ticket Sellers (2).** Wages approx. £4.50 per hour. To work full and/or part-time over the summer months. Period of work May-September. Min. period of work July/August. Some experience in working with the public and handling cash is preferred. No accommodation is available.
*Applications* from March to Andrew Howard. Interview required.

**CHESSINGTON WORLD OF ADVENTURES:** Human Resources Dept, Thorpe Park and Chessington World of Adventures, PO BOX 125, Chessington, KT9 2WL(☎0870-444 4678; fax 01372 731570; www.chessington.com). One of the top theme parks in the South, located off Junction 9/10 of the M25 and accessible via trains from Waterloo to Chessington South.
**Ride Operators, Retail Staff, Cleaners, Guest Services, Photography, Catering, Admissions, Games and Warehouse Staff.** Pay £4.65-£7.00 per hour. Benefits include free uniform, free parking, staff canteen and 10 complimentary tickets to any Tussaud's attraction. Flexible hours available.
Enthusiastic and friendly people of all ages are required to join the teams. **Apply** to the above address from January.

**GLL:** Middlegate House, The Royal Arsenal, Woolwich, London SE18 6SX (☎020-8317 5000 ext. 4020; fax 020-8317 5021; e-mail gll.hrm@greenwich.gov.uk). The largest leisure centre operator in London, with 27 centres. As a worker-owned and controlled organisation GLL offers opportunities and benefits that far exceed the rest.
**Leisure Assistants (many).** National Pool Lifeguard qualification an advantage but not essential.

**Catering Assistants (20).** Experience only required.
**Kids Activity Instructors (40).** No experience required.
**Assistant Receptionists (20).** Experience required.
Wages of £5.20 per hour for up to 48 hours work per week. Min. period of work of 7 weeks. Positions are available from June to September. Foreign applicants welcome with appropriate permits. Minimum age 18. No accommodation available but can help locate some. Subsidised training courses are also offered to those who want to build a career in the leisure industry.
*Applications* should be made from early June onwards to Lorraine Patrinos, Human Resources Department, at the above address. Interview necessary.

**LEGOLAND WINDSOR:** Winkfield Road, Windsor, Berkshire SL4 4AY (Human Resources Department ☎01753-626150; fax 01753-626143; e-mail jobs@legoland.co.uk). Legoland Windsor is a theme park dedicated to the imagination and creativity of children, where the kids are king. It draws on the inspiration of the world-famous Lego toys and models. The operating season lasts from June to October during which staff are employed in the following positions:
**Admission Assistants (20), Food and Beverage Assistants (100), Retail Assistants (50), Rides and Attractions Assistant (100), Environmental Services Assistants (20), Security Guard (10), First Aiders (5).** Wages are £4.80 per hour (2002 figure).
To work an average of 40 hours over 5 days (variable, including weekends). Part time positions also available in the above areas. Min. period of work 8 weeks. Staff required from March to October. Help is available to find accommodation. Fluent English essential. Minimum age 16. No previous experience necessary; training will be given in all departments.
Applicants must have a passion for serving others, an exuberant personality and a natural affinity with children. To be part of the Legoland team staff need to be willing to work hard and have fun whatever the weather (many positions involve working outside).
*Applications* should be made to Jenny Webb or Lesley Carrothers from February. Interview necessary.

**THE LONDON AQUARIUM:** County Hall, Westminster Bridge Road, London SE1 7PB (☎020-7967 8010; fax 020-7967 8029). The biggest aquarium in the UK.
**Ticket Office Staff (4), Customer Service Staff (4)** required to work between June and September selling entry tickets and dealing with members of the public, including conducting tours and talking about the marine life exhibits. Wages £4.50 per hour. No experience required, just enthusiasm.
*Applications* to Human Resources at the above address.

**THE SHERLOCK HOLMES MUSEUM:** 221B Baker Street, London NW1 6XE (☎020-7738 1269; fax 020-7224 3005; e-mail sherlock-holmes.co.uk; info@sherlock-holmes.co.uk).
**Victorian Maids (2)** to receive visitors attending the museum. Minimum age 24; knowledge of other languages would be an asset.
**Sherlock Holmes Lookalike** to dress up as Sherlock Holmes and give out promotional literature to tourists. Must be slim, at least 6′ tall and well spoken.
Wages £5 net per hour; no accommodation available. Period of work from May to September. *Applications* to Grace Riley, Manager, at the above address.

**THORPE PARK:** Human Resources Dept, Thorpe Park & Chessington World of Adventures, PO Box 125, Chessington, KT9 2WL; ☎0870-4444 678; fax 01932-566367; www.thorpepark.com). One of the top theme parks in the South, located off junction 11/13 of the M25 and accessible via trains from Waterloo to Staines; a short bus ride will take you to the park.
**Staff** for shops, rides and attractions, photography, cleaning, catering, admissions, games and warehouse. Rates of pay £4.65 to £7.00. Flexible hours available. Benefits include free uniform, free parking, staff canteen, social nights, discounted merchandise and 10 complimentary tickets to any Tussaud's group attraction. Enthusiastic and friendly people of all ages are required to join the teams.
*Applications* to the above address from January.

**THE TUSSAUDS GROUP, LONDON SITES:** c/o Madame Tussauds, Marylebone Road, London NW1 5LR (☎020-7487 0289; fax 020-7465 0860; www.madame-tussaurds.com). The Tussaud's Group is one of Europe's largest operators and developers of visitor attractions with over 10 million guests a year. The London sites incorporate Madame Tussaud's and the London Planetarium.
**Guest Services Assistants, Catering Assistants, Retail Assistants, and Photographers.** Positions are available from late June to mid September. Experience in a customer focused environment will be an advantage.
For *applications* please send your CV and covering letter to Human Resources at the above address.

# Hotels and Catering

**THE BERKELEY:** Wilton Place, Knightsbridge, London SW1X 7RL (☎020-7201 1645; fax 020 7201 1643; e-mail info@the-berkeley.co.uk). A five star deluxe hotel on the corner of Knightsbridge and Wilton Place and has achieved the 'Investor in People' status. Opened in 1972, it has 214 luxurious bedrooms.
**Day Room Attendants (5).** Wages approx. £11,000 per annum, pro rata; to work 40 hours per five-day week. To clean 8-11 rooms a day. Good command of English and experience as a room attendant is desirable.
**Commis Chefs (4).** Wages approx. £10,400+ per annum pro rata; to work 45 hours per five-day week. Duties include assisting other chefs in preparation and service of food, maintaining high standards of hygiene and ensuring tidiness and cleanliness of designated sections.
Other jobs may also be available, including waiting work. Previous experience is required.
Minimum period of work is 6 months. Overseas applicants with excellent spoken English are welcome. An interview is required. All candidates must demonstrate a high standard of personal presentation.
*Applications* from March to David Naish at the above address.

**BRIGGENS HOUSE HOTEL:** Briggens Park, Stanstead Abbotts, near Ware, Herts. SG12 8LD (☎01279-829955; fax 01279-793685).
**Casual Waiting, Bar and Banqueting Staff.** £4.25 per hour. Period of work May to October. Min. age 18 and experience essential. Overseas applicants welcome. Very important; minimum period of work is 6 months.
*Applications* to the Gail Needham at the above address.

**THE BULL HOTEL:** Oxford Road, Gerrards Cross, Bucks SL9 7PA (☎01753-278804; fax 01753-880116; e-mail kfindlay@saroua.co.uk). 111 bedroom busy

hotel. Frequent weddings and functions. Tranquil and picturesque. Many live-in staff. Community spirit.
**Housekeeping Staff (5).** Wages from National Minimum Wage. 40 hours per week and overtime to be considered. Prefer 18+.
**Night Porter.** Wages of £5.22 per hour. 40 hours per week and overtime to be considered. Prefer 21+.
**Receptionists (2).** Wages of £10,500 p.a. pro rata. 40 hours per week. Prefer 18+.
**Restaurant Staff (4).** Wages from National Minimum Wage. 40 hours per week. Prefer 18+.
**Bar Staff (2).** Wages of £4.74 per hour. 40+ hours per week. Prefer 21+.
**Conference Assistant.** Wages of £4.08 per hour. 40 hours per week. 16+.
Duties are various and hotel is very busy. Board and accommodation available for £35 per week. Min. period of work 3 months. Positions are available from April onwards.
*Applications* should be made to Human Resources from March onwards. Interview required, by telephone if necessary.

**CATAMARAN CRUISERS:** Embankment Pier, Victoria Embankment, London WC2N 6NN (☎020-7695 1824; fax 020-7839 1034; e-mail nicola.gilbert@bateauxlondon.com or sally.elsdon@bateauxlondon.com). London pleasure boat company operating between central London and Greenwich, providing river cruises with commentary and refreshments.
**20-25 positions in retail, hosting, ticket agency and pier supervision** Wages are £4.89-£5 per hour, with bonus and commission applicable to some positions. Contracts available April to October. Applicants must have experience of dealing with the public in front line situations, a positive attitude and a happy smile. Second language an advantage. Foreign applicants with reasonable English welcome. No accommodation available.
*Applications* to Nicola Gilbert or Sally Elsdon at the above address from March onwards. Interview necessary.

**THE CROWN HOTEL:** 7 London Street, Chertsey, Surrey KT16 8AP (☎01932-564657; fax 01932-570839). The hotel dates back to Queen Victoria's reign.
**Chefs (2), Bar Staff (4), Waiting Staff (3), Receptionist.** Pay negotiable depending on experience. Work is 5-days split shifts, 39 hours per week. Possibility of accommodation.
*Applications* to D. Fiddes, General Manager.

**DOWN HALL HOTEL:** Hatfield Heath, Bishop's Stortford, Herts. CM22 7AS (☎01279-731441; fax 01279-730416; e-mail personnel@downhall.co.uk). A Victorian mansion brimming with charm, style and elegance, with 100 bedrooms.
**Waiting Staff (5/6)** to work in one of two restaurants; casual work in conference and banqueting also available. Staff needed at any time of year; to work five out of seven days, 8 hours per day. Salary at the equivalent of £8,000 p.a. There is a charge for accommodation. Overtime is paid at the basic rate.
**Room Attendant (1-2)** to work from June to September. Same terms as waiting staff (see above).
Minimum age 16; training will be provided. *Applications* to the Personnel and Training Manager.

**EURO PAIR AGENCY:** 28 Derwent Avenue, Pinner, Middlesex HA5 4QJ (☎020-8421 2100; fax 020-8428 6416; e-mail europair@btinternet.com; www.euro-

pair.co.uk). The agency takes great care in the selection of posts available and has a back-up service if things do not work out.
**Hotel Work (50+).** Wages of £150 for approx. 8 hours work over five days plus free board and accommodation. Min. period of work of 26 weeks. Positions are available all year round. Applicants should be 18+, have service industry experience and speak reasonable English. Only EU applicants are welcome.
*Applications* should be made at any time to Mrs C Burt at the above address. Telephone interview required.

**FMC:** All England Lawn Tennis and Croquet Club, Church Road, Wimbledon, London SW19 5AE (☏ 020-8947 7430; fax 020-8944 6362; e-mail resourcing@fmccatering.co.uk; www.fmccatering.co.uk). FMC have grown to be one of the larger outdoor event caterers in Europe. Their portfolio now covers some of the most prestigious events in the society calendar including Wimbledon, celebrity cricket matches, company launches, Langan's Brasserie at the Volvo PGA Golf, Rugby at Twickenham and numerous other events.
**Staff of all categories, including management and chefs,** needed to work at events. The Wimbledon Tennis Championships require 1,500 staff between Monday 23 June and Sunday 6 July inclusive. Hours of work and rates of pay are by arrangement. Applicants must be aged at least 18 and have either a National Insurance number or the relevant work permit documents if coming from abroad. For all events applicants should be people who are outgoing and fun loving with good communication skills.
Applicants should contact the Personnel Department at the above address for an *applications* pack.

**FRED (UK) 2000 LIMITED:** Copthall House, Victoria Road, Aldershot, Hampshire (☏ 01252-315544; fax 01252-342727; e-mail freduk2000@hotmail.com). Specialised recruitment agency.
**Catering Staff (5-10).** Wages from £5-£18 per hour. Hours vary. Positions are available all year. Positions open depend on qualifications. Foreign applicants entitled to work in the UK and with acceptable spoken English welcome. Accommodation available for some positions.
*Applications* should be made at any time to a Recruitment Consultant at the above address. Interview necessary, by telephone is sufficient.

**FULLER, SMITH & TURNER:** The Griffin Brewery, Chiswick Lane South, Chiswick, London W4 2QB (☏ 020-8996 2000; fax 020-8996 2013; recruitment.manager@fullers.co.uk; www.fullers.co.uk). UK pub group.
**Bar Staff, Assistant Managers and Chefs.** Wages £4-5 per hour for bar staff; other wages discussed at interview. Hours by arrangement. Positions available all year round. B & L sometimes available. Placements mainly in the London area but some around the UK. Minimum age 18. Foreign applicants with permission to work in the UK welcome.
*Applications* to the Recruitment Advisor at the above address.

**GARFUNKELS:** 103 Charing Cross Road, London WC2H 0QZ (020-7440 5501; fax 020-7440 5503; e-mail 106404.3075@compuservecom). A restaurant chain with branches in Bath, Cambridge, Sutton, Edinburgh, Glasgow, Heathrow Airport, Gatwick Airport, and all over London.
**Waiting Staff and Kitchen Staff.** Wages to be arranged. Flexible hours. Staff required throughout the year, mainly between June and September. Minimum period of work 3 months. Kitchen staff must have good knowledge of food hygiene. Foreign

applicants with high standard of spoken English considered. Accommodation not available. All applicants should be available for interview.
*Applications* all year round to the Manager of the appropriate branch.

**HILTON LONDON METROPOLE:** Edgware Road, London W2 1JU (☎020-7616 6474; fax 020-7616 6471). The largest conferencing and banqueting centre in Europe. A cosmopolitan four star hotel with 1,058 bedrooms and 40 meeting rooms in central London.
**Waiting Staff.** £200 per week (Min. age 18). Must have a good command of the English language and customer service experience.
**Cleaning Staff.** £200 per week. Must be physically fit and have a basic command of the English language.
**Sales Researcher (1).** £170 per week. Intelligent and studying for a degree in sales and marketing.
To work 39 hours per week. Staff required all year round. No accommodation available. Minimum period of work 6 months.
*Applications* at any time to the Human Resources Department, FAO the Human Resources Manager.

**HILTON COBHAM:** Seven Hills Road South, Cobham, Surrey KT11 1EW (☎01932-864471; fax 01932-867067). A four star hotel with 158 bedrooms, 13 function rooms and a leisure club facility. Set in 40 acres of woodland in Surrey; half an hour from London by train.
**Food and Beverage Servers** to work in the Café Cino Bar, Zuccotta Restaurant or Conference & Banqueting Operations. Wages £4.12 per hour (live in), £4.64 per hour (live out). Some experience preferred.
**Room Attendants.** Wages £3.91 per hour (live in) and £4.64 per hour (live out).
A good level of English is important for all front line positions. All positions are based on 39 hours per week and for a minimum of 6 months. Accommodation is subject to availability. A telephone interview is sufficient if applicants enclose a photo with their CV as well as references.
*Applications* should be addressed to Rachel Holland or Alison Dobbie, Human Resources Department.

**HILTON ST ANNE'S MANOR HOTEL:** London Road, Wokingham, Berkshire RG40 1ST (☎0118-977 2550; fax 0118-977 2526). A four star 180 bedroom luxury conference based hotel, set in 25 acres of gardens.
**Bar Persons, Room Attendants, Banqueting/Restaurant Waiting Staff.** Wage for all positions approx. £4.50-£5 per hour. To work hours as required. Accommodation may be available for £20 per week, inclusive of bills and food. Min. period of work 6 months. Minimum age 18. Training will be given. Overseas applicants with good knowledge of English considered.
*Applications* to Michaela Cassa, HR Manager. An interview is necessary.

**HOLIDAY INN BRENT CROSS:** Tilling Road, Brent Cross, London NE2 1LP (☎020-8201 8686; fax 020-8967 6372). Owned by Bass, the hotel is part of the Holiday Inn chain.
**Food and Beverage Assistants (2/3)** to perform bar and waiting work. Wages £4.25 per hour.
**Receptionist (1)** to greet and check in guests. Wages £4.25 per hour. Must have hotel reception experience.
All staff work 30-40 hours a week depending on business. Accommodation

is available at a cost of £70 per week inclusive. Min. period of work 4 months. Overseas applicants who are suitably qualified and speak English well are considered. Interview may be necessary if applicants are in the UK.
*Applications* to Natalie Moran from January.

**HOLIDAY INN MAYFAIR:** Berkeley Street, London W1J 8NE (☎020-7493 8282; fax 020-7412 3008). A busy 4 star hotel situated in Mayfair that caters for business and leisure clients.
**Room Attendants (5)** to clean 14 rooms a day to a high standard. Wages £9,400 per annum. To work 5 days a week according to a rota. No accommodation is available. Min. period of work 6 months all year round.
   Commitment and enthusiasm are more important than experience. Overseas applicants with work authorisation are considered.
   *Applications* should be made after arrival in the UK to the Personnel Department. Interview necessary.

**THE IMPERIAL LONDON HOTELS LTD:** 6 Coram Street, Russell Square, London WC1N 1HA (☎020-7278 3922; fax 020-7278 9318; e-mail personnel@imperialhotels.co.uk; www.imperialhotels.co.uk). Group of 6 prestigious hotels based in central London.
**Chamber Staff** Wages from £169.50 per week. To work 34 hours per week. Min. period of work of 3 months. Positions are available from June to August. Shared accommodation and full board available for £120.50 per week. Intermediate English essential. Minimum age 18. No previous experience necessary. Foreign applicants with correct work permits are welcome.
   *Applications* should be made from April onwards to the Personnel Departmnet. References essential.

**JARVIS ELCOT PARK HOTEL:** Elcot, Newbury, Berkshire RG20 8NJ (☎01488-658100; fax 01488-658288). A 75 bedroom hotel with 9 conference rooms and a leisure club set in 16 acres of countryside.
**Restaurant Attendants (1-2).** Wage £3.90 per hour if living in, £4.47 if living out. To work 39 hours over 5 days a week. Paid overtime available. Min. period of work 2 months between May/June and August/September. Accommodation subject to availability at a cost of £22.23 per week (2002 figure). Meals and uniform provided.
   Applicants must be over 18 with some experience of restaurant work. Interview necessary, but can be conducted over telephone. Overseas applicants entitled to work in the UK considered.
   *Applications* from March to the Personnel and Training Manager.

**KENSINGTON POSTHOUSE:** Wrights Lane, Kensington, London W8 5SP (☎0870-400 9000; fax 020-7937 8289). A 550 bedroom hotel serving international professional clients located in central London.
**Housekeeping and Waiting Staff.** Wages on application for 36½ or 39 hours a week or hours to suit. Min. period of work 3 months between June and September.No accommodation available. Overseas applicants welcome.
   *Applications* from May to the Personnel Officer. Interview necessary.

**KENTCHOICE SITE SERVICES:** 58 Park Road, Hampton Hill, Middlesex TW12 1HP (tel/fax 020-8941 8900; e-mail kentchoice@aol.com)
**Waiting Staff, Bar Staff, Contract Cleaners, Labourers, Chefs and Kitchen**

**Staff** aged over 17; details of work by arrangement.
*Applicants* should contact Mr G. Povey at the abovce address.

**LONDON HOSTELS ASSOCIATION LTD:** 54 Eccleston Square, London SW1V 1PG (☎020-7834 1545; fax 020-7834 7146; www.london-hostels.co.uk). Established in 1940, recruits residential staff for 10 London hostels run for young employed people and full-time bona-fide students.
**General Domestic Staff** to do housework and help in kitchens. Wages by arrangement, paid monthly with B & L provided. To work an average of 30-39 hours per week (mornings and evenings). Minimum period of work 3 months throughout the year. Work available all year round, long stays welcome. Opportunities to attend courses and improve English skills.
**Voluntary jobs** also available, working only 20 hours per week in exchange for board and lodging. Minimum stay 8 weeks.
   Min. age 18 years. Common sense and willingness to tackle variety of jobs required. Foreign applicants with permission to work in the UK welcome.
   *Applications* should be sent 2 months before date of availability to the Personnel Manager, London Hostels Association, at the above address.

**MAYDAY TEMPORARY CATERING STAFF:** See below for addresses. Arranges temporary and permanent catering jobs to suit all levels of experience. Excellent benefits.
**Chefs.** From £7 per hour.
**Waiting Staff.** From £5 per hour.
**Bar Staff.** £5.25 per hour.
**Deli Assistants.** From £5 per hour.
**Kitchen Porters.** From £4.75 per hour.
**Catering Assistants.** From £4.75 per hour.
**Silver Service** From £6.00 per hour.
   Temporary and permanent positions available all year round. Overtime is available for evening and weekend work and employees are paid weekly.
   *Applicants* should telephone any of the offices listed below or come directly to their nearest office from Monday to Thursday between 10am and 12pm: 2 Shoreditch High Street, London E1 6PG (☎020-7377 1352) (City); 21 Great Chapel Street, Soho, London W1F 8FP (☎020-7439 3009) (West End). All applicants must have a valid work permit and references.

**MELIA WHITE HOUSE HOTEL:** Albany St, Regents Park, London, SW8 4TX (☎020-7387 1200; fax 020-7872 0087; e-mail vida.macdermott@solmelia.com). Sol Media is an international hotel group which has adopted an approach of 'Everything is Possible'.
**Waiting and Catering Staff (25), Porters (3), Room maids.** Wages from £4.04 to £5.09 per hour. Hours of work vary. Min. period of work is 1 week. Positions are available from April to September. Waiting experience may be required. Accommodation is available for £45 per week.
   *Applications* should be made to the HR Officer at the above address from April onwards.

**NATIONAL TRUST ENTERPRISES:** c/o Polesden Lacey, Dorking, Surrey RH5 6BD (☎01372-455033/4; fax 01372-452023; e-mail sensak@smtp.ntrust.org.uk)
**Catering Assistants** to work in 15 National Trust properties catering to the general public in West Sussex, Hampshire and Surrey. Wages vary from property to property

but will be at least £4.20 per hour. Accommodation not available. Please do not apply if accommodation is required. Working hours vary but may include working over weekends and bank holidays. Experience of working in the catering industry and basic food hygiene are desirable but not essential; full training will be given.

Those interested should *contact* Sue Knevett, Regional Catering Manager, or Sylvia Raynor at the above address who will refer them to an appropriate property.

**NORFOLK PLAZA HOTEL:** 29/33 Norfolk Square, London W2 1RX (☎020-7723 0792; fax 020-7224 8770; e-mail enquiries@norfolkplazahotel.co.uk). An 87 bedroom, 3 Star hotel by Paddington Station in London W2. The majority of clients are Europeans on short leisure breaks in London, with a mixture of local UK Corporate customers. The hotel employs approx. 40 staff.
**Hotel Receptionists.** Wages £50 (gross) per 8-hour shift, with 5 shifts per week, plus weekly tips. Uniforms and other benefits provided free. Period of work June to end of September. Min. age 20. Applicants must be able to speak fluent English; knowledge of another Western European language would be an advantage. Experience of working on a computer database system and telephone switchboard essential. Overseas applicants welcome. Two weeks' training will be provided for successful applicants. No accommodation available.
*Applications* should be sent to Mr Ali Muttawa, General Manager, at the above address, or to ali@norfolkplazahotel.co.uk

**ROYAL GARDEN HOTEL:** 2-24 Kensington High Street, London, W8 4PT (☎020-7361 1944; fax 020-7361 1914; e-mail emmabailes@royalgdn.co.uk).
**Room Attendants (10)** to clean 12 rooms a day between 8am-4.30pm, 5 days a week on a rota basis. Wages £150 per week. Staff are required from June until the end of September.
*Applications* should be sent to Emma Bailes, Personnel Administrator, at the above address.

**SAVOIR FAIRE (MARQUEES) LTD:** 1 Woodside Terrace, Cadmore End, High Wycombe, Buckinghamshire HP14 3PE (☎01494-883663; fax 01494-883553; e-mail party@savoirfaire.co.uk; www.savoirfaire.co.uk).
**Marquee Erectors (Up To 10)** Wages from £5 per hour with occasional tips. To work Monday to Friday from 8am to 5 or 6pm plus occasional weekend work at time and a half. Required from April to September. Must be sociable, work well in a small team, preferably strong and at least five feet eight inches in height. No accommodation available.
*Applications* to Richard Hall, Managing Director, at the above address.

**THAMES LUXURY CHARTERS Ltd:** on board HMS Belfast, Tooley Street, London, SE1 2JA (☎020-7378 1211; fax 020-7378 1359; e-mail belinda@livetts.co.uk).
**Silver Service and Bar Staff (20)** required to work on board vessels on the Thames for corporate hospitality events. Hours of work are variable, but mostly evening work; wages from £6.25 per hour plus tips. Applicants must have previous experience, a good command of English and like boats.
*Applications* to Belinda Livett, Company Secretary.

**THISTLE MARBLE ARCH HOTEL:** Bryanston Street, Marble Arch, London W1A 4UR (☎020-7629 8040; fax 020-7629 0628).
**Waiting Staff.** Experience in catering essential.

**Bartender.** Min. age 18 years. Bar experience essential. Wages approx. £4.70 gross per hour. All staff to work 20-40 hours a week in shifts. Some uniform provided, all meals on duty provided. Work offered at all times of the year. Must have excellent presentation. Overseas applicants considered, provided they speak fluent English. All applicants must be available for interview.
*Applications* at any time to Human Resources Manager at the above address.

**THISTLE TOWER HOTEL,** St. Katharine's Way, London E1W ILD (☎020-7481-3745; fax 020-7680-0256; e-mail: hr.tower@thistle.co.uk).
**Waiting Staff** for café, **Haagen Dazs Server, Bar Person, Room Service Staff.** Required throughout the year. Pay from £4.10 per hour for waiting staff to £5.18 per hour for bar work. Minimum age is 18 years.
*Applications* to Helen Warnock, Manager

**THISTLE VICTORIA:** 101 Buckingham Palace Road, London SW1W 0SJ (☎0870-333 9120; fax 020-7868 6293; e-mail hr.victoria@thistle.co.uk). A 4-star hotel in the heart of Victoria, near Buckingham Palace and the West End. 364 bedrooms, a bar, restaurant, lounge and seven conference rooms
**Front of House and Food and Beverage Staff** with excellent customer service skills needed. Wages from £5 to £9 per hour depending on experience. Applicants must be 18 and ideally have leisure and tourism experience (but not essential). Accommodation available for the right candidates. Minimum stay 1 year and all nationalities welcome. The hotel has an Equal Opportunities Policy.
*Applications* to the the Human Resources Department at the above address.

**THISTLE WESTMINSTER HOTEL:** 49 Buckingham Palace Road, London SW1W 0QT (☎020-7834 1821; fax 020-7931 7542; e-mail westminster@thistle.co.uk). A four star central London hotel, with 134 bedrooms, a brasserie style restaurant and a popular bar.
**Waiting Staff (2)** to wait at tables. Wage £175 per week plus tips. To work 39 hours over 5 days a week. Shared accommodation available at a cost of approx. £47.50 per week. Min. period of work 3 months between end of June and end of September.
Applicants must be over 18. Experience not necessary, but interview required. Overseas applicants with excellent English considered.
*Applications* in March/April to the Human Resources Department.

**WILLOW TREE NARROW BOAT TRIPS:** Horsenden Visitor Centre, Horsenden Lane North, Greenford, Middlesex UB6 7PQ (tel/fax 028-8841 2100; e-mail anthony.moss@btinternet.com). A small operator of both public and private narrow boat trips along the Grand Union Canal.
**Boat Crew (1/2)** to carry out food/drink service, bar work and general cleaning duties. Wages £5.50 per hour. To work approx. 30 hours per week, mainly evenings and weekends. Min. period of work of 4 months. Positions available June-September. Foreign applicants with fluent English considered. Minimum age 18. No accommodation available.
*Applications* should be made from April onwards to Mrs Barbara Moss at the above address. Interview required.

**VINCENT HOUSE:** 5 Pembridge Square, London W2 4EG (☎020-7229 1133). Residential club for business people.
**General Assistants** required to help with housekeeping, restaurant and porterage. Wages £107-£115 per week, dependent on age, plus free B & L. To work average of

32 hours per week. Work available all year round but employment is for a minimum period of 4 months. Applicants should be 18 or over. Overseas applicants welcome.
*Applications* to Mr R. Tomkins, Vincent House.

**WOODLANDS PARK:** Woodlands Lane, Stoke D'Arbernon, Cobham, Surrey KT11 3QB (☎01372-843933; e-mail bp@arcadianhotels.co.uk).
**Hotel Staff** Wages from £4.30 an hour with company discounts and uniform provided. To work 40 hours a week. Minimum period of work 6 months all year round. All positions are live-in. Overseas applicants with a high standard of English welcome.
*Applications* at any time to Human Resources Department at the above address.

# Language Schools

**EJO Ltd:** Passfield Business Centre, Lynchborough Road, Passfield, Liphook GU30 7SB (☎01428-751933; e-mail ed@ejo.co.uk)
**Course Directors, Senior EFL Teachers, EFL Teachers** required for residential and non-residential courses. Course Directors and Senior Teachers need to be TEFL qualified with a good degree (MA or TEFL/TESOL Dip preferred)and 2+ years of teaching experience. Teachers need to have CELTA/Trinity TESOL qualification.
**Activity Staff** required for non-residential and residential courses, to work 5-6 days per week. Applicants should be studying towards or graduates in a sports or arts qualification.
**Qualified Lifeguards and First Aiders** required for residential centres.
Staff are required for Easter, June, July and August. Pay varies according to qualifications and experience.
*Applications* to The Education Department, at the above address.

**FRANCES KING SCHOOL OF ENGLISH:** 5 Grosvenor Gardens, London SW1W 0BD. A large language school located on 3 sites in Central London. Their Students come from all over the world, particularly Italy and Spain during the summer months.
**EFL Teachers (30)** Pay on an hourly basis, with accommodation included at centres outside London. to teach up to 30 hours per week at various centres, plus optional leading of groups and taking part in activities with students; residential centres may require extra duties. Period of work from the first week of July-last week of August. Must hold RSA/Cambridge TEFL certificates plus a minimum of one years experience.
*Applications* to R. Stewart, Director of Studies, at the above address.

**HAMPSTEAD SCHOOL OF ENGLISH:** 553 Finchley Road, Hampstead, London NW3 7BJ (☎020-7794 3533; fax 020-7431 2987; e-mail info@hampstead-english.ac.uk). The school has an average of 350 foreign students, and enjoys a reputation for excellence. Staff pride themselves on treating each student as an individual.
**Student Group Leaders (6-8)** to guide foreign language students around London and take care of them while on route to and during their evening engagements. Wages of £6.00 per hour (negotiable); flexible hours ranging from 15 to 40 hours over mainly afternoons and evenings. Work would suit undergraduates aged 19 and over who have successfully completed at least one year of a university course. Work is available from last week of June to early September. Applicants should be energetic, enthusiastic and like dealing with people. No accommodation provided.
*Applications* to Kevin McNally, Principal, at the above address. Applicants must be available for interview.

**HARVEN SCHOOL OF ENGLISH:** The Mascot, Coley Avenue, Woking, Surrey GU22 7BT (☎01483-770969; fax 01483-740267; e-mail harven.school@btinternet.com). A private organisation providing full-time intensive courses in English as a foreign language with a comprehensive social programme for adults and juniors in pleasant surroundings.

**Qualified EFL Teachers (10), Sports/Social Assistants (2)** to work for an English language school in June, July and August. Salary according to qualifications and experience. To work from Monday-Friday or Saturday from 9.30am-4pm approx. and some evenings for the social programme. no accommodation provided. Applicants should have relevant qualifications and experience.

*Applications* to the Director of Studies, at the above address.

**INTERNATIONAL COMMUNITY SCHOOL:** 21 Star Street, London, W2 1QB (☎020-7402 0416; fax 020-7724 2219; e-mail bmurrayskola@aol.com).

**EFL Teachers (10-15)** to work between the start of June and the end of August. Hours of work are full-time, 9am-4.30pm, for wages of £290-£340 per week. Staff should have CELTA/DELTA/PGCE and preferably experience of teaching young learners.

**Social Organiser (1-2)** required for full-time work in July and August. Wages are £300 per week and applicants must have experience of organising social activities for teenagers.

*Applications* to the Director of Studies at the above address.

**KING'S SCHOOL OF ENGLISH (LONDON):** 25 Beckenham Road, Beckenham, Kent BR3 4PR (☎020-8650 5891; fax 020-8663 3224; e-mail info@kingslon.co.uk; kingslon.co.uk). The only all year round recognised school in Beckenham. Takes around 150-250 students from all over the world and specialises in teaching general English to international groups of adult learners. Established in 1966 and British Council accredited.

**EFL Teachers (Approx 10)** to work from mid June to end of August for 16-32 lessons per week programmes (min 4 weeks) for learners aged 16 and over. Only RSA Cambridge qualified applicants to apply from January.

**Travel Manager & Assistant** for the organisation of leisure programme including evening work and weekends, and airport transfers. Must have a good knowledge of attractions in London and South East England. Knowledge of Italian or Spanish or Russian an advantage. Suitably qualified overseas applicants with good English considered. Interview essential.

Salaries by negotiation. Applicants must be EU Citizens or have work permits. *Applications* to the Principal at the above address.

**LANGUAGE LINK:** 21 Harrington Road, London SW7 3EU (☎020-7225 1065; fax 020-7584 3518; e-mail languagelink@compuserve.com). Language Link is accredited by the British Council and is a member of ARELS.

**EFL Teachers (20).** Pay is dependent on qualifications and experience. Monday-Friday. To work from end of June to the end of August. Applicants must be Cambridge, Trinity or equivalent TEFLA certified. No accommodation is available.

*Applications* from June to the Director of Studies at the above address. An interview is required.

**ENGLISH IN LONDON:** 27 Delaney Street, London NW1 7RX(☎020-7388 6644; fax 020-7387 7575). Long established language school; also runs CELTA teacher training courses.

**EFL Teachers** to teach classes of 15 adults or 20 children. Wages starting at £11.55

per hour. To work Monday to Friday, 15 hours (part-time) or 25 hours (full-time). Min. period of work of 4 weeks. Positions are available from late June to early September. CELTA or Trinity certificate required. Experience preferred but not essential. No accommodation available.

*Applications* to David Riddell at the above address from Easter onwards. Interview necessary.

**OISE YOUTH LANGUAGE SCHOOLS:** OISE Youth Language Schools, Newbury Hall, Enborne Road, Newbury RG14 6AD (☎01635-36879; fax 01635-48400; e-mail yloise@btclick.com). Work available throughout Britain.

**EFL Teachers** to teach small groups of foreign students. Must be qualified and have experience.

**Academic Directors.** Qualified EFL teachers with organisational ability.

**Leisure Directors** to run a pre-planned leisure programme and teach half a timetable.

Period of work Easter and July/August. Applicants must be graduates and speak English to the level of a native. Some residential courses available.

*Details* from the Recruitment Administrator, OISE.

**OXFORD HOUSE COLLEGE:** 28 Market Place, Oxford Circus, London W1W 8AW (☎020-7580 9785; fax 020-7323 4582; e-mail principal@oxfordhouse.co.uk). A leading British Council accredited college in central London providing English, Computing, Travel and Tourism and Teacher Training courses.

**EFL Teachers and EFL Teacher/Trainers** required to work for a minimum period of 2 weeks or throughout the year. Applicants must be TESOL/TEFL certified.

*Applications* at any time to the Principal at the above address.

**SELS SCHOOL OF ENGLISH:** 64 Long Acre, Covent Garden, London WC2E 95X (☎020-7240 2581; fax 020-7379 5793; e-mail english@sels.co.uk; www.sels.co.uk). Located in fashionable Covent Garden near the Opera House, the school teaches English at all levels to foreign adults in groups of 5-9 and on a one-to-one basis.

**Assistant** to work in the tea room and clean premises. Wages £4.50 per hour. To work 5-9 hours per day, Monday to Friday and alternate weekends. Period of work by arrangement. Applicants should be aged 18-30 years. Knowledge of Portuguese, Spanish or Italian useful.

**Clerks/Secretaries.** £6+ per hour. To work approx. 20-40 hours per week. Must have typing and word processing experience. Long period of employment preferred.

*Applications* to Mr Y. Raiss, Sels School of English, at the above address.

**SUPERSTUDY UK:** 1-3 Manor Parade, Sheepcote Road, Harrow HA1 2JN (☎020-8861 5322; e-mail superstudy.london@btinternet.com; www.superstudy.uk). Teaches all levels of English to all nationalities, specialising in general English and conversation in a friendly atmosphere. Five minutes walk from Harrow-on-the-Hill Underground station.

**EFL Teachers (2-4).** from £12.23 per hour, exact hours of work to be arranged. Minimum period of work 2-4 weeks between 1 July and 31 August. Accommodation not available. RSA/UCLES, CTEFLA and first degree required.

*Applications* as early as possible to Iain Tebb at the above address.

**TASIS ENGLAND AMERICAN SCHOOL:** Coldharbour Lane, Thorpe, Surrey TW20 8TE (www.tasis.com). Set in 35 acres; approx. 30 minutes train journey from London, the school runs a summer programme for American and International students.

**Counsellors.** To supervise sports and activities such as visits and trips all over

England, and act as teaching aides. Driving licence necessary.
**Teachers.** To teach English as a foreign language and traditional high school maths and English courses. Must be familiar with the American educational system. Wages according to relevant experience. Room and board provided. Applicants must have a standard of English as high as that of a native speaker and have completed at least one year at university.
*Applications,* including CV, should be sent by 15 March to Mr David West, Director of Summer Programmes, at the above address.

**GEOS ENGLISH ACADEMY LONDON:** 16/20 New Broadway, Ealing, London W5 2XA (☎020-8566 2188; fax 020-8566 2011; e-mail cristina@euroaccents.co.uk).
**EFL Teachers (15).** Wages of £8.50-£10 per hour. To work from mid-June to the end of August. Teaching duties are for 3 hours per day Monday-Friday, with the possibility of helping with the social programme in the afternoons. Applicants must have RSA, CTEFLA/CELTA, or Trinity College TESOL.
*Applications* to Jane Flynn, Principal, at the above address.

# Medical

**ABBEY HOMECARE LTD:** Unit 6B, Desborough Industrial Park, Desborough Park Road, High Wycombe, Buckinghamshire HP12 3BG (☎01494-896400; fax 01494-896401; e-mail ann@abbeyhomecare.co.uk; www.abbeyhomecare.co.uk). Established for 6 years, offering all kinds of care to the elderly.
**Care Assistants (9).** Based in Henley, High Wycombe, Hazlemere or Marlow. Wages from £12,000-£22,000 pro rata; hours very flexible. Age 18+ and training is provided.
**Health Care Assistants (10).** Based within a 20 mile radius of High Wycombe. Wages from £15,000-£25,000 pro rata; hours flexible. Must have at least 1 year's experience in care for the elderly or be student nurses.
All staff required from June 2003 to October 2003; minimum period of work of 4 weeks. Accommodation not available. Foreign applicants with work permits and fluent English are welcome provided they preregister with the company.
*Applications* should be made from March to the above address. Interview required.

**ALLIED HEALTHCARE GROUP:** Hollytree Cottage, Bryants Bottom Road, Great Missenden, Buckinghamshire HP16 OJS (☎01494-488040/1; fax 01494-488650; e-mail highwycombe@alliedhealthcare.com). Nursing agency.
**Health Care Assistants (100)** needed for work in the community, hospitals and nursing homes. Wages £6.88-£10.71 per hour. Positions are available all year.
*Applications* should be made to Mrs Vanessa Cracknell. Interview necessary.

**ANCHOR CARE ALTERNATIVES:** 618-620 Kingston Road, London SW20 8DN (☎020-8545 4900). Cares for the elderly and disabled in their own homes throughout the UK.
**Live-In Care Workers.** Wages from £5.78 per hour.
**Daily Care Workers.** Wages from £262.80 per week.
Staff required all year round to care for mainly housebound people. Minimum period of work 1-3 months. Duties include personal care, cooking, housekeeping, laundry, shopping and companionship. Overseas applicants authorised to work in the UK welcome. Applicants must be friendly with a caring attitude.
*Applications* 2-3 weeks before work is required to the Senior Area Manager at the above address.

**COMPLETE CARE CENTRE LTD:** 25 Beynon Road, Carshalton, Surrey SM5 3RL (☎020-8288 0902). A care agency supplying staff to private and local authorities.
**Care Assistants (25+).** Wages of £5-£7 per hour
**Support Workers (30+).** Wages of £6-£9 per hour
All positions involve shift work. Applicants should be over 18, have experience as a care assistant (preferably two years) and a Moving and Handling Certificate. Staff required all year round, with no minimum period of work. Suitably qualified foreign applicants with fluent English welcome. No accommodation available.
*Applications* should be made at any time to Sam, Lesley or Dawn at the above address. Interview required.

**EUROPEAN NURSING AGENCY LTD:** Smallford Works, Smallford Lane, St Albans AL4 O5A (☎01727-825000; fax 01727-825005; e-mail jobs@ena.co.uk).
**Live-in Care Assistants.** to work one-to-one at home for busy young adults disabled by car accidents etc. The clients lead busy lives and enjoy going to the cinema, pub etc; help also needed with personal care, washing, dressing etc. The company takes care to get to know care assistants before placing them, aiming to match personalities as well as experience. Wages from £318-£400, board and accommodation included. To work various hours. Min. period of work of 3 months around the year. Positions are available all year. Applicants should be 21+; previous experience and a clean driving licence are advantages.
*Applications* should be made at any time to Recruitment at the above address.

**FRED (UK) 2000 LIMITED:** Copthall House, Victoria Road, Aldershot, Hampshire (☎01252-315544; fax 01252-342727; e-mail freduk2000@hotmail.com). Specialised recruitment agency.
**Care and Nursing Staff (17).** Wages from £6.45-£50 per hour. To work shifts. Min. period of work of 1 week. Positions are available all year. Positions open depend on qualifications. Foreign applicants entitled to work in the UK and with acceptable spoken English welcome. Accommodation available for some positions.
*Applications* should be made at any time to a Recruitment Consultant at the above address. Interview necessary, by telephone is sufficient.

**KELLS NURSES BUREAU:** 43 The Grove, London N13 5LP (☎020-8886 6589; fax 020-8886-6168).
**Care Assistants (30-40)** to work with elderly and frail people in local authority residential homes in North and Central London. Wages are from £6 p.h. (£7 at weekends). Shifts are from 7.30am-2pm and from 1.30-9pm. Period of work May-September. Minimum age is 20 and experience of working in a similar post for at least 6 months is essential; the work is particularly suitable to nursing and medical students.
*Applications* should be sent to Michael Ganeski, the Manager.

**VICTOR LIM:** 112 Shenley Road, Borehamwood, Hertfordshire WD6 1RB (☎020-8953 9297; fax 020-8386-6941; e-mail: vkl_nursing@hotmail.com).
**Qualified RMN/RGN Nurses** Wages from £11.20-£28.50 per hour. 12 hours per day. Must be registered with the UK Central Council (Nursing).
*Applications* to Victor Lim, Manager, at the above address.

## Office Work

**STRATEGY RESEARCH AND ACTION:** Parkway house, Sheen Lane, London SW14 8LS (☎020-8878 1482; fax 020-8876 1204; e-mail robin@sra.dircon.co.uk) An international marketing and research consultancy concerned with publishing and food distribution.
**Research Assistants (2)** Wages by negotiation. To work 7 hours a day, 7 days a week. Applicants must have studied/be studying business. Research assistants are needed all year round.
*Applications* should be addressed to Robin J Birn and sent to the above address. An interview is required.

## Outdoor

**ALRESFORD MARQUEES:** Ashdell Farm, Headmore Lane, GU34 3ES (☎01420-587444; fax 01420-587444).
**Marquee Labourers (3)** needed from May onwards. £55 per day. Long hours, hot work, good laughs. Must be over 17 years old.
*Applications* to the above address.

**BUCKS WIGWAMS:** Ibstone, near High Wycombe, Buckinghamshire HP14 3XT (☎01491-638227).
**Marquee Erectors (5)** wanted for the summer period until the end of November to put up marquees in the Thames Valley area. Wages from £4.50-£6 per hour according to age and experience. Working hours are 8am-5pm with some overtime and weekend work. Minimum age 18. Must have own transport and be physically fit.
*Applications* should be made in writing to Mr W.M. King, Manager.

**CAM VALLEY PLUMS:** 39 Chiswick End, Meldreth, Royston, Herts. SG8 6LZ (☎01763-262964/260332; fax 01763-260332; e-mail camvalley.plums@virgin.net).
**Fruit Pickers (6)** f Wages at piece-work rates; to work 5-7 days per week. Required for work in September. Caravan accommodation available. Minimum age 18. Applicants must be students authorised to work in the UK.
*Applications* to T.J. Elbourn, Manager, at the above address.

**DIALOGUE DIRECT LTD:** www.funkyjobs.co.uk; email: jobs@dialoguedirect .co.uk; tel:08454-583 901. A successful international fundraising agency working on behalf of charities and NPOs (non-profit organisations). Raising donations *face to face* for well-known charities all over the UK, in mobile teams. Work available year-round with main campaign in the summer months.
**Dialoguers**. OTE £180-£450 per week. (avg £250/ wk for those without previous training/ experience). Accommodation and team car hire paid for. All candidates start as face-to-face fundraisers, communicating directly with the public. Flexible contracts. Work is in small, live-in, UK mobile teams. Must have a positive and flexible attitude towards work and team-life, excellent communication skills and an energy and passion to succeed and represent good causes. Must be able to work and live successfully in a small team.
**Team Guides**: Fast progression for the right candidate to Team Guide. DialogueDirect has in-house training with a yearly seminar for Team Guides from across DD Europe.
All candidates must be over 18yrs and available to work away from home, minimum five week contract. No maximum age limit. Overseas applicants with

fluent English and a working visa welcome, particularly those from New Zealand, Australia, America and South Africa.
Call the local number above for immediate interview.

**CLAREMONT MARQUEES:** Fishers Hill House, Hook Heath Road, Woking, Surrey GU22 OQE (☎01483-720472; fax 01483-724714).
**Marquee Erectors/Labourers (6)** Wages from £5.50-£7.50 per hour Flexible working hours, normally approx. 8 hours a day. Period of work May to September 30. Applicants must be fit and strong. No accommodation available.
*Applications* to Robert Watkins, Owner, at the above address.

**INTENTS MARQUEES CO:** Laplands Farm, Brill, Aylesbury, Bucks HP18 9T2 (☎01844-238466; fax 01844-238870) A family run group operating up to around 50 miles from the base. They hire out and erect marquees and equipment for weddings, parties and corporate functions.
**Marquee Erectors (2)** Wages £5 per hour, for minimum 8 hours per day. Staff are needed from April to October for a minimum of 1 week. Applicants must be over 18, strong and fit, preferably with a driving licence. Must be active, willing to travel and flexible regarding working hours. Foreign applicants are welcome but must speak good English and have a valid work permit. Accommodation is available.
*Applications* to Mr Roger Cope from January 1st at the above address.

**MAIN EVENTS:** MPR House, 5 Island Farm Avenue, West Molesey Trading Estate, West Molesey, Surrey KT8 0UZ (☎020-8941 2411; fax 020-8941 4710).
**Staff (up to 10)** required to set up and man inflatable equipment including bouncy castles at events, activity days etc. £5 per hour. Work is on an ad hoc basis; hours and dates cannot be guaranteed but depend upon company's contracts at a particular time. Min. age 21. Must be able to deal with people and have a sense of fun. First-aid qualification an advantage. No accommodation available; applicants should ideally live locally. Overseas applicants with a good level of English welcome. If possible applicants should be able to attend an interview.
*Applications* at any time to Mr James Feary, Main Events.

**MAMALOUCOS:** The Power Station, Coronet Street, London N1 6HD (☎020-7837 1019; e-mail: mat@mamaloucos.com).
**Tent crew (20)** Wages £60-£70 per day. 4 days per week up to 10 hours per day. Staff required from 15 Aug to 8 Oct. To work on a portable theatre installation for a circus-theatre show transferring from The National to tour. Heavy lifting ability and enthusiasm required. Age 18-35.
*Applications* to M.V. Churchill, Producer at the above address.

**MERIDIAN MARQUEES:** Avoca, Church Lane, Three Mile Cross, Reading, RG7 1HB (☎0118-988 7660; fax 0118-988 7661; e-mail sales@meridian.com; www.meridianmarquees.com).
**Marquee Erectors (6)** wanted between June and September for wages of £5.50-£6 per hour, extensive overtime offered. Hours and other details by arrangement.
*Applications* to M. James, Partner.

**WIDMER FEEDS LTD:** Pink Road, Lacey Green, Buckinghamshire HP27 OPG (☎01844-344765; fax 01844-347446; e-mail widmerfeeds@supernet.com).
**Pet Shop, Livery Yard & Farm Assistants** to work over the summer. Wages and hours by arrangement; the pet shop opens seven days a week. No accommodation

available. Must be helpful, cheery and able to deal with the public and animals.
*Applications* to Cathryn Davies, Owner at the above address.

**E.W. MORRIS** Home Bush, Brox Lane, Ottershaw, Surrey KT16 0LN (☎01932-873050). Small scale herb grower.Family business supplying the wholesale market.
**Outdoor Staff.** To work 5 days per week plus Sunday morning. Positions are available from June to October. No accommodation available. Some tractor driving; driving licence preferred.
*Applications* should be made from mid-May onwards to Jane Morris at the above address. Interview necessary.

# Sport

**BRAY LAKE WATERSPORTS:** Monkey Island Lane, Windsor Road, Maidenhead, Berks SL6 2EB (☎01628-638860; fax 01628-771441; e-mail info@braylake.com). Set next to a 60 acre lake ideal for beginners and intermediate windsurfers, sailors and canoeists. Caters for both adults and juniors. Has a good range of equipment for teaching, hire and demo.
**Seasonal Watersports Instructors (8)** to teach windsurfing, sailing and canoeing. Wages dependant on qualifications. Required from June/July to September to instruct adults and juniors in windsurfing, sailing and canoeing 5 days a week. Instructors should hold RYA Windsurfing, RYA Sailing or BCU Canoeing Instructor's Certificates.
*Applications* should be sent to Simon Frost, Director.

**CHARLIE MANN RACING LTD:** Whitcoombe House Stables, Upper Lambourn, Hungerford, Berkshire RG17 8RA (☎01488-71717; fax 01488-73223; e-mail charlie.mann@virgin.net). One of the top national hunt yards in the country. Located in Lambourn on the Berkshire Downs, they have over 50 top class horses.
**Stable Staff (2)** wanted between May and September. The job consists of mucking out, riding, grooming and leading up at races. Wages are £225-£245 per week before tax. Hours of work are Monday-Friday 6am-12pm, 4-6pm and Saturday 6am-12pm, alternate weekends are Sat 4-5.30pm, Sun 8am-10.30am, 4-5pm. Accommodation available.
Applicants must be over 18, competent riders and experienced with horses.
*Applications* should be sent to Nicole Rossa, Secretary at the above address.

**CONTESSA RIDING CENTRE:** Willow Tree Farm, Colliers End, Ware, Hertfordshire SG11 1EN (☎01920-821 792/496; fax 01920-821496; e-mail contessariding@aol.com; www.contessa-riding.com). Riding school and competition yard with a particular interest in dressage. Set rurally 30 miles north of London; easy access to Cambridge and Stansted Airport.
**Stable Helpers** to perform general yard duties including mucking out, grooming, tack cleaning and horse handling. Horses range from novice to grand prix standard. Pocket money, riding and self-catering accommodation are provided. To work from 8am-5pm (beginning at 8.30am on two days) over 5½ days per week. Applicants must be aged 17; qualifications and experience preferred.
To work throughout the year, especially around the holiday periods. Minimum period of work two months. Applicants should ideally be available for an interview and must apply with references. Brochures available.
*Applications* are welcome year round to Tina Layton at the above address.

**EXSPORTISE INTERNATIONAL LTD:** PO Box 402, Redhill, Surrey, England RH9 8YQ (☎01883-744011; fax 01883-744066; e-mail info@exsportise.co.uk; www.exsportise.co.uk). Founded by Olympic gold medallist Steve Batchelor, Exsportise runs specialised sport and language holidays for children aged 8-18.
**Hockey, Tennis, Cricket, Golf, Swimming, Football and Rugby Coaches.** £100-£300 per week plus B & L. Applicants must be willing to work all hours and organise evening entertainment. Qualifications essential. Opportunity to make extra money by doing airport pick-ups.
**Pastoral Carers and Administrative Staff** needed. £120-£500 per week.
  Period of work 6 weeks between July and August, and during the Easter and Christmas holidays.
  *Applications* to the Course Co-ordinator at the above address or online. Interview required.

**FRENCH BROTHERS LTD:** The Clewer Boathouse, Clewer Court Road, Windsor, Berks SL4 5JH (☎01753-851900; fax 01763-832303; e-mail info@boat-trips.co.uk). French Brothers is a prestigious Thames passengerboat operator.
**Boat Crew, Bar Staff and Caterers** required at any time, though work is usually seasonal. Minimum period of work 6 weeks. Foreign applicants with sufficient English to understand the safety conditions of the business are welcome.
  *Applications* should be made to Chris Brace or Paul Cross at the above address. Interview required.

**GREAT FOSTERS HOTEL:** Stroude Road, Egham, Surrey TW20 9UR (☎01784-433822; fax 01784-472455; www.great.fosters.co.uk). A four star privately owned historic hotel with period bedrooms and superb banqueting facilities. Close to London with excellent train links.
**Swimming Pool Attendants (2)** Wages to be negotiated, with accommodation available. To work 5 days per week, 9.30am-7pm, between May 1st and September. Candidates should be over 18, good swimmers and hold a Bronze Medallion in Life Saving.
**Hall Porter(1)** Wages negotiable, accommodation available.
To work 5 days per week, shift work.
  *Applications* to Angela Collins, Assistant Manager, at the above address.

**GREEN LANE RIDING STABLES:** Green Lane, off Garth Road, Lower Morden, Surrey SM4 6SE (☎020-8337 3853; fax 020-8337-8383; www.greenlaneriding.co.uk). A BHS approved riding school. Majority of pupils are children, lots of school riding activities and thriving pony club, with the opportunity to ride young horses.
**Riding Teacher (1)** Work involves mostly teaching and general yard duties; riding is available. Wages are according to experience; to work either full-time or part-time. Applicants must either have BHSAI qualification or be very experienced with children.
  Suitably qualified applicants are welcome to apply. *Applications* should be sent to the Secretary at the above address.

**LEE VALLEY WATERSPORTS CENTRE:** Banbury Reservoir, Harbet Road, London E4 8QB (☎020-8531 1129; fax 020-8527 0969; e-mail watersports@leevalleypark.org.uk). The centre runs a schools programme in conjunction with a commercial watersports operation.
**Seasonal & Relief Instructors (2-4)** to teach windsurfing, dinghy sailing and

waterskiing. Wages and working hours by arrangement. Needed for work May 1-October 31st. Applicants must be aged at least 18 and need a relevant national governing qualification and knowledge of first aid.
*Applications* to Peter T. Stephenson, Site Manager, at the above address.

**DC LEISURE LTD:** Aldershot Pools Complex, Guildford Road, Aldershot, Hampshire GU12 4BP (☎01252-322750; fax 01252-316499).
**Lifeguards (15)** needed from 24th May-10th September. Wages are currently £4.73 per hour but a pay award is pending. Potential employees must have National Pool Lifeguard Qualification, and First Aid skills would be helpful.
*Applications* should be made in writing to The General Manager at the above address.

# Voluntary Work

## Children

**CHILDREN'S COUNTRY HOLIDAYS FUND (CCHF):** 42-43 Lower Marsh, London SE1 7RG (☎020-7928 6522; fax 020-7401 3961; e-mail clare@childrensholidays-cchf.org).
CCHF is a registered Charity that has been providing holidays for London children in need since 1884. It runs residential summer activity holidays, which provide a variety and balance of activities designed to meet the needs of all the children on them.
**Volunteers** needed during the school summer holidays to work as Camp Supervisors, looking after small groups of children (aged 8-12) under the guidance of an experienced Camp Leader. Relevant experience desirable although full training will be given. Minimum age 18. Supervisors are responsible for the care and welfare of children in their group for the duration of the camp. A camp lasts for 7 days, on a variety of dates in July and August, in residential centres in the south of England.
Accommodation, board, insurance, travel and pocket money are provided. To ensure the safety of the children, applicants must have been residents of England or Wales for five years to enable Police and Social Service checks to be made of them.
*Applications* by May at the latest.

**THE CHILDREN'S TRUST:** Tadworth Court, Tadworth, Surrey KT20 5RU (☎01737-365038-9; fax 01737-373848; e-mail c-trust@netcomuk.co.uk; www.the childrenstrust.org.uk).
Offers care, treatment, and education to approx. 80 children with exceptional needs and profound disabilities, and gives support to their families.
The Trust requires **Volunteers** to work on a residential summer scheme for profoundly disabled and exceptional needs children. The services are provided in a number of specialised nursing and therapeutic child care units and at a residential school. The work involves acting as a friend to the children, organising games, encouraging them to take an active part in daily activities, escorting them on outings and organising evening activities.
Previous experience with children or handicapped children is preferable, but not essential. Only those wishing to go into the caring profession should apply. Creative skills, handicraft or musical ability welcomed. The work is very rewarding but is also physically and emotionally tiring. 9 volunteers are appointed each year.

Minimum age 18. To work a 37½ hour week with 2 days off per week, mid July to first week in September. Students are expected to stay for the duration of the scheme. Accommodation is provided free of charge and an allowance of £51 per week is paid. Travel expenses within mainland England will be paid. Apply before 31 March to Rachel Turner at the above address.

The Residential School also requires volunteers for 6 to 12 months to assist with the daily routine of physical care and education of the children in both the residential home and school. Under the guidance of teachers, therapists and senior care staff, work as part of an interdisciplinary team on the individual planned programmes for the children. Minimum age 18, to work a 37½ hour week, 2 days off per week. Accommodation is provided free of charge and an allowance of £51 per week is paid. Travel expenses within England can be reimbursed.

*Applications* to Rachel Turner, Voluntary Services Manager, at the above address.

**THE OK CLUB:** Christian Holt House, Denmark Road, Kilburn, London NW6 5BP (☎020-7624 6292; fax 020-7372 6598; e-mail enquiries@okclub.org.uk; www.okclub.org.uk).
Christian organisation carrying out a wide variety of work with young people and children.
**Volunteers (40)** to engage in youth work, administration and management committee membership. Part time and full time opportunities available. No minimum period of work for part time volunteers; full time positions are for one year minimum and applicants must be committed Christians. Volunteers required all year round. Reasonable expenses and travel provided for part time volunteers; pocket money and food allowance for full time. Accommodation is available free to full time staff and at a low cost to part time.

Applicants should preferably have experience in youth/children's work or skills such as sports/art/IT etc. Foreign applicants with appropriate permits welcome.

*Applications* should be made to Matt Parker, Administrator, at the above address.

## Conservation and the Environment

**CORAL CAY CONSERVATION LTD:** The Tower, 13th Floor, 125 High Street, Colliers Wood, London, SW19 2JG (☎0870-750 0668; fax 0870-750 0667).
Recruits paying volunteers to help alleviate poverty through research, education, training and alternative livelihood programmes worldwide.
**Assistant Science Co-Ordinators** are required to assist with management, analysis and synthesis of scientific data collected from coral reef and tropical forest conservation expeditions to the Caribbean and Southeast Asia.
**Fundraisers** are required to assist with fund-raising campaigns on behalf of the Coral Cay Conservation Trust, a UK-registered charity which supports conservation education and training projects in developing countries.
**Administration Assistants** are required to help manage Volunteer recruitment campaigns.

The above are needed to work for Coral Cay Conservation (CCC), a non-profit organisation established in 1986 to provide support for the conservation and sustainable use of coastal and marine resources. CCC maintains full-time expedition projects in the Philippines and Honduras.

To work 8 hours a day, 5 days a week at CCC's London offices. Work is available all year round. Board and lodging is not provided, but travel and subsistence costs

are included. The jobs are essentially voluntary but in some cases a basic wage can be negotiated. Volunteers are provided with full training so no previous experience is required.
*Applications* at any time to the above address.

**LONDON AND WEST MIDDLESEX NATIONAL TRUST VOLUNTEERS:** c/o Hughenden Manor, High Wycombe, Buckinghamshire HP14 4LA (e-mail lwmntv@mail.com; www.lwmntv.org.uk).
The largest regional volunteer group of the National Trust, with over 250 members from all over the UK. Members carry out practical conservation all over the country.
**Volunteers** to repair paths, build bridges, clear scrub, repair dry stone walls and carry out other general land management and access work. Volunteers participate in weekend programmes, staying in Basecamps, converted outbuildings on estates; usually dormitory style accommodation with basic facilities. Volunteers work all day Saturday, until lunchtime on Sunday.
Basecamps are supervised by National Trust wardens who provide safety equipment and tools. The group is open to anyone over 16. Volunteers need enthusiasm and old clothes. The weekends have leaders who organise catering and travel. Membership of the group costs £6 per year. A typical weekend will cost around £10 for food, accommodation and travel.
*Contact* the above address for an information pack.

**THE LONDON AQUARIUM:** County Hall, Westminster Bridge Road, London SE1 7PB (☎020-7967 8010; fax 020-7967 8029). The biggest aquarium in the UK.
Volunteers to study a specialised field of the housed waterlife and provide information on this to the public. Any applicants with a proven **Interest In Biology** are welcome at any time.
*Applications*, including CV, to Human resources at the above address.

**SAVE THE RHINO INTERNATIONAL:** 16 Winchester Walk, London SE1 9AQ (☎020-7357 7474; fax 020-7357 9666; e-mail info@savetherhino.org; www.savetherhino.org).
A London based charity raising funds for projects protecting rhinos and other endangered wildlife in Africa and Asia, through endurance challenges, marathons and donations.
**Office Volunteers (5)** needed to carry out general office work including data entry, managing mailings, leafleting and money collections. Volunteers work 10am-6pm with lunch and travel expenses provided. Must be over 18 with some office and financial administration experience. Volunteers are required all year round for a minimum period of two weeks. Foreign applicants with good spoken and written English are welcome.
*Applications* to Kirstie Wielandt at the above address.

# Heritage

**ALEXANDER FLEMING LABORATORY MUSEUM:** St. Mary's Hospital, Praed Street, London W2 1NY (☎020-7886 6528 fax 020-7886 6739; e-mail Kevin.Brown@St-Marys.nhs.uk; www.st-marys.org.uk/about/fleming_museum.htm).
**Volunteer Guides** needed all year round to conduct visitors around the Alexander

Fleming Laboratory Museum, which is based on a reconstruction of the laboratory in which Fleming discovered penicillin. The job includes making a short presentation and retail duties in a small museum shop. Full training will be supplied: knowledge of the subject matter is not required. Hours from 10am to 1pm from Monday to Thursday. Minimum age 16. The museum lacks disabled access.
  *Applications* to Kevin Brown, Trust Archivist and Museum Curator.

**THE ALICE TRUST:** Waddesdon Manor, Aylesbury, Bucks HP18 0JH (☎01296-658252; fax 01296-658403; e-mail TWMMIR@smtp.ntrust.org.uk).
Waddesdon Manor, a National Trust property, is a magnificent French Renaissance-style chateau, home to the Rothschild Collection of 18th century French furniture and decorative arts, with acclaimed Victorian gardens.
**Volunteer Gardeners** required for a diverse range of maintenance tasks, alongside the team of professional gardeners. Residential internships are full time and for a period of one month minimum, although a three month period is preferred. Rent-free accommodation and some assistance with food expenses may be available. No experience necessary but commitment and reasonable fitness are required. Overseas English speaking applicants are considered
In addition, **Volunteer gardeners** are required for the Sunday Task Groups.
**Other volunteer opportunities** within the collection and gardens are available – contact the above address to find out more.
  *Applications* with CV and references to Marian Ridgway (ref SJ3) at the above address.

**THE FORGE MUSEUM AND VICTORIAN COTTAGE GARDEN:** High Street, Much Hadham, Hertfordshire SG10 6BS (tel/fax 01279-843301; e-mail cristinaharrison@hotmail.com).
The Forge Museum is owned by the Hertfordshire Building Preservation Trust. It is situated in the picturesque village of Much Hadham, and houses displays about blacksmithing and village life.
**Volunteer Museum Assistants (2)** These positions are aimed at those interested in gaining museum work experience. To work at least 2 days a week and up to 5 days a week. Applicants must be over 16. No previous experience is necessary.
**Volunteer Conservation Assistants (10)** These positions are aimed at anyone interested in gaining experience of conservation work in museums. No previous experience is necessary as training will be given. To work between 1 and 5 days per week.
  Volunteers are required from July to the end of August for a minimum period of 1 week. *Applications* should be addressed to Cristina Harrison and sent to the above address from May onwards.

**LEIGHTON HOUSE MUSEUM:** 12 Holland Park Road, London W14 8LZ (☎020-7602 3316).
The house was built between 1864-79 to designs by George Aitchison. It is the expression of Leighton's vision of a private palace devoted to art.
**Volunteers** to work at the home of Frederic, Lord Leighton (1830-1896), the great classical painter and president of the Royal Academy. Duties include office work and helping mount exhibitions. Hours are flexible. Applicants must be interested in museums and be graduates or currently studying. No accommodation is available. Min period of work 1 month at any time of year. Overseas applicants with good communications skills are considered. Interview necessary.
  *Applications* at any time to Reena Suleman.

## Physically/Mentally Disabled

**HERTFORDSHIRE ACTION ON DISABILITY:** The Woodside Centre, The Commons, Welwyn Garden City, Herts AL7 4DD (☎01707-324581; fax 01707-371297; e-mail herts_action@dial.pipex.com).
Hertford House Hotel is a 22 bedded seaside hotel which is fully accesible to people with physical disabilities.
**Volunteers (6 per fortnight)** are required to assist with holidays for people with disabilities. Helpers work, aiding the mobility of guests, to give companionship and assist them in dressing, transferring from wheelchair to bed/bathroom/toilet, taking guests in wheelchairs to shops, church, the seafront etc. and escorting them on outings in hotel minibus.
Free return transport to hotel from Welwyn Garden City provided. Period of work all year round. Volunteers usually work for a two-week period. Min. age 20. Experience of working with disabled people would be helpful.
Write a.s.a.p. for an *applications* form, enclosing two character references, to the Manager at the Hertford House Hotel, 11 Parkway, Clacton-on-Sea, Essex CO15 1BJ (☎01255-475994)

**INDEPENDENT LIVING ALTERNATIVES:** Trafalgar House, Grenville Place, London NW7 3SA (☎020-8906 9265; e-mail mail@I-L-A.fsnet.co.uk; www.I-L-A.fsnet.co.uk).
**Volunteers** required to provide support for people with disabilities, to enable them to live independently in their own homes. The work involves helping them get dressed, go to the toilet, drive, do the housework, etc. Volunteers receive £63.50 a week plus free accommodation, usually in the London area or in Cumbria. ILA offers a chance to learn about disability issues and see London at the same time. No qualifications required, except good English. Vacancies arise all year round.
*Applications* should be sent to Tracey Jannaway at the above address.

**INDEPENDENT LIVING SCHEMES:** Lewisham Social Care and Health, John Henry House, 299 Verdant Lane, Catford, London SE 6 1TP (☎020-8314 7239 (24 hours); fax 020-8314 3013; e-mail ken.smith@lewisham.gov.uk).
Part of a local government body which assists disabled people.
**Volunteers (8 At Any One Time)** to help disabled people living independently. Duties include dealing with the personal care and assisting with the leisure and social activities of independent people with severe disabilities (lifting is involved). Allowances of £60 per week and an additional £15 per month are paid, plus free, shared accommodation with all bills covered. To work on a rota basis with other volunteers; usually 24 hours on (sleeping in) followed by 48 hours off.
Volunteers are needed around the year; those who can make a six month commitment are preferred. Applicants should be aged 17 or over and should have a commitment to civil rights for disabled people.
*Applications* to Kenneth Smith, Project Worker, at the above address. An interview in London is usually required before an offer can be made.

**KITH & KIDS:** c/o The Irish Centre, Pretoria Road, London N17 8DX (☎020-8801 7432; fax 020-8885 3035; e-mail projects@kithandkids.org.uk; www.kithandkids.org.uk).
A self-help organisation that provides support for families of children with a physical or learning disability.
**Volunteers** needed to take part in social training schemes working on a two-to-one

basis with learning disabled children and young people, helping them with everyday skills and community integration. Hours of work 9:30am-5pm daily. Minimum period of work 2 consecutive weeks in August or a week at Christmas/Easter. There is also a 3 day training course before each project. Lunch and travel expenses within Greater London provided. Minimum age 16. No experience necessary, but lots of enthusiasm essential. No accommodation available. The organisation does also run a one-week camping holiday in August with accommodation for volunteers.

For *further details* contact the Volunteer Organiser at the above address.

**SHAD (BALHAM):** The Volunteer Development Officer, SHAD Wandsworth, 5 Bedford Hill, Balham, LW12 9E2 (☎020-8365 8528; e-mail shadwand@aol.com). SHAD (Support and Housing Assistance for people with Disabilities) enables people with physical disabilities to live independently in their own homes.
**Volunteers** are required to act as 'arms and legs' for disabled people. Volunteers receive £60 per week, free furnished accommodation, training, adequate support and expenses, 2-3 days off per week, social networking in London, excellent experience, advice on career prospects and insight into disability. No experience is necessary but a minimum commitment of 4 months or more is required. All nationalities are welcome but a good standard of English is essential.

For more *details* and an application form, please contact the above address.

**WOODLARKS CAMP SITE TRUST:** Tilford Road, Farnham, Surrey GU10 3RN (☎01252-716279; e-mail woodlarks1@aol.com).
Woodlarks Camp Site Trust provides a setting for people of all ages with disabilities to expand their capabilities and have fun. This small-scale camping site and woodland activity area has facilities including a heated outdoor swimming pool, an aerial runway, a trampoline, archery and more.
Camps are held weekly from May to September. Campers come mainly from special schools, clubs or organisations for people with specific disabilities. Several camps require volunteer **Carers/Enablers**. Volunteers are normally taken on for one camp lasting a week, though some help on more. Tent accommodation provided. A small fee is usually paid by helpers to cover the cost of food.

Written *applications* to the Honorary Secretary, Kathleen Marshall House, at the above address, enclosing a s.a.e or IRC.

## Social and Community Schemes

**THE GRAIL CENTRE:** 125 Waxwell Lane, Pinner, Middlesex HA5 3ER (☎020-8866 0505; fax 020-8866 1408; e-mail WAXWELL@compuserve.com).
The Grail is home to a community of Christian women. The Elizabethan house has modern extensions and is set in 10 acres of wooded garden, which contain several hermitages for individual retreats.
**5-6 Volunteers** are needed throughout the year to live alongside the resident community and help **Maintain the House and Garden** and assist in running the centre. Much of the work is household/manual. Duties are arranged on a flexible basis and volunteers are required to be available for 7½ hours daily. There is one full day off a week and one day's holiday per 2 weeks worked. Those who need a well defined timetable/ fixed hours would find this pattern unhelpful.

Volunteers are offered board, their own room and an allowance for necessary expenses. Min. age 20; no upper limit. No special skills are required, but goodwill and sense of humour essential. Overseas applicants pay their own fares and arrange the correct immigration clearance but an invitation letter is provided on request.

EU applicants should be familiar with medical cover arrangements between their country and the UK. Others should be insured or prepared to pay the cost of any treatment they may require. Applicants must have enough spoken and written English to function in this very busy household. In-house lessons can be arranged for those interested. Religious observance is not a requirement.

Send a letter, CV and a recent photograph to the Volunteer Co-ordinator at the above address. Early *Applications* are likely to be more successful. All applications must include a s.a.e. or an IRC.

**HACKNEY INDEPENDENT LIVING TEAM:** Richmond House, 1a Westgate Street, London E8 3RL (☎020-8985 5511 volunteer hotline ext. 227; fax 020-8533 2029; e-mail volunteers@hilt.org.uk; www.hilt.org.uk).
Helps adults with a learning difficulty in Hackney to live in the community as independently as possible, and to continue to develop their independence and personal identity.
**Independent Living Support Volunteers (12).** Volunteers may be involved in all projects and activities of HILT. Some of the ways in which volunteers have supported service users include sports, leisure and social activities, arranging and accompanying on holidays and assessing education and training opportunities. Volunteers support service users in personal development and achieving goals. Living allowance of £55 per week, plus weekly zones 1-2 Travelcard. To work 35 hours a week.

Applicants must be over 18 and committed to enabling people with learning difficulties to have as much control over their lives as possible. They should also help provide a service which reflects the cultural, racial and religious needs of service users, and promote anti-discriminatory practice. They should have a willingness to understand service users' emotional needs, and attend regular supervision and communicate ideas and suggestions.

Min. period of work 4 months at any time of year. All volunteers have their own furnished room, including all bills apart from telephone. Food allowance is incorporated into weekly allowance. Overseas applicants must have a good level of conversational English, and the right to enter the UK. Interview necessary.

*Applications* as far in advance of intended start date as possible to the Volunteer Co-ordinator.

**HEALTHPROM:** Star House, 104-108 Grafton Road, London NW5 4BD (☎020-7284 1620; fax 020-7284-1881; e-mail healthprom@healthprom.org; www.healthprom.org).
Healthprom works in partnerships to improve healthcare for the most vulnerable in Eastern Europe and Central Asia. Interesting and some ongoing opportunities exist in administrative, research, communications and fundraising areas. Excellent experience is to be gained by committed and reliable volunteers with an interest in international development work. Local travel and lunch expenses will be paid.

*Applications*, including CV, to Catherine Hine, Business Manager, at the above address.

**HOLY CROSS CENTRE:** Holycross Church, The Crypt, Cromer Street, London WC1H 8JU (tel/fax 020-7278 8687; e-mail cmt@hcct.org.uk).
This centre in the Kings Cross area of London is a social centre for people with mental health issues and drug/alcohol problems.
**Part-Time Volunteers (40)** needed to run the centre, befriending clients, catering and offering peer support in a friendly and informal atmosphere, with the possibility

of teaching arts and crafts and computing. Volunteers work 5 hours per week. Minimum commitment 3 months. In return they receive travel expenses and a meal for each session. Training and support provided.
*Applications* to M.Willett, Centre Management Team, at the above address.

**SIMON COMMUNITY:** PO Box 1187, London NW5 4HW (☎020-7485 6639; fax 020-7482 6305; e-mail simoncommunity@ic24.net).
Living and working in the Simon Community is a unique and challenging way of life offering the chance to meet people and situations as never before while doing vital and rewarding work.
The Simon Community is a community of volunteers and homeless people living and working with those of London's homeless for whom no other provision exists. **Volunteers** are expected to help run its night shelter or one of two residential homes, as well as participate in group meetings, regular outreach work, campaigning and fund raising. The community also has a farm near Canterbury, and conducts tea runs round London and other outreach work.
B & L are provided plus £32.50 per week pocket money. Volunteers are required throughout the year for a minimum of 3 months, but ideally for 6 months or more. All applicants should be aged 19 or over, have a mature and responsible attitude and a good command of the English language. *Initial enquiries* to the above address.

**SOUTHWARK HABITAT FOR HUMANITY:** PO Box 14284, London SE22 8ZH (☎020-7732 0066; fax 020-7732 6060; e-mail southwarkhfh@zetnet.co.uk).
**Volunteer Construction Workers** to work with an innovative community self-help group building houses to provide affordable housing for people with low incomes. Southwark HFH is part of HFH Great Britain, an ecumenical Christian housing ministry working to provide high quality affordable housing to those on low incomes and in need of housing.
The construction programme is continuous throughout the year so help is needed on weekdays and at weekends; volunteers can help for as little as one day. Volunteers must pay for their own transport and provide their own lunch. Applicants should be aged over 16; no building skills or experience are needed as skilled supervisors direct the work.
If interested in making *applications* call the above telephone number.

**THE SUZY LAMPLUGH TRUST:** PO Box 1718, London SW14 8WW (☎020-8876 0305; fax 020-8876 0891; e-mail info@suzylamplugh.org; www.suzylamplugh.org).
Organisation providing advice and services related to personal safety.
**Administrative Assistants (8)** for 2 offices in East Sheen, London. To carry out general tasks including database and accounts work, answering the telephone and packing of resources. Travelling expenses provided, and £3 lunch allowance for volunteers who stay all day. No minimum period, but it is preferred that volunteers stay as long as possible for continuity. No accommodation available. Foreign applicants with fluent English welcome.
*Applications* should be made to Ann Elledge at the above address.

# Vacation Traineeships & Internships

## Accountancy, Banking and Insurance

**ABN AMRO:** 250 Bishopsgate, London EC2M 4AA (www.graduate.abnamro.com).
Global wholesale bank.
**Summer Internships** offered in Client Management, Corporate Finance, Equities, Finance, Global Finance Markets and Loan Markets. Wages £500 per week. Placements last between 8 and 12 weeks in the summer vacation.
Positions are open to penultimate year students of any discipline. Minimum expected degree result must be 2:1. Must have 24 UCAS points and minimum grade C in GCSE Maths and English Language.
More information and online *application form* can be found at www.graduate.ab namro.com.

**BANK OF ENGLAND:** 1&2 Bank Buildings, Princes Street, London EC2R 8EU (www.bankofengland.co.uk).
Central bank of the United Kingdom; at the centre of economic policy making and implementation.
**Summer Placements.** Available to penultimate year undergraduates reading any subject. Must have an interest in economics and finance. Placements are based in London and will last 6-8 weeks in summer 2003. For further information refer to the website above.
*Applications* should be made via the online form at www.bankofengland.co.uk. Interview required.

**BARING ASSET MANAGEMENT:** 155 Bishopsgate, London EC2H 3XY (☎020-7214 1936/1403; fax 020-7214 4163; e-mail fsghumanresources@baring-asset.com; www.baring-asset.com).
**Trainee Fund Administrators** will be responsible for the daily collation and distribution of information relating to the administration (valuing and pricing) of funds (UK and overseas).
**Trainee Registration Administrators** will be responsible for maintaining the register in respect of each unit trust and OEIC Management group. **6 positions in total**
Salaries from £200 per week (GCSE educated) to £250 per week (A level educated). Positions are available for the Summer Vacation only, typically for 6 weeks. These positions are not open to university students and relevant qualifications include GCSE and A level passes at Maths and English or BTEC general or nationals in relevant subjects such as business, finance, economics and statistics. No accommodation available. Foreign applicants with valid work permits and able to arrange their own travel and accommodation are welcome.
*Applications* should be made by 2 June 2003 to Anita Drayton or Jane Quilter, Human Resources Manager, at the above address or via e-mail.

**BLOOMBERG L.P.:** City Gate House, 39-45 Finsbury Square, London EC2A 1PQ (fax 020-7661 5809; e-mail Recruitment@Bloomberg.net; www.careers.Bloomberg .com or www.Bloomberg.co.uk).
**Approx. 60 Internships** in most areas of the business including Sales, Broadcast and Broadcast Operations, HR, IT Support, Networks, etc.
The internships would suit university students or graduates but anyone can

apply. Looking for people with proven interest in Finance. A fluency in a second European language is a bonus. Interships last 12 weeks and the wage is dependent on experience. No accommodation is provided. Overseas students with a UK working permit are welcome.
*Applications* should be sent to Human Resources at the above address.

**EUROMONEY INSTITUTIONAL INVESTOR PLC:** Nestor House, Playhouse Yard, London EC4V 5EX (☎020-7779 8524; fax 020-7779 8513; e-mail jlewington@euromoneyplc.com; www.euromoneyplc.com).
Euromoney Institutional Investor plc is an international publications and events company. Although it has no formal vacation scheme, it often has work available for university undergraduates or gap year students with excellent grades. Students of any subject are considered but economics, law and languages are particularly useful.
**Positions** available include researchers, telesales executives, administrators and data inputters. Periods of employment depend on vacancies as does the wage. No accommodation is provided. Qualified applicants from abroad with excellent English and the relevant work permits are considered.
*Applications* by e-mail only to Julie Lewington at jlewington@euromoneyplc.com

**INSTITUTE FOR FISCAL STUDIES:** 7 Ridgmount Street, London WC1E 7AR (☎020-7291 4800; fax 020-7323 4780; e-mail mailbox@ifs.org.uk).
IFS is an independent research institute which specialises in the economic analysis of public policy, especially the field of taxation policy. It aims to bridge the gap between purely academic research and issues of practical policy. The research is largely orientated towards microeconomic analysis, and has a strong quantitative flavour.
The institute makes use of major UK surveys of households, individuals and firms in order to analyse the impact of taxation and other public policies on individuals' and companies' behaviour. Research is disseminated through conferences, publications, the journal *Fiscal Studies* and other journals. IFS aims to provide impartial information from a politically independent standpoint.
IFS offers approx. **5 Placements** which last for 6 weeks in the summer in London. Trainees can expect to work with a research team on a particular project. Tasks involve the preparation and analysis of data, the conducting of literary searches, and writing up search results. Applicants should have a minimum of 2 years undergraduate experience in Economics or a closely related subject. The salary in 2002 was £245 per week. No accommodation is provided, paid travel expenses to interview within the UK only.
Overseas applicants entitled to work in the UK are considered; interviews take place in London. *Applications* including a CV and covering letter should be sent to Robert Markless by the middle of March.

**MERRILL LYNCH EUROPE PLC:** Merrill Lynch Financial Centre, 2 King Edward Street, London EC1A 1HQ (www.ml.com/careers).
**Approx. 150 Internships** are available within the following business areas: Debt Markets, Equity Markets, Investment Banking, Investment Managers, Research, Securities Services, Financial Operation, Human Resources and Technology.
Internships are aimed at penultimate year university students. There are no required degree disciplines but students should have outstanding academic achievement and be able to demonstrate quantitative and analytical problem solving skills.
Wages very competitive. Internships start in early July and last 10 weeks. No

accommodation is provided, although advice on how to find accommodation may be offered. Foreign applicants are welcome but all applicants must possess a valid work permit.

All *applications* must be made online at www.ml.com/careers by mid-February 2003. Applications are dealt with on a first come, first serve basis so early application may be advantageous.

## Law

**ADDLESHAW BOOTH & Co:** 60 Cannon Street, London, EC4N 6NP (☎0161-934 6000; fax 0161-934 6060; e-mail grad@addleshawbooth.com).

Addleshaw Booth & Co is a leading UK law firm with an international capability. Their client portfolio features a spectrum of high profile companies including J. Sainsbury plc, MyTravel, Rugby Football League and AstraZeneca. The firm has experienced significant growth in size, client base and profitability over the past few years. The firm currently employs over 1,300 staff, including 123 Partners and more than 600 fee-earners

Addleshaw Booth & Co. offer a **2 Week Summer Vacation Scheme**. The scheme provides opportunities to experience work within legal departments and is supplemented by a number of presentations and exercises. The scheme is open to all those who would be in a position to commence a training contract with the firm in September 2005 or March 2006. The scheme is currently remunerated at a rate of £150 per week and assistance with accommodation can be given if required. Placements are located in the Firm's Leeds, London and Manchester offices.

*Applications* will only be considered via the Firm application form, which is available online or can be requested by telephone or e-mail. Applications must be received by 14 February 2003. Send your *application* to Mrs Simran Foote, Graduate Manager, Addleshaw Booth & Co., 100 Barbirolli Square, Manchester M2 3AB.

**ALLEN & OVERY:** One New Change, London EC4M 9QQ (☎020-7330 3000; fax 020-7330 9999; e-mail graduate.recruitment@allenovery.com; www.allenovery.com).

Founded in 1930, Allen & Overy is one of the UK's leading law firms. It has over 300 partners and over 4,000 staff working in 26 major centres on three continents, with an international reputation for serving business, financial institutions, government and private individuals wherever there is a need for decisive legal advice on complex transactions.

Allen & Overy offers **90 Three Week Placements** to penultimate year students (law and non-law) interested in a career in law. Students spend time in two departments, becoming fully involved and making genuine contributions to the work. They will be treated as one of the team; sometimes attending meetings and observing, at other times carrying out research and helping to check documents, but at all times getting an insight into how law is practised in the firm.

Salary is £250 per week in London and £280 outside, with positions also available in Brussels, Frankfurt, London and Paris. Assistance may be given in finding accommodation.

Application forms are available from 1 November and before 28 February. Completed *Applications* should be sent to Graduate Recruitment at the above address.

**ASHURST MORRIS CRISP:** Broadwalk House, 5 Appold Street, London (☎020-7638 1111; fax 020-7859 1800; e-mail gradrec@ashursts.com; www.ashursts.com).

International City law firm with 140 partners, around 450 solicitors and a total staff of 1,400. Main areas of specialism include Company/Commercial, Litigation, International Finance, Real Estate, Tax and Energy, Transport and Infrastructure.

Offers **70 Placements** in the Summer and **30 at Easter**. During the schemes, students are placed in a different department each week and share an office with a solicitor or partner. The main aim is that students become involved in the solicitor's daily workload by completing 'real' tasks such as letter writing, drafting, legal research and attending client meetings. In addition a series of lectures, workshops and social activities are arranged.

Penultimate year law degree students and final year non-law degree students are eligible. Wage is £250 per week. No accommodation is provided but help in finding some can be given. Foreign applicants who speak fluent English are welcome.

*Applications* should be made online to Stephen Trowbridge, Graduate Recruitment, by 31 January 2003, including CV and covering letter.

**BAKER & MCKENZIE:** 100 New Bridge Street, London EC4V 6JA (☎020-7919 1000; fax 0207-919 1999; e-mail london.graduate.recruit@bakernet.com; www.ukgraduates.bakernet.com).

A city law firm offering **30 London Summer Placements** for 3 weeks and **3-5 International Summer Placements** where students divide their time between London and one of our overseas offices. These placements are for students in the 2nd year (or 3rd of a 4 year course) of an undergraduate course, and for the International Summer Placement you must be studying law. Students can expect a high degree of responsibility, being involved in working with, and for, clients. With appropriate supervision students will also participate in various commercial transactions. Training sessions and social events are part of the programme. The salary for 2002 was £250 per week.

No accommodation is provided, however details of suitable accommodation are provided to help students find their own.

*Applications* should be sent to Natalie McGourty at the above address or students can apply on-line by 31.01.02.

**S.J. BERWIN:** 222 Grays Inn Road, London WC1X 8XF (☎020-7533 2268/2393; fax 020-7533 2000; e-mail graduate.recruitment@sjberwin.com; www.sjberwin.com).

S.J. Berwin offer up to **60 Placements** on their vacation training schemes, each one lasting 2 weeks. The placements are open to second year law students (and above) and third year non-law students (and above) who are expecting or have gained a 2:1 degree. Trainees spend 2 weeks working in a department ideally suited to them, gaining hands-on experience in a wide range of legal tasks during the summer. Attendees receive £225 per week and whilst accommodation is not provided suggestions on good hostels and university halls can be made. Suitably qualified applicants from abroad who do not require a work permit are considered.

*Applications* should be sent to Graduate Recruitment by 31 January 2003.

**CAMERON McKENNA:** Mitre House, 160 Aldersgate Street, London EC1A 4DD (0845-3000 491; www.law-now.com).

Cameron McKenna, an international city law firm, offers **two-week placements to students during Easter and Summer and Christmas**. Positions are open to second and final year law students or final year non-law graduates who expect to achieve at least a 2:1 degree. The firm is distinctive, unstuffy and approachable, and is looking for creative, bright, commercially aware, committed people who have the potential

to contribute to its future success.
*Applications* from November 2002; the closing date for is Friday 28th February. For an application form and further details please call 0845-3000 491.

**DENTON WILDE SAPTE:** Five Chancery Lane, Clifford's Inn, London EC4A 1BU (☎020-7242 1212; fax 020-7320 6555; e-mail trainingcontracts@dentonwildesapte.com; www.dentonwildesapte.com).
Denton Wilde Sapte is a large international commercial law firm.
Their vacation schemes are targeted to penultimate/final year law students or final year non law students, looking to make a career in law. **Christmas open days (20/25)** are specifically for non-law students and **Summer Information Weeks (30/35)** are open to both law and non law students. These comprise skills workshops and departmental talks designed to give an overview of the firm.
Wage for summer information week is £250. Positions are open to current university students or graduates from any discipline. Graduates need to have a minimum 2:1 degree result or show a good indication of achieving this. Fluent English essential. Minimum age 18. No previous experience necessary. No accommodation is provided
*Applications* to the vacation schemes should be made using the firm's application form and addressed to Emma Hooper, Recruitment Officer (Trainee Solicitors). This is available on the website or can be requested by telephone. Deadlines are as follows: Christmas open day, 6 December 2002; Summer scheme, 14 March 2003. Overseas candidates are considered.

**MACFARLANES:** 10 Norwich Street, London EC4A 1BD (☎020-7831 9222; fax 020-7831 9607; e-mail gs@macfarlanes.com; www.macfarlanes.com).
Macfarlanes is a leading firm of solicitors based in the City. Areas of work include corporate, property, litigation and private clients.
Macfarlanes run a summer student scheme which offers those seeking a training contract the opportunity to gain hands-on experience of life in a city law firm. There are **40 Positions** available for the 2 week scheme, open to University students with a strong academic record at both A-level and degree level. Students receive a wage of £250 per week and help can be given in finding accommodation. Suitably qualified applicants from overseas are welcome.
*Applications* by 28th February to Graham Stoddart, Graduate Recruitment Officer, at the above address.

**RICHARDS BUTLER:** Beaufort House, 15 St. Botolph Street, London EC3A 7EE (☎020-7247 6555; fax 020-7247 5091; e-mail gradrecruit@richardsbutler.com; www.richardsbutler.com).
Richards Butler is a premier international law firm with its head office in the City of London and 10 other offices worldwide.
Richards Butler offer two 2-week **Vacation Schemes** during the summer to both law and non-law students in their 2nd Year or above. Students partake in work shadowing and research for one week and one week of lectures. Trainees receive £200 per week and are expected to arrange their own accommodation. Foreign applicants eligible to work in the UK are welcome.
*Applications* between November and February should be submitted online via their website www.richardsbutler.com.

**STEPHENSON HARWOOD:** One, St Paul's Churchyard, London EC4M 8SH (☎020-7329 4422; fax 020-7606 0822).

Stephenson Harwood is a City law firm with eight overseas offices and an international practice. Their main areas of work are: financial services, commercial litigation, property, private capital and maritime services.
Stephenson Harwood offer **16 Students** the opportunity to spend 2 weeks workshadowing solicitors. Students spend 1 week each in 2 different departments. Applicants must be 2nd year Law undergraduates or 3rd year non-Law undergraduates. Salary is £250 per week.

Placements last 2 weeks and take place in the last fortnight in June and first fortnight of July in the firm's St Paul's Office. No accommodation is provided but help can be given in finding it.

*Applications* by form only by 21 February 2003 to the Graduate Recruitment Department.

# Media and Marketing

**GLOBE EDUCATION:** Shakespeare's Globe, International Shakespeare Globe Centre, 21 New Globe Walk, London SE1 9DT (☏ 020-7902 1400; fax 020-7902 1401; e-mail education@shakespeares-globe.org; www.shakespearesglobe.org).
Restored Shakespearean theatre on the banks of the Thames with museum, lecture programme and workshop. Caters for 45,000 students each year.

**Administration Work Experience Placements (30).** To work in the main areas of operation, including exhibition, fundraising and communications. Some stewarding and special events work will also be available in the summer.

Positions are unpaid, and expenses cannot be provided. Hours by arrangement. Minimum period of work 3 months, positions available all year round. Foreign applicants with fluent English welcome to apply.

*Applications* should be made to Alexandra Massey, Administration Assistant, at the above address. Interview required.

**INDEPENDENT TELEVISION:**
A limited number of work experience placements are sometimes available with the 19 regional ITV companies. Vacancies are rarely known in advance and demand constantly outstrips supply.

Applicants must be students on a recognised course of study at a college or university; their course must lead to the possibility of employment within the television industry (ideally, work experience would be a compulsory part of the course); and the student must be resident in the transmission area of the company offering the attachment, or in some cases, attending a course in that region. However, opportunities may occasionally exist for students following computing, librarianship, finance, legal, administrative or management courses. Suitably qualified applicants from overseas are considered.

**Placements** vary in length from half a day to several weeks or months, depending upon the work available and the candidate's requirements. Students do not normally receive payment from the company, although those on courses of particular relevance to the industry may be paid expenses. Students from sandwich courses who are on long-term attachments may be regarded as short-term employees and paid accordingly.

*Applications* should be sent to the Personnel Department of the applicant's local ITV Company. General information on working in the television industry can be obtained from Skillset, the National Training Organisation for Broadcast, Film, Video and Multimedia, on 020-7534 5300 and ask for *Skillset Careers Handbook;* or call recruitment on 020-7843 8058 for basic guidance.

**MERIDIAN RECORDS:** PO Box 317, Eltham, London SE9 4SF (☎020-8857 3213; fax 020-8857 0731; e-mail mail@meridian –records.co.uk).
Meridian Records is a small record company specialising in the recording and production of classical records.

In 2002 the company will be seeking **One Or Two Candidates** who can demonstrate motivation and a keen interest in music. No other particular qualifications are required, although applicants should have a general interest in all aspects of running a record company. An ability to read music is useful but not essential. The successful candidate(s) will participate in a wide variety of tasks including the preparation of artwork, accounting, recording, editing and the maintenance of machines, buildings and grounds.

The traineeships are unpaid, though the company may be able to offer accommodation on its premises. The placements run for a varying number of weeks during any of the three main vacations. Overseas applicants will be considered. It is the policy of Meridian Records only to employ non-smokers.

*Applications* should be sent to Mr John Shuttleworth, Director, at the above address.

**PROUD GALLERIES GROUP:** Proud Galleries, 5 Buckingham Street, The Strand, London WC2N 6BP (☎020-7839 4942; fax 020-7839 4947; e-mail info@proud.demon.co.uk; www.proudgalleries.com).
The most popular private photographic gallery in Europe, with up to 10,000 paying customers per show. Launched in autumn 1998 to bring affordable high quality photography to a mainstream market by exhibiting accessible shows with popular themes. Owns two London venues, with Proud Brighton due to open in late 2002.
**Internship.** Involves general assistance with the running of the gallery, organising/ planning of launch nights, hanging and wrapping of prints, customer service, research for future exhibitions, maintaining press books and more. Ideal for anyone interested in learning more about every aspect of the industry, including production, management and sales. Internships last for a minimum of 4 weeks. Positions available all year round. Expenses cannot be provided. Minimum age 18, qualifications important but not essential. Fluent English essential.

*Applications* should be made at any time to the above address.

## Public Sector

**CIVIL SERVICE:** Cabinet Office, Room G14, Admiralty Arch, London SW1A 2WH (☎020-7276 1622; fax 020-7276 1502; www.civil-service.gov.uk/training).
**Summer Development Programme For Ethnic Minorities.** A 6-8 week programme designed to introduce the varied work of the UK Civil Service. Includes a formal residential training course. The course is open to students of any discipline; applicants must be UK nationals from an ethnic minority. Must be able to demonstrate communication skills, creativity, resilience and motivation. A training allowance of £265 per week is provided.

For further details and an *application form*, contact Patrick Brown, Outreach and Events Manager, at the above address.

## Science, Construction and Engineering

**THE AUTOMATION PARTNERSHIP:** York Way, Royston, Hertfordshire SG8 5WY (☎01763-227289; fax 01763-227201; e-mail hr@automationpartnership.com; www.automationpartnership.com).

A hi-tech company which develops and manufactures large, complex and flexible automation systems for the life science industries; further information on the website.
**Summer Placements (4).** Wages approximately £200 per week. Open to undergraduates studying computer science, software engineering and engineering degrees at recognised universities. Placements last for 8-10 weeks between July and August, dependent on student's availability. Based in Royston.

*Applications*, including covering letter, CV and indication of availability for interview, should be made during February, March and April to the Personnel Manager at the above address or e-mail. Interview required.

**BLACK & VEATCH:** Grosvenor House, 69 London Road, Redhill, Surrey RH1 1LQ (☎01737-774155; fax 01737-772767; www.bv.com).
Binnie, Black & Veatch is an engineering consultancy specialising in water supply, public health, environmental engineering, power, telecommunications and energy services. It is an employee-owned company with over 90 offices and 8,500 employees worldwide.

Each year the firm takes two **Pre-University Trainees** for up to twelve months. These students will normally have Mathematics and Science A-levels and will be preparing to read Electrical, Electronics or Mechanical Engineering, Mathematics, Physics or Applied Science. The firm also offers placements over the summer to two or three undergraduate students of Civil Engineering. These traineeships last for up to ten weeks and take place in the firm's Consultancy Services, Water Infrastructure, water process and energy service, Business Units. Suitably qualified applicants from abroad will be considered. Wages discussed on application.

More information can be found at www.bv.com, and *applications* should be sent to Celia Morris, Learning and Development Manager, by Easter.

**CADOGAN TIETZ LTD:** 14 Clerkenwell Close, Clerkenwell, London EC1R 0PQ (☎020-7490 5050; fax 020-7490 2160).
An independent civil and structural engineering consultancy based in lively Clerkenwell.

Cadogan Tietz offers **Summer Placements** to students from university or college who are studying Civil Engineering or related disciplines. All trainees will gain first-hand experience of structural and civil engineering. Suitably qualified applicants from abroad, especially from Germany and France, will be considered. Salary will be discussed at interview.

*Applications* should be sent by April to A.J. Jolly, Director, at the above address.

**DATA CONNECTION LTD:** 100 Church Street, Enfield, Middlesex EN2 6BQ (☎020-8366 1177; e-mail recruit@dataconnection.com; www.dataconnection.com).
Founded in 1981, Data Connection is one of the world's most successful computer technology companies with a worldwide reputation for developing complex high quality products. Customers include some of the biggest names in the IT industry, such as Cisco, Microsoft, IBM and BT. The company has over 250 employees and is based in North London, with satellite offices in Edinburgh, Chester, San Francisco and Washington DC. They offer outstanding students the chance to develop their computing skills at the cutting edge of technology.

**Vacation Work** is offered to exceptional students with an interest in the development of complex software. Applicants typically have all A grades at A level.

Data Connection provides complex and challenging programming assignments, with help and support. A salary of £1,200 per month and subsidised accommodation in the Company House is offered. Many vacation students go on to join Data Connection as full-time employees; some receive sponsorship while still at University.

Interviews are held all year round. However, as vacancies are limited it is best to apply in the autumn term. For more details *contact* Denise Crisp at the above address, or apply on-line following the links from the Website.

**M.W. KELLOGG LTD:** Kellogg Tower, Greenford Road, Greenford, Middlesex UB6 0JA (☎ 020-8872 7000).
M.W. Kellogg Ltd is a world leader in the design, engineering, procurement, constuction and project management of process plants within the oil, gas and petrochemical industries.

It offers traineeships during the summer vacation mainly for **Engineering and IT Positions.** Main degree subjects of interest are chemical engineering, mechanical engineering or computer science or other related degree. Other possible areas include, Purchasing and Supply, Construction, Civil and Structural, Business, CAD, Electrical, Instumentation, Process Control and Materials. Excellent facilites and a work environment condusive to enthusistic innovative team players are offered.

Trainees will be paid around £6 per hour. Placements take place at the head office in Greenford. Help is usually given with finding accommodation, but students must pay for their own board and lodging.

*Applications* should be sent from April to the Recruitment Officer at the above address.

**SIR ROBERT MCALPINE LTD:** Eaton Court, Maylands Avenue, Hemel Hempstead, Herts HP2 7TR (☎ 01442-233444; e-mail a.scarth@sir-robert-mcalpine.com; www.sir-robert-mcalpine.com).
Sir Robert McAlpine is one of the UK's major building and civil engineering contractors, undertaking projects such as industrial plants, marine works, power stations, hospitals, offices, theatres, leisure and retail complexes.

**University Students** reading degrees in construction-related subjects, or **'A' Level Students** considering such degrees, are offered employment lasting a minimum of 8 weeks during the summer. Students assist site engineers and quantity surveyors working on various major construction sites throughout the country. The salary varies according to experience and qualifications and assistance in finding lodgings is provided. Approximate number of vacancies will be between 20 and 50.

*Applications* should be made to the Human Resources Department, at the above address.

# The West Country

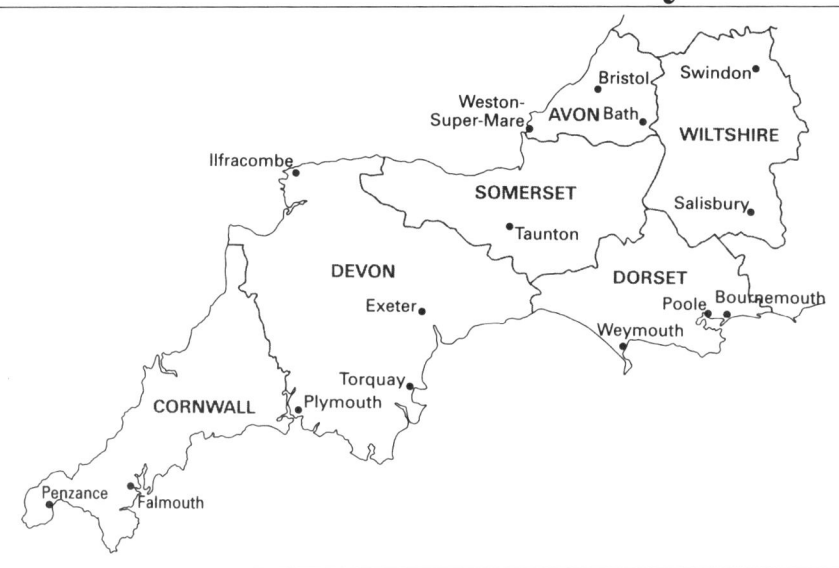

**Prospects for Work.**
The coasts of Dorset, Devon and Cornwall are scattered with hotels which need staffing during the summer season. Bournemouth alone has 20,000 hotel rooms, the largest number outside London. The largest employers of temporary staff are the many holiday camps in the region: Pontins has several centres in the South West, Butlins has its refurbished Family Entertainment resorts and there are a further two camps in St Ives and Hayle. The Jobcentre in Penzance recruits for local caravan parks during both Easter and summer, as well as for employers on the Scilly Isles. Recruitment for the Scilly Isles' particularly long season begins in January. In and around Penzance there are often vacancies for chefs and kitchen/service staff.

There may well be a demand for agricultural workers and fruit pickers at the strawberry farms around Camborne or in Penzance, home to one of the largest bulb farms in the area.

Vacancies in Taunton in Somerset are mainly for administration, retail and the hospitality and leisure industry. There is also a need for temporary fruit pickers and production workers, mainly recruited through employment agencies. It is important to apply early because the demand is high among students. Some temporary jobs are advertised in the *Somerset County Gazette* and vacancies in the region and nationwide can also be accessed on the Jobcentre Plus website www.jobcentreplus.gov.uk or phone Jobseeker Direct on 0845-6060 234. Temporary jobs are also advertised in the town's two Colleges. Bristol is one of the few other areas away from the coast where there is an extensive demand by retailers for more staff over the summer; again, however, the number of students vying for jobs makes it sensible to apply early.

## Business and Industry

**ROCHESTERS EVENT HIRE LTD:** Deer Park Farm, Marshwood Vale, Bridport, Dorset, DT6 5PZ (☎01308-868743; fax 01308-868086).
**Delivery Drivers (2)** needed June to August/September. Hours to be agreed with applicant. Up to 60 hours a week if wanted. Clean driving licence essential.
**Loaders (3)** of washing machine, check orders and pack from June to September. Common sense and sense of humour required.
Wage for all jobs is £5 per hour. *Apply* to Trevor Richards, Director.

## Children

**3D EDUCATION AND ADVENTURE LTD:** Business Support, Osmington Bay, Weymouth, Dorset DT3 6EG (☎01305-836226; fax 01305-834070; e-mail darren@3d-education.co.uk; www.3d-jobs.co.uk). 3D is a specialist provider of activity and educational experiences for young people. Owned by Center Parcs, 3D has been operating since 1991 and gone from strength to strength year on year.
**ACTIVITY INSTRUCTORS (500)** Employed and trained as either multi-activity instructor, field studies instructor, specialist watersports instructor or IT instructor, staff will work with children at specialist holiday centres across the south of England as well as across the UK and Europe with Pontins and Center Parcs.

Field studies instructors must hold or at least be gaining a relevant degree. IT instructors need to have a broad range of IT skills. Any sports coaching awards or national governing body awards are advantageous, if applying for Activity instructor and Watersports instructor positions, although those with relevant experience will be considered. Training courses are held from late January through to July, so there is plenty of opportunity to develop your skills and qualifications.

Most important is an applicant's enthusiasm, personality and energy, coupled with a true desire to work in the outdoor leisure industry. Excellent accommodation and catering packages are offered with payment and working hours as covered by minimum wage and working time legislation. Minimum period of work 14 weeks.

Applicants should telephone 01305-836226 for a recruitment pack or visit http://www.3d-jobs.uk between September and June. Before employment all applicants must complete a residential training programme in the UK.

## Holiday Centres and Amusements

**ALLNATT CENTRES:** 35 Ulwell Road, Swanage BH19 1LG (☎01921-421075;e-mail operations@allnatt.co.uk; www.allnatt.co.uk). Residential outdoor centres providing education, inspiration and play through adventure activities and environmental education to schools, youth and overseas groups.
**Duty Managers, Centre Assistants, Teaching Staff and Catering Staff** Inspirational people required to fill these positions in year round operations at Swanage and on the Isle of Wight. Live-in, work for the season or just a couple of months. Applicants must have an interest in educating young people and a passion for working and playing in the outdoors. More information available from the above address.

*Applications* to the Manager at the above address. Interviews carried out in person or over the phone.

**CREALY PARK:** Clyst St. Mary, Exeter, Devon EX5 1DR (☎01395-233200; fax 01395-233211; e-mail employment@crealy.co.uk).
**Receptionist (1)** Wages £4.50 per hour. To work 4 days per week and alternate

weekends with a fixed day off. Required from Easter to October. Must have excellent telephone manner, good knowledge of IT and outgoing personality.
**Retail Assistants (10-15)** in the Guest Services Department. Pay dependent on age and experience. Flexible hours to suit. Needed for Easter and Summer holidays. Experience in till operation an advantage. Minimum age 16
**Catering Assistants (20)** for fast food outlets during the summer holidays. Flexible hours to suit. Experience not essential.
**Play Supervisors & Ride Operators (15)** for summer work. Must have outgoing personality and be able to adhere to strict working practices to comply with health and safety best practice. Minimum age 16.

Please *apply* to the Personnel Officer at the above address.

**EXMOUTH FUN PARK:** Queen's Drive, The Seafront, Exmouth, Devon EX8 2AY (☎0797-0482 236; e-mail chriswrighty@lineone.net). Family-based amusement park, situated opposite the beach. Friendly holiday atmosphere.
**Assistant Fun Park Manager (1), Fun Park Assistant (2).** Negotiable wage depending on age and experience. To work 30-50 hours per week. Min. period of work of July and August. Positions are available from April to mid-September. These seasonal positions are paid for hours worked which may mean less hours than expected as the site is weather dependent. Reasonable English required. Rugby players particularly welcome! Accommodation not available.

*Applications* should be made from March onwards to Mr C. Wright. Interview necessary.

**FARMER PALMER'S FARM PARK LTD:** Organford, Poole, Dorset BH16 6EU (☎01202-622022; fax 01202-632111; e-mail farmerpalmers@bigfoot.com). A professional farm park with 60,000 visitors per year, aimed primarily at children 8 years and under. The farm also includes a cafe, shop, play areas etc.
**Waiting Staff (2) Potwashers (1) Kitchen Assistants (1).** Wages £3.60- £4.50 per hour; to work 5 hours a day, 5 days a week, possibly more, from Easter to October: Applicants must be over 16. Experience is not essential as skills will be taught, what is more important is a positive and happy attitude.
**Shop Assistant (1)** £4-£4.50 per hour; to work from 10am to 6pm, 3 days a week, Easter to September.

Uniforms are supplied and rolls are provided for lunch breaks. All staff working for over 4 hours must have half an hour break. Accommodation may be available. Staff are required to work for a minimum of 8 weeks. Foreign applicants are considered but must have a reasonable command of English in order to communicate with the other members of staff.

*Applications* should be sent to Miss Sandra Palmer from February onwards at the above address. Interview necessary.

**PARK RESORTS:** Bideford Bay Holiday Village, Bucks Cross, Bideford, Devon EX39 5DU (☎01237-431331; fax 01273-431649).
**Lifeguards.** Wages on application. Must hold National Pool Lifeguard qualification.
**Catering Assistants, Bar Assistants.** Wages on application.

All staff to work 39 hours a week. Posts occur between Easter and end of October. An ability to deal with people is essential. Accommodation available at a small charge. Overseas applicants with good English and eligibility to work in the UK will be considered. Min. age 18 years.

*Applications* from January to the Personnel Manager, Park Resorts.

**HB LEISURE INTERNATIONAL LTD:** c/o Butlins Fer, Minehead, Somerset TA24 5SH (☎0771-505 2009; fax 01643-709932; e-mail minehead@hbLeisure.co.uk). International leisure company specialising in games and amusements.
**Games Operators (10+).** to work on prize-giving midway games. Wages and hours by arrangement. Some accommodation available at £20 per week. Min. period of work of 8 weeks. Positions are available at all times. Minimum age 18.
*Applications* should be made to Nathan Hepinstall at the above address. Interview necessary.

**HENSON & NEAVE:** Cotswold Farm Park, Guiting Power, Cheltenham, Glos. GL54 5UG (☎01451-850307; fax 01451-850423).
**Farm Park Assistant** needed until mid-October to work with small animals and the general public.
**Cafe Staff** to work until 1 October to prepare and serve food, clear tables etc.
**Shop Staff** needed until 1 October to serve in the gift shop and look after school parties and the farm park entrance.
All staff must be aged 18 plus and offer a high standard of customer service.
*Apply* to A.J. Henson, Partner at the above address.

**K'S ENTERTAINMENT CENTRE:** Warren Road, Minehead, Somerset TA24 5BG (☎01643-704186; fax 01643-702134; e-mail mail@ks-entertainment-centres.co.uk; www.ks-entertainment.co.uk). Operates three family entertainment centres on the south-west coast of England.
**General Assistants (15).** Wages £4.10+ per hour, dependent on age and experience. To work 48 hours per week. Minimum period of work 6 weeks. Positions available from 1 April to 31 October. No accommodation available. Foreign applicants with permission to work in the UK considered.
*Applications* should be made to Gemma or Dom at the above address from 1 December 2002.

**OCEANARIUM:** Pier Approach, West Beach, Bournemouth (☎01202-311993; e-mail oceanarium@reallive.co.uk).
**Front Of House/Retail Assistants (5-10)** to serve customers, operate tills, stock up and for light cleaning, selling guide books, and leafleting.
**Catering Assistants (5-10)** to prepare food, work tills, clean, serve customers and clean tables.
**Welcome Hosts/Hostesses (5-10)** to greet customers, entertain, give talks and for face painting.
All positions are from July to September. Wages £3.70 to £4.00 p.h. Minimum age is 16.
For *applications,* contact, the Personnel Manager at the above address.

**WESTERMILL FARM HOUSE:** Exford, nr Minehead, Somerset TA24 7NJ (☎01643-831216). Campsite, six self-catering cottages and farmhouse cottage on 500-acre working hill farm by a river in the middle of Exmoor National Park.
**Farm Campsite Assistants (2).** Wages on application. Large caravan provided, meals with family. Long hours, with 1 day off a week. Duties include signing people in and out, cleaning shower and loo block, working in the shop, grass cutting and weeding, checking and cleaning cottages, log cottage painting and some domestic jobs including cooking.
Must be non-smokers, conscientious, intelligent and hard working, with a practical nature. One assistant needed from the end of June, the other from the end

of July; to work until early September. Overseas applicants welcome.
*Applications* and further details (enclosing s.a.e./IRC, c.v and small photo) from January to Mrs O.J.C. Edwards at the above address.

# Hotels and Catering

**ABBOTSBURY OYSTERS:** Ferrymans Way, Ferrybridge, Weymouth, Dorset DT4 AYU (☎01305-788867; fax 01305-760661). A friendly, busy seafood bar connected to a working oyster farm.
**Waiting Staff (3)** will also involve some kitchen work. Wages £3-£4 per hour; to work 6-25 hours a week. Applicants must possess empathy, responsibility, consistency and efficiency.
Staff are required from Easter to September. Accommodation is not available.
*Applications* should be sent to Martin Syvret at the above address from 1st March.

**ANCHOR HOTEL AND SHIP INN:** Porlock Harbour, Somerset TA24 8PB (☎01643-862753; fax 01643-862843). Attractive hotel 10 yards from water's edge in a small picturesque harbour set in the beautiful scenery of Exmoor.
**BAR STAFF. Min. age 18. Experience preferred. Min. period of work July to September.**
**KITCHEN ASSISTANTS, SILVER SERVICE WAITING STAFF. Min. age 17. Min. period of work July to September.**
 All staff receive around £155 a week for 5 days' work. Split shifts including weekends. B & L available for £25 per week. *Applications* in writing, enclosing s.a.e., from January to the Personnel Department, The Anchor Hotel and Ship Inn.

**AZTEC HOTEL:** Aztec West, Almondsbury, Bristol BS32 4TS (☎01454-201090; fax 01454-201593). A busy 4 star hotel with 128 bedrooms and 16 meeting/syndicate rooms. Old-style design and philosophy aims to make guests feel welcome.
**Bar Staff (2).** Must be over 18.
**Waiting Staff (2).** Must be over 17.
 Wages on application. Full and part-time work available from April until October. No accommodation is available. Overseas applicants with good language skills considered.
*Applications* from January to Sandra Hart. Interview necessary.

**BATH HOTEL:** Lynmouth Street, Lynmouth, North Devon EX35 6EL (tel/fax 01598-752238). A family run seasonal hotel with approximately 14 members of staff during the season.
**Chamber Person (1).** Wages £128 per week, live-in; to work 39 hours over 6 days. Must be over 18.
**Waiting Staff (2), Bar Person (1), Kitchen Porter (1).** Wages £140 per week, live-in; to work 39 hours per week over 5½ days. Must be over 18.
 Staff required from April-October for a minimum period of 4 months. Foreign applicants with a good level of English are welcome.
*Applications*, from March to June, to Sharon Hobbs at the above address.

**BOURNEMOUTH HIGHCLIFF MARRIOTT HOTEL:** St Michael's Road, Westcliff, Bournemouth, Dorset BH2 5DU (☎01202-557702; fax 01202-293155; e-mail HR.Bournemouth@marriotthotels.co.uk). Following £5.6 million of refurbishment by Whitbread, they consider this the premier hotel in Bournemouth.

**Restaurant Staff(5), Pool Bar Staff(3), Leisure Club Pool Staff (2)**. Wages from £4.10 per hour.
**Chef de Partie(1)**. Approx. £5.91 per hour.
**Night Porter (1)**. Approx. £5 per hour
Limited accommodation available. Full training, leisure club membership and excellent staff facilities are provided. To work 39 hours over 5 days per week (30-40 for pool attendant). Min. period of work of 2 months between June and September. Good level of English required: pool staff should be RLSS/National Pool Lifeguard qualified.

*Applications* should include a referee and be made to the HR Manager at the above address from March onwards. Interview in person or by phone will be required.

**COLLAVEN MANOR HOTEL:** Sourton, Devon EX20 4HH (☎01837-861522; fax 01837-861614; e-mail collavenmanor@supanet.com). A small 4 Crown, AA two star country house hotel with 9 bedrooms. Situated in a rural location admidat lovely scenery, the hotel is recommended in the *Good Hotel Guide*.
**Waiting Staff (1)**. Wages £4.00 per hour.
**Kitchen Assistant (1)**. Wages £3.50 per hour.
**Sous Chef (1)**. Wages £4.50 per hour.
Accommodation is provided. Period of work June to September. All staff must be adaptable and flexible, and prepared to assist in the general running of the hotel. Applicants must be over 16. Overseas applicants who speak English considered

*Applications* from December to Mrs J. Mitchell. References must be provided if an interview is impossible.

**THE CHINE HOTEL:** 25 Boscombe Spa Road, Bournemouth BH5 1AX (☎01202-396234; fax 01202-391737; e-mail reservations@chinehotel.co.uk).
**Waiting Staff (4)** needed for restaurant and pool service; some silver service. Wages £4.20 per hour plus tips. To work 40 hours per 5-day week; some casual work available. Period of work mid-June to early September. Live out. Food hygiene certificate, previous experience and references needed.
**Chamber Staff (3)** needed to clean bedrooms and public areas. £4.20 per hour. 30-40 hours work per 5-day week. Period of work mid-June to early September. Live out. Previous experience and references required.

*Apply* to Mr R. Douglas, Hotel Manager.

**THE COTTAGE HOTEL:** Hope Cover Kingsbridge, South Devon TQ7 3HJ (☎01548-561555; fax 01548-561455; e-mail info@hopecover.com).
**General Assistants (1-2)** needed to work for as long as possible over the summer and around the year. Duties may include working in the restaurant or beach café, housekeeping, portering, depending on suitability. Wages at the national minimum wage (possibly more for experienced staff) plus tips and meals. To work a 39 hour week with 1½ or 2 days off per week depending on rota. Applicants should be aged at least 17, must speak excellent English and have previous experience of hotel work.

*Applications* to Sarah Ireland, Director, at the above address.

**CROWN HOTEL:** Exford, Exmoor, Somerset TA24 7PP (☎01643-831554; fax 01643-831665; e-mail info@crownhotelexmoor.co.uk; www.crownhotelexmoor.co.uk). Award-winning seventeenth century coaching inn set in the heart of beautiful Exmoor National Park. Internationally-renowned cuisine.
**General Assistants.** needed for waiting in the restaurant, bar work, cleaning rooms and washing-up duties. Wages £170 per week minus B & L. To work 39 hours

per week. Min. period of work of 2 months. Positions are available from April to September inclusive. Fluent English essential. Minimum age 19. B & L available, cost to be arranged. Suitably qualified foreign applicants welcome
*Applications* should be as soon as possible to Mr Hugo Jeune at the above address.

**THE CROWN HOTEL:** Blockley, Gloucester GL56 2PF (☎01386-700245; fax 01386-700247)
**Dining Room Staff (2), General Assistants (2)** for the summer period June to October. £4 per hour plus tips and accommodation. 40 hour week split shifts. Some experience preferred. Minimum age 18 years.
*Applications* to Mr Kertai, Manager.

**EARLE HOTELS LTD:** Whitsand Bay Hotel, Portwinkle, Cornwall PL11 3BU (☎01503-230276; e-mail earlehotels@btconnect.com; www.cornish.golf.hotels.co.uk). A manor house hotel with golf course and leisure facilities.
**Restaurant and Housekeeping Staff** required all year round to work in a relaxed atmosphere. Staff accommodation is available.
*Apply* to J. da Rosa, Manager.

**THE EAST CLOSE COUNTRY HOTEL:** Lyndhurst Road, Hinton St Michael, nr Christchurch, Dorset BH23 7EF (☎01425-672404; fax 01425-674315; e-mail eastclosecountryhotel@yahoo.co.uk).
**Waiting Staff (3), Chamber Assistant.** Must be aged at least 17.
**Bar Assistant.** Must be aged at least 18.
All the above for restaurant and function work, including weddings. Wages of £142 per week plus tips and accommodation. Period of work by arrangement from May.
*Applications* to the above address.

**FAIRHAVEN SEA FRONT HOTEL AND RESTAURANT:** 40 The Esplanade, Weymouth, Dorset DT4 8DH (☎01305-760200; fax 01305-760300).The Hotel is part of a family owned group of hotels and restaurants in Weymouth. Weymouth is a holiday resort on the South coast with a sandy beach and 17th century harbour.
**Waiting Staff (5), Chefs and Grill Cooks (3), Kitchen Assistants (2).** Wages by arrangement plus tips. Meals provided and accommodation may be available. To work 6 days a week. All staff must be available from the end of May to September. Some jobs are suitable for overseas students wishing to perfect their English.
Send *Applications* (with photograph) from March onwards to the Manager, Fairhaven Hotel.

**HOOPS INN:** Horns Cross, Bideford, Devon EX39 5DL (☎01237-451222; fax 01237-451247). A 13th century 2 star historic inn and hotel with 12 rooms, close to the coastal path. Renowned for its cooking and traditional coaching inn atmosphere.
**General Assistants** for duties including waiting, housekeeping, kitchen and bar work. 40-45 hours per week. Minimum age 18. Experience preferred.
**Chefs** also needed. Experience essential.
Staff required for spring, summer and winter seasons. Accommodation available.
*Applications*, including recent photograph, to Mrs Gay Marriott at the above address.

**HUNTSHAM COURT:** Huntsham Valley, near Tiverton, Devon EX16 7NA (☎01398-361 365; fax 01398-361 456; e-mail andrea@huntsham.co.uk; www huntsham.co.uk ). A gothic Victorian country manor hotel that specialises in group parties, conferences and weddings. Set in a countryside location, it has a reputation for being unique and special.
**Waiting Staff (2-4), Chamber Staff (2-4), Experienced Chefs/Cooks (2), Carpenter/Tradesman.** Wages from £100 to £130 a week inclusive of accommodation and meals. Min. period of work 12 weeks, staff required all year round. Applicants must have knowledge of English, a neat appearance, and be a team worker.

*Applications* with photo and s.a.e./IRC to Andrea Bolwig, Director, Huntsham Court.

**JESSOP HOUSE HOTEL:** 65 Church Street, Tewkesbury, Gloucestershire GL20 5RZ (☎01684-292017; fax 01684-273076; e-mail LesThurlow@aol.com). A small hotel in the centre of a small town.
**General Hotel Help(s).** To work mornings and some evenings doing a variety of tasks including breakfast preparation, serving, room servicing, bar work and reception duties.
Wages to be discussed at interview. Minimum period of work of 3 months between April and October. Foreign applicants with work permit and good English will be considered. Previous experience not essential, as applicants can be trained. Minimum age 18. Accommodation unlikely to be available.

*Applications* should be made from March onwards to Les or Jenny Thurlow at the above address. Interview required.

**KNOLL HOUSE HOTEL:** Studland Bay, near Swanage, Dorset BH19 3AH (☎01929-452233/450450; fax 01929-450423; e-mail staff@knollhouse.co.uk; www.knollhouse.co.uk). A country house holiday hotel superbly located in a National Trust Reserve overlooking Studland Bay. Independent and family run, it has a reputation for service and care of its guests, many of whom return annually.
**Waiting Staff (6-10)** for dining room including wine service. £4.20 per hour.
**Housekeeping Staff (6-10).** £4.40 per hour. No experience required.
**General Assistants (2-3)** to care for children. £4.40 per hour.
**Kitchen Assistants (2-3)** washing up and helping in kitchens. £4.40 per week.
**Chefs (4).** Salary dependent on experience. 706/1 or equivalent not always necessary.

All staff to work 38 hours with two days off per week. Deduction made for B & L, available in single rooms. Positions available for a min. 6 weeks between March to October. A happy disposition and a good attitude are more important than experience. Min. age 17 years. Easter and summer vacation positions also available, as well as further positions not mentioned here but only available for the entire season. EU applicants with good spoken English welcome.

Interview is not always necessary. *Applications* from the start of the year to the Staff Manager, Knoll House Hotel.

**LAND'S END AND JOHN O'GROATS COMPANY:** Land's End, Sennen, Penzance, Cornwall TR19 7AA (☎0870-458 0044; fax 01736-871812; e-mail info@landsend-landmark.co.uk). A leading tourist attraction in Cornwall located in a spectacular setting. It comprises various exhibitions and trading units which operate throughout the year. In winter the operation is reduced.
**Catering Personnel, Retail Staff** for various jobs at Land's End from spring to early

autumn. Wages by arrangement; hours depend on the level of business. Applicants should be aged over 16, those with previous experience preferred.
*Applications* to Personnel at the above address.

**LIMPLEY STOKE HOTEL:** Lower Limpley Stoke, Near Bath BA3 6HZ (☎01225-723333; fax 01225-722406).
**Waiting Staff (3), Cleaner, Chamber Staff (3), Bar Staff (3), Night Porter, General Assistants (2).** Wages to be discussed depending on position applied for and previous experience. Period of work by arrangement.
*Applications* to Nick Gray, Managing Director at the above address.

**LUCKNAM PARK HOTEL:** Colerne, Chippenham, Wilts SN14 8AZ (☎01225-742777; fax 01225-743536; e-mail personnel@lucknampark.co.uk; www.lucknampark.co.uk). A four star hotel with a 2 rosette restaurant, set in 500 acres of parkland, 7 miles from the historic town of Bath.
**Restaurant Staff (2-4).** Restaurant experience essential.
**Chefs.** must be qualified and experienced.
All staff to work full-time, shift hours. Min. period of work 6 months. Min. age 18 years. Accommodation available. All staff are entitled to use the hotel's extensive leisure spa facilities. Overseas applicants with good spoken English welcome; applicants in England will be required to attend an interview. All applicants should be smart in appearance, able to work with others and have a friendly, helpful nature.
*Applications* to Michelle Pepper at the above address.

**LUNDY COMPANY:** The Lundy Island Shore Office, The Quay, Bideford, Devon EX39 2LY (☎01237-470074; fax 01237-477779; e-mail info@lundyisland.co.uk). Lundy is an island off the North Devon coast owned by the National Trust with 23 letting properties, a pub and a shop.
**Tavern Staff (4)** to help run the pub. Wages are variable, with free B & L; to work a 5 day week. Staff are required from April to September. Applicants must have previous bar/kitchen experience.
*Applications* from January to Paul Roberts at the above address. Interview necessary. Also see under *Heritage* in the Voluntary Work section.

**MR & MRS I.S. MACDONALD:** The Flat, 1 Barton Road, Woolacombe, North Devon (☎01271-870752). Fish and chip takeaway in a popular resort, a few minutes' walk from the sea.
**Counter Assistants (3).** £195-£200 per week, on an hourly basis. Serving takeaway food, plus some general cleaning when preparing food and shutting shop. Need little training but lots of sympathy.
**Assistant Fryer.** Training given. £230-£240 per week, on an hourly basis.
All staff to work 48 hours per 6-day week. Free B & L in comfortable flat with excellent facilities. Min. period of work 6 weeks between May and September. Must have pleasant appearance and sense of humour. Excellent English essential.
*Applications* (enclosing s.a.e. and photograph) from March to Mr & Mrs I. S. MacDonald at the above address.

**MILL ON THE BRUE ACTIVITY CENTRE:** Trendle Farm, Bruton, Somerset BA10 0BA (☎01749-812307; fax 01749-812706; e-mail millonthebrue@compuserve.com). A family-run outdoor activity centre (2 hours from London, 1 hour from Bath and Bristol) offering activities such as canoeing, climbing, archery etc. and with many young, energetic staff.

**Housekeeping Assistants (2)** for cleaning rooms and dining room duties. £142.20 per week. Staff work 7½ hours per day, 5½ days a week. Min. period of work 2 months. Residential post, deductions made for accommodation. Full training provided.
**Group Leaders** needed from June/July until end of August. First Aid Qualifications an advantage. Must be available for 24 hour selection process in March and a training week. Minimum age 19 years.
**Long Term Instructors** employed from January to November. Residential post, 44 hour week with deductions for board and lodgings.

Overseas applicants welcome. All applicants for Group Leader/Instructor positions should be available for interview.

*Applications* from Ruth Braithwaite at the above address.

**MOUNTAIN WATER EXPERIENCE:** Courtlands, Kingsbridge, Devon, TQ7 4BN (tel/fax 01548-550675; e-mail mwe@mountainwaterexp.demon.co.uk).
**General Assistant** needed for April-November. The work involves general kitchen and housework duties plus bar work. No qualifications are required, but candidates need to be over 18 and have a good sense of humour.

For *applications* and for details of wages and hours please contact Mark Agnew, Operations Manager, at the above address.

**NARRACOTT GRAND HOTEL:** Beach Road, Woolacombe, Devon EX34 7BS (☎01271-870418). Sea-front 100 bedroom hotel with extensive leisure facilities situated in a small coastal village near a surfing beach surrounded by National Trust land, and overlooking Woolacombe Sands.
**Waiting Staff, Porters, Kitchen Staff and Room Staff.** Wages specified on application. Short period of work between February and January. Longer periods possible.

*Applications*, including details of work experience and photo, to Mr Wyld, Narracott Grand Hotel.

**NORFOLK ROYALE HOTEL:** Richmond Hill, Bournemouth, Dorset BH2 6EN (☎01202-551521; fax 01202-299729). A luxury 4 star hotel owned by the English Rose Hotels Group.
**Bar Staff, Waiting Staff.** Wages on application. Part-time and full-time work available for both positions. Previous experience helpful.
**Chamber Staff.** Wages on application. Full-time and part-time work available.

No accommodation is available. Staff are required for periods of 6 weeks or longer (although shorter time will be considered). Overseas applicants with work permits are considered.

*Applications* at any time to Personnel. Interview necessary.

**OLD STOCKS HOTEL:** The Square, Stow on the Wold, Glos GL54 1AF (☎01451-830666; fax 01451-870014; e-mail theoldstocks@btinternet.com). A small 18 bedroom family run hotel with a friendly team of caring staff. Located in the highest point of the Cotswolds, a Grade II listed building.
**Housekeepers (2), Waiting Staff (2), Kitchen Assistants (2), Bar Staff (2).** Wages approximately £170 per week for 40 hour, 5 day week. Minimum period of work one month between April and November. Accommodation available. Previous experience not necessary as full training will be provided.

*Applications* should be sent to Julie Rose, Proprietor at the above address.

**PENKERRIS:** Penwinnick Road, St. Agnes, Cornwall TR5 0PA (tel/fax 01872-

552262; e-mail info@penkerris.co.uk; www.penkerris.co.uk). Attractive detached house with garden in unspoilt Cornish village. Dramatic cliff walks, beaches and good surfing nearby.
**Guesthouse Assistant** required, to work on an *au pair* basis. Accommodation provided. Pocket money according to duties and season. Afternoons free to visit the beach or explore the cliff walks. The guesthouse is open throughout the winter. Min. work period 3 months; much longer preferred, but 3 weeks acceptable over Christmas and Easter. Overseas applicants welcome: the job is ideal for students wishing to perfect their English as they can study at Truro college nearby. The owner can also help with English as she has years of experience in EFL teaching
*Applications* a.s.a.p. to Mrs Dorothy Gill-Carey at the above address.

**RIVIERA HOTEL:** Burnaby Road, Alum Chine, Bournemouth, Dorset BH4 8JF (☎01202-763653; fax 01202-768422). A large family holiday orientated hotel based 20 minutes walk from the centre of Bournemouth and 2 minutes walk from the beach.
**Waiting Staff (2).** Wages on application, plus tips. To work 36 hours/6 days per week. Experience required.
**Chamberperson.** Wages on application, plus tips. To work 36 hours over 6 mornings per week. Experience preferred.
Wages may be increased depending on experience. Accommodation is available. Min. work period 3 months between March and November. Min. age 18. All applicants must have a friendly personality. Previous experience preferred. Overseas applicants eligible to work in the UK welcome.
Send *applications* with s.a.e. in February to the General Manager, Riviera Hotel.

**ROSKARNON HOUSE HOTEL:** Rock, Wadebridge, Cornwall PL27 6LD (☎01208-862785/862329).
**General Assistant (1/2).** Min. of £80 for working 45 hours basic a week, plus overtime. To work 6 days per week. Any catering or housekeeping knowledge useful.
**Assistant Cook, Kitchen Porter.** Wages and hours negotiable. Free B & L provided. Min. period of work 6 weeks from 25 May to 12 October. Work also available for 2-4 weeks at Easter. Overseas applicants eligible to work in the UK welcome.
*Applications* in late March to Mr Veall at the above address.

**ROYAL BEACON HOTEL:** The Beacon, Exmouth, Devon EX8 2AF (☎01395-264886; fax 01395-268890). Georgian Coaching House overlooking the sea, known for its old world charm and high standard of service. Two minutes walk from the beach.
**Chamber Staff (2), Receptionists (2), Bar Staff (2), Kitchen Assistants (2), Porter (1), Waiting Staff (2).** Pay by arrangement. To work 38 hours per 5-day week. Deductions made for B & L. Min. work period 4 months between 1 April and 31 October. Also vacancies at Christmas, lasting 3-4 weeks. French, Spanish and German applicants welcome.
*Applications* with photo to Bill Ellis, Royal Beacon Hotel.

**THE ROYAL CASTLE HOTEL:** 11 The Quay, Dartmouth, Devon TQ6 9PS (☎01803-833033; fax 01803-835445). A busy three star hotel which employs around 50 staff. Investors in People awarded.
**Waiting Staff (4-6), Bar Staff (4-6).** Wages from £4.40 per hour. To work 40 hours

over 5 days a week. Work available all year round. Accommodation is available at a cost of £35 per week. No experience necessary, just a bright personality, the right attitude, and the ability to work hard and play hard.

*Applications* about 3 weeks prior to desired start to the Duty Manager. Interview sometimes required.

**THE ROYAL YORK AND FAULKNER HOTEL:** The Esplanade, Sidmouth, South Devon EX10 8AZ (☎01395-513043; fax 01395-577472; e-mail work@royalyorkhotel.net; www.royalyorkhotel.net). Regency resort hotel occupying a superb position on the Esplanade of Sidmouth, a charming coastal resort. 70 rooms. Family business.

**Waiting Staff.** Wages £4.46 per hour. To work 40 hours per week.

**Bedroom Cleaners/Dining Room Relief.** Wages £4.64 per hour. To work approx. 40½ hours per week.

Accommodation and full board available for £25 per week. Staff needed all year round. Min. period of work 3 months.

*Applications* to Mr Peter Hook, Managing Director.

**SUNNYDENE HOTEL:** 11 Spencer Road, Knyveton Gardens, Bournemouth, Dorset BH1 3TE (☎01202-552281). A family run hotel with 11 bedrooms situated midway between Boscombe and Bournemouth and catering for a wide range of customers.

**General Assistant.** £60 a week plus free B & L. To work 6 days a week in mornings: 8am-1pm. Assistants must be prepared to help with any aspect of hotel work including cooking, cleaning, waiting on tables, and bedroom work. Must like children, and have a very even temper, lots of patience and a lively sense of humour.

Min. period of work 10 weeks between mid July and mid September. Must be prepared to stay at least until 11 September. Overseas applicants welcome.

*Applications* from March enclosing a recent photograph and s.a.e./IRC, to Mrs L.H. Hackett, Proprietor, Sunnydene Hotel.

**TORS HOTEL:** Lynmouth, North Devon (☎01598-753236; fax 01598-752544; e-mail Torshotel@torslynmouth.co.uk; www.torslynmouth.co.uk). A 3 star 4 crown 33 bedroom hotel situated on the North Devon coastline with stunning sea views across the Bristol Channel to Wales.

**Silver Service Waiting Staff.** £125 a week. Experience or the ability to learn required. 39 hours, 5½ days; split shifts. Wages dependent on experience.

**Chamber Person, Porters, Kitchen Porters.** £125 a week. To work 39 hours a week. No experience needed. Wages dependent on experience.

All staff work 6 days a week. Free B & L provided. Season lasts from March to January. Period of work must be for the whole period from April until September, applicants only available for summer vacation need not apply. Bonus paid on completion of season.

Send *Applications* with details of previous experience and photograph a.s.a.p. to the Manager, the Tors Hotel.

**TOWNGATE PERSONNEL LTD:** 3 Alum Chine Road Bournemouth, Dorset BH4 8DT (☎01202-752955; fax 01202-752954; e-mail enquiries@towngate-personnel.co.uk). A recruitment agency specialising in recruitment within the hotel and catering industry.

**Short-term live-in assignments** available in hotels in the west country and throughout England.

**Hotel Receptionists (20).** Wages £200 per week; to work 8 hours a day, 5/6 days a week. Hotel reception experience essential.
**Silver Service Waiting Staff (30).** Wages £180-£200 per week; to work split shifts, 6 days a week. Silver service experience essential.
**Chefs (30).** Wages £200-£400 per week; to work split shifts, 6 days a week. Must have relevant experience.

All positions are in 3 or 4 Star hotels in the Channel Islands. Accommodation is available at a cost of £40 per week. Staff are required from March to October for a minimum of 5 months. Applicants from the EU/EEA and others on working holiday visas considered.

*Applications* from February to James Tucker, Operations Manager, at the above address. Telephone interview required.

**TRALEE HOTEL LTD:** West Hill Road, Bournemouth BH2 5EQ (☎01202-556246; fax 01202-295229; e-mail personnel@tralee.co.uk). A busy 68 bedroom holiday and conference hotel.
**Waiting Staff (1).** Overtime available. Must have experience and be over 18
**Kitchen Porter (1).** Overtime available. Must be over 18. No experience necessary.
**Room Attendant (1).** No overtime. Must be over 18. Experience preferred.
**Bar Attendant (1).** Overtime available. Must have qualifications and experience and be over 18.

Wages on application. To work 40 hours a week over 5 days. Staff should be professional, courteous, co-operative and flexible. Overseas applicants considered.

*Applications* to the Personnel Department 4 weeks prior to intended arrival. Interview necessary.

**TRESCO ESTATE:** Tresco, Isles of Scilly, Cornwall TR24 OQQ (☎01720-424110; fax 01720-422807; e-mail personnel@tresco.co.uk.)
**Waiting Staff (5), Housekeeping Staff (3), Kitchen Porters (3), Retail Assistant, Chef de Partie** needed to cover all duties in one of the Estate's three luxury hotels. Wages £4.20 per hour (£4.75-£4.90 for *Chef de Partie*) with tips split at the end of season and live-in accommodation. To work 40+ hours per week, generally split shifts over 5-5 1/2 days per week. Period of work from May to October (May-September for retail assistant).
**Farm Worker** needed in May to assist the farm manager with beef herd and flower picking. Wages negotiable.
**Assistant Mechanic** needed in June to assist the island's mechanic with all vehicle repairs and general mechanical duties.

Minimum age 18 for all roles. *Applications* to Gill Knight, Personnel Manager at the above address.

**TREYARNON BAY HOTEL:** Treyarnon Bay, St Merryn, Padstow, Cornwall PL28 8JN (☎01841-520235; fax 01841-520239).
**Kitchen Porter** to work 6-8 hours per day providing general kitchen clean-up and help with preparing vegetables and starters. Applicants must have a basic hygiene certificate.
**Chef/Cook** to work 8-10 hours per day preparing, breakfast, lunch, dinner and for the overall running of a clean kitchen. Must have a Basic/Intermediate food hygiene certificate and NVQ.
**Bar Staff (3-4)** for general bar duties 6-8 hours per day, experience preferred but not essential.

**Housekeeper/Room Cleaner (1-2)** to clean rooms and some hotel areas for 5-6 hours per day, there is also some laundry work (although most of it is sent out). All staff are required from July to September, and must be over 18, wages are between £3.75-£4.50 per hour according to experience, except for the chef whose wages will be £4-£5.50 per hour with accommodation available.

To apply *contact* Jennifer Kenley at the above address.

**TWO BRIDGES HOTEL:** (Warm Welcome Hotels) Two Bridges, Dartmoor, Devon PL20 6SW (☎01822-890581; fax 01822-890575). A 29 bedroom hotel in the middle of Dartmoor with a busy pub trade restaurant and function suite for weddings, dinners and conferences. Friendly working atmosphere.
**Bar Assistant, Waiting Staff (4), Reception Assistant** to work a 5 day week of approx. 40 hours, with extra time available.
**Housekeeping Staff (2)** to work approx. 30 hours per week.

Required from the beginning of July to the end of October. Wages min £4.25 per hour if living out (or some limited opportunities for living in, wages negotiable) plus tips. Previous experience and qualifications not necessary, but bar assistant must be aged over 18.

*Applications* with recent photograph to the Personnel Manager, at the above address.

**THE VICTORIA and BELMONT HOTELS:** The Esplanade, Sidmouth, Devon, EX10 8RY (☎01395-512555/512651; fax 01395-579101; e-mail info@victoriahotel.co.uk /info@belmont-hotel.co.uk). 4 star hotel hotels that boast a relaxed atmosphere and a young and enthusiastic team. Located on the beautiful Devon coastline in Sidmouth, famous for its International Folk Festival.
**Room Attendants (2)** to service guests' rooms. Wages £135/£150 per week, dependent on age, to include all meals and accommodation. To work 5 days per week, mostly straight shifts 7am-3pm or 8:30am-4:30pm. Required for a minimum of 3 months to include September. Full training given.
**Silver Service Waiting Staff (2)** to serve breakfast, dinner and three lunches. Wages £140/£160 per week, dependent on age, plus tips, to include all meals and accommodation. To work 5 days per week. Required for a minimum of 3 months to include September. Full training given.

Candidates should be of smart appearance, with a pleasant outgoing personality and sense of humour, and ideally be between 18-26 years old. Must be EU citizens or possess UK work permit.

*Applications* to Mr M. Hext, Personnel and Training Manager, at the above address.

**SANDBANKS HOTEL:** 15 Banks Road, Poole, Dorset, BH13 7PS (☎01202-707377; fax 01202-708885; e-mail personnel@sandbankshotel.co.uk). AA 3 star hotel. 116 bedrooms. Situated on beautiful Blue Flag beach. Excellent service and food.
**Waiting Staff (8).** Wages from £4.50-£5.00 per hour. To work 5 days out of 7, split shifts, 40 hours or casual, overtime available. Good level of English.
**Room Attendants (8).** Wages from £4.25-£4.75 per hour. To work 5 days out of 7, straight shifts, 37½ hours or casual.

Limited board and accommodation available for £30 per week. Min. period of work of 2 months. Positions are available from July to September. Applicants should be 16+, no previous experience necessary. Overseas applicants welcome as long as they have a good understanding of English.

*Applications* should be made to the Human Resources Manager. Interview necessary.

**WATERSMEET HOTEL:** Mortehoe, Woolacombe, Devon EX34 7EB (☎01271-870333; fax 01271-870890). A 3 star high quality country house hotel with 25 bedrooms set on the National Trust's North Atlantic Coastline and overlooking a sandy beach.
**Restaurant/Bar Staff (2), Housekeeping Staff (2), Kitchen Staff (2).** Wages £110 a week including B & L. 40-42 hours per week over 6 days. Min. period of work 3 months between May and October. Min. age 18 years. Experience an advantage.
*Applications*, with CV and photograph, from January to Mr Neil Bradley at the above address.

**WOOLACOMBE BAY HOTEL:** Woolacombe, Devon EX34 7BN (☎01271-870388; fax 01271-870613). A family hotel situated near 3 miles of golden sands and a surfing beach.
**Waiting Staff, Room Staff, Kitchen Staff, Bar Staff, Porters.** £4.50 per hour (live-in). To work 44 hours per week. . Min. period of work 4 months between Easter and October. Staff are also required over Christmas and New Year (approx. 22 December to 2 January). Minimum age 18.
*Applications* from March to The Manager, Woolacombe Bay Hotel.

# Language Schools

**ALBION LANGUAGE TOURS:** c/o 151 Woodlands Avenue, Hamworthy, Poole, Dorset BH15 4EZ (☎01202-677734). A German organisation that has been bringing students to the UK for a number of years. Offers packages including language tuition, activity programme and accommodation.
**EFL Teachers(15-20)** needed to teach English to monolingual classes of German students aged 13-19. Wages £10 per hour. To work 9am-midday or 2:15pm Monday to Friday (not Bank Holidays). Min. period of work of 2 weeks. Positions are available from Easter to October. TEFL qualification required. No accommodation available.
*Applications* should be made from February 2003 to Diana Scovell at the above address. Interview required.

**ANGLO-CONTINENTAL EDUCATIONAL GROUP:** 33 Wimborne Road, Bournemouth BH2 6NA (☎01202-557414; fax 01202-556156; e-mail english@anglo-continental.com).
**EFL Teachers (up to 100)** for English language summer courses for adults. To teach 20, 25 or 30 lessons per week. Cambridge CELTA/Dip. TEFL or equivalent qualifications required, plus experience of TEFL.
**EFL Teachers (20)** for 8-16 year olds in residential and non-residential schools. TEFL or equivalent qualifications preferable, but candidates with enthusiastic and outgoing character may also be considered.
**House Staff (6)** for residential junior centre. To work 6 days per week, mostly in the afternoons and evenings. Experience with children needed.
**Sports Staff (8)** on both residential and non-residential junior courses. Cert.Ed/PGCE preferable; experience with children essential.
Salaries approximately £140-£240 per week according to qualifications and experience. No accommodation, except on some residential junior courses. Min. age 20. Period of work between 10 June and 24 August.

*Applications* from the beginning of March to Ms J. Haine, Anglo-Continental Educational Group.

**BOURNEMOUTH TEACHING SERVICE LTD:** 139 Charminster Road, Bournemouth, Dorset BH8 8UH (tel/fax 01202-521355). A small language school with 9 members of staff; established in 1980.
**EFL Teachers (2).** Wages £240-£290 per week. To work 22½ hours per week. Min. period of work of 4 weeks. Positions are available from late June to end of August. RSA cert TEFL or RSA DIP TEFL required. Accommodation not available.
*Applications* should be made from April onwards to Stephen Laughton. Interview necessary.

**CHANNEL SCHOOL OF ENGLISH:** Country Cousins Ltd., Bicclescombe, Ilfracombe, Devon EX34 8JN (☎01271-862834; fax 01271-865374; e-mail help@country-cousins.com; www.country-cousins.com). Situated on the beautiful North Devon coast, the school offers a range of English courses with 12, 15 or 21 hours of lessons per week to those aged 7 to adult.
**EFL Teachers (3)** Wages £9.70 per hour; to work 24 hours per week, July-August. Must have TEFL qualification and should have experience with the age range 11-18.
**Social Organisers** to work July and August, supervising children and young adults on the school's sports and excursion programme. Wages £4.60 per hour. – Ideally candidates would be trainee teachers.
*Applications* to John Swan, at the above address.

**DORSET INTERNATIONAL COLLEGE:** Cambridge House, 7 Knyveton Road, Bournemouth BH1 (☎01202-316611; fax 01202-318811; e-mail info@dorsetinternationalcollege.co.uk). A British Council accredited small language school which runs junior and adult courses all year round. Situated near the centre of a seaside town ½ hour from the New Forest, and 1½ hour's train journey from London.
**EFL Teachers (1-5)** to work 9am-5pm. 2 years' experience of teaching English required.
**Activity Leaders (2).** 4 hours a day. 2 years' experience required.
**Receptionist (1/2)** to work 9am-5pm. Min. age 19. GCSEs required.
Staff wanted from July to September. Min. period of work 1 month. Accommodation not available. Overseas applicants welcome.
*Applications* from 1 June to the Administration Manager at the above address.

**EAGLE INTERNATIONAL SCHOOL:** Tiami, 55 Elms Avenue, Lilliput, Poole, Dorset BH14 8EE (tel/fax 01202-745175; e-mail eaglesch@aol.com).
**Teacher/Leaders (15)** needed to work with overseas students in the 11-17 age range. Wages £200 per week. Work available over the Easter and Summer vacations. Duties will involve giving classes in English conversation and supervising students on the activity programme. Periods of work will be EasterPreference given to B.Ed and P.G.C.E. Modern Languages and English/Sport/Drama students.
*Applications* to J. Rees, Principal.

**THE ENGLISH CENTRE SALISBURY:** The Duchess of Albany Building, Ox Row, Salisbury, Wiltshire SP1 1EU (☎01722-412711; fax 01722-414604; e-mail info.ecs@twinschool.co.uk). Small but expanding language school in the centre of Salisbury. Offers English tuition to groups of international students in a friendly work environment.

**EFL Teachers (5).** £13.33 per hour minimum. To work mornings and some afternoons. Applicants must be TEFL qualified with experience teaching multilingual groups.
**Social Activity Organisers (2).** From £5 per hour. To work afternoons and some weekends. Applicants must have proof of organisational skills. Minimum age 18.
Staff required from June-September. Board and accommodation is not provided. Enthusiasm and energy needed. *Applications* from March to the Principal at the above address.

**THE ENGLISH COUNTRY SCHOOL:** 18 Riverside, Winchcombe, Cheltenham, Gloucestershire GL54 5JP (tel/fax 01242-604067). A British Council accredited English language summer school in Southern England and Scotland, for children and teenagers providing 'fun, friendship and learning in a healthy, natural environment'.
**EFL Teachers (8)** to teach English and assist with sports and crafts. Wages from £300 per week live-in, with time off. Must have EFL qualifications, and/or PGCE/B.Ed.
**Sports Organisers (2).** Wages from £300 per week live-in, with time off. Must have relevant sports coaching qualifications.
Min. period of work 3 weeks between mid July and mid August.
*Applications* from April to the Director. Interview necessary.

**HARROW HOUSE INTERNATIONAL COLLEGE:** Harrow Drive, Swanage, Dorset BH19 1PE (☎01929-424421; fax 01929-427175; e-mail andrew.kirby@harrowhouse.co.uk). An all year round school in a beautiful location with superb facilities, catering for all ages of students from over 45 different countries.
**EFL Teachers (20).** Wages from £300-£400 per week. To work 6 days a week. Possibility also of helping with evening activities and one full day excursion every week, both paid extra. Applicants must have CELTA, TESOL, BEd or QTS, be at least 21 years old and have some knowledge of foreign languages.
**Residential Sports Staff (20).** Wages £200 per week. To work 6 days a week. Must have coaching certificates/BSc Sports Science. Should be aged 18-25.
**Catering Staff (15).** To work 40+ hours per week.
Accommodation is available. All postions available June-August.
*Applications* to Andrew Kirby, Principal, at the above address.

**THE INTERNATIONAL SCHOOL:** 1 Mount Radford Crescent, Exeter EX2 4EW (☎01392-254102; fax 01392-434432; e-mail kim@internationalschool.co.uk). An International School providing English as a foreign language courses all year round, mostly for adults.
**EFL Teachers (25).** Wages £8.60 per 45 minute lesson; to teach 20-40 lessons per week. Must possess a recognised TEFL certificate and have teaching experience. Accommodation may be available for £70 per week. Teachers needed from June to September for a minimum period of 1 week. Applicants with a high fluency in English are welcome.
*Applications* from March to Kim Stephens at the above address.

**KING'S SCHOOL OF ENGLISH:** 58 Braidley Road, Bournemouth BH2 6LD (☎01202-293535; fax 01202-293922; e-mail info@kingsschool.uk.com). A private school of English for overseas students. Offers courses for all ages, but much of their work is with teenagers and children.
**EFL Teachers (40).** Wages from £200-£350 per week, to give 20-40 lessons per

week. Must have TEFL certificate or diploma, and preferably a degree and relevant experience.
**Social and Sports Supervisors (20).** Wages from £150-£250 per week, working full time 5-6 days per week. Must have relevant sports and social activities experience/qualifications.
**Administrative Assistants (10).** Wages from £150-£225 per week, working full time 5-6 days per week. Must have good computer, organisational and interpersonal skills.
**Course Directors (4)** Wages from £300-£375 per week, working full time. Must have a diploma in TEFL, university degree and considerable TEFL experience.

Min. period of work 2 weeks. Positions are available between 1 July and 31 August 2003. Foreign applicants may be considered for positions other than teaching posts. Fluent English absolutely essential. All applicants must be enthusiastic, versatile and enjoy working with young people. Accommodation not usually available, but included for teachers on residential courses.

*Applications* should be made from April onwards to the School Principal at the above address. Interview required.

**THE LANGUAGE PROJECT:** 27 Oakfield Road, Clifton, Bristol BS8 2AT (☎0117-9090 911; fax 0117-9077 181; e-mail info@languageproject.co.uk). A small school with a focus on innovative teaching techniques and use of the latest materials; also performs a lot of teacher training. Its students come from all over the world.
**EFL Teachers (3).** who can deliver topic-based lessons using authentic materials of their own making. Wages £220 per week. To work 18 hours per week. Min. period of work of 4 weeks. Positions are available from June to August. TEFL at A or B grade plus 2 years' experience teaching adults required. Accommodation available at a charge of £90 per week. Foreign applicants welcome.

*Applications* should be made from May onwards to Dr Jon Wright at the above address. Interview necessary.

**MIDLAND SCHOOL LTD:** 7 Alverton Hall, 33 Westcliff Road, Bournemouth BH4 8AY (☎01202-759595; fax 01202-303265).
**EFL Teachers (up to 10).** Wages £209-£305 per week. Hours approx. 9am-5pm Monday to Friday, including one excursion day a week and one extra-curricular evening. Most weekends off. Must have at least a B.Ed, preferably with TEFL. Should be keen, able to discipline large groups and enjoy team work.

No accommodation provided but free lunches usually available. Min. period of work 2 weeks in either July or August. Contractual problems make it difficult for positions to be offered to overseas applicants. All applicants must be available for interview.

*Applications* a.s.a.p. to Miss A. Burton, Director, Midland School Ltd.

**RICHARD LANGUAGE COLLEGE:** 43-45 Wimborne Road, Bournemouth, Dorset BH3 7AB (☎01202-555932; fax 01202-555874; e-mail acadman@rlc.co.uk; www.rlc.co.uk).
**EFL Teachers (20).** £252-£270 per week depending on qualifications and experience. Hours 8.30am-4.30pm Monday to Friday. Teaching 6 or 7 lessons of 45 minutes per day to adults of mixed levels and different nationalities, in classes of about 10 students. Min. work period 2 weeks between 1 June and 30 August. Must have first degree in foreign languages/English literature and RSA Prep. Certificate in TEFL.

Help cannot be given in finding accommodation. Applicants from America, Canada, New Zealand and Australia will be considered.
*Applications* from 28 February to the Academic Manager, Richard Language College.

**SOUTHBOURNE SCHOOL OF ENGLISH:** 30 Beaufort Road, Bournemouth BH6 5AL (☎01202-422300; fax 01202-417108; e-mail details@southbourneschool.co.uk; www.southbourneschool.co.uk). A family run school, working for 34 years teaching English as a foreign language. British Council accredited and a member of ARELS and STB.
**EFL Teachers (20).** Wages £9.00 per hour; to work 15-30 hours per week. Must have one of the following qualifications; PGCE, B.ed., Cert Ed., RSA Cert EFL, RSD Diploma EFL, TESOL, Trinity Diploma.
**Sports Organisers/Assistants (8).** Wages £180-£300. Either residential or to work 30 hours a week. Sports training useful. Minibus driver useful.
Free accommodation on residential courses. Staff required from mid June-end August.
*Applications* from Easter to the Principal, at the above address.

**SUL LANGUAGE SCHOOLS:** 7 Woodland Avenue, Tywardreath, Par, Cornwall PL24 2PL (☎01726-814227; fax 01726-813135; e-mail claire@sul-schools.com). A well-established business that provides language holiday courses in Cornwall, Devon, Somerset, Midlands, Ireland and Scotland for foreign teenagers. Courses run for 2-4 weeks from April to September.
**EFL Teachers.** Wages dependant on experience and qualifications but are usually from £23 per morning of 2½ hours. To work mornings and possibly afternoons, supervising activities. Teachers required from April-August for a minimum period of 2 weeks. Applicants should be TEFL qualified or hold a languages degree or teaching qualification. Accommodation is available at some centres.
*Applications* from January to Claire Frost at the above address. Interview usually required.

**TORBAY LANGUAGE CENTRE:** Conway Road, Paignton, Devon TQ4 5LH (☎01803-558555; fax 01803-559606; e-mail tlc@lalschool.org). A large school with very good resources. CELTA training centre so there is excellent teacher support and guidance. Maximum class size of ten students. Also runs a small residential centre in North Devon.
**EFL Teachers (40).** Wages £8.50 per hour; to teach an average of 22½ hours per week. Teachers required from last week of June to the third week of August for minimum of 2 weeks. Must be CELTA or equivalent or PGCE with TEFL experience. No accommodation available.
*Applications* from 1 March to the Director of Studies at the above address.

# Medical

**DAMARIS UK LTD:** Suite H, Astoria House, 165/6 Victoria Road, Swindon SN1 3BY(☎01793-617378; fax 01793-495150;e-mail nursingagency@damarisuk.co.uk).
**Care Assistants** needed all year round for shifts in nursing homes, residential homes etc. for a nursing agency. Wages from £6.15 per hour. Must have experience in care field. Age 18+. Own transport essential.
*Applications* to R. Battersmell, Director.

**ELITE CARE NURSING AGENCY:** 14 Silver Street, Barnstaple, Devon, EX32 8HR (☎01271-346666).
**Qualified Nurses (20)** To work in hospitals, nursing homes etc. Must be RGN/RMN.
**Care Assistants (30)** to work in clients' own homes or nursing homes as live-in carers. Carers must be at least 18 and have carework experience.
**Nursing Auxiliaries (30)** to work in district and cottage hospitals. Must be experienced carers and at least 18 years old.
Work available around the year. *Applications* to M. Eastaugh, Branch Manager at the above address.

**EXERCISE INDEPENDENCE:** 1 The Green, East Knoyle, Salisbury (tel/fax 01747-830504; e-mail live.aware@virgin.net; www.livingfocus.net). A disabled teacher of remedial exercise needs help from a team to establish a project from his own home around exercise, diet and living independently. Some group work and meditation.
**Carers/Personal Assistants (2).** to run house, look after and be part of an organised team in order to enable an active and disabled person to live a normal and healthy alternative lifestyle. Also train to assist in the community with exercises.
Wages negotiable, full board and accommodation. To work variable hours. Enquiries/applications invited all year round, especially mid-June, September and spring. Fluent English required.
*Applications* and enquiries should be made as soon as possible to Michael Mitchell at the above address, by e-mail or online.

**THORNBURY NURSING SERVICES:** 7 & 9 Whiteladies Road, Clifton, Bristol, BS8 1NN (☎0117-923 8443; fax 0118-973 2546; e-mail recruitment@thornbury-nursing.com).
**Registered and Auxilliary Nurses** to work nationwide carrying out day and night-shift agency nursing work in NHS and private hospitals and nursing homes. Wages are from £16.50 per hour for registered nurses, or from £9 per hour for auxiliary nurses, with holiday pay on top of the basic rates. Candidates must have 6-12 months experience (dependent on specialism) within the last two years of clinical nursing and NMC Registration for qualified nurses. All applicants must pass an interview prior to being accepted.
To obtain positions *contact* the agency at the above address.

# Outdoor

**BOLDSCAN LIMITED:** Unit 4 Tonedale Business Park, Wellington, Somerset TA21 OAW (☎01823-665849; fax 01283-665850). Manufactures marquees and hires them out to the event industry.
**Marquee Erectors (15-20)** Work involves the erection of marquees for local events, weddings and shows. Wages £4.00-£4.50 per hour, to work 40-60 hours per week. Applicants must be at least 18 years old. Period of work from April 1st to September 30th for a minimum of 4 weeks. Accommodation not available.
Applicants should *apply* from mid February to Mr P.Cornish at the above address. Interview necessary.

**BURNBAKE CAMPSITE:** Rempstone, Corfe Castle, Wareham, Dorset BH20 5JJ (☎01929-480570; e-mail info@burnbake.com; www.burnbake.com). Long established campsite.

**Campsite Assistants.** to handle enquiries, serve the shop, help with cleaning and rubbish collection and carry out general site maintenance and customer service duties. Wages of £170 per week with free mobile accommodation. To work 8am-12pm and 5pm-7pm over a 6 day week.

One required 5 May to 8 September, two needed 11 July to 5 September. For *applications* or further details, contact Tim Bircham at the above address.

**J.F. COLES t/a V.T. COLES:** Stephens Farm, Spaxton, Near Bridgwater, Somerset TA5 1BU (☎01278-671 281; fax 01278-671530).
**Pea and Bean Pickers (20).** Piece work rates, hours 7am-4pm. Minimum period of work 6 weeks between June and September. Accommodation: own tents required, water and portaloos available. No experience necessary. Overseas applicants welcome.

*Applications* from end of May to Mr and Mrs Coles at the above address.

**K.S. COLES:** Cheston House Farm, Cheston, Wellington, Somerset TA21 9HP (☎01823-664244; fax 01823-660325; e-mail kscoles@btinternet.com). Situated in one of the most attractive areas of England, K.S. Coles have been trading for over 30 years and now supply several of the major multiples with fresh produce.
**Pea Pickers (60 Or More).** Period of work approx. mid June to end August. Piece work at £2.50 per 21 lb picked. 5-6am start; 4.30pm finish. Minimum age 18.

*Applications* to Mrs C.M. Coles, Partner, or Miss S. Coles, at the above address.

**THE COURTS:** Holt, Trowbridge, Wiltshire BA14 6RR (tel/fax 01225-782340). A twentieth century creation in the style of Hidcote Manor, 7 acres in total, with an arboretum.
**Gardener (1).** To work with three others maintaining an important National Trust garden. To work variable hours from 1 March to November. Min. period of work one month. Min. age 20. Applicants should be motivated with some experience. Overseas applicants welcome. Free accommodation available.

*Apply* from 1 March to the Head Gardener, at the above address. Note that it is preferable for candidates to be available for an interview.

**CUTLIFFE FARM:** Sherford, Taunton, Somerset TA1 3RQ (☎01823-253808).The farm is within easy walking distance from Taunton town centre, with all the facilities available in a large country town.
**Fruit Pickers (30+)** to pick strawberries, raspberries, runner beans, plums, etc. Wages at piece work rate plus bonuses. Period of work late May to early August. Some accommodation may be available in caravans. Min. age 18. Overseas applicants welcome, provided they have obtained the necessary work visa.

*Applications* to A.P. & S.M. Parris at the above address.

**M. J. DAVISON:** Ploddy House, Newent, Gloucestershire GL18 1JX (☎01531-820240).
**Farm Assistants.** Varied range of work to be performed on arable and poultry farm. Wages at Agricultural Wages Board rates or piecework rates. Min. period of work of 1 month between May and October. Early starts when required. Applicants must be over 18 and authorised to work in the UK. Accommodation will be in own tent but washing, cooking and toilet facilities are available.

*Applications* to M. J. Davison, Owner, at the above address from March onwards.

**THE DORSET BLUEBERRY COMPANY:** Hampreston, Wimborne, Dorset BH21 7LX (☎01202-579342; fax 01202-579014; www.dorset-blueberry.com/jobs). Britain's primary producers of fresh blueberries for major supermarkets.
**Pickers and Packers** required. Wages are calculated by kg performance and good workers can earn high wages. Positions availaby from July to September.
*Applications* only accepted through the above website.

**GRAND WESTERN HORSEBOAT CO:** The Wharf, Canal Hill, Tiverton, Devon EX16 4HX (☎01884-253345; www.horseboat.co.uk). A family run business operating horsedrawn barge trips on a delightful canal providing peace, tranquility, wildlife and nature.
**Crew Member** for the horsedrawn barge. Will include working with heavy horses, steering, roping and team work. Pay meets National Minimum Wage. From 4 days per week, longer in high season. Position available from May to September. Must be flexible, fit, polite and of clean appearance. Applicants should be 25+ and hold a driving licence. Accommodation not available.
*Applications* should be made to Mrs P. Brind from 1 April at the above address.

**HAYLES FRUIT FARM LTD:** Winchombe, Cheltenham, Glos. GL54 5PB (☎01242-602123; fax 01242-603320; e-mail jobs@hayles-fruit-farm.co.uk; www.hayles-fruit-farm.co.uk). A very friendly family run mixed fruit farm in a beautiful rural location in the Cotswolds. A subsidised hot meal can be provided every evening for people staying in tents.
**Fruit Pickers (10)** to work 8am to 4pm, picking apples, pears, plums or nuts. Piecework rates, approx. £20-£35 per day. No experience necessary. Min. period of work 3-5 weeks between August and end of September. Min. age 21 years. No accommodation provided. Campsite available.
*Applications* from 1 July to Mr Martin Harrall at the above address.

**MICHAEL H. KEENE & SON LTD:** The Moat, Newent, Gloucestershire GL18 1JG (☎01531-820363). A family run farming company producing apples for supermarkets, cider apples for the cider industry and blackcurrants for the blackcurrant juice market. Situated in an attractive tourist area within easy reach of shops in Cheltenham and Gloucester.
**Apple Pickers (12)** required for careful hand-picking. Payment is by recognised hourly rates. To work from 8am to 4pm, starting 1 September. Instruction will be given in how to pick carefully. A campsite with showers, toilets and electric cooker is available, but must bring own tent, cooking utensils, wet-weather clothes and boots. There is some mobile home accommodation: please check for availability. A sitting area with TV also provided. No dogs allowed. Please note that applicants from outside the EEA must have permits to work in the UK.
For *applications* call 01531-820363 or 07973-764166 in early August to confirm starting dates.

**KENTON FRUIT:** 2 Ford Farm Court, Manihead Road, Kenton, Exeter EX6 8LZ (☎01626-891871; fax 01626-891750; e-mail kentonfruit@aol.com). Situated on the edge of a village with pubs and easy transport to Exeter (4 miles).
**Strawberry Pickers (up to 6).** Piece work rates of £1.50 for a tray of ten half pound punnets, i.e. 30p per pound picked, which should ensure an hourly rate in excess of the Minimum Wage. Workers can choose their own working hours to suit themselves. Period of work from June 1-September 30. Accommodation not provided, but it may be possible to pitch a tent on site. Applicants should be physically fit with a good pair

of hands and the ability to sustain physical work for several hours each day.
*Applications* to Brian Berman, Proprietor, at the above address.

**J.G. MARQUEES:** Nettwood Farm, East Harptree, Bristol, BS40 6DA (tel/fax 01761-221372).
**Marquee Erectors.** Wages from £4.30-£5.50 per hour. To work 8.30am-5.30pm Monday to Friday. Positions are available from mid-June to September. Applicants must be able to drive to get to work.
*Applications* should be made to Jeremy Griffin, Proprietor, at the above address.

**NEWTOWN FARM:** Newent, Gloucestershire GL18 1JX (☎01531-820240).
**Assistants (20+)** to plant and cut lettuce. Wages at Agricultural Wages Board rates or piecework. To work 5-6 days a week when required. Early start necessary, often 6am. Period of work May to October: preference given to those who can start in May. Accommodation provided on a campsite with shower and toilets; some self-catering accommodation also available at a charge. All applicants must be over 18 and physically fit. EU/EEA nationals and overseas applicants with work permits welcome.
*Applications*, enclosing s.a.e., to Mr J. Davison at Ploddy House, Newent, Glos. GL18 1JX.

**POWNEY BROTHERS:** 16 Jockey Lane, Bromham, Chippenham, Wilts SN15 2EZ (☎01380-850340).
**Vegetable Harvester/Planter** to work from June to October. £3.80 per hour, variable hours. Accommodation possible. Age 16+.
*Applications* to D. Powney, Owner.

**PENROSE MARQUEES:** Trevellas, St Agnes, Cornwall TR5 0XS (☎01872-552494; fax 01872-554106).
**Marquee Erectors (2-3)** Wages dependent on experience; hours of work vary so employees must be available 7 days a week. Positions available between May and September.
*Applications* to Rik Evans at the above address.

**SHULDHAM SOFT FRUIT GROWERS LTD:** East Stoke House, Stoke-sub-Hamdon, Somerset TA14 6UF (☎01935-822300; fax 01935-824596; e-mail shuldham@aol.com). Set in beautiful countryside in southeast Somerset. Nearby towns for good shopping and nightlife. Excellent transport links. Family business, small and friendly.
**Pickers/General Farm Hands (8)** needed from 20 May to 31 August to pick soft fruits including strawberries, blackberries, tayberries, gooseberries, raspberries and redcurrants, weather permitting during harvest. After the harvest, to carry out general husbandry of the farm and land. To work up to 6 days a week 6-8 hours per day. May involve early starts (6-6.30am) usually finishing at about midday. Some late afternoon picking. Minimum of £4.10 p.h., up to £6/£7 per hour possible. No accommodation provided but camping with own gear if necessary at nearby campsites. Applicants should be strong, determined and conscientious. Foreign applicants with appropriate permits or visas welcome.
*Applications* to Simon Shuldham, Managing Director.

**SIMPSON & SIMPSON MARQUEE HIRE:** Unit 8, Elm Tree Business Park, Sheepway, Portbury, Bristol, BS20 7TF (☎01275-372237; fax 01275-372728; e-

mail enquiries@marquees-simpson.co.uk).
**Marquee Erectors (6)** required from mid-June until mid-September to erect marquees. The work is paid at £4 per hour and is usually made up of ten hours or more per day over a 5 day week, with some weekend work. Employees must be over 18 and a full driving licence would be helpful, but not essential.
*Applications* should be made to G. Davies, Operations Manager.

**SOUTH DEVON ORGANIC PRODUCERS LTD:** Wash Bath, Buckfastleigh, Devon TQ11 0LD (☎01803-762100; fax 01803-762100; e-mail sdop@farmersweekly.net). Organic vegetable growers.
**Casual Field Staff (10-20)**. To weed, plant and harvest organic field scale vegetables. Minimum agricultural wage. To work 39 hours plus overtime; flexible hours. Positions are available from June to September/October. No previous experience necessary. Foreign applicants with necessary work permits welcome; fluent English not essential. Minimum age 17. No accommodation available.
*Applications* should be made from the end of May onwards to Mrs Michael Vanstone at the above address. Telephone interview sufficient.

**STUART LINE CRUISES:** 5 Camperdown Terrace, Exmouth, Devon EX8 1EJ (☎01395-279693; fax 01395-279693; e-mail info@stuartlinecruises.co.uk). Passenger boat operator in Devon.
**Boat Crew(2)**. Wages from £100-£150 per week. Flexible hours. Positions available for the summer. Fluent English helpful. No accommodation available. No experience necessary as full training is given. Minimum age 16.
*Applications* should be made to Ian Stuart at the above address. Interview required.

**WHITE MOTOR BOATS:** 7 Old Station Road, Upwey, Weymouth, Dorset DT3 5NQ (tel/fax 01305-813246; mobile ☎0777-8286892). Tourist passenger boat operators plying between Weymouth and Portland.
**Coxswain (1/2)**. Wages £6 per hour. Boatmasters grade 1 or 2, VHF certificate, sea survival, basic first aid, and fire fighting certificate.
**Coxswain's mate (1/2)**. Wages £4.50 per hour. No qualifications required as training given but boating experience useful.
To work 8 hours for 7 days a week but could be full or part-time. Positions are available from April 1 to October 31. Good customer skills plus public safety, smart appearance and dress code important. Foreign applicants welcome if English is proficient. No accommodation available.
*Applications* to Mr Ian Robertson at the above address from February. Interview necessary.

# Sport

**CHRISTCHURCH BOROUGH COUNCIL:** Civic Offices, Bridge Street, Christchurch, Dorset BH23 1AZ (☎01202-495000; fax 01202-482200; g.foyle@christchurch.gov.uk). Christchurch's beaches are friendly, neighbourhood beaches which have not been commercialised with the lively, cosmopolitan town of Bournemouth close by. Christchurch is a great place to work, rest and play.
**Beach Lifeguards (4)**. Wages £4.75 per hour. To work 9:30am-6pm Thursday-Tuesday. Period of work July-September. NARS Beach Lifeguard preferable, but will accept RLSS Bronze Medallion (with training).
**Seasonal Leisure Assistants (4)**. Wages £4.75-£6 per hour. To work 9am-5pm

Thursday to Monday. Needed April-September. Leisure qualifications would be an advantage.
**Patrol Boat Crew (4)** Wages £5-£6 per hour. Hours vary according to local tides. Needed April-September. RYA Powerboat Level 2 and above.
*Applications* to Gary Foyle, Leisure Operations Supervisor.

**GREENBANK SWIMMING POOL:** Wilfrid Road, Street, Somerset BA16 0EU (☎01458-442468). A very busy, privately run open-air swimming pool with over 1,000 bathers during hot periods.
**Lifeguards (3)** to lifeguard and clean the pool and premises. Wages from £4.30 per hour. To work a minimum of 35 hours per week on a rota basis. Standby required during busy periods. Min. period of work of May to September. Royal Life Saving Society's National Pool Lifequard Qualification expected. No accommodation available.
*Applications*, including a reference, should be made from between 1 March and the end of April to Mr D. Mogg, Pool Manager, at the above address. Interview necessary.

**KNOWLE MANOR & RIDING CENTRE:** Timberscombe, Minehead, Somerset TA24 6TZ (☎01643-841342; fax 01643-841644; e-mail knowlemnr@aol.com; www.ridingholidaysuk.com). Knowle Manor is a residential riding holiday centre based in Exmoor National Park. Set in 80 acres of grounds with indoor heated swimming pool, trout lake, croquet and badminton areas.
**Riding Instructor** to work 5 days a week. Salary £160+ per week. Applicants must have B.H.S.A.I.
**Ride Leaders (2)** to work approx. 40 hours a week. Salary £144+ per week. Experience with horses essential. Recommended B.H.S. Riding and Road Safety. Mature outlook also needed. Minimum age 18.
**Domestic Helpers (3)** to clean and to perform waiting duties in hotel. Wages £147 per week. To work approx. 35 hours a week. No experience necessary but applicants must be cheerful.
Minimum period of work for all positions July to end of August or preferably September/October. B & L charge calculated on hourly rate and deducte from wage (wages listed are approximate after deductions). Suitably qualified foreign applicants welcome.
*Applications* from February onwards to Sue Lamacraft at the above address.

**MENDIP OUTDOOR PURSUITS:** Laurel Farmhouse, Summer Lane, Banwell, Weston-Super-Mare BS29 6LP (☎01934-820518; www.outdoorpursuits.uk.com). A multi-activity mobile centre established in 1987 for clients aged 8 years and above. Training available in safety, education, technical skills and NVQs.
**Instructors.** £180+ per week. Min. age 21.
All instructors to work 5 days per week. Must hold qualifications in outdoor pursuits. Accommodation is **not** provided. Min. period of work 2 weeks between June and September. Overseas applicants able to communicate well in English welcome. All candidates must be available for interview.
*Applications* to J. Hayward at the above address.

**MILL ON THE BRUE ACTIVITY CENTRE:** Trendle Farm, Bruton, Somerset BA10 0BA (☎01749-812307; fax 01749-812706; e-mail millonthebrue@compuserve.com). An outdoor activity centre (2 hours from London, 1 hour from Bath and Bristol) offering activities such as canoeing, climbing, archery etc.

**Domestic Staff.** £155-£162 based on 42 hour week. Accommodation and board provided. Min age 17 years. English lessons provided for overseas applicants. Needed January to beginning of December.
**Group Leaders.** Wages from £142.20 to £162 per week; based on a 46 hour week with deductions made for board and accommodation. Min. age 19. Qualifications such as First Aid and advantage. Staff required from June/July until the end of August. Applicants must attend a 24 hour selection in March and a training week. Overseas applicants welcome though require good level of English. Long term instructors, residential post, employed January-November.

*Application* forms from Ruth Braithwaite, Mill on the Brue Activity Centre.

**ROCKLEY WATERSPORTS:** Poole, Dorset BH15 4RW (☎01202-677272; fax 01202-668268; e-mail info@rockleywatersports.com). Based in beautiful Poole Harbour and South-West France, Rockley teach watersports to all abilities and ages and are one of Europe's most highly regarded watersports centres.
**Watersports Instructors (50).** Experienced instructors, senior instructors and sailing managers required.
**Couriers (10)** for duties including assisting in the kitchens, cleaning and general site duties.
The jobs offer the opportunity to gain watersports experience and use all the centre facilities. Staff required for the summer season, March to October.

For an *application form* contact Richard Percy at the above address.

**WEST-ANSTEY FARM EXMOOR:** Dulverton, Somerset TA22 9RY (☎01398-341354). A working farm and stables adjoining open moorland four miles from Dulverton, the nearest town. Lovely riding county, moorlands, fields and woods.
**Riding Assistants (2).** Must be able to take out rides and lead beginners when necessary. Hours vary depending on schedule of activities. Min. age 16. Must be fairly light, a good rider and with experience of going on riding holidays or of conducting treks and caring for ponies, horses and people. Sense of fun, helpfulness and a cheerful disposition essential. Must also be willing to help indoors when necessary.

Pocket money plus B & L provided. Applicants must be non-smokers and able to get on with both adults and children. Accommodation only available for females. Work available all year round. Min. work period 8-10 weeks.

*Applications* with a contact phone number and photograph a.s.a.p. to the Proprietor, West-Anstey Farm Exmoor.

# Voluntary Work

## Conservation and the Environment

**THE MONKEY SANCTUARY:** Looe, Cornwall PL13 1NZ (☎01503-262532; e-mail info@monkeysnctuary.org; www.monkeysanctuary.org). Home to a colony of Woolly Monkeys and Rescue Centre for ex-pet Capuchins. The Sanctuary is a community dedicate to conservation, sustainable living and animal welfare. Education of the public in these areas is their main summer activity.
**Volunteers** are required to work 40 hours per week in the sanctuary, and are essential in allowing the team of keepers to care for the colony. Help is needed in the kiosk, and with cleaning while the sanctuary is open to the public between April and September; during the closed season (October to March) volunteers assist with general

maintenance work and cleaning. No qualifications are necessary but workers must have an interest in animal welfare and conservation.
Food and accommodation are provided, and volunteers are asked to make a voluntary donation to the Monkey Sanctuary Trust (suggested £35 per week waged, £30 per week students/unwaged). Min. age 18. Overseas applicants with a good standard of English welcome.

*Applications*, four or five months in advance, should be made to Mike Brown at the above address, enclosing stamped s.a.e. or International Reply Coupon.

## Heritage

**LUNDY COMPANY:** Lundy Island, Bristol Channel, North Devon EX39 2LY (☎01237-431831; fax 01237-431832; e-mail warden@lundyisland.co.uk).
Lundy is an island off the North Devon coast managed by the Landmark Trust with 23 letting properties, a pub and a shop.
**Volunteer Positions.** There are various outdoor positions available involving conservation and farm work and general island duties. The jobs are variable according to the time of year. Volunteers need no experience but must have lots of enthusiasm. Accommodation is provided free of charge and there is a reduced fare on boat trips. Volunteers are required from April to September for a minimum of 1 week.

*Applications* should be sent to the Warden at the above address from January onwards.

## Social and Community Schemes

**LEE ABBEY COMMUNITY:** The Warden, Lee Abbey, Lynton, Devon EX35 6JJ (☎01598-752621; e-mail relax@leeabbey.org.uk; www.leeabbey.org.uk).
A Christian holidays and conference centre run by a community working for the renewal and refreshment of the church.
**Volunteers.** Board, lodging and pocket money provided. Minimum stay 1 year. Minimum age 18. Volunteers must be committed Christians. No qualifications necessary. Foreign applicants with fluent English welcome.

*Applications* should be made to the above address. Applicants should give information about themselves, their background and why they would like to join the community.

# Vacation Traineeships & Internships

## Law

**BURGES SALMON SOLICITORS:** Narrow Quay House, Narrow Quay, Bristol BS1 4AH (☎0117-902 7733; fax 0117-902 4400; e-mail alexandra.van-hattum@burges-salmon.com; www.burges-salmon.co.uk).
Burges Salmon is a leading regional law firm with a reputation for quality and an ability to attract people and clients normally regarded as the preserve of City firms. Based in Bristol some 75% of the firm's clients are situated outside its South West base and over recent years, Burges Salmon has witnessed an extraordinarily high and sustainable rate of growth. The firm provides national and international clients with a full commercial service through five departments: Company Commercial, Commercial Litigation, Property, Tax and Trusts, and Agriculture,

Property Litigation and Environment (APLE). Specialist areas of the firm include: agribusiness, banking, competition, corporate finance, dispute resolution, e-commerce, environment, human resources, IP and IT, and transport.
Full fees are paid for both the CPE and LPC and maintenance grants of £4,500 LPC and £5,000 CPE (£2,000 p.a.).
**Places** for 2003: 34; Duration: 2 weeks; Remuneration; £150 per week; Closing Date; 21 February 2003, 20-25 training contracts for September 2005.
*Applications* and queries to Miss Alexandra van Hattum, Graduate Recruitment Officer, at the above address.

## Science, Construction and Engineering

**DEVONPORT MANAGEMENT LIMITED:** Devonport Royal Dockyard, Devonport, Plymouth P21 4SG (☎01752-605665; fax 01752-323656; nicola.bleddyn@devonport.co.uk; www.devonport.co.uk)
Traineeships are offered in Production, Projects, Nuclear Safety and Design Areas. There are available **6 Sixth-form Placements** for 10 weeks, **6 Undergraduate Positions** for 16 weeks during the summer, and there are **6 Sandwich Year Positions (YIA).**
Applicants should be Sixth-formers wishing for a career in Engineering and Undergraduates should be reading Engineering Degrees. Wages are available on request.
The traineeships are based in Devonport. No accommodation is provided but help is available for arranging lodgings and finding contacts.
Any suitably qualified applicants will be considered but all applicants will need to be cleared with the Ministry of Defence Security. This is not possible for many non-nationals.
*Applications* should be made to the HR Manager (GPGS) at the above address, preferably by e-mail.

**MESSIER-DOWTY LTD:** Cheltenham Road East, Gloucester GL2 9QH (☎01452-712424; fax 01452-713821; e-mail sarah.powell@messier-dowty.org; www.messier-dowty.com).
Messier-Dowty is a world leader in the design, development and manufacture of landing gear systems, with an annual turnover of US$540 million. The company's capability is the supply of fully integrated landing gear systems for a wide range of aircraft including large commercial, regional, business, military and helicopters.
**3 or 4 Engineering and Manufacturing based Traineeships** are offered which will be over the summer or for a full year. Wages of approx £1,000 per month. Summer positions will be for a period of 12 weeks, the offer of a year in industry is mostly for post A-level students lasting from September to August. Traineeships will be in Gloucester. Some assistance may be provided to find accommodation.
*Applications* should be made from as soon as possible to Sarah Powell at the above address.

**RENISHAW PLC:** New Mills, Wotton-under-Edge, Gloucestershire GL12 8JR (☎01453-524432; fax 01453-524404; e-mail recruitment@renishaw.com; www.renishaw.com).
A British engineering company specialising in metrology. They design and manufacture high precision metrology equipment and systems, and exports account for 90% of its sales. Employs 1,200 people in 20 countries.
**Work Placements.** Wages from £200-220 per week. Placements last between 6

and 13 weeks. Available to undergraduates currently studying towards a degree in engineering or physics. Placements are based in rural Gloucestershire, so students must have their own transport.

*Applications* should be made in January to the above address, e-mailed in Microsoft Word format or made online. Interviews take place in mid-February.

**TYCO ELECTRONICS UK LIMITED:** Faraday Road, Dorcan, Swindon, Wiltshire SN3 5HH.

Tyco specialises in the design and development of radiation chemistry techniques for commercial applications and applied technologies for industrial use. It has invested large amounts of research money into the treatment of plastics by high energy electronic beam radiation.

The company offers limited **Vacation Placements** to students reading for degrees in Chemistry, Physics, Electronics, Electronic, Mechanical or Manufacturing Engineering and Materials Technology, although other scientific disciplines may also be appropriate. Experience is useful but not essential. Positions are available between June and October and are based in Swindon.

*Applications* should be sent by the end of March to Tyco Electronics Recruitment, c/o Pertemps Recruitment Partnership, 102 Commercial Road, Swindon, Wiltshire, SW1 5PT.

# The South Coast

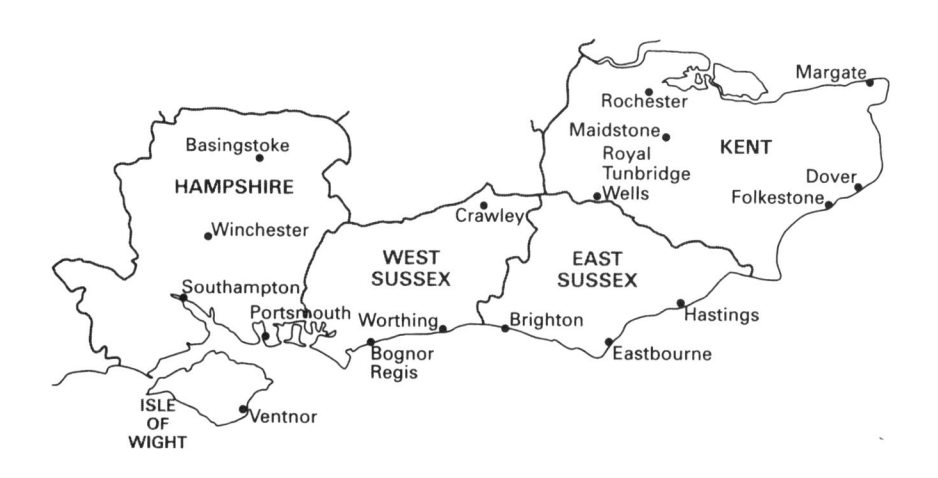

**Prospects for Work.**
Hotel and catering jobs should not be too hard to come by along the southern coast as long as you begin your search in good time. In Hastings, for example, many hotels open just for the holiday season and vacancies are generally for unskilled workers. Early enquiries are advisable in view of the likely difficulties in finding accommodation. Holiday camps in the area, such as the Combe Haven Holiday Park or Pontins at Camber Sands, always need seasonal summer staff. For details of work in the Hastings area contact Hastings Jobcentre on 01424-784300.

Eastbourne has roughly ten times as many hotels as Hastings and throughout the season all types of hotel and catering vacancies are available. A large number of seafront kiosks also need staffing throughout the summer. Eastbourne hosts an annual Airborne week that attracts hundreds of thousands of visitors and staff are required to sell programmers, act as stewards and clean up afterwards. Eastbourne Jobcentre (1-3 Langney Road, Eastbourne BN21 3QF; ☎01323-532444) operates a student register throughout the summer and Christmas seasons that endeavours to match students to suitable vacancies. Anyone wanting to look for work in the area can contact Jobseeker Direct at Ashdown House Jobcentre on 0845-6060 234; for the price of a local telephone call staff can complete a comprehensive jobsearch of vacancies locally or nationwide. You can also search for yourself at www.worktrain.gov.uk.

Holiday camps in West Sussex always need seasonal staff too. Bognor Regis Jobcentre (01243-224200) is the main contact for Butlins, the largest employer in the region. Butlins is just one of the many holiday camps along the South Coast; others include Sussex Beach Holiday Village, Sussex Coast Holiday Village, Church Farm Holiday Village and Pontins Ltd in Combe Sands, near Rye. Most of these provide live-in accommodation as well.

Eastbourne has roughly ten times as many hotels as Hastings, and hotels always have a problem recruiting staff. A large number of seafront kiosks also need staffing throughout the summer. Eastbourne also hosts an annual Airborne Week which attracts hundreds of thousands of visitors and staff are always needed. Eastbourne Jobcentre (1-3 Langney Road, Eastbourne BN21 3QF, ☎01323-532444) operates a student register that endeavours to match students with suitable summer work.

As well as work connected with the tourist industry, southern England is a good area for agricultural work, particularly in the hop fields and orchards of Kent (the 'Garden of England') during September. Around Ramsgate on the south Kentish coast, greenhouses require people to pick tomatoes for much of the summer season. Thanks to technology and new crops, it is possible to find agricultural work at any time of year. Wages are not bad, but be prepared for an early morning start. Seasonal jobs of this kind are advertised in the Ramsgate Jobcentre (☎01843-258258), although they note that the amount of work available has reduced, so you need to start looking reasonably early.

The South Coast is one of the principal areas for English language schools, which require teachers, youth leaders and supervisors. The majority of schools can be found at coastal resorts: Hastings, Bexhill, Eastbourne, Brighton, Hove and Bognor Regis, and in Tunbridge Wells, Thanet and Canterbury inland.

Sporting activities, like Cowes Week on the Isle of Wight (end of July/beginning of August) generate a short-term requirement for staff to help with catering, marshalling and car parking. In Southampton, exhibiting companies employ canvassers during the weeks running up to the Boat Show at Olympia in London. Southampton Jobcentre can be contacted at 61-64 High Street, Southampton (☎023-8053 8600) for more information.

Both Jersey and Guernsey have thriving tourist industries, and the fact that Jersey is exempt from VAT, capital gains tax or inheritance tax means that financial services thrive there. However, potential jobseekers should be aware that Jersey retains the right to deport non-UK Nationals; even EEA/EU citizens need a work permit before they can be employed in the Channel Islands.

# Business and Industry

**CHILSTONE GARDEN ORNAMENTS:** Victoria Park, Fordcombe Road, Langton Green, Kent TN3 ORD (☎01892-740866; fax 01892-740249). Manufacturers of reconstituted stone architectural items and garden ornaments.
**Workshop Helpers (20)** to help with the mixing, etc. Must be strong and energetic.
**Office Assistant** to help with general office duties. Typing would be an advantage.
Wages and hours by arrangement. Interesting and varied work available throughout the year. Applicants must find own accommodation.
*Applications* to the Manager at the above address.

**LE COCQS STORES:** Alderney, Channel Isles GY9 3TR (☎01481-824646; fax 01481-824189; e-mail shop@lecocqs.com).
**Staff (4)** to operate the check out, fill the shelves, deliver and warehousing duties. Wages of £4.40-£5.00 per hour beach; flights to Alderney provided free of charge. Flexible working hours. Period of work from June to September. Cheap local accommodation available on campsite by the beach. Minimum age 20.
*Applications* to Noel Hayes, Director, at the above address.

**ORDNANCE SURVEY:** Romsey Road, Maybush, Southampton, Hampshire SO16 4GU (☎023-8079 2141 fax 023-8079 2572; e-mail recruitment@ordsvy.gov.uk.
**Temporary Staff** required; *contact* the above address for details.

**REGENT LANGUAGE HOLIDAYS:** 40-42 Queens Road, Brighton BN1 3XB (☎01273-718620; fax 01273-718621; e-mail holidays@regent.org.uk; www.regent.org.uk). Regent operates five high quality residential centres in Southern England. They specialise in summer language holidays.
**Administrative Assistants (4).** £200-250 per week. Full board and accommodation provided. Graduate, proven accounting/banking experience/skills.
*Applications* at any time to Recruitment at the above address.

**SATURDAY VENTURE ASSOCIATION:** PO Box 9, Chichester, West Sussex PO20 7YD (tel/fax 01243-513464; e-mail SVA2@btinternet.com; www.SVA2@talk.com.) A small national charity currently promoting disability awareness in the community. Sets up projects to form nationwide support for clubs and activities for young disabled people.
**Project Workers (2).** Involves research, correspondence and fund raising. Wages from £5 per hour. To work 15-20 hours weekly. Must have own transport and be a non-smoker. A-Level plus and graduates preferred. No accommodation available.
Positions are available from January 2003. *Applications* should be made as soon as possible to Jenny Bembridge via fax or telephone (as above).

**SYSTEMSOLID LTD:** The Sanderson Centre, 15 Lees Lane, Gosport, Hampshire PO12 3UL (☎02392-524331; fax 02392-510287; sales@sanderson-centre.com).
**Decorator/Handy Person (1)** needed from 1 July to 30 September to perform general decorating and other manual duties. Hours from 9am-5pm. Wages on application.
*Contact* Mr A.C. Smith, Director.

**TONY FRESKO ICE CREAM:** Warren Farm, White Lane, Ash Green, Aldershot, Hampshire GU12 6HW (☎01252-315528; fax 01252-334537; e-mail icecream@tonyfresko.freeserve.co.uk). Mobile ice-cream outlet, with a fleet of fifteen vans.
**Drivers (25)** for mobile ice cream sales at various shows and fetes and on rounds of industrial and housing estates. Wages from £7 to £10 per hour. To work approx. 11am-9pm, 7 days of the week available. Min. period of work of 6 weeks. Positions are available from March to October. Full driving licence required. Foreign applicants with appropriate work permits and acceptable spoken English welcome. No accommodation available.
*Applications* should be made from February onwards to Mr J Sawyer at the above address. Interview necessary.

# Children

**DWEEZILS ADVENTURE CENTRE:** c/o Asda Stores, Newgate Lane, Fareham, Hants PO14 1TT (☎01329-221956). Provides a warm, friendly and safe environment for childrens play, parties and various playgroup activity sessions. Looks after children for very short periods whilst their parents shop in the adjoining supermarket.
**Playleader (2)** to work flexible hours at a creche open seven days a week from July 24 to September 3. Jobs involves interaction with children from 2 years nine months to nine years, cash handling and minimal paperwork. Some childcare

experience necessary; some qualifications in childcare preferable. Minimum age 18. Accommodation *not* available.
*Applications* to Marie Hooper, Centre Manager.

**3D EDUCATION AND ADVENTURE LTD:** Business Support, Osmington Bay, Weymouth, Dorset DT3 6EG (☎01305-836226; fax 01305-834070; e-mail darren@3d-education.co.uk; www.3d-jobs.co.uk). 3D is a specialist provider of activity and educational experiences for young people. Owned by Center Parcs, 3D has been operating since 1991 and gone from strength to strength year on year.
**Activity Instructors (500)** Employed and trained as either multi-activity instructor, field studies instructor, specialist watersports instructor or IT instructor, staff will work with children at specialist holiday centres across the south of England as well as across the UK and Europe with Pontins and Center Parcs.

Field studies instructors must hold or at least be gaining a relevant degree. IT instructors need to have a broad range of IT skills. Any sports coaching awards or national governing body awards are advantageous, if applying for Activity instructor and Watersports instructor positions, although those with relevant experience will be considered. Training courses are held from late January through to July, so there is plenty of opportunity to develop your skills and qualifications.

Most important is an applicant's enthusiasm, personality and energy, coupled with a true desire to work in the outdoor leisure industry. Excellent accommodation and catering packages are offered with payment and working hours as covered by minimum wage and working time legislation. Minimum period of work 14 weeks.

*Applicants* should telephone 01305-836226 for a recruitment pack or visit http://www.3d-jobs.uk between September and June. Before employment all applicants must complete a residential training programme in the UK.

**HOLIDAY CLUB 4KIDS:** Vinalls Business Centre, Neptown Road, Henfield, West Sussex BN5 9DZ (☎01273-494455; fax 01273-494451; info@holidayclub 4kids.com).
**Activity Coaches (25)** £40 per day. Hours 8.30am to 4.30pm. To run a range of activities for children aged 4-11 years including sports, art and crafts, dance, drama and music. Teaching qualifications useful, but not essential. Must like children and some experience of working with them. Minimum age 17. No accommodation provided.
**Programme Managers (4)** for management of holiday club's team of coaches. £65-£85 per day. Childcare or teaching qualifications required.
All positions available from 29th July to 23 August. *Apply* to Lyn Povey.

**LEISURE SERVICES:** Council Offices, Rushmoor Borough Council, Farnborough Road, Farnborough, Hampshire GU14 7JU (☎01252-398745).
**Playleaders** needed every school holiday to help organise a daily programme of activities and events for children aged 5-11. Wages £5.38 per hour. Accommodation is not available. Hours: 8:30am-5:30pm (with a break for lunch) from Monday to Friday. Period of work every school holiday except Christmas. Min. age 18. Applicants should have experience of working with children and be good organisers. Sports coaching qualifications and arts and crafts skills would be an advantage. 2 day training course provided.
*Applications* all year round to D.A. Wall at the above address.

**LTC INTERNATIONAL COLLEGE:** Compton Park, Compton Place Road, Eastbourne, East Sussex BN21 1EH (☎01323-727755; fax 01323-728279; e-mail l

earnenglish@ltccollege.demon.co.uk). A friendly private language school running residential courses for young learners. Set in a mansion house in its own park, 20 minutes walk from Eastbourne town centre.
**Residential Social Organisers (4)** Wages £165 per week for 40 hours per week; must be flexible as hours not 9-5. Free board and lodging. Would suit people interested in sport and/or music who like working with young students aged 10-16.

Contact the above address for *further details*.

**VILLAGE CAMPS:** Personnel Office, Dept 815, Rue de la Morache 14, 1260 Nyon, Switzerland (☎+41 22-9909400 (English); fax +41 22-9909494; e-mail personnel@villagecamps.ch; www.villagecamps.com). Village Camps has been organising camps, tours and activity holidays for children for over 25 years. Set up in 1972 to serve the international community in Geneva, it has now developed into an organisation that leads sports, language, activity and leadership camps for children throughout Europe.
**Support Staff (Chefs, Kitchen Staff, Bar/Tuck Shop Staff, House Keepers, House Counsellors), Drivers, Counsellors and Activity Specialists** in swimming, archery, tennis, outdoor education, soccer, arts and crafts, mountain biking, gymnastics and drama.
**Nurses.** Qualified RSN or equivalent.

All the above required to work in childrens' spring, summer, autumn and winter camps in the UK and Europe. Experience of working with children and knowledge of a second language is an advantage. Accommodation and board are provided. Accident and liability insurance is provided, along with a generous allowance. All staff must be 21 or over. Minimum period of work 2 weeks. Suitably qualified foreign applicants are welcome. A telephone interview is required.

Go to the above website for more information or contact the above address for an *application pack*.

## Holiday Centres and Amusements

**ATHERFIELD BAY HOLIDAY CAMP:** Chale, Ventnor, Isle of Wight PO38 2JD. Small family owned holiday centre providing holidays for school parties, families and the over 50s. Situated 8 miles from Ventnor on a cliff top, in 14 acres of grounds, and on own foreshore.
**Waiting Staff (8), Kitchen Porters (8), Bar Staff (2), Snack Bar Assistants (4), Stillroom Assistants (2).** Basic weekly wage £90, Free B & L.

All staff to work approx. 36 hours a week. Employment from 5 May to early October. Min. period of work 12 weeks. Experience not essential but must have friendly personality. Use of camp facilities when off duty. Min. age girls 16, boys 17. Training given.

*Applications*, which must include a s.a.e. for a quick reply, from 15 March to Mrs M. Williamson, Atherfield Bay Holiday Camp.

**BRIGHTON SEA LIFE CENTRE:** Marine Parade, Brighton, Sussex BN2 1TB (01273-604234; fax 01273-681840).
**Catering/Retail/Admission Staff (1-2).** Work entails stocking up and pricing goods, including one stock-take, light cleaning, till work, greeting the public and selling the centre's guide book. Wages on application.

*Applications* to the Personnel Manager at the above address. Interview necessary.

**BUCKLEYS YESTERDAY'S WORLD:** 89/90 High Street, Battle, East Sussex TN33 0AQ (☎01424-774269; e-mail info@yesterdaysworld.co.uk; www.yesterdaysworld.co.uk). Voted Top Attraction in the South East 2002, England for Excellence Awards. Tourist attraction incorporating an interactive museum of shopping and social history and a gift shop selling nostalgic items.
**Customer Care Assistants (3)** National minimum wage. To work variable hours including one day at weekends. Must be smart and reliable with a pleasant personality and good customer service skills. Min. age 15. To work between Easter and September during Easter/Whitsun/Summer vacations. No accommodation available.
*Apply* to the Manager before May at the above address. Note all applicants must be available for interview.

**HARBOUR PARK LTD:** Seafront, Littlehampton, West Sussex BN17 5LL (☎01903-721200; fax 01903-716663; www.harbourpark.com) A family enertainment centre situated right on the sea front with rides and attractions for all ages including a coffee bar, burger bar and ice cream parlour.
**Ride Operators and Catering Staff.** Wages £3.50 per hour plus accomodation. To work 5/6 days per week including weekends. Period of work June-September: must be able to work July and August.
Minimum age 18 years. Overseas applicants eligible to work in UK welcome.
*Applications* must be received by end of April.

**SAUSMAREZ MANOR:** St Martin, Guernsey, Channel Islands GY4 6SG (☎01481-235571; fax 01481-235572; e-mail peter@artparks.co.uk; www.guernsey.org/sausmarez; www.artparks.co.uk). House and show garden open to the public with Sculpture Park, seen on TV and in national print media.
**Housekeeper** to do housework on a regular basis and clean the Manor House which is open to the public. Wages £4 per hour (£100 per week) plus free food and lodging. To work 4 hours per day. Afternoons and most evenings free. Period of work May to October although it is understood that one person may not be able to work the entire period. Should ideally have experience of working en famille. Sons, nephews and nieces (young twenties) are in and out all the time.
**Horticultural/Garden Design Student** also welcomed to work with the groundsman in sculpture park/garden for some/all the summer. Wages at £4 per hour plus food and lodging. Working hours plus or minus 4 hours a day.
Overseas applicants welcome. Interview necessary, but can be conducted by phone. Early application is advised and appreciated because applicants generally either come back the following year or send a friend because they enjoy it so much.
*Apply* from January to Peter de Sausmarez at the above address.

**SUSSEX BEACH HOLIDAY VILLAGE:** Earnley, nr Chichester, West Sussex PO20 7JP (☎01243-671213). A secluded holiday village by the sea which caters for up to 600 guests. Facilities include outdoor heated pool, tennis courts, crazy golf and shop.
**Bar Staff (4).** To work split shifts. Min. age 18 years. Must have experience and be trustworthy with money.
**Counter Assistants (3) and Grounds Person.** Experience not essential, training provided.
All staff (22 years and over) receive £4.10 per hour (plus tips for bar and waiting staff). Hours: 39 over 6 days. Min. work period 5 weeks between March and November. Must be adaptable, trustworthy and of smart appearance. Overseas

applicants eligible to work in the UK and with good English welcome.
*Applications* to Mr Allan Chamberlain, Operations Manager, Sussex Beach Holiday Village.

**VECTIS VENTURES LTD:** Blackgang Chine, Ventnor, Isle of Wight PO38 2HN (☎01983-730330; fax 01983-731267; e-mail vectisventuresltd@btinternet.com). Blackgang Chine and Robin Hill are 2 visitor attractions on the Isle of Wight with a range of family amusements. Open daily throughout the summer, attractions include a small number of rides and also activity play areas.
**General Park Assistants (15)** to work on rides, in retail outlets and catering facilities and for gardening and car parking. Wages are £4.50 per hour, to work 5-6 days a week. Staff are required from April to September/October and must work from July to August a minimum period of 8 weeks.
Applicants should be aged between 18 and 25. No experience is necessary but applicants should be friendly and outgoing.
Overseas applicants are welcome but must have good English. No accommodation available.
*Applications* should be sent to Pam Wyeth, Front of House Manager at the above address between January and April. Interview necessary.

**WIGHT CITY LEISURE PLC:** Culver Parade, Sandown, Isle of Wight PO36 8AT (☎01983-403658; fax 01983-406115; e-mail admin@bogeys.co.uk).
**Bar Staff (4)** to work in the bar and on food counters. Wages £4.65 per hour.
**Arcade Assistants (2)** to work in the amusement arcade. Wages £4.50 per hour. Period of work from June to October. Applicants should be aged at least 18 years old.
*Applications* to Helen Witts, Manager at the above address.

# Hotels and Catering

**THE ANGEL HOTEL:** North Street, Midhurst, West Sussex GU29 9DN (☎01730-812421; fax 01730-815928; e-mail Angel@hshotels.co.uk).
**Waiting/Bar Staff (2)** needed from June to September for 40 hours p.w. maximum. Wage up to £200 per week plus accommodation. Minimum age is 18 years.
*Applications* to T. Gilmore, General Manager.

**BAILIFFSCOURT HOTEL:** Climping, Nr. Littlehampton, West Sussex BN17 5RW (☎01903-723511; fax 01903 723107; e-mail bailifsfscourt@hshotels.co.uk). Built by Lord Moyne of the Guinness Empire in 1927, situated in 30 acres, 200 yards from the beach. A chapel dating back to the 13th Century is situated in the hotel grounds.
**Restaurant Staff (2/3).** Wages £4 per hour; to work 8 hours a day. Must be 18 years or older and have silver service experience.
**Porters (2).** Wages £4 per hour; to work 8 hours a day. Duties include luggage handling, serving morning coffees and afternoon teas and the setting up of conferences. Accommodation is available free of charge, with a £100 key deposit refunded at the end of employment. Period of work from mid May to late September/ October. Minimum period of work 3 months.
*Applications* to Karen Wilson, Training and Personnel Manager, from the beginning of April.

**BALMER LAWN HOTEL:** Lyndhurst Road, Brockenhurst, Hampshire SO42 7ZB

(☎01590-623116; fax 01590-623864; e-mail BLH@btinternet.com).
**Waiting Staff (2-4)** to work 39 hours per week, including weekends, serving breakfast 6.30-10.00am, lunch 12-2pm, and dinner 6.30-11pm, on shift basis.
Wages on application minus £20 for accommodation. Applicants should be over 20 years old and while previous experience of the hotel industry is an advantage training will be given.
*Applications* to Mrs Joanne Hamilton, Personnel and Training Manager.

**CAREYS MANOR HOTEL:** Lyndhurst Road, Brockenhurst, New Forest, Hampshire SO42 7RH (☎01590-623551; fax 01590-622799; e-mail careysmanor @btinternet.com; www.careysmanor.com). An attractive 3 star hotel in the beautiful countryside of the New Forest with 79 bedrooms, 2 restaurants, and a health and fitness club with 500 members. Employs 120 staff.
**Restaurant Staff (3) and Kitchen Staff (2)** Wages of £160-£200 per week. Board and lodging is available for £35 per week. To work a 50 hour week. Min. period of work 1st July to 15th September. Applicants must be over 16 and have qualifications. Overseas applicants considered.
*Applications* from April to the General Manager.

**COMFORT INN ARUNDEL:** Junction A27/A284, Crossbush, Arundel, West Sussex BN17 7QQ (☎01903-840840; fax 01903-84984; e-mail admin@gb642.u-net.com). The Comfort Inn Arundel is a new 53-bedroomed hotel located near Arundel town centre. It offers spacious en-suite rooms, a restaurant and bar.
**Sous Chef (1)** Part-time or full-time.
**Receptionist (1)** to work 5 days a week, 7am-3pm or 3pm-11pm shifts. Wage at least National Minimum Wage.
**Waiting Staff (2/3).** Part-time and full-time positions available. Wages on application. Must be at least 16.
No accommodation is available but meals are provided whilst working. Foreign applicants with a good knowledge of English, especially spoken, are welcome. Permanent positions are available.
*Applications* any time to the Duty Manager at the above address.

**CONGRESS HOTEL:** 31-41 Carlisle Road, Eastbourne, Sussex BN21 4JS (☎01323-732118; fax 01323-720016).
**Staff** £130 per week plus B & L. To work 37½ hours over 5½ days per week. Period of work March to November. Min. period of work 3 months. Min. age 18 years.
*Applications* to Sandie Howlett, Director, Congress Hotel.

**COPTHORNE HOTEL EFFINGHAM PARK:** Copthorne, West Sussex RH10 3EU (☎01342-711705; fax 01342-716039; e-mail lisa.benham@mill-cop.com). A 4 star hotel situated in 40 acres of parkland with 122 bedrooms, healthclub, tennis courts, a 9 hole golf course and extensive conference and banqueting facilities.
**Restaurant Staff, Bar Staff** Wages are £173 per week; to work 40 hours per week over 5 days. Whilst experience is preferred it is not essential. References are required.
**Conference Waiting & Bar Staff** for casual work. Wages £4.10 per hour; hours are as required Work is available throughout the year. No experience is needed.
Accommodation is available at a charge of £33.50 per week. Some items of uniform are provided, as are all meals. There are on and off job training opportunities. Overseas applicants are welcome to apply only if they have a work permit and subject to a telephone interview.

*Applications* to the Personnel and Training Manager at the above address at any time.

**DUKE OF NORMANDIE HOTEL:** Lefebvre Street, St. Peter Port, Guernsey GY1 2PJ (☎01481-721431; fax 01481-711763; e-mail dukeofnormandie@gtonline.net). 2 star hotel catering for guests in a friendly, informal, homely way. One minute's walk from the town.
**Chamberpersons, Plate Service Restaurant Staff And Bar Waiting Staff.** Salaries by negotiation. Live-in accommodation provided. Hotel experience essential. Permanent positions available.
*Applications* any time to the Manager, Duke of Normandie Hotel.

**FARRAR'S HOTEL:** 3-5 Wilmington Gardens, Eastbourne, East Sussex BN2 4JN (☎01323-723737; fax 01323-732902).
**Room Assistants (2)** to work from 8am-2pm. Wages of £3.50 per hour plus tips.
**Day Porters (2)** to work from 10am-2pm and 5pm-9pm. Wages of £3.50 per hour plus tips.
**Restaurant Staff (2)** to work from 7-11am and 6-9pm. Wages £3.50-£4 per hour. Needed to begin work as soon as possible. Minimum age 20.
*Applications* to the Manager at the above address.

**GRAND HOTEL:** Grand Parade, St. Leonards, Hastings, East Sussex TN38 0DD (☎01424-428510/0870-225 7025; fax 01424 428510).
**General Hotel Workers (2)** to clean bedrooms and work in the laundry and kitchen. Wages £3 per hour. Accommodation available for one person only. Work available all year round. Overseas applicants welcome.
*Applications* to Mr Peter Mann at the above address.

**THE GRAND HOTEL GROUP:** The Grand Burshin Hotel, The Harbour, Folkestone, Kent CT20 1TX (☎01303-854513; fax 01303-854549). The hotel is perfectly positioned overlooking Folkestone Harbour.
**Waiting Staff, Kitchen Assistants.** Must be aged 18+.
**Bar Staff, Housekeeping Staff.** Must be aged 18+.
Payment at National Minimum Wage rates. Variable working hours. Min. period of work of 2 months. Positions are available from June to October. Intermediate English required. Accommodation not available.
*Applications* should be made from May onwards to Chris Muckell. Interview necessary.

**GRANGE MOOR HOTEL:** St Michaels Road, Maidstone, Kent, ME16 8BS (☎01622-677623; fax 01622-678246; e-mail reservations@grangemoor.co.uk). 50 bedroom family run hotel with banquet room seeks staff for office christmas dinners/parties.
**Waiting Staff (10), Washers Up (6)** Wages £5 per hour, cash paid weekly. To work hours to suit between 1st and 23rd December for lunches and evening meals. Some Christmas Day work available between noon-5pm at double time. Waiting staff required to provide plated service for Christmas dinners, full training will be given, applicants must be over 17, friendly, helpful and polite. No accommodation available.
*Applications* to Mrs Christine Sedge, at the above address.

**HIGHFIELD COUNTRY HOTEL:** Route d'Ebenezer, Trinity, Jersey JE3 5DT (☎01534-862194; fax 01534-865342; e-mail reservations@highfieldjersey.com).

Situated 4 miles from St Helier, the hotel is a short distance from beaches on the North Coast.
**Second Chef (1).** Wages on application. Must be over 20 and hold a 7061/2 qualification.
**Dining Room Staff (2).** Must have experience and be over 20.
**Bar Person (1).** Must have experience and be over 20.
**Porters (2).** Must have experience and be over 20.
**Receptionists (2).** Should be computer trained. Preferably over 25.

All positions on application ,work 42 hours a week. Live-in accommodation is available. Period of work 23 March to 31 October. Overseas applicants considered. Interview not necessary.

*Applications* from February to David Lord.

**HILTON AVISFORD PARK HOTEL:** Walberton, Arundel, West Sussex BN18 0LS (☎01243 551215). With 139 bedrooms, conference and banqueting for up to 600 and extensive leisure facilities.
**Restaurant, Banqueting and Bar Staff** required to work in busy food and beverage departments. Wages from £4 per hour.

*Applications* to Karen Amos, Senior Human Resources Officer, at the above address.

**HILTON BASINGSTOKE:** Old Common Road, Black Dam, Basingstoke, Hampshire RG21 3PR (☎01256-460460; fax 01256-840441).
**Restaurant Attendants (5)** needed for full-time (39 hours per week) or part-time work. Wages are £4.37 per hour.

*Applications* to Rebecca Gwilliam, Human Resources Manager, at the hotel.

**HOTEL L'HORIZON:** St Brelade's Bay, Jersey, Channel Islands JE3 8EF (☎01534-494404; e-mail hotelhorizon.@jerseymail.co.uk; www.hotelhorizon@jerseymail.co.uk). A 4 star 107 bedroom hotel, located on one of the island's beautiful beaches. Hotel L'Horizon offers a unique work experience for employees who prove themselves to be dedicated, responsible and efficient, with further employment prospects after the seasonal contracts terminate.
**Food and Beverage Service Attendants, Room Attendants, Kitchen Porters.** To work a 6 day week.
**Commis Waiting Staff/Chef de Rangs.** To work a 5 day week.

All applicants must be presentable, have excellent customer care skills and have worked within a similar environment before. Uniform and meals on duty and accommodation provided. Overseas applicants who have good English considered.

*Applications* should be made by application form available together with further information from the above address and website.

**LAKE HOTEL:** Shore Road, Lower Bonchurch, Ventnor, Isle of Wight PO38 1RF (☎01983-852613; e-mail richard@lakehotel.co.uk; www.lakehotel.co.uk). A small hotel (20 rooms) in a quiet, peaceful location. Very busy and a high standard of service and cleanliness. Family run. Close to beach.
**Chamber Staff (2).** To work 39 hours a week. Shifts: 7.30am-12.30pm and 6.30-8.30pm.
**Waiting Staff (2).** To work 40 hours a week. Shifts as above.

All staff work 6 days for £150 a week, plus free B & L. Min. period of work 3½ months between May and end of October. No replies for shorter availability. Some experience required, and applicants should have a sense of humour, be tidy and polite, and be able to work quickly and under pressure. Overseas applicants with

good English welcome.
*Applications* from January to Mr Wyatt, Lake Hotel.

**LONSDALE, SMITH'S, EDEN AND PALM COURT HOTELS:** 51-61 Norfolk Road, Cliftonville, Margate, Kent CT9 2HX (☎01843-221053; fax 01843-299993). A family run group of private hotels. Hotels have indoor heated swimming pools and sports facilities. All rooms are en suite and have telephones, colour TVs and tea and coffee making facilities.
**Restaurant Staff / Room Attendants (4).** Wages £70 per week including food and accommodation.
**Chefs.** Pay on application.
To work 40 hours over 5 days a week (usually on split shifts) with no overtime. Must be over 18. Min. period of work 3 months all year round. Overseas applicants welcomed.
*Applications* from January to Mrs Ann Smith. Interview not necessary.

**LUCCOMBE HALL HOTEL:** Luccombe Hall Hotel, Luccombe Road, Shanklin, Isle of Wight PO37 6RL (☎01983-862719; fax 01983-863082; e-mail reservations @luccombe.co.uk). Luccombe Hall Hotel is on a popular I.O.W. beach with tennis, squash, indoor and outdoor pools, gym, sauna etc.
**Kitchen Staff (1-2), Waiting Staff (1-2), Room Attendants (1-2)** for the school holidays. Live in or out. Pay £80 per week while training, and £100 per week thereafter (live-in); or £4.25 per hour (live out). Split shifts, 5/6 days per week. Hotel will train if no previous experience: applicants should be cheerful, reliable and sober.
*Applications* to Miss Claire Wells, General Manager.

**THE MASTER BUILDERS HOUSE HOTEL:** Buckler's Hard, Nr Beaulieu, Hampshire SO42 7XB (☎01590-616253; fax 01590-6162978; e-mail res@themasterbuilders.co.uk).
**Commis Waiting Staff** to work in the 2-rosette Riverview Restaurant. Serve at breakfast, lunch, afternoon teas, dinner and conference set-up.
**Bar Staff** in the bar and galley to serve drinks and pub food.
**Chamberstaff** servicing guestrooms and evening turndown.
Wages £4.08-£4.32 per hour plus tips. Accommodation may be available; single room (£30pw), shared (£25pw), including 3 meals daily. Positions available from end April/May to end August/September. Applicants need good English; a pleasant outgoing personality; to enjoy countryside; and be good team players in international team.
*Applications* to Sam Brinkman, General Manager, at the above address.

**MORVAN FAMILY HOTELS:** 57 Rouge Bouillon Street, St Helier, Jersey JE2 3ZB (☎01534-731684; fax 01534-768804; e-mail morFamho@itl.net). A company in operation for 45 years which runs 5 hotels on the picturesque island of Jersey.
**Staff** required for various posts ranging from head chefs through to chamber staff. Wages by arrangement; accommodation is available at a cost of £43.50 per week, plus meals. Min. period of work 6 months between March and October. Overseas applicants considered.
*Applications* from January to Adrian T. Gordon, Group Personnel Manager. Interview not necessary.

**NATIONAL TRUST ENTERPRISES:** The Restaurant, Chartwell House, Mapleton Road, Westerham, Kent TN16 1PS (☎01732-866368).
**Catering Assistants (8).** Wages on application. Hours negotiable.
*Applications* at any time to the above address.

**NEW WAVE WINES LTD:** Tenterden Vineyard, Smallhythe Road, Tenterden, Kent TN30 7NG (☎01580-763033; fax 01580-765333; e-mail tourism@newwavewines.com). The largest wine producer in the UK, making mainly white, red and sparkling wines. A popular tourist attraction in the heart of the Kent countryside.
**Waiting Staff.** Wages to be arranged; uniform provided. To work 37 hours per week full time; part time positions also available. Experience would be an advantage, but training will be given.
**Shop Staff.** Wages to be arranged; uniform provided. Part time positions with varied hours. Job involves lifting.
**Winery Staff.** Wages to be arranged. Seasonal, short term position working full time hours. Manual work; workers need to bring old clothes.
　　Staff required from April-November. Fluent English essential. All applicants must be over 18 and have their own transport. No accommodation available.
　　*Applications* should be made to Mrs V. Gould at the above address from March onwards. Interview required.

**OCKENDEN MANOR HOTEL:** Ockenden Lane, Cuckfield, Haywards Heath, West Sussex RH17 5LD (☎01444-416111; fax 01444-415549; e-mail ockenden@hshotels.co.uk; www.hshotels.co.uk).
**Commis Waiting Staff** to work in the restaurant and bar and at functions. Wages of at least £140 per week plus tips and accommodation; to work split shifts over a 5-day week.
　　Period of work by arrangement around the year for a minimum of 12 months. Applicants must be aged at least 18 and have restaurant experience; silver service experience desirable.
　　*Applications* to Adam Smith, Manager, at the above address.

**PAYNE AND GUNTER:** Goodwood Racecourse, Goodwood, Chichester, West Sussex PO18 0PS (☎01243-775350; fax 01243-784490). Payne and Gunter are the caterers for Goodwood Racecourse, supplying waiting, bar and catering staff on race days and motorsport events.
**Waiting Staff, Silver Service Staff, Porters, General Catering Assistants, Table Clearers and Washing Up Staff.** Between 400 and 1,000 staff are employed per event on a casual basis. Wages are £4.50-£5.50 per hour. Must be at least 18, no experience necessary. To work on various race days from May to September. Meals are provided on duty and free transport from various pick-up points is provided.
　　*Applications* from March/April to the Staffing Manager, at the above address.

**PORTELET HOTEL:** St Brelade, Jersey, Channel Islands JE3 8AU (☎01534-741204; fax 01534-746625). A family hotel situated on the coast, catering for 160 guests.
**Hall Porters, Commis Barman, Commis Wine Waiting Staff** needed. Wages from £172 a week. To work 42 hours per week over 6 days. Period of work May to October; min. 4 months. Min. age 18. Full-board accommodation is available at £52 a week. Foreign applicants with permission to work in the UK and good English considered.
　　*Applications* from April onwards to Mr Mario Dugini, Manager, at the Portelet Hotel.

**THE PRIORY BAY HOTEL:** Priory Drive, Seaview, Isle of Wight PO34 5BU (☎01983-613146; fax 01983-616539; e-mail jane@priorybay.co.uk; www.priorybay.co.uk).
**Kitchen Porters, Waiting Staff, Bar Staff, Room Attendants, Chefs:** Many

**Vacancies.** Wages by arrangement plus tips and accommodation provided. To work up to 48 hours per week. To work the summer season, beginning in May/June. All applicants should have experience in the catering or hospitality trade and a working knowledge of English.

*Applications* should be sent to the Personnel Department, at the above address.

**HOTEL REX:** St Saviours Road, St Helier, Jersey JE2 4GJ (☎01534-731668; fax 01534-766922; e-mail hotelrex@localdial.com; www.localdial.com/users/hotelrex/ ). Established 40 years ago, the hotel is 5 minutes from St Helier.
**Receptionists (2).** Wages £175 per week plus bonus. Must have computer experience.
**Day Porter (1).** Wages £165 per week plus bonus. Should have some experience.
**Waiting Staff (4).** Wages £165 per week plus bonus. Must have silver service experience.
**Commis Chef (1).** Wages £165 per week plus bonus. Must be experienced.
**Kitchen Porter(1)** Wages £155 per week plus bonus.
All staff work 42 hours a week. Accommodation is available at a cost of £47 per week. Staff share accommodation, with a max. of 2 per room. Uniforms are supplied by the hotel. Min. period of work 6 months between April and October. French and Italians are encouraged to apply.

*Applications* form 1st March to N. Berenguer, Hotel Manager. Interview necessary.

**ROYAL BEACH HOTEL:** South Parade, Southsea, Portsmouth, Hants PO4 0RN. A three star, 115 bedroom, seafront hotel commanding stunning views over to the Isle of Wight.
**Waiting Staff (3)** to serve breakfast, lunch and dinner and functions as required.
**Room Attendants (2)** to be responsible for cleaning guest bedrooms, bathrooms and corridors.
National minimum wage applies, plus tips. Accommodation available plus meals/uniform.To work 5 days per week in shifts. Min. period of work 12 weeks. Overseas applicants welcome.

*Applications* to the Personnel Manager at the above address.

**THE ROYAL HOTEL:** Belgrave Road, Ventnor, Isle of Wight PO38 1JJ (☎01983-852186; fax 01983-855395). The only AA 4 star hotel on the Isle of Wight. Pleasant working conditions and friendly staff.
**Waiting Staff (4), Chamber Staff (4).** £140-£160 per week. To work at least 45 hours per week. Training available. Accommodation provided at no extra cost. Staff required from April to October; min. period of work the three months of July, August and September. Overseas applicants welcome, members of staff from France, Spain and South Africa already employed.
Interview required or trial work period is necessary. *Applications* from March 1st to the Personnel Manager/General Manager at the above address.

**ROYAL ESPLANADE HOTEL:** Ryde, Isle of Wight PO33 2ED (☎01983-562549; fax 01983-563918). Owned by Shearings Hotels, the hotel has an 11 month season and is closed in January. It offers various benefits of working for a large company. Hotel is situated on the seafront.
**Waiting Staff, Kitchen Porters, Chamber Staff, Bar Staff.** From £3.60 per hour plus tips. Free B & L. To work 39 hours per week. All staff work 6 days per week. No experience needed. Full in-house training is given. Max. age 28 years.

*Applications* enclosing photograph to Mrs C. Davies, General Manager.

**SEYMOUR HOTELS OF JERSEY:** 1 Wharf Street, St Helier, Jersey JE2 0ZX (☎01534-875926; fax 01534-780726; e-mail brightfuture@seymourhotels.com; www.seymourhotels.com). The largest hotel group in the Channel Islands, with 4 hotels catering for all aspects of the leisure, business and conference markets.
**Receptionists (20).** Wages were £195 per week in 2002. Some previous experience is required. Computer skills and languages are an advantage. Must be over 18.
**Waiting Staff (35).** Wages were £187 per week in 2002. Some positions require specific skills eg. silver service. Must be over 18.
**Bar Staff (15).** Wages were £187 in 2002. Previous experience needed. Must be over 18.
**Commis Chefs, Chefs De Parti, Sous Chefs (20).** Wages were £186-£250 in 2002. Applicants must have experience relevant to the level of the position.
**Room Attendants (20).** Wages were £173 per week in 2002. Some experience would be useful.
**Porters (10).** Wages were £190 in 2002. Some experience would be useful.

All staff work 42 hours a week over 5/6 days. Accommodation is provided at a cost of £52 per week (reviewed annually), including meals and uniforms. Min. period of work 6 months between March/April and end October. Full training is provided where appropriate. There are opportunities for career development and permanent employment. Foreign applicants with permission to work in the UK considered; must have a basic level of spoken English.

*Applications* from February to Mrs S. Armes, Group Personnel and Training Manager. Interview necessary, but may be conducted by telephone.

**STOCKS ISLAND HOTEL:** Sark, via Guernsey, Channel Islands GY9 0SD (☎01481-832001; fax 01481-832130; e-mail stocks@sark.net; www.stocks-sark.com). Sark is a beautiful and remote rural island 20 miles from France; fishing, farming and eco-tourism provide the main local employment.There are no motor cars and no airport. Stocks is a traditional old farmhouse and home of the Armorgie family.
**Silver Service Waiting Staff** for general waiting and some cleaning duties in an award-winning restaurant. Must possess silver-service skills, a pleasant personality and caring attitude.
**Kitchen Porter** for general kitchen cleaning duties and some vegetable preparation in a high quality kitchen with a brigade of qualified chefs. Must work extremely cleanly, efficiently and quickly. Overseas applicants considered.
**Bistro Staff** for general waiting and cleaning duties in busy but informal Bistro restaurant. Must be attractive with pleasant personality and very good references. The ability to work quickly, cleanly and efficiently are essential.

Wages £110 per week, tax-free with no deductions. B & L provided. Private medical health cover provided. To work maximum of 60 hours per week over 6 days. Fifteen members of staff required to work from April until October, with two additional workers between June and September. Overseas applicants welcome but must speak the standard of English of a native. Preferred age group 20-35.

Sark is an isolated and unspoilt island. Applicants must be able to adapt to the unique working environment. For further details *contact* Mr Paul Armorgie, Stocks Island Hotel and Restaurants.

**THISTLE BRIGHTON HOTEL:** Kings Road, Brighton, BN1 2GS (☎01273-763237; fax 01273-820692; e-mail hr.brighton@thistle.co.uk). Award-winning hotel

company whose policy is to put its guests at the heart of everything it does. 56 hotels nationwide – discounted staff accomodation scheme.
**Waiting Staff** required to provide food service in the hotel's restaurant. Wages £4.18 per hour plus tips. To work between 5 and 39 hours a week in shifts (6.30am-3pm, 10am-5.30pm, 3-11.30pm).
**Bar Person** needed to serve in a Mediterranean style cafe-bar. Wages £4.18 per hour plus tips. To work between 5 and 39 hours per week. Applicants must be over 18 years of age.
**Room Attendants** wanted to carry out housekeeping and room cleaning work. Wages £4.10 per hour. Hours of work 9.30am-4.30pm with 8-39 hours of work available per week.
**Concierge/Hall Porter** wanted for front reception, guest liaison and to carry luggage. Wages £4.27 plus tips. To work a 39 hour week, either 7am-3.30pm or 3-11.30pm. Applicants must be over 21 for insurance purposes.
**Night Guest Services Porter** Wages £4.84 plus tips. To work 39 hours per week, 11pm-7.30am. Tasks include general setting up duties, some food preparation and hotel security. Applicants must be over 25.

All remuneration schemes include a company benefits package. *Applications* or requests for further details should be made to Jason Fox, Area Human Resources Manager at the above address.

# Language Schools

**CICERO LANGUAGES INTERNATIONAL:** 42 Upper Grosvenor Road, Tunbridge Wells, Kent TN1 2ET (☎01892-547077; fax 01892-522749; e-mail enrolments@cicero.co.uk; www.cicero.co.uk). A small, friendly and professional language school accredited by the British Council and a member of ARELS. Students are mainly in their 20s and 30s, from over 70 countries.
**EFL Teachers** to teach students of many nationalities (average age 25). Salary £11-£13 per hour. Hours of work variable. Period of work mid July to end of August, min. period of employment 4 weeks. Accommodation is not available. Applicants must have a degree and TESOL/CTEFLA qualifications. Experience also important. Punctuality and a professional attitude are essential.
*Applications* from April to the Director of Studies, Cicero Languages International.

**CONCORDE INTERNATIONAL SUMMER SCHOOLS LTD:** Arnett House, Hawks Lane, Canterbury, Kent CT1 2NU (☎01227-451035; fax 01227-762760; e-mail info@concorde.ltd.uk; www.concorde.ltd.uk). Concorde International has been organising summer schools for over 29 years in the south of England. They have a high return rate of international students and teachers.
**EFL Teachers (approx. 150).** To teach in summer schools. Wages £235-280 a week depending on course. An average working week consists of 15 hours tuition and supervising 20 hours of activities, but weeks vary according to individual programmes. Both residential and non-residential positions are available. Applicants should have the RSA CTEFLA or Trinity College certificate TESOL or equivalent or PGCE in an appropriate subject, and some summer school experience.
**Course Directors (approx. 6)** to ensure the smooth running of the centre and liaise with Head Office, the local host family organiser and the group leader. Other duties include holding staff meetings and weekly in-house training sessions, briefing teachers and standing in for them if required. Wages £400 a week. Both residential and non-residential positions are available, depending on the centre. Applicants must

hold a RSA Dip. TEFL or Trinity College diploma in TESOL and have a minimum of 5 years' summer school experience.
**Assistant Directors of Study (approx. 68)** to ensure the smooth running of the centre, liase with Head Office, oversee the daily routine and give support to staff, in addition to 15 hours' tuition a week. Wages £290 a week. Positions are residential and non-residential. Applicants must hold RSA Dip. TEFL or Trinity College London Diploma and have several years' teaching experience.
**Centre Managers (approx. 6)** to ensure smooth running of the social programme and take care of the students' health and welfare. Other duties include checking transfer arrangements, liasing with Head Office, and regular staff at the centres. Positions are residential. Wages £310 per week. Applicants should preferably hold a qualification in leisure management although other management qualifications/ experience will be considered.
Period of work June, July and August for all positions. *Applications* to the Vacation Course Director at the above address.

**EASTBOURNE SCHOOL OF ENGLISH:** 8 Trinity Trees, Eastbourne, E.Sussex BN21 3LD (☎01323-721759; fax 01323-639271; e-mail english@esoe.co.uk). Runs language courses for students aged 16 and over from all around the world. The freetime programme is lively and varied.
**Assistant Social Organiser (1).** Wages £175 per week. Responsible post suiting someone energetic, enthusiastic and reliable. Some experience with overseas students an advantage. Min. age 20. To work 6 days per week (flexi-time). Required from mid June to mid September. Accommodation not available. Interview necessary.
*Applications* with a CV to Graham White, Principal, from early 2002 at the above address.

**EMBASSY CES:** Lorna House, 103 Lorna Road, Hove, E. Sussex, BN3 3EL. (Web site www.embassyces.com ☎+44 1273 322353; E-mail vacjobsuk@embassyces.co m; Fax: +44 1273 322381.) Embassy CES is a division of Study Group International, part of the Daily Mail and General Trust family of companies, and is a world leader in quality international education. Embassy CES organises summer schools for international students, combining English lessons and an activity/excursion programme at schools and universities around the UK.
**Activity Leaders** to organise a variety of daytime, evening and weekend activities. Experience of working with children or in the leisure or tourism industry is desirable, but full training will be given. All applicants must speak fluent English, have enthusiasm and initiative, and be hardworking.
**EFL Teachers** to teach and participate in the activity programme. Previous experience is desirable. Full board accommodation is available at residential centres.
*Apply* from February onwards either online at www.embassyces.com (click on the Summer Jobs in the UK link) or contact the Recruitment Department for an application pack.

**EMBASSY CES:** Palace Court, White Rock, Hastings, TN34 1JY (Tel: 01424-720100; Fax: 01424 720323; e-mail hastings@embassyces.com; www.embassyces.com). All year round language school with large summer centre.
**EFL Teachers** wanted for July and August to teach adults and children; to also assist with a programme of social activities/excursions. Residential posts available. Cambridge CELTA (formerly CTEFLA) certificate required. Applications from January to the above address.

**Sports & Social Activity Organisers** required during July and August. Graduates and Undergraduates, min age 20. Qualifications in sports coaching, first aid, arts and crafts etc. an advantage. Accommodation available. Work includes running a full activity programme: discos, excursions, sports, local visits etc. Applicants should have common sense and a good sense of fun. Overseas applicants with a sufficient knowledge of English considered.

*Apply* from February onwards either online (click on the UK Summer Jobs' link) or contact the Recruitment Department for an application pack. Interview necessary, usually by telephone.

**HASTINGS ENGLISH LANGUAGE CENTRE (HELC):** St Helens Park Road, Hastings, East Sussex TN34 2JW (☎01424-437048/441549; e-mail clive@helc.co.uk; www.helc.co.uk). Adult only British Council accredited school.
**EFL Teachers (10)** £130-£230 for 15-24 hours per week. Degree and CELTA (or equivalent) required. Staff wanted from mid June to October. Min. period of work 4 weeks. Accommodation not available.
*Applications* from middle of March to Hastings English Language Centre at the above address.

**ITS ENGLISH SCHOOL:** 43-45 Cambridge Gardens, Hastings TN34 1EN (☎01424-438025; fax 01424-438050; e-mail itsbest@its-hastings.co.uk). A small, professional, language school situated in the centre of Hastings and accredited by the British Council.
**EFL Teachers.** All applicants must have Trinity College Cert. TESOL or RSA CELTA: £141 for 15 hours per week, £225.60 for 24 hours per week. Applicants with Trinity College Diploma TESOL or RSA DELTA: 15 hours per week – £162: 30 hours per week – £324. Non residential.
Minimum period of work 3 weeks, between June 20th and September 16th.
*Contact* Richard Thompson after April 1st at the above address.

**KENT SCHOOL OF ENGLISH:** 3 Granville Road, Broadstairs, Kent CT10 1QD (☎01843-874870; fax 01843-860418; e-mail enquiries@kentschool.co.uk). A medium-sized school specialising in short courses for groups from 21 countries; a dynamic, energetic, enthusiastic and friendly place to work.
**EFL Teachers (30), Social Activity Assistants (6).** £150-£250 per week. To work 30-35 hours per week from Monday to Saturday. Min. period of work of 4 weeks. Positions available mid-June to mid-September. Applicants should be over 18 and teachers require the relevant TESOL or CELTA certificte.
*Applications* welcome from 1 March to Chris McDermott at the above address.

**LTC INTERNATIONAL COLLEGE:** Compton Park, Compton Palace Road, Eastbourne, East Sussex BN21 1EH (☎01323-727755; fax 01323-728279; e-mail learnenglish@ltccollege.demon.co.uk). A friendly private language school running courses for adult students and residential courses for young learners. Set in a mansion house in its own park, 20 minutes walk from Eastbourne town centre.
**EFL Teachers (5).** Wages from £205 per week, with free B & L. To teach 15 lessons per week; includes evening and some weekend social and residential duties. Minimum of RSA/Cambridge CELTA or Trinity Cert. TESOL required.
**Residential Welfare Officers (4).** Wages from £165 per week, with free B & L. To work 40 hours per week, including evenings and weekends. Would suit a student. First Aid an advantage.
Staff required from 25th June-2nd September. Overseas applicants for teaching

posts must have competence in English to the standard of a native speaker.
*Applications* from February to Paul Clark, Director of Studies, at the above address.

**PASSPORT LANGUAGE SCHOOLS:** 37 Park Road, Bromley, Kent BR1 3HJ (☎020-8466 5925; fax 020-8466 5928; e-mail dos@passport.uk.com). Runs language programmes in different centres from Durham to Worthing for students mainly from Europe and the Far East. Courses take place throughout the year, but summer is the busiest time.
**EFL Teachers.** Required at various centres throughout Britain to teach international students aged 11-17 and assist with afternoon and evening leisure activities. Salary £160-£300 per week depending on experience and position. Board and accommodation provided in residential schools. Approx 15-30 hours over a 6-day week for 2-10 weeks between July and August. Min. age 21. Applicants must have RSA/UCLES, CELTA or Trinity College Certificate TESOL or be state qualified teachers with EFL experience. Training day is held. Teachers must arrange own travel and insurance.
*Applications* to the Director of Studies at the above address.

**ST BEDE'S INTERNATIONAL SUMMER SCHOOL:** The Dicker, Hailsham, East Sussex BN27 3QH (☎01323-443818; fax 01323-848188; e-mail summer.school@stbedesschool.org).
**EFL Teachers (10).** £250 p.w. plus accommodation. Needed from 30 June to 17 August to teach 15 hours per week plus pastoral care and assisting with sports and activities. Must hold either CERT TEFL, D. TEFLA or QTS.
Apply to Nigel Heritage, Director.

**REGENCY SCHOOL OF ENGLISH:** Royal Crescent, Ramsgate, Kent CT11 9PE (☎01843-591212; fax 01843-850035). A British Council recognised school and a member of ARELS.
**Temporary EFL Teachers (15).** Guaranteed 14 hours of teaching per week, but up to 28 hours usually available. Must hold at least a Trinity College or RSA Certificate. £10 per hour (2002 figure).
**Activity Leaders (3).** £100 per week (2002 figure) for 20-30 hours' work. Must be sporty and enthusiastic.
Min. period of work 6 weeks between June and September. Overseas applicants with a standard of English as high as that of a native speaker considered. The school has hotel accommodation but this is often full during the summer.
*Applications* from April to Jocelyn Flaig, Director of Studies, Regency School of English.

**REGENT LANGUAGE HOLIDAYS:** 40-42 Queens Road, Brighton BN1 3XB (☎01273-718620; fax 01273-718621; e-mail holidays@regent.org.uk; www.regent.org.uk). Regent operates five high quality residential centres in Southern England. They specialise in summer language holidays.
**EFL Teachers (40).** Wages from £225-£255 per week for 15 hours tuition and 6 afternoon or evening sessions. Will assist in social programme. RSA/Trinity qualified.
**Centre Managers (4).** Wages from £400-500 per week. Graduate, preferably Masters/RSA/Trinity qualified with appropriate management experience and a proven and successful track record.
**Welfare Assistants. (4)** Wages from £175-£225 per week. Graduate, preferably

social or youth work experience.
Full board and accommodation provided. *Applications* at any time to Recruitment at the above address.

**RICHARD LEWIS COMMUNICATIONS:** Riversdown House, Warnford, Hants SO32 3LH (☎01962-771111; fax 01962-771050; e-mail steve.allison@rlcglobal.com; www.crossculture.com). An international company committed to providing training solutions in the areas of language, cross culture and communication skills. The company operates in 5 continents, and offers career opportunities to travel.
**EFL Teachers.** Wages from approximately £280 per week depending on experience/qualifications, with food and accommodation provided. To teach from 9am-5pm; will also be expected to attend dinner daily and perform one evening duty such as escorting a trip to a pub or the theatre a week. To work from June to September. Applicants should have a university degree, RSA/Trinity TEFL certificate and at least 1 year's teaching experience.
*Applications* to Steve Allison, Director of Studies, at the above address.

**SCANBRIT SCHOOL OF ENGLISH:** 22 Church Road, Bournemouth, BH6 4AT (☎01202-428252; fax 01202-428926; e-mail info@scanbrit.co.uk; www.scanbrit.co.uk).
**EFL Teachers (10)** Wages between £9.10-£10.70 per hour. To teach for 20-30 hours a week from 9am-4pm Mon-Fri over the summer. Applicants should have some teaching experience and a minimum RSA Certificate TEFL qualification.
*Applications* via CV to the above address.

**SCHOOL OF ENGLISH STUDIES FOLKESTONE:** 26 Grimston Gardens, Folkestone, Kent CT20 2PX (☎01303-850007; fax 01303-256544; e-mail info@ses-folkestone.co.uk). Founded in 1957, the School of English Studies Folkestone is a serious, professional and successful language school.
**EFL Teachers (10)** Wages £300-£350 per week; to work 35 hours per week. Applicants must have a UK degree and a TEFL qualification.
**Sports & Activities Co-Ordinators (4)** Wages £250 or more per week; to work 35 hours per week. Applicants must be 21 or over and have some appropriate qualifications.
Both positions available involve working with students of English from overseas. Accommodation is not available. Staff are required from 27 June to 23 August for a minimum period of 4 weeks.
*Applicatons* to David Foley, Principal at the above address from February onwards.

**STAFFORD HOUSE SCHOOL OF ENGLISH:** 8/9 Oaten Hill, Canterbury, Kent CT1 3HY (☎01227-452250; fax 01227-451685; e-mail enquiries@staffordhouse.com). The summer school has mixed nationality classes with a max. of 15 students per class. Ages 12-adult. Emphasis is on productive skills and fluency-based activities.
**EFL Teachers (35).** Rates of pay on application. Min. period of work 1 week between June and September. TEFL qualifications such as RSA/Trinity Certificate or RSA/Trinity Diploma required. Reliability, energy and enthusiasm essential.
*Applications* to Naomi Cooper at the above address.

**WARNBOROUGH UNIVERSITY:** International Offices, 8 Vernon Place, Canterbury CT1 3WH (☎01227-762107; fax 01227-762108, e-mail admin@warnborough.edu, www.warnborough.edu or warnborough.ac.uk). An

international university offering undergraduate and graduate degree programmes by Distance Learning and/or Onsite through affiliated campuses worldwide. Scholarships available to all nationalities.
**Mentors, EFL Teachers, Tour Guides, Translators, Activity Organisors** sought regularly. Payments vary depending on teaching and other employment offered. Please see website for all openings.
*Apply* on line (viceprez@warnborough.edu) or by fax/post to the Vice President for Administration.

# Medical

**CAREWATCH (EASTBOURNE AND HASTINGS):** Unit 14, Swan Business Centre, Hailsham, East Sussex BN27 2BY (☎01323-849444; fax 01323-849222) Carewatch is a provider of homecare services to the elderly and less able.
**Carers (10)** Wages £5-£10 per hour, hours and period of work to suit. Applicants must be 18 or over; no qualifications are needed but applicants must be able to provide 2 references. Applicants from abroad are welcome but must be English speaking. No accommodation available.
*Applications* should be sent as soon as possible to the Manager at the above address. An interview is necessary.

**HOME COMFORTS COMMUNITY CARE LTD:** Suite 6, Quarry House, Mill Lane, Uckfield, East Sussex TN22 5AA (☎01825-762233; fax 01825-762234; e-mail lance@homecomforts-1.fsbusiness.co.uk. Care agency/employer with clients all over Sussex. Established 1995.
**Full Time/Part Time Care Workers (15-20)** to work various shifts in nursing homes, residential homes and homes for adults with learning disabilities in East Sussex, West Sussex and Kent. Some personal care: washing, dressing etc. Wages of £6.50 per hour plus travel expenses; own transport essential. Positions available at all times of year. Applicants must be aged at least 18. Basic training will be given in first aid and manual handling; a caring nature would be useful for this work. Foreign applicants with fluent English and eligibility to work in the UK welcome.
*Applications* to Marie Ingram, Personnel Director, at the above address.

**HOME HELP UK:** Old Forest Barn, Kiln Lane, Buriton, Petersfield, Hampshire GU31 5SL (☎01730-266866; fax 01730-710164; e-mail: philipm@homehelpuk.co.uk).
**Carer/nursing assistants (10).** About £6 per hour. Flexible hours to suit worker. Needed all summer and other holiday periods for looking after elderly/vulnerable people in their own homes, helping to dress and get up/get ready for bed and social support. Generally mornings and evenings (including weekends). Minimum age 18. Experience not needed as training given. Own transport useful.
*Applications* to Philip Marshall, Director, at the above address.

**OPTIONS TRUST STAFF RECRUITMENT:** 4 Plantation Way, Whitehill, Bordon, Hampshire GU35 9HD (☎01420-474261, e-mail optionstrust@pvm.ndo.co.uk).
A non-profit making organisation, set up and run by a number of disabled people who employ personal assistants to enable them to live in homes of their own homes in the community.
**Personal Assistants (10-12).** to carry out personal care, domestic duties and driving. £100-£200 a week plus free B & L. Min. period of work 6 months at any time of year.

Min. age 18. Driving licence required but no previous experience is necessary.
*Applications* to Mrs V. Mason at the above address.

## Outdoor

**ABOUT MARQUEES:** 12 Oval Waye, South Ferring, Near Worthing, West Sussex, BN12 5RA (tel/fax 01903-246302; e-mail: aboutmarquees@lineone.net).
**Marquee erectors (2)** £5.50 per hour. Must be flexible about hours which are mainly Friday pm through to Sunday pm, about 10 hours per day. Needed from May to October. Work is largely manual. Must be fit.
*Applications* to Kelvin Smith at the above address.

**ADRIAN SCRIPPS LTD:** Moat Farm, Five Oak Green, Paddock Wood, Tonbridge, Kent TN12 6RR (☎01892-832406; fax 01892-832721).
**Hop Pickers.** Approx. £150 a week. Period of work 4-5 weeks from 1 September. Work involves mechanical picking of hops.
**Piecework Fruit Pickers** to pick apples and pears growing on small trees for 4-5 weeks from early September.
Self-catering accommodation provided. Min. age 18.
For more details and *applications* write to Adrian Scripps Ltd. at the above address, enclosing s.a.e, after 1 June. Please note that no bookings are taken before July 1.

**AMBERVALE FARM:** North Common Lane, Sway, Lymington, Hampshire SO41 8LL. New Forest farm five minutes away from the sea by car.
**Live-In Assistant** to help with horses and manual work on the farm; tidying, gardening and building. All accommodation, home cooked meals included as well as horse riding and swimming.
**Experienced All-Round Builder (1-2)** to work on the farm. Food, pocket money and mobile home accommodation provided.
*Applications* enclosing a s.a.e. only to Mrs C.M. Nicholson-Pike at the above address.

**S.C. AND J.H. BERRY LTD:** Gushmere Court Farm, Selling, Faversham, Kent ME13 9RF(☎01227-752205/752838). A family run farm in a beautiful area of Kent, which grows a range of crops to sell to supermarkets, wholesalers and brewers.
**Apple Pickers/Hop Pickers (15).** Wages at standard Agricultural Wages Board Rates. Apple picking mostly paid at piece work rates. To work a standard 39 hours per week, plus up to 16 hours overtime. Workers are needed for the entire period between 25th August and 28th September. Work cannot be guaranteed during wet weather. Self-catering accommodation in caravans available for approx. £14 a week: blankets, pillows and separate kitchen, lounge and shower facilities are provided, as well as TV room and various sporting facilities. Applicants should bring their own sleeping bags, towels, etc. as well as wellington boots and waterproof clothing.
Applicants should be students over 18 years old. EEA applicants considered. Possession of a driving licence would be an advantage.
*Applications* (with s.a.e. or IRC) should be sent from 1 May to Mr J.P.S. Berry at the above address.

**BRAMSHOT HOUSE:** Fleet, Hampshire GU13 8RT (☎01252-617304). A family who need help with their large garden, chickens, ducks, general repairs and maintenance. Would suit anyone wanting a working holiday. 45 minutes by train from London. The helper may often be taken along on trips to places of interest with

the family.
**Gardeners/Painters/Carpenters (1-2).** £20 pocket money per week. Flexible working arrangement averaging 3-5 hours per day. Plenty of free time for sightseeing. Self-contained fully furnished flat provided, also produce from the garden when available and use of bicycle, tennis court and swimming pool. Some skill in painting, gardening or carpentry essential. Overseas applicants welcome.

*Applications* to Mrs P.A. Duckworth at the above address.

**BUTLER BROS. (MARDEN):** Cornwells Farm, Marden, Tonbridge, Kent, TN12 9NS (☎01622-831385; fax 01622-832939; e-mail butlerbros@farmline.com).
**Supervisors (2)** wanted for May-July.
**Tractor Drivers (2)** wanted for May-July.
**Strawberry Pickers (12)** wanted May-July.
**Apple Pickers (6)** needed in September/October.
**Supervisors (2)** needed for August/October.
**Tractor Drivers (2)** needed for August/October.
All positions are paid at above minimum wage rates, with some accommodation available. Employees work a 5 day week plus overtime and some weekend work, previous experience is useful but not essential.

For *applications,* contact J.M. Lutener, Partner, at the above address.

**CHANDLER & DUNN LTD:** Lower Goldstone, Ash, Canterbury, Kent CT3 2DY (☎01304-812262; fax 01304-812612; e-mail chandlerdunn@btclick.com; http://home.btclick.com/chandlerdunn).
**Fruit Pickers (numbers variable)** for periods between the end of May and the end of September; most pickers needed for strawberries in June and apples in September. Most picking is piecework so opportunity for fast pickers to earn more. Daily paid casual fruit picking Monday to Saturday from 8am to 4pm approximately.
No accommodation on farm but good campsite very close. Must be aged at least 16 and possess a valid work permit if necessary; please note that the farm does not use the Seasonal Agricultural Workers Scheme (SAWS) and therefore cannot get foreigners a work card.

*Applications* to Anne, Farm Secretary, by e-mail, fax or post, as above.

**CHARRINGTON FRUIT FARMS:** Old Cryals, Cryals Road, Matfield, Tonbridge, Kent TN12 7HN (☎01892-72 2372; fax 01892-72 3311).
**Fruit Pickers (6-10).** Casual rate paid, flat rate during harvest time. Minimum age 18 years. Usual min. period of work 1 week between end of August and first week of October. No accommodation available so applicants should live locally. Must be healthy and willing to work hard and for long hours when the weather permits. Overseas applicants welcome but must have work permit and visa if coming from non EU countries.

Please *apply* from July to Charrington Fruit Farms at the above address/e-mail.

**S.H. CHESSON:** Manor Farm, Oldbury, Ightham, Sevenoaks, Kent TN15 9DG (☎01732-780496; fax 01732-780509; e-mail andrew@manorfarm1.demon.co.uk; www.manorfarm1.demon.co.uk). Situated approx. 64km from London. Approx. 2km from station and shops.
**Fruit Pickers (20)** to work 6 days per week picking strawberries (June-Sept) and apples/pears (Sept/Oct). Piecework rates in region of £125-£175 per week. Hours of work vary depending on the nature of the job. Start time 6.30am-8.00am; finish 2-5pm. Day off alternate Sat/Sun Minimum work period 4 weeks between 1 June and

10 October. Campsite charges £11.20 per week; kitchen, showers, laundry, tv/video room, canteen, outdoor recreations, outings and entertainment provided. Bring your own tent. Minimum age 18. EU/EEA citizens welcome. Non EU/EEA citizens must apply for necessary work permit through Concordia.
*Apply* in writing for an application form, from March 1 to Mr A.T. Chesson at the above address. All applicants must enclose a s.a.e. Visit their Website at www.manorfarm1.demon.co.uk.

**ELPHICKS FARM:** Scuffits, Hunton, Maidstone, Kent ME15 ORY (☎01622-820758; fax 01622-820754). A family owned company supplying top quality fruit to all the national supermarkets.
**Apple Pickers (6).** Wages above the minimum wage. To work 8-9 hours per day. Period of work mid-August to end of September. Caravan accommodation provided. Min. age 19 years. Overseas applicants must have valid working visas.
*Applications* (enclosing s.a.e. or IRC) to be sent no earlier than 1 April to Mr S.S. Day, Elphicks Farm.

**EWELL FARM:** Edward Vinson Ltd., Graveney Road, Faversham, Kent ME13 8UP (tel: 01795-539452; fax 01795-539509). A friendly fruit growing company with several farms.
**Fruit Pickers** to work June to October. Wages at piecework rates; £30-£50 possible depending on ability. No accommodation available. Hours flexible, but typically 7am-3pm; weekend work available but time off as needed without restrictions. Applicants should be at least 16 and reasonably healthy.
*Applications* to the Harvest Manager, at the above address.

**S. FERMOR:** Oakdene Farm, Sutton Valence, Maidstone, Kent ME17 3LS (☎01622-843332; fax 01622-843332). Small fruit farm.
**Fruit Pickers (5).** Paid at piecework rates.
To work Monday-Friday; possibly 7 days per week. Basic accommodation available. Min. period of work 1 week between June and September. Min. age 18.
*Applications* at any time to Mrs J. Fermor at the above address.

**H.E. HALL & SON LTD:** Little Pattenden, Marden, Kent TN12 9QL (☎01622-831376; fax 01622-831654).
**Fruit Pickers (10).** Paid piecework based on £4.10 per hour. 8am-3pm, Mon-Fri, but flexible hours and days dependent on weather and crop. Min. period of work 1 day between mid August and mid October. Basic self-catering accommodation available at no cost. Min. age 20. No previous experience necessary but it is useful. Overseas applicants considered if work authorisation is in order and English is spoken.
*Applications* from June onwards to Peter Hall by telephone.

**HILL FARM ORCHARDS:** Droxford Road, Swanmore, Hampshire SO32 2PY (☎01489-878616; e-mail hifol@farmline.com). Pleasantly situated between Portsmouth and Southampton, with shops and pubs nearby. Packing apples and pears for high class outlets.
**Apple Packers (up to 10).** Pay as set by Agricultural Wages Board and piece work rates at the height of the seasons. To work 8.00am-4.30pm Monday to Friday, with occasional weekends. Min. period of work 1 month. Positions available November to January. Min. fee accomodation available. Applicants must be eligible to work in the UK.
*Applications* by post to Mr Paul Roberts, Farm Manager, at the above address.

**JERSEY CYCLETOURS:** 2 La Hougue Mauger, St. Mary, Jersey, JE3 3AF (☎01534-482898; fax 01534-484060). The company's bikes (Trek, Giant, Dawes) are the best maintained and equipped hire bikes in Jersey; it needs people who are keen and able to maintain our standards.
**CYCLE MECHANIC, BIKE ISSUER** needed from April to the end of September. Mechanic must have experience in bike building and repair. Issuer should be clear headed and enjoy cycling and helping people. Wages are aae. Working week 20-40 hours per week.
Contact Daniel Wimberley at the above address.

**LANGDON MANOR FARM:** Seasalter Road, Goodnestone, Faversham, Kent ME13 9DA (☎01795-530035).
**Soft Fruit Pickers & Agricultural Workers** required to pick and pack all types of soft fruit to a very high standard. Minimum age 18. Pickers will be trained and should be hard working and conscientious. Min. work period of 4 weeks between mid May and October. Pickers especially welcome in June. Hours 6am to 3pm with some work in evenings. Piecework rates paid. Workers will be expected to pick at the required speed. Some tractor driving work, etc. also available.
Accommodation available in mobile homes, cost £21 per week. Facilities include showers, toilets, mess room, kitchen, bus to shops. Group outings, discos and barbecues organised. English lessons given 2 nights per week. Easy access to London (by train 50 minutes). Early booking advised; notification of acceptance March. Overseas applicants welcome but those from outside the EEA must hold a valid work permit.
*Applications* to the above address enclosing a s.a.e. or IRC to ensure a reply.

**LAUREL TREE FRUIT FARM:** Boar's Head, East Sussex TN6 3HD (☎01892-661637 or 01892-654011; mobile 07768-980308; fax 01892-663417).
**Pickers (20)** for top fruit picking (apple and pear). Wages £4+ per hour, to work 6 hours per day. Period of work depends on harvest, but probably 20 days between 25th August and 30th September (approx). No accommodation available, but limited camping is permitted. Overseas applicants with valid working visas welcome. No interview necessary.
*Applications* from 20th August onwards to Robert Booker (mobile phone 07768-980308) or evenings at the above number.

**F.W. MANSFIELD & SON:** Nickle Farm, Chartham, Canterbury, Kent CT4 7PL (☎01227-731441; fax 01227-731795).
**Fruit Pickers And Packers (50-100)** to pick and pack apples, pears, strawberries, plums, cherries and pumpkins. National minimum wage or piecework rate; to work variable hours a week, plus overtime - as they wish. Accommodation in caravans for £25 per week with communal kitchen and washing facilities. Cash daily during harvest. Workers needed from May-November, must be aged at least 18, fit and hard working.
*Applications* to the Farms Manager at the above address.

**C.E. MURCH LTD.:** Amery Court Farm, Chapel Lane, Blean, Canterbury, Kent CT2 9HF (☎01227-471774; fax 0207-6812014; e-mail cemurch@aol.com).
**Fruit/Asparagus Pickers (8).** Wages at piecework rates, equivalent to around £5 per hour; to work 6-8 hours per day. Accommodation in shared caravans is available at a cost of £20 per week. Workers required for a minimum of 2 weeks. Work is available from May 1st to mid July, then from September 5th to October 5th.

Foreign applicants with a good understanding of English and a valid work permit are welcome; please do not apply unless you have a valid work permit.
*Applications* from April to the above address.

**A.R. NEAVES & SONS:** Little Sharsted Farm, Doddington, Near Sittingbourne, Kent ME9 OJT (☎01795-886263; fax 01795-886470). A friendly family run business which has been running for sixty years and supplies fruit to the supermarkets.
**Strawberry Pickers (20)** for casual work. Wages on a piecework basis, to work 8 hours a day Monday to Saturday. Applicants must be over 18; no experience is necessary. Pickers are required from June 1st to July or August for a minimum of 6 weeks, however as there are other fruits (cherries, plums, apples) there could be up to 3 months work available.
Overseas applicants with a valid work permit are welcome. Accommodation is available at a charge of £15 per week.
*Applications* should be sent to Sarah Neaves/Martin Harman from the beginning of May onwards at the above address.

**NEWMAFRUIT FARMS LTD:** Howfield Farm, Howfield Lane, Chartham, near Canterbury, Kent CT4 7HQ (☎01227-738221; fax 01227-738086; e-mail Enquiries@Newmafruit.co.uk). A fairly large organisation, with a personal supervisor for all the students; a new accommodation area has just been built.
**Fruit Pickers/Packers.** Wages national minimum wage or piecework rate. Accommodation available at £20 per week. Workers required from 6th June to 30th September. Overseas applicants are recruited through Concordia (see Work Permits and Special schemes section).
*Applications* from March to Mr Melvyn Newman at the above address.

**R.H. NIGHTINGALE & PARTNER:** Gibbet Oak Farm, Appledore Road, Tenterden, Kent TN30 7DH (☎01580-763492; fax 01580-763938). Ideally situated only 2 miles from town with all amenities, campsite and mobile homes with usual facilities.
**Strawberry Pickers** to work from May to July.
**Apple Thinners** to work from June to July.
**Apple/Pear Pickers** (up to 15) to work from 25 August to 30 September.
To work 5-9 hours per day, depending on ripening of crops. Payment at piecework rates. Applicants should be fit, willing and able; age not important. Overseas applicants welcome, but those from outside the EU must hold a valid work permit.
*Applications* to P.J. Nightingale at the above address.

**PERRYHILL ORCHARD:** Bolebroke Lodge, Edenbridge Road, Hartfield, East Sussex TN7 4JJ (☎01892-770595).
**Fruit Pickers (8-10).** Wages £20-£45 per day. To work 4-8 hours per day picking mainly apples and top fruit. Work available during August, September and October. Must be aged at least 18 and have plenty of common sense.
Please *apply* to Mr J. Smith at the above address.

**POSTERN HEATH FARM:** Heath Farmhouse, Postern Lane, Tonbridge, Kent TN11 0QU (tel/fax 01732-354230; e-mail johnclevely@freenetname.co.uk). A small farm offering plenty of work; within walking distance of the town and railway.

**Fruit Pickers (8)** to pick apples and pears. Paid per bin picked with good rates for good pickers; overtime by arrangement. Period of work 9th-29th September approx. Job can involve driving the tractor (not essential). Accommodation available in caravans and possibly tents, with cooking and shower facilities available in the farm. Applicants with previous experience preferred; must be aged 18 or over.
*Applications* to Mrs M. Clevely, Owner, at the above address.

**REDSELL GROUP:** Nash Court, Boughton, Faversham, Kent ME13 9SR (☎01227-751224 or 07889-308731; e-mail pat.goode@redsell.com; www.redsell.com).
**Hop And Fruit Pickers (30-40)** needed to work on 200 acres of hops and 300 acres of top fruit. Piecework rates for fruit; Hops are picked on an hourly rate based on a 52-hour week. Period of work about four weeks from around 25th August. Basic accommodation provided free of charge. Workers must provide own bedding and cooking utensils. Non-EU students need to obtain their own work permits.
*Contact* Pat Goode.

**SOUTHERN MARQUEES:** 22 Peters Road, Locksheath, Southampton, Hampshire SO31 6EQ (☎01489-575372; e-mail sales@southernmarquees.co.uk). Excellent reputation for marquee hire, particularly for weddings, corporate events and parties. In operation 11 years.
**Marquee Erectors (4).** Wages £5 per hour. To work 30 hours per week plus overtime. Min. period of work of 4 months. Positions are available from end of April to the end of September. Need to be aged over 21 and have a minimum of 7 feet of reach, a strong back and loads of stamina; job involves heavy lifting. Clean driving licence. No accommodation available.
*Applications* should be made from end of March onwards to Hugh and Mandy Reigate at the above address. Interview necessary.

**SUNRISE FRUITS:** The Street, Stourmouth, nr. Canterbury, Kent CT3 1HY (☎01227-721977; fax 01227-728633).
**Strawberry/Raspberry Pickers** to work from June to October. Also some general farm work. To work approximately 40 hours per week; good piecework rates paid. Accommodation is available at a small charge; a £5 booking fee is returnable after the first working week. Minimum period of work 4 weeks. No experience or qualifications needed but applicants should be self-motivated.
Early *application* is recommended to the above address.

**TILMANSTONE SALADS:** Wigmore Lane, Eythorne, Near Dover CT15 4ND (☎01304-382061/833061; fax 01304-382443). A part of Geest foods, Tilmanstone salads prepares and packs salad and deli products.
**Production Operatives (100)** To prepare and pack salad products. Wages £5.05 per hour; to work alternate 6 and 4 day weeks for 8 hours a day. No experience is required. Applicants must be at least 21 years old.
Staff are required from March to September for a minimum period of 1 month. Overseas applicants are welcome but must have a valid work permit and understand enough English to comply with health and safety and food safety training.
*Applications* should be sent to Personnel at the above address from February onwards.

**VIBERT MARQUEES:** Manor Farm, Rue du Manoir, St Ouen, Jersey, JE3 2LF (☎01534-482970; fax 01534-482905; e-mail vibmarq@localdial.com). Long established, family-run business with 6 full-time and 20 seasonal workers.

**Marquee Erectors (10).** Wages from £6 per hour. To work from 8am to finish, varied hours including overtime and weekends, approx. 50 hours per week. Period of work runs April-September; min. period of work of July to September. Applicants must be 17+ and hard working. Foreign applicants who speak good English are welcome. No accommodation available, but there is a campsite within walking distance. Working shirts are provided free; shorts are recommended.

*Applications* should be made from January onwards to Gary Vibert at the above address.

**R.J. WALKER:** Little Postern, Postern Lane, Tonbridge TN11 0QU (☎01732-353290).
**Apple Pickers (5)** Piecework rates. To work for three weeks during September. Min. age 18. No accommodation available.

*Applications* by mid-August to Mr Walker at the above address.

**L. WHEELER & SONS (EAST PECKHAM) LTD:** Bullen Farm, East Peckham, Tonbridge, Kent TN12 5LX (☎01622-871225; fax 01622-872952). A hop farm within an hour's journey of London. Local facilities such as shops and pubs are available.
**Apple Pickers (20).** 6 hour day, 5½ days a week.
**Hop Pickers (20).** 8-9 hour day, 5½ days a week.
Wages approx. £4.10 per hour with the possibility of bonuses. Minimum period of work 5 weeks between 26 August and 30 September. Accommodation available with just a charge for electricity. Overseas applicants authorised to work in the UK welcome.

*Applications* from June to the Manager at the above address.

**L. WHEELER & SONS (YALDING) LTD:** Bockingfold, Marden, Tonbridge, Kent TN12 9PH (☎01892-730224/07808200404; fax 01892-722532). Farm is in mid Kent, near Paddock Wood railway station. Needs pickers for Gala and Bramley apples.
**Fruit Pickers** required for apple picking. Wages paid at piece rate per bin filled, hours flexible with low cost accommodation available. Work available from September 1st approx. for 3 weeks to a month. Applicants must be fit.

*Applications* to M.J. Wheeler, Director, at the above address.

**M.J.M. & G.A. WYANT AND SON:** The Packhouse, New Place Farm, Ickham, Canterbury, Kent CT3 1RA (☎01227-728538; fax 01227-721110). A family run horticultural business growing and packing vegetables for major supermarkets to a very high standard.
**Vegetable Harvest Workers (50), Vegetable Packhouse Staff (25).** Wages at piecework rates, some hourly work at £5 per hour. To work 40 hours per week plus overtime. Staff required for a minimum of 1 month between mid-July and early-October. Must have energy, dexterity, self-motivation, common-sense and the ability to follow instructions. Accommodation available. Overseas applicants with excellent English are considered.

*Applications* from 1st June to Geraldine Wyant at the above address.

**WORKING WONDERS:** Wapsbourne Manor Farm, Sheffield Park, Uckfield, East Sussex TN22 3QT (☎01825-723414; fax 01285-722451; e-mail info@wowo.co.uk; www.wowo.co.uk) A specialised working holiday company for gap year students/travellers situated in the East Sussex countryside, one hour south of London.

**Light Industrial and Service Industry Work;** Wages are minimum of £4.10 per hour. Weekend work is available. The sometimes demanding work requires flexibility, motivation and plenty of spirit. Applicants should be self disciplined with good social skills, a valid working visa and advanced English language skills. Minimum stay 13 weeks; ages 18-26; registration deposit required.

Meet and greet, accomodation, transport, holiday pay, bank account, national insurance, recreation and excursions are all services the company provides for an inexpensive weekly charge.

*Applications* to Working Wonders at the above address.

# Sport

**ALBOURNE EQUESTRIAN CENTRE:** Henfield Road, Albourne, West Sussex BN6 9OE (☎01273-832989; fax 01273-833392). An approved British riding school and livery yard, also Council approved. Regularly hold affiliated and unaffiliated shows and clinics.
**Working Pupils (2-3)** training for BHS exams. Work will consist of general yard work, riding tuition and the opportunity to compete at shows and events.Wages depending on experience; to work 5½ days a week from 8am to 5.30pm. Staff are required at any time for a minimum of 3 months. Applicants must be 16 and over. Accommodation is available at a charge of £30 per week. Students of all nationalities are considered; some experience with horses is prefered.

*Applications* should be sent to Megan Hughes at the above address. References required.

**ARUN DISTRICT COUNCIL:** Arun Civic Centre, Maltravers Road, Littlehampton, West Sussex BN17 5LF (☎01903-737662; fax 01903-733059). Local authority employer.
**Beach Lifeguards (12).** Wages £5 per hour. To work a 37-hour week; overtime possible. Min. period of work 6 weeks. Positions are available from May to September. Boat handling, powerboat driving, PWC and beach life guard training are all advantageous. Foreign applicants with permission to work in the UK and good English considered. Minimum age 17. No accommodation available.

*Applications* should be made from January onwards to Peter Knight, Foreshore Officer, at the above address. Interview necessary.

**CALSHOT ACTIVITIES CENTRE:** Calshot Spit, Fawley, Hampshire SO45 1BR (☎023-8089 2077; fax 023-8089 1267; e-mail calshot.ac@hants.gov.uk; www.hants.gov.uk/calshot). One of the biggest outdoor adventure centres in Britain, overlooking Southampton Water and the Solent, Calshot is perfectly located. It provides lessons, courses, short breaks and holidays in a wide range of water and land-based activities.
**Activity Instructors (10).** Wages £220+ per week. To work February to October. Applicants must be over 21 and have experience and qualifications in dinghy sailing, canoeing, windsurfing, etc. Experience in skiing or climbing or other outdoor activities an advantage.
**Visiting Instructors** to work all year round for single sessions, days, weekends. Must be fully qualified applicants over 18. Activities include dinghy sailing, canoeing, windsurfing, powerboating, rock climbing, skiing, and snowboarding.
**Summer Helpers** to assist with activities and pastoral care of youngsters aged 10-16. Pay at National Minimum Wage. To work July/August. Applicants must be over 18.
**Gatekeeper** to work 5 weeks July to August, £5.50 per hour

High levels of training and staff development are undertaken. Staff accommodation normally available. Good opportunities exist for internal promotion.

*Applications* to Calshot Activities Centre at the above address. From September 2002 for Activity Instructor positions.

**GIRLGUIDING UK:** Clayhill, Lyndhurst, Hants SO43 7DE (☎023-8028 2638; fax; 023-8028 2561; e-mail foxlease@girlguiding.org.uk). A centre owned by the Guide Association and used by schools, guides and scouts throughout the summer months. Residential and camping; canoeing, archery, climbing and swimming pool all on site.

**Activity Instuctors (4).** Wages £4.50 per hour; to work 40 hours per week or more if desired. Accommodation is available at a charge of £30 per week. Staff required between April and September; minimum stay is July and August. Applicants must be 18 or over at have at least two of the following: BCU (canoeing), GNAS (archery), Single Pitch Supervisor (climbing), National Pool Lifeguard. Suitably qualified foreign applicants are considered.

*Applications* from November to Hilary Chittock at the above address.

**HILSEA LIDO:** c/o Victoria Swimming Centre, Anglesea Road, Portsmouth PO1 3DL (☎023-9282 3822; fax 023-9287 1781).

**Casual Lifeguards (20)** required for the open-air Hilsea Lido between 26 May and 14 September. Wages are £4.50 per hour (2002 figure). To work from 11am-7pm daily with overtime as required, although the work is dependant on the weather. Applicants must be over 16 and have a National Pool Lifeguarding Qualification.

*Applications* in writing from May to A.D. Baker, Manager, at the Victoria Swimming Centre.

**MEDINA VALLEY CENTRE:** Dodnor Lane, Newport, Isle of Wight PO30 5TE (☎01983-522195; fax 01983-825962; e-mail info@medinavalleycentre.org.uk). An outdoor education and activity centre providing fieldwork courses for schools in Biology and Geography, Key Stage 2 to A-level. Also provides RYA sail training for adults and children.

**Seasonal Temporary RYA Dinghy Sailing Instructors** needed from the end of July to August. Must have RYA dinghy sailing instructor qualifications.

*Applications* to Peter Savory.

**REGENT LANGUAGE HOLIDAYS:** 40-42 Queens Road, Brighton BN1 3XB (☎01273-718620; fax 01273-718621; e-mail holidays@regent.org.uk; www.regent.org.uk). Regent operates five high quality residential centres in Southern England. They specialise in summer language holidays.

**Programme Co-ordinators(4).** £250-£300 per week. PGCE sports qualified. Full board and accommodation provided.

*Applications* at any time to Recruitment at the above address.

**SHEPWAY DISTRICT COUNCIL:** c/o Hythe Swimming Pool, South Road, Hythe, Kent CT21 6AR (☎01303-269177).

**Beach Lifeguards(4)** to perform patrol services including litter picking and normal lifeguard duties on Folkestone Beach. To work 8 hours per day. Usual period of work is 8 weeks. Positions are available from July to early September. Should be aged 18+, beach lifeguard qualifications required, English essential. People living locally can be given training at Hythe Pool. Overseas applicants welcome with appropriate qualifications and if they can arrange their own accommodation.

*Applications* to be made directly to Hythe Pool, enclosing a CV.

**TRAVEL CLASS LTD: 14 Queensway, New Milton, Hampshire BH25 5NN (☎08705 133773; fax 08705 133774; e-mail admin@travelclass.co.uk).** A premier UK provider of adventure activity and environmental programmes for primary age children. Heroic and enthusiastic role models required.
Activity Instructors, Group Leaders and Support staff required for a summer job with a difference, to work with children in glorious coastal locations across the south of England at Travel Class' JCA Adventure and Environmental Activity Centres. Training and qualifications provided but applicants require enthusiasm, dedication and an affinity with children. Great lifestyle working as part of a multi-national, young and vibrant team. Positions available from March until September, excellent wages, superb food and quality accommodation.
Call or e-mail at any time for an application pack.

# Voluntary Work

## Conservation and the Environment

**CELIA HAMMOND ANIMAL TRUST:** High Street, Wadhurst, East Sussex TN5 6AG (☎01892-783820; fax 01892-784882; http://web.ukonline.co.uk/chat).
A animal rescue and re-homing service and sanctuary that also offers low cost neutering and vaccination clinics.
**Volunteer Rescue Workers (4), Volunteer Administrative Staff (4).** Hours are negotiable.
**Veterinary Nurses (4), Veterinary Surgeons (4), Veterinary Receptionists (2).** Wages and hours are negotiable. A love of animals and an interest in animal welfare are essential. Accommodation is available at a cost to be negotiated. Staff are required all year round. An interview is required.
*Applications* to Miss Roma Brawn at the above address.

## Festivals and Special Events

**BROADSTAIRS FOLK WEEK:** Pierremont Hall, Broadstairs, Kent CT10 1JH (☎01843-604080; fax 01843-866048; e-mail info@folk-week.demon.co.uk; www .broadstairsfolkweek.com).
The Broadstairs Folk Week Trust, a registered charity, organises events throughout the year and an annual festival. 2003 will be the festival's 38th year. The whole town and its promenade, jetty, bandstand, taverns, halls, churches and streets becomes the venue for international music, song and dance.
**Volunteers (120+)** are needed as door stewards, information and shop staff, PA and sound technicians, drivers, campsite stewards and collectors. Volunteers are also needed to handle publicity and liaise with international personnel. Posts are unpaid, but staff receive a season ticket for access to all events. Free camping is available. Volunteers work 4 hours a day. Minimum period of work 3 days between 8th and 15th August. Overseas applicants with good English are considered.
*Applications* from March to Jane de Rose. Interview is not necessary

## Heritage

**HAMMERWOOD PARK:** Hammerwood, near East Grinstead, Sussex RH19 3QE (☎01342-850594; fax 01342-850864).
A Grade I listed building built in 1792, open to the public and providing exclusive, limited accommodation. The restoration of the house and garden is a family project; the estate was derelict in 1982. 28 miles from central London and same distance from the south coast.
**Voluntary Staff (2+)** required to help in all aspects of running a historic house and garden. No wages are paid but full board and accommodation are provided. To work 3-4 days per week. Staff required from Easter to the end of September for a minimum period of 1 month. Applicants must have the ability to deal with the public and be able to carry out tasks as they arise, even the mundane. Suitable foreign applicants with a good level of English are welcome. An interview is desirable.
*Applications* from January to David Pinnegar at the above address.

**MID HANTS RAILWAY (WATERCRESS LINE):** Railway Station, Alresford, Hampshire SO24 9JG (☎01962-733810; fax 01962-735448; e-mail watercressline @compuserve.com; www.watercressline.co.uk)
A preserved steam railway running trains between Alresford and Alton.
**Volunteers Needed:** work available, both full-time and part-time. Tourism students are particularly encouraged to apply, and there is the possibility of work for engineering students.
Staff are required from May to September for a minimum of 2 months. *Applications* should be sent to Volunteer Recruitment at the above address from the beginning of February.

## Social and Community Schemes

**THE SATURDAY VENTURE ASSOCIATION:** PO Box 9, Chichester, West Sussex, PO20 7YD (☎01243-511023; fax 01243-513464; e-mail sva2@btinternet.com).
A small national charity currently promoting disability awareness in the community. Sets up projects to form nationwide support for clubs and activities for young disabled people.
**Residential Worker.** To live as part of a family. Working in fundraising, repairing jewellery, cultivating plants for re-sale and similar chores. Part-time hours. IT competence an advantage. Must be a non-smoker, preferably with a driving licence. Would suit gap year student. Wide range of activity. Pocket money provided.
*Applications* to Jenny Bembridge on the above telephone or fax number.

# Vacation Traineeships & Internships

## Science, Construction and Engineering

**GIFFORD AND PARTNERS:** Carlton House, Ringwood Road, Woodlands, Southampton SO40 7HT (☎023-8081 7500; fax 023-8081 7600; e-mail bruce.cozens@gifford-consulting.co.uk; www.gifford-consulting.co.uk).
Gifford and Partners is a firm of consulting engineers particularly interested in the design of building and highway structures and in marine works worldwide. Each

summer the firm takes on up to **Six Students** to work in its Head Office and in the regional office in Chester. Student engineers work within a design team in a multidisciplinary consultants design office. Disciplines include civil, structural, building services, environmental and geotechnical engineering; also land surveyors and archaeologists.

Traineeships last for up to three months and are open to students reading Civil or Structural Engineering at university. Suitably qualified applicants from abroad are welcome. Salary discussed at interview.

Interested candidates should *contact* Mr Bruce Cozens, Personnel Manager, by 1 March.

## Travel and Tourism

**HOTEL HOUGUE DU POMMIER:** Castel, Guernsey, Channel Islands (☏ 01481-256531; fax 01481-256260; e-mail hotel@houguedupommier.guernsey.net; www.h otelhouguedupommier).

An attractive farmhouse style hotel on the west coast of Guernsey. Busy in summer with visitors from the UK, France, Germany and Switzerland.

Hotel Hougue du Pommier does not offer formal traineeships, but certain positions are open to **Students Of Catering** hoping to develop their skills and gain valuable work experience. The positions are mainly in the restaurant.

B & L is provided free of charge. Applicants are not required to attend an interview. Further details about jobs available and *applications* from Mr Steven Bone, General Manager, at the above address.

# East Anglia

**Prospects for Work.**
East Anglia is not one of the most promising of areas in which to look for temporary summer employment. However, Norfolk and Cambridgeshire are major agricultural areas and fruit picking, packing and processing work provide comparatively good prospects. King's Lynn, Wisbech and East Dereham (near Norwich) are the principal centres.

In and around King's Lynn the *Lynn News* carries general job advertisements. Factory work is the main source of summer employment in the town, as local food factories employ temporary production operators between June and September. The Jobcentre in King's Lynn keeps a register of people looking for work, though you are still advised to check in person on a regular basis. Priority is given to the local unemployed or students whose permanent home is King's Lynn. A lot of this work is governed by the weather, and is therefore irregular. King's Lynn Jobcentre can be contacted at Lovell House, St Nicholas Street, King's Lynn PE30 1LR (01553-734900). The *Eastern Daily Press*, which is circulated throughout Norfolk and in northern Suffolk, also lists general job vacancies.

Temporary tourism and holiday-related jobs are most easily found in Hunstanton, Cromer, Lowestoft and above all Great Yarmouth which, after Blackpool, is Britain's major entertainment resort. You can contact Great Yarmouth Jobcentre at Copperfield House, The Conge, Great Yarmouth NR30 1EJ; ☎01493-633300. Lowestoft Jobcentre (The Marina, Lowestoft, NR32 1HL; ☎01502-403200) has seasonal vacancies for local holiday camps from around February each year, particularly in catering and retail. Hunstanton has a number of large hotels which consistently require staff, particularly in the summer season. While some live-in accommodation is provided by employers in Hunstanton, this is harder to come by in King's Lynn and Wisbech (where rented lodgings are also in short supply). Wisbech Jobcentre (☎01945-675800) has general job adverts in the *Fenland Citizen*, which comes out every Wednesday, and the *Wisbech Standard*, which comes out every Friday. Temporary factory work for local large employers and lots of seasonal picking/packing work is available as well as many vacancies requiring skilled workers that cannot be filled.

In Ipswich it is worth visiting the JobShop at Westgate House, 5 Museum Street which is solely dedicated to job vacancies. The *Evening Star* has a pull-out jobs section every Wednesday which services not only Ipswich, but the surrounding areas.

As a major tourist attraction and language school centre, a number of associated jobs can be found in Cambridge. The town's Jobcentre (Henry Giles House, 73-79 Chesterton Road, Cambridge CB4 3BG, ☎01223-545000) usually has summer opportunities for catering staff and jobs teaching English as a foreign language. The burgeoning science and technology parks on the outskirts of the city can also be a lucrative source of vacation traineeships and internships. There is agricultural work available in the area picking soft fruits and later in the year, picking potatoes. A major local agricultural contractor uses the Earl of Derby pub car park on Hills Road as a pick-up point in the early morning for those wanting work. The contractor also offers agricultural work on a camping basis in many parts of England. The *Cambridge Evening News* newspaper advertises job vacancies on Wednesdays and Fridays.

Felixstowe, on the Suffolk coast, is usually a good source of temporary work, particularly catering and retail together with a few jobs in leisure. Felixstowe Jobcentre is at 29-31 Hamilton Road, Felixstowe, Suffolk IP11 7AZ; ☎01394-623300. Ipswich Borough Council and Suffolk County Council usually need to recruit temporary staff over the summer too.

# Business and Industry

**GRAND UK HOLIDAYS:** The Old Bakery, Queens Road, Norwich, Norfolk, NR1 3PL (☎01603-886751; fax 01603-886702). Britain's largest coach tour operators catering exclusively for the over 55s in over 140 resorts and destinations throughout the UK.
**Couriers (25).** £175 net per week plus optional excursion and tips. To work on eight-day coach tours. Applicants must be friendly and have an outgoing personality and the ability to relate to those aged over fifty-five. Accommodation and food provided. Staff needed from April to October.

*Applications* to the above address.

# Children

**EXPERIENCE UK LTD:** 48 Fitzalan Road, London N3 3PE (☎020-8922 9739; fax 020-8343 0625; e-mail xuk@xkeys.co.uk; www.campsforkids.co.uk). Residential camps in East Anglia for children aged 6-17 years.
**Childrens Leaders, Cooks, Kitchen Assistants, Cleaners.** Competitive wages plus free board. Qualifications or experience in first aid, life saving, arts/crafts, sports, or teaching are helpful. Applications from teachers or student teachers preferred.

More details and *application* forms available on the above website.

**F.A.C.E.S. KIDS CLUB:** Hedley Walter School, Sawyers Hall Lane, Brentwood, Middlesex CM15 9DA (☎01277-204018; janedupreez@hotmail.com).
**Playworkers (2-3).** To supervise, play and be creative with children aged 4-12 years in the summer holidays (July/August). Pay from £4.10 depending on age, qualifications and experience. Must like children. Will need to be police-checked. NVQ II or III in playwork desirable but not essential.
*Applications* to Jane Dupreez at the above address.

**IPSWICH BOROUGH COUNCIL:** Civic Centre, Civic Drive, Ipswich IP1 2EE (☎01473-433514; fax 01473-433636; e-mail jane.hennell@ipswichgov.uk).
**Playworkers (12)** Wages £4.10 per hour.
**Playsupervisors (3) Sportscheme Leaders (3) Daycamp Leaders (2)** Wages £4.97 per hour; to work Monday to Friday. Applicants must be aged 18+ and have experience of working with children.
Applicants should *apply* to the Leisure Services (01473-435000) at the above address from early March.

**KIDS KLUB:** The Lodge, The Hall, Great Finborough, Stowmarket, Suffolk IP14 3EF (☎01449-742700; fax 01449-742701; e-mail info@kidsklub.co.uk).
**Activity Supervisors (30).** Salary at least £100 per week. Min. age 18.
**Activity Instructors (15).** Salary at least £125 per week. Must have National Governing Body awards. Min. age 18.
**Matrons (4).** Salary at least £125 per week. Must have first aid or nursing qualifications. Min. age 21.
**General Assistants (4).** Salary at least £75 per week. Min. age 16.
All positions are for 6 days per week. Staff are required from March 1st or July 1st to August 31st. Min. period of work 4 weeks. Accommodation is available at no extra charge.
Applicants from overseas welcome; a phone or personal interview is required.
*Applications* from January to Ian Lewis at the above address.

## Holiday Centres and Amusements

**ADVENTURE ISLAND:** Western Esplanade, Southend-on-Sea, Essex, SS1 1EE (☎01702-468023; fax 01702-601044).
**Ride Operators, Catering Staff, Cashiers (50-60)** required for the summer, wages and hours by arrangement, staff must be over 18.
*Applications* to the Personnel Department, at the above address.

**CAMP BEAUMONT DAY CAMPS LTD:** Beaumont Lodge, Overstrand Hall, Overstrand, Norfolk. NR27 0JJ (☎01263-579666; fax 01263-576312; e-mail jobs@campbeaumont.com). Vacancies are currently available for all camps, which run for six weeks during July and August.
**Group Leaders (250)** (minimum age 18 years) These posts require previous leadership experience with young people and/or a well developed interest in sports, music, drama, arts and crafts or any recreational pursuits as the job entails looking after and instructing groups of children.
**Activity Instructors** (minimum age 21 years). The role is similar to that of a Group Leader, but with responsibility for planning and instructing a particular activity or group of activities. Applicants must either hold the appropriate recognised qualification and/or be highly experienced in that particular activity.
**Nursery Leaders** (minimum age 18 years) must have NNEB/BTEC or equivalent qualification or trainee Nursery Nurses. They need to have proven communication

skills in relation to children and the ability to create structured activity sessions that allow incidental learning to take place.
**Camp Nurse/First Aider** must be a Registered nurse and/or first aid qualified (Red Cross or St John's Ambulance 'First Aid at Work' qualification).
**Camp Director/Assistant Camp Director** Need relevant management experience, activity camp knowledge, leadership flair, co-ordination and planning ability is essential, and the ability to communicate at various levels – with children, parents, overseas teachers (residential camps) and staff, and to take overall responsibility for the running of camp, including areas such as: programming, personnel management, customer care, diplomacy, transport, financial control and health and safety.

For further details and *applications* regarding any of these posts, camp locations and salary information, please contact the Recruitment Co-Ordinator.

**COLCHESTER ZOO LTD:** Maldon Road, Colchester, Essex CO3 5SL (☎01206-331292; fax 01206-331392; e-mail admin@colchester-zoo.co.uk). The zoo has gained a reputation as one of the most modern and forward-thinking zoos in the UK.
**Retail Staff (12), Catering Staff (12), Site Cleaners (4), Face Painters (3), Gardeners (2).** No accommodation available.

To request an *application form* please send a s.a.e. to Colchester Zoo. Note all applicants must be available for interview.

**IMPERIAL WAR MUSEUM:** Duxford, Cambs CB2 4QR (☎01223-499300; fax 01223-837267). Duxford was a former RAF fighter airfield during the Battle of Britain and is steeped in history. Today Duxford is Europe's premier aviation museum and visitor attraction.
**Museum Assistants (6-9)** to invigilate within the museum, assist visitors, monitor exhibitions and carry out cleaning duties. Wages £9,695 per annum, pro rata, to work 40½ hours a week. Must be 17 or over, hold a driving licence and be eligible to work in the UK. Period of work from March to October. Foreign applicants with good understanding of English welcome.

*Applications* before March to the Personnel Office at the above address. An interview is required.

**PLEASURE AND LEISURE CORPORATION plc:** Pleasure Beach, South Beach Parade, Great Yarmouth, Norfolk NR30 3EH (☎01493-844585; fax 01493-853483; e-mail GYPBeach@aol.com or Nigelthurs@aol.com). A family company operating a major leisure and amusement park with over 25 rides, two amusement arcades and a social club over 9 acres. More than 1 million visitors every year.
**Ride Operators (50).** At least National Minimum Wage, plus full uniform and staff concessions on rides and food outlets. Working hours are variable according to the time of the season. Min. period of work of 4 weeks. Positions are available from March to September. Must be aged 18+ and with good spoken English. No previous experience necessary as training provided. Accommodation not available.

*Applications* should be made from March onwards to Nigel Thurston, Personnel Manager. Interview necessary.

# Hotels and Catering

**ALEXANDERS INTERNATIONAL SCHOOL:** Bawdsey Manor, Bawdsey, Woodbridge, Suffolk IP12 3AZ (☎01394-411633; fax 01394-411357; e-mail englis h@alexandersint.demon.co.uk). An international summer school for 11-18 year olds from all over the world. English Language tuition plus specialist sports courses.

**Domestic Assistants (6) and Estate Workers (6)** Wages commensurate with experience; to work 40 hours a week including weekends. Must be 21 or over. Period of work from 18th June-28th August. Minimum period of work 2 weeks. Free accommodation is available.
*Applications* to the Administration Office from March to the above address.

**ARUNDEL HOUSE HOTEL:** Chesterton Road, Cambridge CB4 3AN (☎01223-367701; fax 01223-367721; e-mail info@arundelhousehotels.co.uk; www.arundelhousehotels.co.uk). A 2 Star private hotel in the centre of Cambridge with 103 bedrooms, à la carte restaurant, bar and conservatory.
**Waiting/Bar Staff (5).** Wages £4.55 per hour; to work 39 hours per five day week. Overtime paid at single time. Staff required at Easter and from June-October for a minimum period of 8 weeks. No accommodation is available. Applicants should be 18 or over; experience is not essential.
*Applications* in writing to Ms Lynn Moulding at the above address.

**BRIDGE HOTEL:** Clayhythe, Near Waterbeach, Cambridge CB5 9HQ (☎01223-860252; fax 01223-440448).
**Bar Staff (2)** wanted for June, July and August. Wages £4.50 per hour. Applicants must be over 18.
To *apply* contact Maggie Manson, Owner, at the above address.

**GREAT ADVENTURES:** Grafham Water Centre, Perry, Huntingdon, Cambridgeshire PE28 0BX (☎01480-810521; fax 01480-812739; e-mail grafham.water@education.cambridgeshire.gov.uk; www.grafham-water-centre.co.uk).
**Catering Assistants (3)** to work May-July. To work 8 hours per day; wages of £184 per week plus food and accommodation. Applicants need a basic food hygiene certificate. Domestic assistants also required.
*Applications* to Mr Ian Downing, Manager, at the above address.

**HAVEN PASSENGER CRUISES LTD:** P.O.Box 401, Cambridge, CB4 3WE (☎01223-307694; fax 01223-307695; e-mail info@georgina.co.uk). The Georgina is a fully-appointed passenger craft on the river Cam, taking mainly private bookings for weddings, birthdays, corporate events and the group travel market.
**Crew (5/6)** for the Riverboat Georgina. Wages of £5.00 per hour plus tips. To work between May and September. Job involves bar work, serving food and general crewing tasks (tying/untying ropes, opening/closing locks on river). Full training given. Applicants must be at least 18 and proficient in English.
*Applications* to Nick Bennett, Operations Manager.

**HILTON NORWICH HOTEL:** Cromer Road, Norwich, Norfolk NR6 6JA (☎01603-410544; fax 01603-487701; e-mail personnel.manager@norwich.stakis.co.uk). Close to Norwich International Airport, the hotel has 121 rooms, a busy á la carte restaurant and large banqueting rooms.
**Bar Hosts, Banqueting Hosts, Waiting Staff (20-30 in total).** Wages up to £5 per hour. To work part-time or full-time shifts - must be flexible. Positions are available all year; accommodation not available Minimum age 18. Overseas applicants welcome.
*Applications* should be made to Karen Lawrence, Personnel Manager, as soon as possible. Interview necessary.

**KENTWELL HALL:** Long Melford, Sudbury, Suffolk CO10 9BA (☎01787-310207; fax 01787-379318). A redbrick Tudor mansion in rural Suffolk offering

re-creations of Tudor domestic life. Staff on the 20th century side ensure smooth running of event for the public.
**Retail and Catering Staff (10)** to serve in a temporary shop/restaurant in a marquee during 16th century re-creations; duties also include marshalling school parties. Wages by arrangement; must make own arrangements for accommodation. Minimum age 16; applicants need a pleasant manner and to be fit as they will be on their feet all day. Period of work 4 weeks from 20th June-16th July.
*Applications* should be sent to Dawn Champion, Administrator, at the above address.

**THE LODGE HOTEL:** Old Hunstanton Road, Hunstanton, Norfolk PE36 6HX (☏01485-532896; fax 01485-535007). A Grade II listed Hotel close to a beach with 22 ensuite bedrooms; popular with bird watchers and golfers.
**Waiting and Bar Person and Housekeeping Staff.** Wages £4-£4.30 per hour, depending on age and experience.required for 20-40 hours per week from early July to late September. Min. period of work 6 weeks. Accommodation can be provided. Must have some relevant experience. Overseas applicants welcome.
*Applications* should be made as soon as possible to Mr A.G. Best, Proprietor, at the above address.

**MARLBOROUGH HOTEL:** Sea Road, Felixstowe, Suffolk IP11 2BJ (☏01394-285621; fax 01394-670724).
**Housekeeper/Waiting Staff (2) and Commis Chef (1)** £90, plus laundry, per week plus tips, food and accommodation. To work a maximum of 45 hours per week.
**Receptionist (1)** £90, plus laundry, per week plus tips, food and accommodation. Shift work 7am-3pm or 3-11.30pm.
All staff needed to work 5 days in 7 from May to October inclusive. Minimum age 18. Applicants must be able to speak English.
*Applications* to Sharon Petley, General Manager at the above address.

**OASIS LEISURE CENTRE:** King's Lynn & West Norfolk Borough Council, Central Promenade, Hunstanton, Norfolk PE36 5BD (☏01485-534227; fax 01485-534227). A seafront leisure centre comprising pools, slides, roller skating, café, squash and tennis courts.
**Catering Assistants (6).** Experience of fast food service required, plus basic food hygiene certificate. Wages National Minimum Wage. To work up to 47 hours, 6 days per week. Period of work April to October. Accommodation is not available. Applicants should be available for interview.
*Applications* from February onwards to the Manager at the above address.

**STOKE BY NAYLAND CLUB:** Keepers Lane, Leavenheath, Colchester, Essex CO6 4PZ (☏01206-262836; fax 01206-263356). A 30-bedroom hotel with two 18-hole golf courses and a leisure centre.
**Bar/Waiting Staff and Cleaners** needed. Hours and wages to be discussed at interview. Accommodation possibly available, at an approximate charge of £25 per week. Foreign applicants with fluent English welcome; applicants must be 17 or over (18 for bar staff).
*Applications* to Jeff Hunt at the above address. Interview required but may be done by telephone.

**TOPSAIL CHARTERS LTD:** Cooks Yard, The Hythe, Maldon, Essex CM9 5HN (☏01621-857567; fax 01621-840567; e-mail info@top-sail.co.uk). Based in

Maldon but also working in London and Ipswich. Private functions and public trips on historic sailing barges. A small company, very customer-orientated, with a great team of staff on board.
**Bar Worker, Host/ess, Catering Assistants (3)** for work on Thames sailing barges. Wages approx. £6 per hour. Must be flexible about hours, up to 50 per week. Positions are available from April to September. Some bar/catering experience preferable; must be flexible and combine galley and bar work. No accommodation provided.
*Applications* to Stephanie Valentine from Easter onwards. Interview necessary.

## Language Schools

**ALEXANDERS INTERNATIONAL SCHOOL:** Bawdsey Manor, Bawdsey, Woodbridge, Suffolk IP12 3AZ (☎01394-411633; fax 01394-411357; e-mail office@alexandersschool.com). An international summer school for 11-18 year olds from all over the world. English Language tuition plus specialist sports and activities courses.
**Residential Sports Assistants (24).** Wages £200-£245 per week; to work 48 hours per week over 6 days, including weekends. Applicants must be undergraduate sports teachers or qualified professional coaches and 21 years or older.
**EFL Teachers (24).** Wages approx. £350 per week; to work 6 days a week including a Saturday or Sunday. Must be RSA certified TEFL or better and 23 years or over. Period of work June-August inclusive. Minimum period of work 4 weeks. Free accommodation is available.
*Applications* to the Administration Office, from March to the above address.

**ASPECT ILA:** 75 Barton Road, Cambridge (☎01223-357702; fax 01223-311939; e-mail enquiries@aspectworld.com). Long-established year-round english language school with large junior summer school.
**EFL Teachers (30), Social Organisers (30), Director of Studies, Centre Manager.** Wages from £250 to £340 according to position. Work is full-time. Min. period of work is two weeks. Positions are available from July to end of August. CELTA is required for all teachers, DELTA for the centre manager, and sports coaching experience is preferable for the social organisers. Accommodation is available for £70 per week.
*Applications* should be made to Jane Bloomfield from March onwards. A telephone interview will be required.

**BELL YOUNG LEARNERS:** Lancaster House, South Road, Saffron Walden, Essex CB11 3DP (☎01799-581880; fax 01799-516690; e-mail staff.yl@bell-centres.com). The Bell Educational Trust runs residential courses for overseas students aged 8-17 during the summer period at five independent UK schools.
**Sports & Social Staff** From £40 per day. Required June-August.
**Course Assistants** From £20 per day. Non-teaching.
**Course Directors** From £65 per day. Required July-August. Must have degree and teaching qualifications.
**Directors Out-of-Course Activities** From £50 per day. Degree in sports sciences/ drama/tourism and managerial experience.
**House Supervisors** From £40 per day. Degree and preferably a teaching qualification. Acts a bit like a house warden, responsible for the welfare of all students.
**Director Of Studies** From £50 per day. Degree and RSA/Cambridge Dip. TEFLA or equivalent experience of teaching EFL to young learners.
**EFL Teachers** From £40 per day. Degree, TEFL qualification and teaching

qualification preferred.
**Nurses** to run morning and evening surgery and help with pastoral and welfare matters. From £45 per day.
**Team Leaders** From £40 per day. Graduate or equivalent and teaching qualification.
**Activity Leaders** From £33 per day. Preferably a graduate and have special skills to offer, e.g. trampolining coach.
**Activity Assistants** £25 per day. Preferably undergraduates. Age 20 years plus and responsible for children.
All positions include full B & L and 24 hours leave per week. Full job descriptions can be obtained from Bell Young Learners.
*Applications* to Sue Nellis, Recruitment Secretary.

**BRIAR SCHOOL OF ENGLISH:** 8 Gunton Cliff, Lowestoft, Suffolk NR32 4PE (☎01502-573781; fax 01502-589150; e-mail briareducation@fsbdial.co.uk). Situated in the pleasant seaside town of Lowestoft. Established in 1958 and offers English courses to international students aged 12-25.
**EFL Teachers.** From £8 per hour. TEFL qualifications or experience preferable. Applicants must possess either a degree or a teacher's certificate.
**Sports Instructors.** From £6 per hour. Must hold at least an L.T.A. Part 1 certificate.
To work up to 6 hours per day. Min. period of work 3 weeks between end of June and end of August. Successful applicants for both jobs can earn extra pay by leading excursions on Saturdays to Norwich, Cambridge, London and other local places of interest. Accommodation is not available.
Teaching *Applications* should be sent to Ms H. Sterne and Sports Instructor applications to Mr N. J. Doe, at the above address.

**CAMBRIDGE ACADEMY OF ENGLISH:** 65 High Street, Girton, Cambridge CB3 0QD (☎01223-277230; fax 01223-277606; e-mail sheila@caeco.demon.co.uk). Situated in the leafy suburb of Girton, the Academy runs non-residential courses for teenagers and young adults, and residential courses for the 10-13 age group.
**EFL Teachers** to teach teenagers and young adults. Required for 3 week courses between June 23 and August 22; wages of approx. £800 per course. The job involves 21-24 hours teaching a week. Must have RSA TEFL/Trinity College certificate or equivalent and experience.
*Applications* to S. Levy at the above address.

**THE EAST SUSSEX SCHOOL OF ENGLISH:** 92 Portland Road, Hove, BN3 5DN (☎01273-736404; fax 01273-770672; e-mail esse@mistral.co.uk).
**EFL Teachers (5)** required for July and August, working hours negotiable. Wages according to qualifications and experience. Applicants must have at least PGCE, CELTA or DELTA qualifications.
*Applications* to Tony Gill, Principal, at the above address.

**CAMBRIDGE CENTRE FOR LANGUAGES:** Sawston Hall, Church Lane, Sawston, Cambridgeshire CB2 4JR (☎01223-835099; fax 01223-837424; e-mail ar70@dial.pipex.com).
**EFL Teachers (6+), Activities Organisers (3), Social and Welfare Officers (1-2).** Wages £250 per week with free accommodation. Required July-August to staff residential summer camps for children aged 10-17.
For details and *applications* contact John F. Sullivan at the above address.

**EFL INTERNATIONAL LANGUAGE SCHOOLS:** 221 Hills Road, Cambridge CB2 2RW (☎01223-240020; fax 01223-412474; e-mail pippa.cusimano@ef.com).
Leaders required to work with adults and/or juniors during the summer. Responsibilities include organising events, entertainment and excursions. You will be expected to attend the events and to act as courier/guide on excursions. The hours of work are varied and will include evenings and weekends. Minimum age 18 with good communication skills; experience of working with young people an advantage.
*Applications* to Pippa Cusimano, School Director.

**STUDIO SCHOOL OF ENGLISH:** 6 Salisbury Villas, Station Road, Cambridge CB1 2JF (☎01223-369701; fax 01223-314944; e-mail richard.mountford@studiocambridge.co.uk; www.studiocambridge.co.uk). The oldest of the permanently-established Cambridge language schools, and a founder member of the ARELS organisation
**EFL Teachers** for young people's courses (age 10-14 and 14-17). Applicants should have CELTA, TESOL and/ or EFL experience.
**Activity Organisers** for young people's courses (ages as above). Applicants should have interests/abilities in sport, art, music or drama, and need stamina, initiative and enthusiasm.
**Course Directors and Assistant Course Directors** (ages as above). Applicants should have good organisational and managerial skills. Some EFL or summer camp experience preferred.
 Residential and non-residential posts available, mainly between July and August but also at other times of the year; only those who speak English as if it were their first language need apply.
*Applications* to Richard Mountford at the above address.

# Medical
**ESSEX NURSING SERVICES:** 3rd Floor, St Botolphs Street, Colchester, Essex CO2 7PU (☎01206-578600; fax 01206-577899; e-mail opportunities@ensrg.co.uk ). A busy employment agency covering homecare, nursing homes and hospitals.
**Care Staff.** Unlimited positions available for those with at least 6 months experience in a care environment. Wages from £5-10 per hour, full or part time and at any time of the year. Suitably qualified foreign applicants welcome, but fluent English is essential. Accommodation is not available.
*Applications* should be made at any time to Linda Jones at the above address. Interview required.

# Outdoor
**1ST CHOICE PERSONNEL:** Fenberry Farm, Peters Point, Sutton Bridge, Spalding PE12 9UX (tel/fax 01406-351044). Small family-run employment agency.
**Factory and Farm Workers.** to carry out various tasks including factory tasks with fruit or flowers, picking, potato grading and fruit preparation. Wages £200 per week. To work 9-10 hours, 5½ days a week. Min. period of work of 2 weeks. Positions are available all year. Foreign applicants with fluent English welcome. No previous experience necessary. Accommodation available for £40 per week.
*Applications* should be made at any time to Keith Hargreaves at the above address.

**BOXFORD (SUFFOLK) FARMS LTD:** Hill Farm, Boxford, Sudbury, Suffolk CO10 5NY. (☎01787-210348; fax 01787-211106). A family owned company supplying fruit to major supermarkets. Situated in beautiful countryside within an hour's train journey from London.
**Fruit Pickers and Fruit Packers** required to work on farms and packhouse situated on the Suffolk/Essex border. The work involves the picking and packing of soft and top fruit (strawberries, raspberries, apples etc). The season is from June to July for soft fruit and the middle of August to the end of October for apples. Hours of work and wages are variable subject to the crop and weather. Self catering caravan accommodation is available and the camp has toilets, showers, laundry facilities and TV. Workers must be over 18 years old with a liking for outside work and with valid working visas and work permits. It is essential that the farm is contacted 24 hours before arrival.
*Applications* to the Personnel Manager at the above address.

**C & I MARQUEES:** Cornsland, Hall Lane (north of A1277), Upminster, Essex RM14 1TX (☎01268-584736). A family run business that manufactures and hires marquees throughout the South East.
**Marquee Erectors (5).** Wages £4.00 per hour; to work 7am-5pm Monday to Friday. No accommodation is available. Staff required for a minimum of 4 weeks between 1st June and 15th September. Must be 16 or over; no experience necessary, just commitment and fitness. Foreign applicants with good spoken English are welcome.
*Applications* from April to the above address.

**CHELMER MARQUEES LTD:** Waltham Road, Boreham, Chelmsford CM3 3AY (☎01245-450033; fax 01245-451133; e-mail hire@chelmermarquees.co.uk).
**Marquee Erectors (5).** Wages from £5-5.50 per hour; time and a half paid on Sundays and Bank Holidays. To work 7:30am-6:30pm or longer Monday to Friday; 8am to 6pm Sundays. Staff required from April to end September 2003. Work involves erecting and lacking down marquees and equipment, cleaning and driving. Minimum age 18. Must have a clean driving licence.
*Applications* should be made to G.R. Anstee, Director, at the above address.

**FIVEWAYS FRUIT FARM:** Fiveways, Stanway, Colchester, Essex CO3 5LR (☎01206-330244; fax 01206-330828; e-mail fiveways.fruit.farm@farming.co.uk). A medium sized farm run by two brothers growing mainly strawberries, cherries and apples. Situated in a rural oasis on the outskirts of Colchester with shops close by.
**Fruit Pickers (17-22).** Wages at piece work rates, approx. £100-£250+ per 5-7 day week. Hours flexible, start at 6am with hourly work also available. No overtime. Strawberry picking from May-September; apple picking from August but principally from September to October; orchard work and many semi-skilled jobs in propagation tunnels and French tunnels etc.; packing fruit for supermarkets.
Minimum period of work 4 weeks. Meadow next to farm available for camping. Caravans on site with all facilities, including showers, cooking facilities and television. Charge £20 per week. Supermarket, post office, off-licence and launderette within a 5 minutes walk from the farm. Overseas students aged over 18 welcome.
*Applications* from the beginning of the year to Alistair Mead, c/o Fiveways Fruit Farm.

**FRIDAYBRIDGE INTERNATIONAL FARM CAMP:** March Road, Fridaybridge, Wisbech, Cambridgeshire PE14 0LR (☎01945-860255; fax 01945-861088). A very friendly, family run company offering the chance to meet people from all over the world.

**General Agricultural Workers** to harvest strawberries, apples, broccoli, potatoes and salads and to help with many other jobs. To normally work 5-6 days per week, although this cannot be guaranteed. . Vacancies available April-November. Min. period of work 3 weeks. Basic accommodation, breakfast and dinner provided at a reasonable weekly charge, payable in advance.

Club, disco, swimming pool, tennis courts, basketball, volleyball, day trips, free English lessons (conversational) and many other facilities provided. Staff vacancies also available for drivers, bar work, shop staff, kitchen asistants, administrative staff and English teachers. EU students aged 16-30 welcome.

Send s.a.e./IRC for brochure (*Applications* on official forms only) to Bookings, Fridaybridge International Camp.

**G'S MARKETING LTD:** Hostel, Barway, Ely, Cambridgeshire CB7 5TZ (☎01353-727314; fax 01353-727255).
**Production Operatives.** Wages at piecework rates (average £180 per week). Required from October to the end of April to trim, pack and label salad and vegetable crops plus some farming positions. Must be fit and willing to work. Evening meal and accommodation provided on site. Minimum age 18.
*Applications* to Sharon Gudgeon, Hostel Recruitment Officer, at the above address.

**G.E. ELSWORTH & SON:** Park Fruit Farm, Park Lane, Great Holland, Frinton-on-Sea, Essex CO13 OES (☎01255-674621; e-mail s.elsworth@farmline.com).
**Fruit Pickers (15)** to pick apples in September. Wages at National Minimum rates. To work flexible hours between 9am and 5pm. No accommodation available.
*Applications* to S.Elsworth, Partner, at the above address.

**HADLEY MARQUEES LTD:** Unit 9, Minton Enterprise Park, Oaks Drive, Newmarket, Suffolk, CB87YY (☎01638-663777). A friendly company where good work is rewarded highly.
**Marquee Erectors (4-6)** Wages £6 per hour; to work 10 hours a day Monday to Saturday, no overtime paid. No accommodation available. Applicants must be prepared to work flexible hours, weekends and occasional long hours. It is important to be physically fit as the job involves lifting heavy materials. Staff are required from the end of April to September/October. Overseas applicants are welcome.
*Applications* should be sent to the above address from February onwards. Interview necessary.

**HIGHFIELD TIFFANY MARQUEES:** Klondyke Farm, Broads Road, Burwell, Cambridge CB5 OBQ (tel/fax 01638-743860; e-mail the info@thehighfieldsgroup.co.uk; www.thehighfieldsgroup.co.uk).
**Marquee Hire Labourers (Up To 4)** to assist with marquee hire from June to August. Long hours available subject to workload. Wages from National Minimum Wage. Accommodation can be arranged at a cost to be advised. Must be physically fit.
*Contact* Gary Chapman, Proprietor.

**HAWK TRADING LTD:** Hawk Farm, Weeley, Clacton-on-Sea, Essex CO16 9AG (☎01255-830251; fax 01255-830060 e-mail hawktrading@1c24.net).
**Fruit Workers (20)** Wages £4.20 per hour and piecework up to £10 per hour. Variable hours up to six days per week. needed from June to September. Must be able-bodied and willing to work outdoors.
*Applications* to Mr. R. Rendall at the above address.

**INTERNATIONAL FARM CAMP:** Hall Road, Tiptree, Essex CO5 0QS (☎01621-815496; e-mail ifc@tiptree.com).
**Fruit Pickers.** Pay at piecework rates. Hours 8am-4pm Monday to Friday; some weekend work. Full B & L provided for approx. £60 a week. Must be aged 20-25 years. Min. work period 2 weeks between early June and mid-July.
Overseas applicants welcome, but places for non-EEA nationals are open only to full-time students who have not completed their studies. *Applications* to be sent as early as possible to the above address: s.a.e. (or IRC if writing from abroad) essential for reply.

**A.E. MARSHALL FARMS:** Old Shields Farm, Ardleigh, Colchester, Essex CO7 7NE (☎01206-230251; fax 01206-231825).
**Fruit Pickers (20-40)** to work from the end of May to July. Wages by arrangement, paid out weekly. To work from 8am-4pm, 6 days per week. Min. age 18 years. Camping and dormitory accommodation available for around 15 people, own equipment is required.
*Applications* should be sent to Gail Marshall at the above address.

**M & B MARQUEES:** Hawk Cove, Battles Bridge, Essex SS11 7RL (☎01268-562622; fax 01268-574228; e-mail sales@mb-marquees). Family-run business, established 25 years ago.
**Marquee Erectors (up to 10).** Wages negotiable. Positions are available from May to September. Applicants should be 21+, driving licence an advantage. No Accommodation available. Foreign applicants welcome.
*Applications* should be made from April onwards to Mr S Moxey at the above address.

**MAYFAIR MARQUEES:** 3 Horizon Works, Dereham Road, New Costessey, Norwich NR5 OSE (☎01603-747200; fax 01603-749100; e-mail mayfair.marquees@zoo.co.uk). A small marquee and furniture hire business covering Norfolk, Suffolk and Cambridgeshire.
**Marquee Erectors (5).** Wages £4.40 starting rate; to work 40 hours per week but also overtime paid at 1½ times the starting rate. Staff are required from mid May to the end of September. Applicants should be at least 5'11 and 19 years old or over. Overseas applicants are welcome. No accommodation available.
*Applications* should be sent to Andrew Cocker at the above address from January onwards. Interview necessary.

**D.A. NEWLING & SON:** Turnover Farm, Decoy Road, Gorefield, Wisbech, Cambridgeshire PE13 4PL (☎01945-870749; e-mail p9ear@aol.com). A family fruit farm with a small and friendly workforce.
**Apple and Pear Pickers(10).** Piecework rates, average £40-£50 per day depending on how hard you work. To work 8 hours per day with some overtime. Min. period of work of 4 weeks. Positions are available from 30 August-30 September. Accommodation generally not available, but possible for the right candidates at £10 per week (no board). Applicants must be 17 or over, clean, healthy and able; foreign applicants with sufficient English to understand instructions welcome. No previous experience necessary.
*Applications* should be made from April onwards to Edward Newling at the above address.

**OUTBACK INTERNATIONAL LTD:** Jark House, Beechhurst, 8 Commercial Road, Dereham, Norfolk NR19 1AE (☎01362-691608; fax 01362-691593).

Recruitment agency that require staff all year round for production work in and around the Norfolk and Suffolk area.
**Production Staff** to pick, pack, cut, sort, label and box fruits, vegetables, meats, poultry, toys, dairy products, flowers and much more. Wages from £4 to £6 per hour plus overtime and holiday pay. Self-catering accommodation is available for £57.50 per week. Catered accommodation is available for approx. £82.50 per week, including 3 meals, laundry, wake-ups, tel/fax and transport to and from work.

Min. period of work 12 weeks at any time of year. Applicants must be 18-35 years old. Overseas applicants with EU/EEA passport or work authorisation, and good English are considered. Interview not necessary.

*Applications* with I.D. at least 2-3 weeks before arrival date to Natalie Aston or Irene Abru (Spanish and Portuguese).

**R. & J.M. PLACE LTD:** Church Farm, Tunstead, Norwich NR12 8RQ. Large soft fruit growers in the centre of the Broadland National Park.
**Fruit Picking,** weather permitting, details on application. Accommodation available for £49.70 per week, including breakfast, in purpose-built dormitory blocks. Tents and caravans are not permitted. Must be in good health. No previous experience necessary. Social activities in camp include tennis, volleyball, badminton, basketball, football, pool and many other activities. Open between end of February and November. Overseas applicants welcome.
*Applications* with s.a.e. to the Administrator, R. & J.M. Place Ltd.

**H.R. PHILPOT & SON LTD:** Barleylands Farm, Barleylands Road, Billericay, Essex CM11 2UD (☎01268-532253; 01268-290222; e-mail robert@barleylandsfarm.co.uk). Established arable farmers with farms in Essex and Suffolk.
**Tractor Drivers (10)** Wages £5 per hour; to work from the end of June until the end of September. Hard physical work during pea vining and general harvest. Must be adaptable to take on any job when asked. Applicants must have a valid driving licence.

Staff are required to work for 3 months. Accommodation is available for £20 per week and a £120 Bond deposit which is returned at the end of employment. Overseas applicants are considered but must have a valid work permit for the UK and be able to understand and speak English.

*Applications* should be sent to Robert Willy at the above address from February onwards.

**C & A SANDERSON:** Bramley House, Cox's Lane, Wisbech, Cambridgeshire PE13 4TD (☎01945-583023). A small family run farm, which is situated just 1 mile from town, growing fruit for processing and wholesale markets.
**Strawberry Pickers (8-10).** Piecework rates. To work Monday to Friday and sometimes Sunday mornings. Pickers must be willing to work hard, with early start common. Free campsite, washroom with hot and cold water and toilet. Period of work approx. 3-4 weeks, commencing late June. Overseas applicants welcome.
*Applications* to Mr A. Sanderson, Bramley House.

**STOKE FARM:** Battisford, Stowmarket, Suffolk IP14 2NA (☎01449-774944; fax 01449-616045; e-mail davidupson@talk21.com). A family run fruit farm.
**Fruit Pickers (5+)** To pick apples and pears. Wages as set by the Agricultural Wage Board; to work 6 or more hours a day. Applicants must be over 18 and should state whether they have had previous experience.

Staff are required from September until the end of picking for a minimum period of

1 week. Please note that no accommodation is available.
*Applications* should be sent to David Upson at the above address from July onwards.

**WALLINGS NURSERY LTD:** 38 Harwich Road, Lawford, Manningtree, Essex (☎01206-230163; fax 01206-230863; e-mail dtdunn@talk21.com). Three hectares of glasshouses growing strawberries off the ground.
**Strawberry Pickers (10).** Wages £200 per week, for 8 hours per day, 6 days per week. Minimum period of work 6 weeks. Positions available from 20 March to 1 June. Board and accommodation available in communal converted barns for £20 per week. EU and Commonwealth citizens with permission to work in the UK welcome; fluent English not essential. Work also available in the packhouse.
*Applications* should be made from February/March onwards to Christopher Batchelor at the above address.

**PAUL WILLIAMSON LTD:** Church Farm, Bradfield Combust, Bury St Edmunds, Suffolk IP30 OLW (☎01284-386333; fax 01284-386155).
**Horticultural Staff (10)** wanted from mid May to mid October mainly for work picking strawberries, raspberries, apples and pears. Wages at Agricultural Wages Board rates. To work mainly from 8am to 4pm Monday-Friday with some Saturday work. Applicants should be aged over 18. Plenty of space available for tents (own equipment required) with showers, toilets and kitchen and washing facilities available.
*Applications* to Mr P.R. Williamson, Director, at the above address.

# Sport

**BRADWELL ENVIRONMENTAL & OUTDOOR CENTRE:** Bradwell Waterside, nr Southminster, Essex CM0 7QY (☎01621-776256; fax 01621-776378: e-mail adventure@bradwell.freeserve.co.uk). A local authority-run high quality multi-activity residential centre for young people and adults. Based on the edge of the River Blackwater in Essex, it is an excellent site for all water and land based activities.
**Sailing (4) Canoeing (2) and Archery Instructors.** Wages negotiable. To include B & L. To work approx. 8 hours per day. RYA Instructors Certificate essential or BCU/GNAS. Min. work period 4 months between April and October inclusive.
*Applications* in January/March to the Principal, Bradwell O.E Centre.

**OASIS LEISURE CENTRE:** King's Lynn & West Norfolk Borough Council, Central Promenade, Hunstanton, Norfolk PE36 5BD (☎01485-534227; fax 01485-534227). A seafront leisure centre comprising pools, slides, roller skating, café, squash and tennis courts.
**Pool Attendants (12-14).** National Pool Lifeguard Qualification essential, experience of leisure industry an advantage. Wages £3.83 per hour. To work up to 47 hours/6 days per week. Period of work February to October. Accommodation is not available. Applicants should be available for interview.
*Applications* from February onwards to the Manager, at the above address.

# Voluntary Work

## Archaeology

**SEDGEFORD HISTORICAL AND ARCHAEOLOGICAL RESEARCH PROJECT:** Moonstones, 8 Rose Court, Sedgeford, Norfolk PE36 5LR (e-mail rosie@moonstones.fslife.co.uk; www.sharp.org.uk)
A long-term investigation of an English parish concentrating at present on Iron Age, Saxon and medieval periods.
**Archaeological & Historical Fieldworkers (75)** wanted from mid July to late August. Subsistence charge of approx. £120 per week. Hours 8.30am-5pm, 6 days a week with Saturdays off. It is recommended that students come for a minimum of two weeks. No professional qualifications needed.
Request for *application form* with SAE to Mrs Chris Kelly at the above address.

## Festivals and Special Events

**HESSE STUDENT SCHEME:** Hesse Student Scheme, Aldeburgh Productions, Snape Maltings Concert Hall, Snape, Saxmundham, Suffolk IP17 1SP (☎01728 687100; fax 01728 687120; e-mail enquiries@aldeburgh.co.uk).
Aldeburgh Productions has grown out of the Aldeburgh Festival founded in 1948 by Benjamin Britten, Peter Pears and Eric Crozier. Inspired by this legacy, Aldeburgh Productions today ensures that the Suffolk Coast remains a world-renowned meeting place for artists, students, academics and audiences.
The Hesse Student Scheme enables **Volunteers** to assist in the varied duties involved in the day-to-day running of the Aldeburgh Festival of Music and the Arts 6-22 June. Duties can include programme selling, page turning, invigilating exhibitions, assisting with stage moves and bus conducting on the coaches that run from Aldeburgh to all concert venues. In addition, students are also expected to devise, rehearse and perform in a concert of their own - one of the free events publicised in the Aldeburgh Festival booking brochure. In exchange, two groups of 12 students are awarded a grant which covers tickets to all Festival events together with bed and breakfast accommodation in Aldeburgh for each half of the Festival.
Applications are welcomed from anyone between the ages of 18 and 25 (on 1 June) irrespective of current course or occupation. Applications from overseas are particularly welcomed. A willingness to help, no matter how mundane the task, together with a passion for music are essential.
For further details and an *application* form contact Clare Lovell, General Administrator. The closing date for applications is 30 April.

## Heritage

**KENTWELL HALL:** Long Melford, Sudbury, Suffolk CO10 9BA (☎01787-310207; fax 01787-379318).
A privately owned Tudor mansion, situated in park and farmland, approximately 1.5 miles from the historic town of Long Melford, famous for its annual recreation of Tudor life which takes place for 3 weeks during June and July. Up to 1,500 schoolchildren visit on weekdays and the public at weekends.
**Volunteer Tudors (700)** needed for historical re-creations. Duties consist of demonstrating 16th century life and activities to visiting schoolchildren and the

public. The re-creations run for 7 days a week for 4 weeks; most volunteers stay one or two weeks during June/July. Take 16th century skills or learn them there. All ages and Nationalities welcome.

All meals, evening entertainment and space on campsite provided for volunteers only. Applicants can be of any age; an interest in the 16th century would be helpful.

*Applications* should be sent to Dawn Champion in January/February at the above address.

## Physically/Mentally Disabled

**BREAK:** 1 Montague Road, Sheringham, Norfolk, NR26 8LN (☎01263-822161; e-mail office@break-charity.org; www.break-charity.org). Registered charity no. 286650.

BREAK provides holidays and respite care for children and adults with learning and physical disabilities. Volunteering with BREAK can be a life-enriching experience and an opportunity to increase awareness, make lifelong friendships and boost your CV.

**Residential Volunteers** are needed to work alongside experienced staff assisting with guests' care and joining in with a programme of activities. Food and accommodation in a self-contained flat with other volunteers is provided; UK travel expenses and weekly out-of-pocket expenses covered. Placements of between six weeks and 12 months are available.

Overseas applicants are welcome but must be able to understand and speak English to a reasonable standard. Anyone aged between 18 and 25 is welcome to apply.

*Applications* to the Residential Volunteer Co-ordinator at the above address, or complete an online form at www.break-charity.org.

# Vacation Traineeships & Internships

## Law

**MILLS AND REEVE:** 112 Hills Road, Cambridge CB2 1PH (☎01223-222336; fax 01223-355848; e-mail graduate.recruitment@mills-reeve.com; www.mills-reeve.com).

Mills and Reeve is a leading law firm based in Norwich, Cambridge and Birmingham who offer a full range of corporate, commercial, property, litigation, and private client services to a mix of regional businesses and national household names.

Mills and Reeve offer a **Formal 2 Week Placement Scheme** at each of their offices. Students gain experience in four main departments, attend seminars and take part in extra curricular events. There are 25-30 placements throughout June or July; preference is given to penultimate year law students, final year law students and all those who have already graduated and are interested in a legal career. Wages are £150 per week. Overseas applicants are welcome but must have a valid work permit.

*Applications* should be sent to Fiona Medlock, Graduate Recruitment, at the above address before 1 March 2003.

## Media and Marketing

**BRITTEN-PEARS SCHOOL FOR ADVANCED MUSICAL STUDIES:** Snape Maltings Concert Hall, Snape, Saxmundham, Suffolk IP17 1SP (tel: 01728 687100; fax 01728 687120; e-mail: enquiries@aldeburgh.co.uk). Under the management

of Aldeburgh Productions, the Britten-Pears School, set in the inspirational surroundings of Sname, Suffolk, has a distinguished tradition of training emerging professional musicians.
**Intern.** An opportunity for one or two students/recent graduates to work on a voluntary basis in the Britten-Pears School for Advanced Musical Studies to support a small permanent team during the height of the season. Ideally, one intern to be appointed for the months of June and July and a second for the months of August and September. An invaluable opportunity to gain an insight into the workings of an internationally renowned arts organisation and to gain a grounding in arts administration which will be useful in furthering a career in this field. This position would suit an enthusiastic, energetic, level headed individual who would like to learn more about the running of a busy, unusual arts organisation. Previous office experience is not as essential as the willingness and ability to learn and to adapt. Duties will include driving the school car or minibus (if over 21), assisting with keeping files and databases in good order and providing clerical support to the school staff. Excellent secretarial and organisational skills together with a sound knowledge of English and its written and spoken use essential; knowledge of classical music desirable. Accommodation in Aldeburgh and a per diem to cover all meals will be provided.
*Applications* to the above address.

## Science, Construction and Engineering

**GARDLINE SURVEYS:** Admiralty Road, Great Yarmouth, Norfolk, NR30 3NG (℡ 01493-850723; fax 01493-852106).
The largest independent survey company which operates a fleet of 6 fully equipped vessels. The vessels operate worldwide, covering Europe, the Far East and West Africa. Gardline Surveys is involved in hydrographic and marine geophysical surveys. The company offers a variable number of **Placements** in several different fields, including Seismic/Hydrographic survey work for surveyors, geophysicists and electronic engineers; there will also be some office work. The company recruits a maximum of two trainees for each area.
Vacancies are open to students on relevant degree courses, with a preference for those in their second or third year of study. Overseas applicants are welcome. Trainees are based in Great Yarmouth from where they will be sent to work on survey. Shared accommodation is sometimes available. The salary for 2002 was £7,250 p.a. pro rata, plus 26 per day field allowance.
Applicants should *contact* Dr K.P. Games, Geophysical Director, at the above address, preferably in the New Year.

**SYNTHOMER LTD:** Central Road, Templefields, Harlow, Essex CM20 2BH (℡ 01279-436211; fax 01279-444025; e-mail personnel@synthomer.com).
Synthomer, part of the Yule Catto polymers division, is a world-class supplier of synthetic polymers to industries ranging from paints and adhesives to textiles, speciality papers and plastics. They are the only manufacturer of polyvinyl alchohol in the UK and the market leader in suspending agents for the PVC industry.
Synthomer Ltd offers **Vacation Traineeships** to two students each summer. These are to work within Research & Development or Technical Service Laboratories. The placements last for 6-8 weeks and are open to university undergraduates reading for a degree in Chemistry or related subject. Accommodation is not provided.
*Applications* should be made in April or May to the Personnel Manager, at the above address.

**RAYTHEON SYSTEMS LTD:** The Pinnacles, Harlow, Essex CM19 5BB(☎01279-426862; fax 01279-407286; e-mail clare.lane@raytheon.co.uk). Raytheon Systems Ltd is a world leader in the design and delivery of high technology products and systems for both the defence and commercial sectors. Already employing 2,000 people across the UK, we see the new millennium providing the challenge of significant growth as we continue to bring the best and most innovative technical solutions to our UK and overseas customers.

Each year Raytheon Systems offers **1-2 Opportunities** for students to work in hardware support and electronic engineering. On-the-job training will be provided. Applicants should preferably be students who have successfully completed one year of their university course.

Placements last all summer with the possibility of follow-on work at Christmas and Easter. Placements are located at Harlow. The company can help in finding accommodation, but would prefer applicants to live locally.

*Applications* by February to Claire Lane.

# The Midlands

**Prospects for Work**
The Midlands region includes a number of large industrial towns, the most notable of which is Birmingham. Temporary jobs in these centres tend to involve warehouse and factory work or the retail trade; the main glut of vacancies arises from September onwards for the run up to Christmas. In addition, the larger local authorities, such as Birmingham and Coventry, take people on as playleaders and recreation assistants (Birmingham Jobcentre: Centennial House, 100 Broad Street, Birmingham B15 1AU). Some car dealers require people to deliver cars around the country.

Tourism in the Midlands is concentrated in Warwick and Stratford-upon-Avon, the Cotswolds and Herefordshire. In this last county, the town of Ledbury has been a good source of work in the past although this now varies from year to year; rented accommodation is scarce there. Fruit farmers in the area mainly recruit foreign students as pickers. Ledbury Jobcentreis at Crown Buildings, Bye Street, Ledbury, Herefordshire HR8 2AB. Hereford is likely to be a better base, with the *Hereford Times* (Thursday) and the *Hereford Admag* (Wednesday) both displaying local job vacancies; alternatively, contact the Hereford Jobcentre at Bath Street, Hereford HR1 2LG. In Staffordshire, Alton Towers Leisure Park always recruits temporary ride attendants, shop staff and so on, and has recently extended to include a large swimming and hotel complex, creating even more and varied jobs.

Fruit and hop picking jobs are available in the Vale of Evesham, Herefordshire and Lincolnshire, but in general the Midlands is an area where 'pick your own' farms are popular. Spalding and Boston in Lincolnshire are centres for agricultural packing. In Lincoln itself, most temporary jobs are in the retail or hotel trade. There is now a very strong retail trade in Lincoln with the Tritton Road area attracting several large new employers, the most recent being Debenhams. There are good opportunities for employment at the Lincolnshire Show, a two day event that is held yearly in mid June; job vacancies are advertised from April. To apply for work either visit the Lincoln Jobcentre (280 High Street, Lincoln LN2 1LL) or call 01522-342061/342065 in May or early June. The *Lincolnshire Echo* is the best local newspaper for job vacancies.

Oxford is a popular centre for language schools and there are opportunities not only for EFL teachers but also for sports instructors and social organisers. Another source of casual employment may be the university's colleges, which have a high turnover of cleaning and catering staff and often host conferences and courses during the summer. These and other jobs may be advertised in the *Oxford Times* (out on Friday) and the *Oxford Mail* (daily). Alternatively, for up-to-the-minute information on both jobs and accommodation look out for the coloured spreadsheet *Daily Information* (daily in term time, weekly during vacations) on noticeboards, in shop windows etc. There is, of course, competition for any summer jobs from those students at the city's two universities who choose to stay in Oxford for the summer.

The industrial heartlands of the Midlands provide plentiful opportunities for Vacation Traineeships and Internships, particularly in the fields of science and engineering.

# Business and Industry

**ADVANCED ALCHEMY LTD:** St Edburgs Hall, Priory Road, Bicester, OX26 6BL (☎01869-3637036; fax 01869-363710; e-mail info@advanced-alchemy.com).
**Telephone Interviewers** wanted to work for at least 15 hours per week. Researchers with all European languages required to conduct interviews by telephone; no selling involved. Wages £6.50-£7.50 an hour. To work for a minimum of 15 hours a week; flexible hours between 8am and 5.30pm. Cosmopolitan working environment.
*For details* call Marlies on 01869-363703 or e-mail recruitment@advanced-alchemy.com.

**BOMFORDS:** Manor Farm, Luddington, Stratford upon Avon, Warwickshire CU37 9SJ (☎01789-751126).
**Trials Team Member** in the quality assurance department for grower and packers of fresh produce to check quality of produce as it is packaged in the factory. Wages £5.13 per hour. To work 7 days a week on a rota basis. Summer only. Should be enthusiastic, adaptable and a good team player. Minimum age 17.
*Applications* to Margaret Reynolds, Manager at the above address.

**CATHEDRAL SECRETARIAL AGENCY:** 2nd floor, Akrill House, 25

Clasketgate, Lincoln, LN2 1JJ (☎01522-530955; fax 01522-530721; e-mail jean@cathedralsecretarial.co.uk).
**Temporary Secretaries, Temporary Office Staff.** Pay above minimum wage, applicants should have keyboard skills and experience is an advantage.
**Legal Secretaries** required at good rates of pay.
*Applications* to Mrs J. Albans, Proprietor, at the above address.

**DISCOVER TRAVEL & TOURS:** Pierpoint Street, Worcester, WR1 1YD (☎0870-225 8000; fax 0870-225 8001). Discover Travel & Tours is the UK's largest supplier of accommodation and services to the international travel trade in Europe.
**Temporary Reservation Assistants** required to take reservations, make bookings and load details onto computer. Wages from £4.85 per hour. To work 37½ hours per five day week with possible overtime. Minimum period of work of three months. Positions are available between March and September. Applicants must be computer literate. Knowledge of German, French, Italian, Spanish and English required. No accommodation available.
*Applications* from January/February to the above address.

**FARMSHOP.NET:** Swan Lodge, Station Road, Upper Broughton, Melton Mowbray, Leics. LE14 3BH (☎0800-169 7009; e-mail ian.jalland@farmline.com; www.farmshop.net). Home delivery company. Young, energetic company.
**Boxpackers (1-2)** Wages at National Minimum Wage rate; to work variable hours. Possibility of accommodation.
*Applications* to Ian Jalland, preferably by e-mail.

**PORTABLE FLOORMAKERS LTD:** Redhill Marina, Ratcliffe on Soar, Nottingham NG11 0EB (☎01509-673753; fax 01509-674749; e-mail sales@portablefloormakers.co.uk).
**Labourers (4)** needed from May to September to work on a production line packing, loading and assembling floor panels. Wages a minimum of £4 per hour possibly rising to £6 per hour, plus piecework.
*Applications* to the above address.

**PALETHORPES:** Maer Lane, Market Drayton, Shropshire TF9 3AW (☎01630-692394; fax 01630-658785; e-mail marie.toth@palenthorpes.co.uk).
**Operatives (100)** to work on a factory line producing savoury products. Wages from £4.53 per hour plus a shift allowance. A 24 hour operation, all shifts available. Min. period of work of 1 week. Temporary or permanent positions are available from July onwards; placements also available for periods of 3 weeks over Christmas. A range of benefits typical of a large organisation is offered. No qualifications required, although food hygiene or first aid would be an advantage. Minimum age 16. No accommodation available.
*Applications* should be made to Marie Toth at the above address.

**RUTLAND WATER CYCLING LTD:** Whitwell Cycle Centre, Rutland Water, Nr Oakham, Rutland LE15 8BL (☎01780-460705; fax 01780-460792; e-mail sales@rutlandwater.co.uk). Most successful commercial cycle hire operator in the UK.
**Retail Staff (4).** Wages from £4.20 per hour. To work 3 to 5 days a week. Positions are available from Easter to September. Fluent English essential. Minimum age 17. Must be fit, healthy and able to use a computerised till. Foreign applicants with work permits and very good spoken English welcome. No accommodation available.
*Applications* should be made by March to Paul Archer at the above address. Interview required.

**K.H. TAYLOR LTD:** The Freezing Station, Sheffield Road, Blyth, Worksop, Notts (☎01909-590000; fax 01909-590001). Frozen vegetable processors and packers situated 2 miles off the A1, 10 miles south of Doncaster.
**Inspection and Quality Control Personnel, Packers, Stackers (Approx. 50).** Wages £4.34 per hour. To work 8 hours per day in shifts 6am-2pm, 2-10pm or 10pm-6am, Monday to Friday, with some weekend work available. No experience or qualifications needed. Must have own transport.
*Applications* (quoting telephone number) from the beginning of June to K.H. Taylor Ltd at the above address.

# Children

**ACTIVE TRAINING AND EDUCATION TRUST:** Kildare, Manby road, Malvern, Worcs. WR14 3BD (☎01684-562400; fax 01684-562716; e-mail enquiries@te.org.uk). A charitable trust running residential 'super-weeks' in school holiday periods for children from a variety of schools, areas and backgrounds.
**Monitors (20)** to look after children on residential holidays. Staff receive pocket money only; free B & L. To work for 7-10 days at various times in July and August. Minimum period of work is 1 week. Applicants must be over 17 and must be able to attend a 7-day residential training course in the Easter vacation.
Overseas applicants are welcome to apply but must speak good enough English to follow the course and take responsibility for children. A suppporting letter is required from someone who has known the applicant well for at least 5 years.
*Applications* should be sent to Chris Green, Director at the above address.

**LEICESTER CHILDREN'S HOLIDAY CENTRE:** Mablethorpe, Quebec Road, Mablethorpe, Lincolnshire LN12 1QX (tel/fax 01507-472444). A charity that provides free holidays for children from the inner city of Leicester, based on the East Coast of England. For anyone interested in working with children this is a fairly unique opportunity offering practical experience and an excellent grounding for a future career.
**Activity Leaders (12). Kitchen/Dining Room Staff (4).** Wages paid at National Minimum Wage, based on a 48 hour week.
**Cook/Chef.** National min. wage is paid, based on a 48 hour week. To work a 6-day week. Deduction made for B & L.
**Activity Leaders** required to organise, instruct and supervise an outdoor activities programme for children aged 7-12 years. Energy, enthusiasm and a good sense of humour essential.
Staff needed from beginning of May to end of August. Min. age 18.
Write for an *application* form (enclosing s.a.e.) from December to H. Eagle-Lanzetta at the above address.

**CITY LEISURE:** Oxford City Council, Third Floor, St Aldate's Chambers, Oxford OX1 1DS (☎01865-252181; fax 01865-252783; e-mail tstevens@oxford.gov.uk). City leisure manage 9 sports and leisure centres for Oxford City Council - including swimming pools, an ice rink, sports halls, etc.
**Playscheme Assistants/Leaders (12+).** Wages from £5.20 per hour for assistants and £7.30 per hour for leaders. To work Monday to Friday 10am-3pm. Min. period of work of 6 weeks. Positions are available from May to August. 16+, desirable to hold a Community Sports Leaders Award. Spoken English required. Accommodation not available.
*Applications* should be made from March onwards to Tim Stevens. Interview necessary.

**PGL TRAVEL:** Alton Court, Penyard Lane (874), Ross-on-Wye, Herefordshire HR9 5GL (☎01989-767833; e-mail pglpeople@pgl.co.uk; www.pgl.co.uk/people). PGL Travel provides adventure holidays and courses for children. PGL has 25 activity centres located in the UK, France and Spain. Each year 2,500 people are needed to help run these adventure centres. Staff needed in Shropshire, Oxford and the Wye Valley.
**Experienced Activity Instructors** in canoeing, sailing, windsurfing, pony trekking, multi-activites, drama, arts and crafts and English language. Qualifications not essential as full training will be provided. Minimum age 18.
**Group Leaders** also needed to take responsibility for groups of children, helping then to get the most out of their holiday. Previous experience of working with children is essential. Minimum age 18.
From £50-85 per week plus free B & L. Vacancies available for short or long periods between February and October.
*Applications* can be made online, or request a form from the above address.

# Holiday Centres and Amusements

**THE ABBEY COLLEGE:** Wells Road, Malvern Wells, Worcs WR14 4JF (☎01684-892300; fax 01684-892757; e-mail abbey@cix.co.uk; www.abbey-college.co.uk). A beautiful residential campus with students from over 30 nations.
**Activities Staff/Sports Staff (15).** £130-£150 per week for 6 days' work. Min. age 18.
**Welfare And Admin. Staff (3).** £130 per week for 6 days' work.
Sports qualifications and experience of summer schools preferred. Accommodation, meals and laundry facilities provided for all staff, plus free use of all sports and leisure activities and excursions. Work available from beginning of June to end of August. Overseas applicants welcome to work 3 weeks and get 1 week's free English classes and accommodation free of charge, worth £410.
*Applications* from February to the Personnel Department at the above address.

**ALTON TOWERS:** Alton, Staffordshire, ST10 4DB (☎01538-704039; fax 01538-703007; e-mail human.resources@alton-towers.com). Part of the Tussauds group, Alton Towers is a large and nationally known rides and theme park. New Hotel and Waterpark development due to open early 2003. Culture of teamwork and high level of customer service. Up to 1200 seasonal positions are available.
**Rides and Shows:** Operators, Ride Assistants, Services Assistants, Hosts
**Retail:** Food and Beverage, Games, Shops, Ride Photos.
**Front of House:** Admissions, Call handling and Guest Services.
**Security, Medical and Traffic:** Security Officers, Nurses, Traffic assistants.
**Finance:** Strongroom team members.
**Hotel:** Housekeeping, Restaurant and Bar, Conference and Events, Chefs and Kitchen Teams, Reception, Leisure.
**Lifeguards:** To work within the new Waterpark development.
Wages at national minimum rate and above depending on position. To work 2,3,4,5 or 7 days per week including weekends and bank holidays. Positions are available from March to October. No specific qualifications or experience are required as training is given. Minimum age 16. Foreign applicants with work permits welcome. Help with finding accommodation can be given.
*Applications* should be made from February onwards to the HR Department or the Employment Service at the above address. Interview necessary which may be by telephone.

**BJ's LEISURE LTD:** Sea Lane, Ingoldmells, Skegness, Lincolnshire PE25 1NU (☎01754-874212; fax 01754-871805; e-mail bjsleisure@barclays.net). Amusement arcades, combining ten pin bowling, go-karts, family showbar and diners.
**Bar Staff, Catering Staff, Play Area Staff, Floor Walkers, Cleaners, Bowling Receptionist.** Wages and hours on application. Min. period of work of 26 weeks. Positions available from March to October. No accommodation available.
*Applications* should be made from February onwards to Patricia Harrison at the above address. Interview required.

**BUTLINS SKYLINE:** Roman Bank, Skegness, Lincolnshire PE25 1NJ (☎01754-761502).
**Staff** to work in residential/retail catering, leisure and sports, technical services, retail shops/supermarkets, housekeeping, security, finance/administration/bookings, as lifeguards, in retail bars, environmental and gardens, entertainments and funfair, guest
services and nursery. Competitive rates of pay and benefits. Accommodation available to those who live 25 miles away or more. Staff needed around the year; fixed term contracts available. Minimum age 18.
*Applications* to above address marked for the attention of Recruitment. Interview required.

**DRAYTON MANOR PARK LTD:** near Tamworth, Staffordshire B78 3TW (☎01827-287979; fax 01827-288916; info@drayton manor.co.uk; www.draytonmanor.co.uk). A family owned and run theme park of 54 years standing, one of the top 5 theme parks in the UK. Owns a catering company and three hotels.
**Seasonal Caterers (100), Seasonal Ride Operators (100), Ticketing Staff (30), Retail Staff (30), Hygiene Staff (10).** Wages by arrangement, but paid at an hourly rate; hours negotiable. Period of work from the end of March to the end of October. No experience necessary as full training is given. Applicants must be 16 or over. Foreign applicants with a work permit and able to arrange their own accommodation are welcome. Fluent English is not essential. No accommodation is available.
*Applications* from January 1 to Tim Sadler at the above address. Interview is generally necessary, but they do not expect applicants to travel long distances for one.

**FANTASY ISLAND:** Blue Anchor Leisure Ltd., Sea Lane, Ingoldmells, Skegness, Lincolnshire PE25 1RH (☎01754-874668; fax 01754-874146). Fantasy Island is the largest indoor theme park in Britain, with a large funfair.
**Maintenance Staff (20+).** Wage negotiable. To work 6 days a week.
**Ride Operators (100+), Cleaners (20+), Security (20+), Arcade Floorwalkers (20+), Cashiers (12+)** required for seasonal work. Wage from £3.50 at 18 or £4.10 at 21 per hour to work a six day week. No accommodation is available. Period of work from 1st March-31st October. Full training is provided and foreign applicants who speak English are welcome.
*Applications*, including 2 named photos, should be made from January to the Human Resources Department at the above address.

**HATTON COUNTRY WORLD:** Hatton Country World, Hatton House, Warwick CV35 7LD (☎01926-843411; fax 01926-842023; www.hattonworld.com).Two unique attractions: Hatton Shopping Village, comprising 25 craft and gift shops, antiques centre and farm shop; and Hatton Farm Village with farm animals and adventure playground.

**Retail Assistants, Farm Village Guides, Restaurant Staff.** Wages on application. Hours are from 10am-5pm on a rota basis which includes weekends and bank holidays. Required for the summer holidays and other bank holiday periods. Must have own transport to rural location.
*Applications* to the Personnel Department at the above address.

**THE OXFORD STORY:** 6 Broad Street, Oxford OX1 3AJ (☏01865-790055; fax 01865-791716).
**Centre Operators** to work part-time from June to September. Wages negotiable; to work flexible hours 3-4 days per week. Work involves customer service, some retail duties, ticket selling etc. Applicants should be aged at least 18, friendly, have good communication skills and outgoing personalities.
*Applications* to Mr Nick Davis at the above address.

## Hotels and Catering

**ABBEY COLLEGE:** Wells Road, Malvern Wells, Worcs., WR14 4JF (☏01684-892300; fax 01684-892757; e-mail abbey@cix.co.uk; web site www.abbey-college.co.uk).
**Catering and Cleaning Staff (5)** Salary £100 per week. Accommodation, meals and laundry facilities provided for all staff, and free use of all sports and leisure activities and excursions. To work 40 hours per week. Work available from mid June to the end of August. Relevant experience an advantage. Overseas students are welcomed, to work 3 weeks and get 1 weeks free English classes and accommodation, worth £410.
*Applications* from March to the Personnel Department at the above address.

**THE BANBURY HOUSE HOTEL:** Oxford Road, Banbury, Oxon OX16 9AH (☏01295-259361; fax 01295-270954; e-mail banburyhouse@compuserve.com; www banbury-house.co.uk). A three star 63 bedroomed hotel in the heart of Oxfordshire. An extensive menu is offered and the hotel caters for company dinners, weddings and conferences.
**Waiting Staff (4)** to serve food and beverages to customers and be responsible for hygiene and general preparation. Areas of work include bar (must be over 18), restaurant, and function rooms.
**Room Attendants/Cleaners (2-3)** to service the guest bedrooms and public areas to a high standard; daytime hours.
**Commis Chef (2)** to assist in the preparation of food for all outlets and maintain a clean, safe and hygienic environment
    Min. rate of pay £4.25 per hour live-out or £75 per week including accommodation and utilities. Meals provided. Various shifts and hours available.
*Applications* to Debbie Churchman at the above address.

**THE BRANT HOTEL:** The Brantings, Groby, Leicester LE6 ODU (☏01162-872703; fax 01162-321255). A traditional country inn set in a rural position, yet only minutes away from the city centre. Comprises a comprehensive bar and restaurant which is open 7 days a week.
**Bar Staff (3), Restaurant Staff (3)** for full or part-time work June-September. Wages by arrangement. Minimum age 18. Foreign applicants with work permits and acceptable spoken English welcome.
*Applications* to Karen Pollard at the above address.

**CROWNE PLAZA HOTEL:** Central Square, Birmingham B1 1HH (☎0121-224 5020; fax 0121-224 5113).
**Food And Beverage Assistants (5)** to help clear tables and serve guests' meals. Wage National Minimum. To work up to 40 hours a week.
**Housekeeping Assistants (10).** Duties include cleaning guests' rooms and public areas. Wage £4.10 per hour. To work up to 40 hours a week.
Staff are required from 1st of June to 31st September. No accommodation is available. An interview is required.
*Applications* from 1st May to Kim Davies, Training Department.

**DE VERE CARDEN PARK HOTEL:** Chester, Cheshire CH3 9DQ (☎01829-731000 or 01829-731005; fax 01829-731575; e-mail debbie.corbett@devere-hotels.com).
**Waiting Staff, Room Assistants, Kitchen Porterss (20)** Wages currently under review. To work 40 hours per week, either full-time or on various part-time shifts.
*Applications* to Human Resources at the above address.

**DONNINGTON PARK FARMHOUSE HOTEL:** Melbourne Road, Isley Walton, Nr Derby DE74 2RN (☎01332-862409; fax 01332-862364; e-mail info@parkfarm house.co.uk). A small family run hotel with friendly young staff (mostly in their mid 20s). The hotel has 16 bedrooms, a function barn and a caravan park. Located next to Donington Park Motor Racing Circuit.
**General Assistant (1-2)** Wages £4.70 per hour. To work 42 hours over 5 days a week; mainly split shifts in all areas (bar, breakfast serving, evening waiting, washing up, room cleaning etc). Min. period of work 4 months between March and October. Accommodation is provided.
Previous relevant experience preferred but not essential. Overseas applicants with good spoken English will be considered. Interview preferred, unless distance makes this difficult.
*Applications* from February to John or Linda Shields.

**GROVE HOUSE:** Bromesberrow Heath, near Ledbury, Herefordshire HR8 1PE (☎01531-650584; e-mail rossgrovehouse@amserve.net). This large country house is set only 3 miles outside Ledbury and has a tennis court and next door swimming pool for use of students who are treated as part of the family. The Malvern Hills are within walking or biking distance.
**General Assistants (1/2)** to work in a guest house, providing general maintenance both in and out of doors, gardening etc. Wages £35 per week including free B & L and outings on day off. Applicants should be physically strong. Work available all year round for any length of time. Riding occasionally available.
*Applications* with CV and photo, to Mrs E. M. Ross at the above address.

**THE HOLT HOTEL:** Oxford Road, Near Steeple Aston, Oxfordshire OX25 5QQ (☎01869-340259; fax 01869-340865; e-mail info@hothotel-oxford.co.uk). Fifteenth-century coaching inn with 86 bedrooms, 9 conference suites and an AA Rosette restaurant.
**Kitchen Porters** required for busy kitchen. Basic wage £200 a week. To work minimum 40 hours a week with overtime available. Accommodation available at £35 a week all in.
**Chamber Staff** also required to service bedroom and keep hotel public areas clean. £175 a week basic. To work minimum 40 hour week. Accommodation available at £35 a week all in

All nationalitities welcome. These positions and others are available all year round; minimum stay 8 weeks. For details *contact* Andrew Timms, Manager, at the above address.

**HOTHORPE HALL CHRISTIAN CONFERENCE CENTRE:** Theddingworth, Leicestershire, LE17 6QX (☎01858 881500; e-mail sheila@hothorpe.co.uk; web site www.hothorpe.co.uk). 18th century manor house surrounded by beautiful countryside catering for up to 150 residents and with 50 full and part-time staff.
**Team Assistants (3 or 4)** are required throughout the year. Duties include serving meals to guests, washing up, and servicing guest bedrooms. Salary (approx. £100 per week) plus full B & L provided. To work approx 36 hours/6 days a week. Min. age 18. Minimum period of work 3 months. Overseas applicants authorised to work in the UK who can speak and understand English well are welcome. All applicants should be committed Christians.
*Applications* form and further information from Mrs Sheila Dunning, Director, Hothorpe Hall.

**HOW CAPLE GRANGE HOTEL:** How Caple, Herefordshire HR1 4TF (☎01989-740208/740668; fax 01989-740301). Set in a rural location approx. 3 miles from the M50 motorway. Business is mainly party bookings and function trade.
**Chef/Cook (1-2).** Approx. £180-£200 per week plus free B & L. To work approx. 40 hours per week. Staff needed between Easter to October and Christmas period. No experience necessary but must be willing to work within other aspects of hotel work. Own transport absolutely essential. Min. age 18.
*Applications* to the Proprietor, How Caple Grange Hotel. Please telephone to check for vacancy availability.

**THE JERSEY ARMS HOTEL:** Middleton Stoney, Oxon OX6 8SE (☎01869-343234; fax 01869-343565; e-mail jerseyarms@blestwestern.co.uk; www.jerseyarms.co.uk). A privately owned and managed high-class country inn with 20 bedrooms.
**Housekeeping Assistant (1).** Wages £500 per month. To work 45 hours over 5 days a week. Min. period of work 1 month at any time of year. Accommodation and meals provided for £30 per week. Uniform is provided. Min. age 18.
*Applications* to Mrs Livingston at the above address.

**KILDARE HOTEL:** 80 Sanbeck Avenue, Skegness, Lincolnshire PE25 3JS (☎01754762935). A family hotel in the process of building up its business, looking for someone to work as part of a team.
**Chamberperson (1).** Wages of £4.00 per hour. To work for 2 hours per day, 6 days per week. Foreign applicants with work permit and fluent English welcome. No previous experience necessary. No accommodation available.
*Applications* should be made from March onwards to Mrs Barham at the above address. Interview required.

**MARRIOTT FOREST OF ARDEN HOTEL and COUNTRY CLUB:** Maxstoke Lane, Meriden, Warwickshire CV7 7HR (☎01676-526101; fax 01676-521025; e-mail juliet.hewens@whitbread.com).
**Bar Staff** to provide bar and table service, minimum age 18.
**Waiting Staff** for food and beverage service, minimum age 16.
**Commis Chefs** for food preparation and cooking, would suit a catering college student.

**Room Attendants** needed to clean and service guest rooms. Minimum age 16.

Wages are £4.32 per hour for all posts except for Commis Chef, Demi Chef de Partie and Chef de Partie. Bar and waiting staff may also get tips. Hours of work can vary between 20-40 per week, with overtime possible; staff get 2 days off in every 7. All positions available from May-September, although posts can be from July-September to fit in with school/college holidays. Some accommodation is a available subject to availability at a cost of £50 per week (deducted from wages).

*Applications* should be made to Juliet Hewens, HR Co-ordinator, at the above address.

**THE NATIONAL TRUST:** Belton House, Grantham, Lincolnshire NG32 2LS (☎01476-566116; fax 01476-579071). The National Trust was founded in 1895 to preserve places of historic interest or natural beauty for the nation to enjoy.
**Catering Assistants** to work in a busy assisted service restaurant. To work Wednesday to Sunday, including bank holiday Mondays. Staff needed from end of July-end of September. Experience of working with the public desirable. No accommodation available.

*Applications* from February/March to Hazel Hook, Visitor Services and Administration Manager, at the above address.

**NOW 'n ZEN:** Lower Wilcroft, Bartestree, Hereford HR1 4BE (e-mail jobs@nowandzen.co.uk). Now 'n Zen is one of the most popular caterers at music festivals. Working from marquees and selling great world foods, this is an efficient, happy and people-friendly organisation.
**Catering Assistants** needed to help in busy vegetarian world food stalls, working at summer music festivals. Duties include vegetable preparation, serving, light cooking, cleaning, packing etc. Pay of approx. Wages £3.75 per hour. Tent accommodation and food provided.

Applicants should be able to work happily in a team, have lots of stamina, be lively, conscientious, adaptable, good humoured and like music and the festival scene.

*Applications* to Ron Zahl, Proprietor.

**OXFORD THAMES FOUR PILLARS HOTEL:** Henley Road, Sandford-on-Thames, Oxford OX4 4GX (☎01865-334444; fax 01865-334400; e-mail Thames@four-pillars.co.uk; www.four-Pillars.co.uk). A four star hotel. Banqueting in 3 different suites at any one time for up to 300 and up to 4 bars open. Weddings every weekend. Very food and beverage orientated.
**Casual Bar Staff (3)** with bar experience.
**Casual Waiting Staff (3)** with silver-service experience.

Wages for both positions £4 per hour. Working hours are varied. Min. period of work 4 months between June and September. No accommodation is available. Applicants must be over 18. Overseas applicants entitled to work in the UK considered.

*Applications* from spring to Celia Lewis, Deputy General Manager. Interview required.

**PARADISO RISTORANTE ITALIANO:** Drummond Road, Skegness, Lincs PE25 3EB (☎01754-767866; e-mail helen@lanzetta.freeserve.co.uk).
**Waiting Staff, Kitchen Staff.** Wages and hours to be arranged. Required throughout the year, mainly May to October. Minimum period of employment 3 months. Some accommodation is available. Must be 18 years or over and have a good level of

English. Outgoing personality and desire to work hard essential.
*Applications* at any time to Gerardo Lanzetta, at the above address.

**PEN-Y-DYFFRYN COUNTRY HOTEL:** Rhydycroesau, Nr Oswestry, Shropshire SY10 7DT (☎01691-653700; fax 01691 650066; www.peny.co.uk). A small family run hotel located 5 minutes from Oswestry.
**General Hotel Worker (1), General Kitchen Assistant (1).** Wages £4.50 per hour with accommodation provided. To work 4/5 days a week. Min. period of work 6 weeks between May and October. Overseas applicants considered.
*Applications* at any time to Miles Hunter. Interview necessary.

**QUALITY HOTEL WARWICK:** Chesford Bridge, Kenilworth, Warwickshire CV8 2LN (☎01926-858331; fax 01926-858153).
**Housekeeping/Restaurant Staff (2-3).** Wages £4.25 per hour; to work 5 days out of 7. Staff are required all year round. Minimum period of work 10 weeks. Accommodation is available at £22 per week. No experience necessary. Minimum period of work 10 weeks.
*Applications* to the Manager at the above address at any time.

**PRINCESS RIVER CRUISES:** c/o The Park Yacht Inn, Trent Lane South Colwick, Nottingham NG2 4DS (☎0115-9100 400; e-mail endtrent@aol.com). Nottingham's largest and most luxurious river cruiser. Day and evening cruises on the river Trent, specialising in corporate entertainment.
**Saloon Staff (8)** to perform general bar and waiting work. Work is very service orientated. Wages £4.10 per hour. To work 37½ hours per week. Min. period of work of 3 months. Positions are available from April to October. Applicants should be 21+ with previous experience preferred but not essential. No accommodation available.
*Applications* should be made from March onwards to Stuart, Ian or Suzanne at the above address. Interview necessary.

**THE RANDOLPH HOTEL:** Beaumont Street, Oxford OX1 2LN (☎01865-247481; fax 01865-791678; www.heritage-hotels.com). Oxford's premier hotel.
**Housekeeping/Catering Assistants** needed to work at The Randolph in Oxford, The Eastgate hotel in Oxford, The Bear Hotel in Woodstock and The Upper Reaches in Abingdon. Wages on application. To work 39 hours over five days per week. No accommodation available. To work from June to September; min. period of work eight weeks. Overseas applicants with good English welcome. Minimum age 18.
*Apply* from April to the Human Resources Manager at the above address.

**ROWTON HALL COUNTRY HOUSE HOTEL AND HEALTH CLUB:** Whitchurch Road, Rowton, Chester CH3 6AD (☎01244-335262; fax 01244-335464). Set in eight acres of award winning grounds, Rowton Hall is renowned for fine food and wine and its wedding and conference facilities.
**Waiting Staff.** Wages £4.50 per hour. To work a five-day week. Staff are required from April-October. Accommodation is available at a cost of £50 per week.
*Applications* including a CV at any time to Linda Formstone at the above address.

**SEASONAL STAFF UK:** Old Mining College, Queen St, Chasetown, Staffordshire WS7 8QH (☎01543-678707; fax 01543-672046; e-mail admin@seasonalstaff.co.uk; www.seasonalstaff.co.uk). Agency placing students, graduates, working travellers etc in seasonal jobs.

**Country Inn and Pub Work.** Wages at least National Minimum. All positions live-in with on-duty meals provided. Staff required all year round. Applicants must be aged 18-28 and be motivated and well presented. No experience necessary as training will be given. Foreign applicants with permission to work in the UK and good English welcome.
*Application forms* can be downloaded from the company website.

**SHILLINGFORD BRIDGE HOTEL:** Shillingford Hill, Wallingford, Oxfordshire OX10 8LZ (☎01865-858567; fax 01865-858636).
**Hotel Work** of all types, full-time. Varying rates of pay. Limited accommodation. Min. period of work 3 months.
*Applications* to the Duty Manager at the above address.

**STOURPORT STEAMER CO:** 99 Areley Common, Areley Kings, Stourport-on-Severn, Worcs DY13 0NL (☎01299-871177; fax 01299-824646; e-mail sales@Ri verboathire.co.uk). Passenger boat operator, trips long and short, day and evening. Party groups.
**Bar and Catering Staff (6).** Wages from £4.80 per hour. To work various hours, mainly evenings and part-time. Min. period of work of 8 weeks. Positions are available from June to September. Excellent English essential as loud music can make it difficult to hear. Must be capable of team work and of keeping work and public areas clean and clear of glasses and plates.
*Applications* should be made from Easter onwards to Mrs Sue May.

**STRATFORD MOAT HOUSE:** Bridgefoot, Stratford-Upon-Avon, Warwickshire CV36 4SA (☎01789-279988; fax 01789-298589). 251 bedroom hotel in town centre location. Busy, friendly environment. Part of Queen's Moat House Hotels.
**Waiting and Bar Staff (4-6).** Wages £4.15 per hour. To work varied hours. Min. period of work of 3 months. Positions are available from June to early October. Good English essential. Minimum age 18. Training provided but applicants need customer service skills. Some accommodation available at £130 per month.
*Applications* should be made as early as possible to Heidi Morris, Recruitment Manager. Interview necessary.

**WESTWOOD COUNTRY HOTEL:** Hinksey Hill Top, Oxford OX1 5BG (☎01865-735408; fax 01865-736536; e-mail reservation@westwoodhotel.co.uk ; www.westwoodhotel.co.uk). Situated in lovely woodland settings just 2½ miles from Oxford city centre, the hotel is recently refurbished and offers high quality food and accommodation.
**General Assistants (2).** Min. £120 per week plus B & L. To work approx. 45 hours per 5½ day week. Hours by arrangement with flexible day off. Min. period of work 3 months between May and October. Min. age 18. Tidy appearance required. Overseas applicants welcome.
*Applications* to Mr Tony Healy, Proprietor, at the above address.

**WESTON PARK ENTERPRISES LTD:** Weston Park, Weston-under-Lizard, Shifnal, Shropshire TF11 8LE (☎01952-852100; fax 01952 850430; e-mail howard@western-park.com) A large stately home offering a very high standard of cuisine and service.
**Summer Staff** are required in the following areas: **Housekeeping, Cleaning, General Catering, Waiting, Event Assistance, Ticket Selling And Gate Staff.** Wages above the National Minimum Wage; hours variable dependent on position.

Staff are required all year round. Minimum age 16. No accommodation available. Overseas applicants with appropriate work permits welcome.
*Applications* should be sent to the Personnel Officer at the above address as soon as possible. Interview required.

**WORCESTER STEAMER CO:** Severn Street, Worcester, WR1 2NF (☎01905-354991; fax 01905-351477; e-mail events@worcestersteamer.co.uk; www.worcestersteamer.co.uk).
**Bar Staff/Crew Members (10) to perform mostly general bar duties.** Wages from £4 per hour plus bonus scheme. To work mostly evenings and weekends. Positions are available from Easter to October. Good English essential. Minimum age 18+. No accommodation available.
*Applications* should be made as soon as possible to V. Hooper at the above address. Interview required.

## Language Schools

**THE ABBEY COLLEGE:** Wells Road, Malvern Wells, Worcs WR14 4JF (☎01684-892300; fax 01684-892757; e-mail abbey@cix.co.uk; www.abbey.college.co.uk). A beautiful 70 acre residential campus with students from over 30 nations. Has developed, over the last 30 years, an English course to meet every requirement alongside the main academic school. Wide range of on-site facilities.
**EFL Teachers (15).** £230-£310 per week. Accommodation, meals and laundry facilities provided. Min. period of employment 3 weeks. Work available from the beginning of June to the end of August. All year positions also available. Must hold at least an RSA/Trinity Prep. Certificate. Previous summer school experience preferred. Free use of all sports and leisure activities and excursions open to all employees.
*Applications* from March to Personnel Department at the above address. Interview necessary.

**ASPECT ILA OXFORD:** 108 Banbury Road, Oxford OX2 6JU (☎01865-515808; fax 01865-310068). A language school in North Oxford with a young and lively atmosphere.
**EFL Teachers (10-15).** Teaching general English to mixed nationality groups aged 16+. CELTA or equivalent required. Minimum age 21.
**Social Assistants (1-2).** To assist the social organiser with arranging and promoting social events and sporting activities. Minimum age 18.
**Accommodation Assistant.** To assist the accommodation officer, mainly by recruiting and inspecting new host families. Minimum age 18; must have access to a car.
**Administration Assistant.** To undertake general administrative duties; computer literacy an advantage. Minimum age 18.
All jobs are on a full-time basis with wages to be arranged. Some accommodation may be available in student residences; this is free if 'warden' responsibilities are undertaken. Staff are required from May/June until the end of August, and an interview is necessary. Overseas students with valid working visas are welcome.
*Applications* from March/April to the Principal at the above address.

**CONCORD COLLEGE:** Acton Burnell Hall, Acton Burnell, Shrewsbury, Shropshire SY5 7PF (☎01694-731631; fax 01694-731219; e-mail summercourse@concordcollegeuk.com; www.concordcollegeuk.com). An independent international school. Fully residential with excellent facilities on campus.

**Residential Summer Course EFL Tutors (10-15)** Applicants must hold as a minimum the RSA Certificate in TEFL.
**Summer Course Sports Tutor (2-4)** Applicants must have the appropriate coaching qualifiations.
For both positions working hours are variable and the salary is dependent on qualifications and experience. Accommodation is provided at no charge. Staff are required from the start of July to August 25th for a minimum period of 3 weeks.
*Applications* and enquiries should be sent to John Leighton, Director of Summer Courses at the above address as soon as possible.

**EF INTERNATIONAL SCHOOLS BV:** Cherwell House, 3rd Floor, 1 London Place, Oxford OX4 1BD (☎01865-200720; fax 01865-243196; www.ef.com).
**EFL Teachers, Leaders, Activity Coordinators** needed to teach teenage overseas students and organise leisure activities between June and the end of August. Teachers are paid £20+ per half day session (or £28+ if with a TEFL qualification); leaders are paid £206+ per week. Applicants should be university students aged at least 19. Good knowledge of Oxford and London required.
*Applications* to the Manager at the above address.

**GLENFIELD ENGLISH COURSES:** Glenfield, Boars Hill, Oxford (☎01865-735370; fax 01865-730246). An extremely friendly residential school offering itensive EFL together with a range of sports, excursions and social activities to overseas students aged 10-18.
**EFL Teachers (2-3)** live-in, to teach students on residential courses. Salary subject to contract but roughly £275 per week with all meals and own study bedroom provided. Periods of work: usually July only or July/August. Minimum age 21, maximum age 25. Sporting ability, particularly in tennis or sailing and some TEFL experience useful but applicants must speak English perfectly, that is, as well as a native speaker.
**General Domestic Assistant** to help with cooking, housework etc. Salary subject to contract but roughly £90 per week. Live-in, with meals and own study bedroom provided. To work from 20th June for either 5 or 9 weeks. Minimum age 20. Overseas applicants especially welcome. Knowledge of English is not essential. Applicants must be legally entitled to work in the UK.
*Applications* for all posts to Mr or Mrs Horwood at the above address. Applicants must be available for interview in May or early June. In exceptional cases interviews may be arranged in Paris or Madrid and candidates preferring this option should say so.

**OISE YOUTH LANGUAGE SCHOOLS:** OISE House, Binsey Lane, Oxford OX2 0EY (☎01865-258323; fax 01865-244696; e-mail ylsrecruit@oise.com). Part of the OISE education group. Offers summer language courses to foreign teenagers. Courses are intensive and fully structured.
**EFL Teachers (100).** Wages £10 per hour, with free accommodation on residential courses. Flexible hours. Min. period of work 2 weeks. Positions are available in June and August. Applicants must have a degree and a CELTA or Trinity TESOL qualification. Fluent English essential.
*Applications* should be made from May onwards to the above address. Interview required.

**OXFORD ENGLISH CENTRE:** 66 Banbury Road, Oxford, OX2 6PR (☎01865-516162; fax 01865-310910; e-mail office@oxfordenglish.co.uk). A year-round

school of English recruiting staff in July and August for summer courses.
**EFL Teachers (5-10)** Wages by arrangement based on qualifications. To work 20 hours per week in July and August. Applicants should have at least a first degree and RSA Prep. certificate.
**Activities Helpers (4)** to work full or part-time between June and September. Applicants should be at least 19, job suits students on vacation.
**Cafe Staff (2)** Wages of £5 per hour. To work from 8am-3pm in July and August. Training given but applicants should be clean, quick and have good presentation skills.
*Applications* to Graham Simpson, Principal.

**OXFORD HOUSE SCHOOL OF ENGLISH:** 67 High Street, Wheatley, Oxford OX33 1XT (☎01865-874786; fax 01865-873351; e-mail oxford.house@dial.pipex.com; www.oxford-house.co.uk). Small, personal school near Oxford, catering for mixed nationality students (individuals and small groups only). A friendly working environment.
**Admin/Secretarial/Social Organiser (1)** from May to September. Approx. £150 per week. 3 hour day; flexible but mainly 3 hours per morning Monday to Friday, plus two hours evenings twice per week. Minimum age 20. Qualifications: knowledge of languages, first aid, secretarial and office skills.
**EFL Teachers (1-2)** Wages approx. £285 per week. 23 hours of class contact per week plus occasional supervisory/social duties. Required from July to the end of August or September. Min. RSA Certificate, TEFL or equivalent plus relevant experience.
*Applications* a.s.a.p. to Mr R.I.C. Vernede, Principal, Oxford House School of English.

**SEVERNVALE ACADEMY:** 25 Claremont Hill, Shrewsbury, Shropshire SY1 1RD (☎01743-232505; fax 01743-272637; e-mail enquiry@severnvale.co.uk). A small school running English courses for foreign students, both adults and juniors.
**EFL Teachers (5-10).** £250 a week. To teach Monday to Friday daytime. . Min. period of work of 4 weeks. Period of work 1 July to 20 August. Degree and TEFL qualification (e.g. RSA/UCLES/TESOL certificate) and experience necessary. Spoken English to the standard of a native required. Board and accommodation available for £84 per week.
*Applications* from Easter onwards to Mr J.W.T. Rogers, Principal, Severnvale Academy. Interview required.

**ST CLARE'S OXFORD:** 139 Banbury Road, Oxford OX2 7AL (☎01865-552031; fax 01865-310002; e-mail shortcourses@stclares.ac.uk; www.stclare.ac.uk). An educational charity which operates a range of courses for students from around the world throughout the year and has residential premises in North Oxford.
**EFL Teachers (20).** To teach 15-26 hours per week. From £15 per hour. Dip. TEFLA preferred; CTEFLA plus experience minimum.
**Activity Staff (20).** £200 per 40 hour week. Min. age 20 years. Experience of organising activities and sport essential.
Accommodation available free to those who choose to undertake pastoral duties. Min. period of work 3 weeks between June and September. All applicants must be available for interview.
*Applications* from March to the Director of Short Courses at the above address.

**SUL LANGUAGE SCHOOLS:** 7 Woodland Avenue, Tywardreath, Par, Cornwall PL24 2PL (☎01726-814227; fax 01726-813135; e-mail claire@sul-schools.com). A well-established business which provides language holiday courses in Cornwall,

Devon, Somerset, Midlands, Scotland and Ireland for foreign teenagers. Courses run for 2-4 weeks from April to September.
**EFL Teachers.** Wages dependent on experience and qualifications but are usually from £23 per morning of 2½ hours. To work mornings and possibly afternoons, supervising activities. Teachers required from April-August for a minimum period of 2 weeks. Accommodation is available at some centres. Applicants should be TEFL qualified or hold a languages degree or teaching qualification.
*Applications* from January to Claire Frost at the above address. Interview usually required.

# Medical

**ABACUS CARE NURSING AGENCY:** P.O. Box 1298, E. Oxford D.O., Oxford, Oxfordshire OX4 1PW (☎01865-245900; fax 01865244747; e-mail oxford.swe@abacuscare.com)
**Nurses (5-20)** of all grades for temporary positions in Oxford, Oxfordshire and the Cotswolds. A variety of positions available in nursing homes, private and community hospitals and with private patients and the prison service. Minimum wage £17 per hour. Shift work. Must possess current UK nursing qualifications and be able to provide proof of permanent National Insurance number.
**Care Assistants (5-30)** for temporary positions in residential and nursing homes and with private patients. Minimum wage £7 per hour. Must have had previous experience and be able to prove permanent national insurance number.
**Support Workers (1-5)** to work in learning disability units. Minimum wage £7 per hour. Must have previous experience.
All the above positions are temporary and are available at all times of year.
*Applications* to the above address.

**BELVADERE CARE LTD:** Suite B-1, 56 Teville Road, Worthing, West Sussex BN11 2LX (☎01903-537499; fax 01903-521654).
**Care Assistants** required for agency work in nursing and rest homes and to work with people with learning/physical disabilities. Wages are between £5.70-£6.90 per hour. Applicants must be over 18.
*Applications* to Celia Madgwick, Director, at the above address.

**BNA:** 12 Clarendon Place, Leamington Spa CV32 5QR (☎01926-883653; fax 01926-886652; e-mail bna@bna.uk.com). A nursing agency supplying regular staff to various sectors including private patients, nursing homes, residential homes and NHS hospitals.
**Auxiliary Nurses And Care Assistants** to work with private patients and in nursing and residential homes. Wages approx. £5.13-£11.63 per hour. Job may involve working at night and weekends. Applicants must be aged 18+; no experience is necessary as training will be given. Vacancies are ongoing and there is no minimum period of work. Overseas applicants are welcome.
*Applications* should be sent to Sara Higgins, Manager, at the above address. Two references are needed.

**CARING HANDS:** Suite 3, Georgian Mews, 24a Bird Street, Lichfield, Staffordshire WS13 6PR (☎01543-417874/fax 01543-418546).
**Community Care Workers** to assist elderly clients with day-to-day activities in their own homes. Duties include assisting with personal hygiene and some practical assistance around the home. Wages from £5 per hour. Enhanced pay at bank holidays

and weekends. Hours to suit between 7am and 10pm Mon-Sat. Staff needed around the year. Own car and telephone essential.
*Applications* to. C Bradshaw.

**NIGHTINGALES CARE AT HOME LTD:** Suite G15, Devonshire Business Centre, Works Road, Hollingwood, Chesterfield, Derbyshire S43 2PE (☎01246-476999; fax 01246-476333).
**Mobile Community Care Assistants (6)** Hourly wages £4.20 for work Monday-Friday, £4.36 for Saturday and £4.50 for Sunday, plus £1.00 for travel for each call. Applicants must be available to work flexible hours including alternate weekends and some evening work.
 Needed for full and part time work June-September. Possession of car/telephone essential, previous experience of providing care desirable. Students studying care-related subjects such as occupational therapy, medicine or health/social care would be at an advantage.
*Applications* to the above address.

**OHSB:** Holly Grove, Pitchcroft Lane, Chetwynd Aston, Newport, Shropshire (☎01952-813246; fax 01952-813360; e-mail julie.wassell@ukgateway.net; www.occ-health.demon.co.uk). Providers of occupational health staff and trainers in all aspects of health and safety.
**Bank Nurses.** Wages from £10-25 per hour. To work 8-hour shifts. Must be RGN or EN(G) qualified, with occupational health experience.
**First Aid Trainers.** Wages £70 per day. Must be trained first aid instructors. To work 8-hour shifts.
All positions available all year round; minimum period of work is one shift. Work involves working alone in an industrial environment. Suitably qualified foreign applicants with perfect English welcome. No accommodation available
*Applications* should be made at any time to Julie Wassell at the above address. Interview required.

**OXFORD AUNTS CARE AND NURSING AGENCY:** 3 Cornmarket Street, Oxford OX1 3EX (☎01865-791016/7; fax 01865-242606). Providing live-in help to enable elderly and disabled people to remain in their own homes.
**Temporary Positions** for nurses and carers for the elderly and disabled. Experience and good references essential. Overseas applicants must have a good standard of English and be eligible to work.
 For *applications*, everyone must be able to attend an interview and provide three references.

# Outdoor

**AI MARQUEES:** 25 Castlecroft Road, Finchfield, Wolverhampton, West Midlands WV3 8BS (☎01902-765353; fax 01902-765353).
**Marquee Erectors (3+)** Wages £4.50 per hour. Hours flexible, sometimes long. Needed from May to September to erect marquees, load and unload, set up furniture, carpet interiors, clean etc. Must be fit and willing to work hard.
*Applications* to the Proprietor at the above address.

**ALFRESCO MARQUEES:** Unit 31, Barnwell Workshops, Barnwell, Peterborough, Lincolnshire PE8 5PL (☎01480-861858; fax 01480-861021; e-mail alfrescomarquees@aol.com).

**Marquee Erectors (7).** Wages on application. To work 5 or 6 days per week, plenty of overtime available. Positions are available from June to September. An HGV or 7.5 tonne lorry driver an advantage but not necessary. Minimum age 18.
*Applications* should be made at any time to Kate Maltby at the above address.

**AMBERLEY MARQUEES:** Unit C, The Knoll, Leicester Road, Earl Shilton, Leicestershire LE9 7TA (☎01455-841445; fax 01455-846984; e-mail marquees@amberley.fsbusiness.co.uk).
**Marquee Erectors (3).** Wages £5 per hour plus time and a quarter overtime. Work is 8 hours a day starting at 8am Monday to Friday with possibility of weekend work and evenings as overtime. Desired period of work from May to October. Applicants should hold a clean driving licence, and being over 25 is preferable but not essential. No accommodation available.
*Applications* should be made from February onwards to Stewart Brices at the above address. Interview and CV necessary.

**APEX MARQUEES:** The Old Forge, Bradbury Street, Sheffield S8 9QQ (☎01142-589626; e-mail info@apex-marquees.co.uk). Private company erecting marquees within a 50 mile radius of Sheffield.
**Marquee Erectors(10).** National minimum wage. To work 60 hours per week. Min. period of work of 1 month. Positions are available from May to September. Foreign applicants with work permits welcome to apply; fluent English is not essential. No previous experience necessary. No accommodation available.
*Applications* should be made from March onwards to the Senior Manager at the above address.

**BARFORD NURSERIES:** Barford, Norwich, Norfolk NRG 4AR (☎01603-759446; fax 01603-758100).
**Horticultural Workers (1 or 2)** for the summer season. £4.10 per hour. Full-time or part-time.
*Applications* to Bill Mansfield, Proprietor.

**D.M. & J. BIDDLE:** Tye Hall Farm, Roxwell, Essex CM1 4NH (☎01245-248006; fax 01245-823948; e-mail: tye.hall@talk21.com).
**General Farm Worker(s) (1 or 2)** from June to November, to carry out general farm work, possibly also gardening and babysitting etc. Agricultural wages rate. Hours by arrangement. Overtime for weekends and extra hours. Cottage available.
*Applications* to Julia Biddle.

**C. DE ANGELIS & SON:** 333 London Road, Wyberton, Boston, Lincs. PE21 7AU (tel/fax 01205-722891; e-mail peter_de_angelis@hotmail.com). A medium size family run farm, growing fruit and vegetables for the processing industry.
**Soft Fruit Pickers (100)** required from 23 June for about 3 weeks.
**Plum Pickers (50)** required from 20 August for about 3 weeks. Includes ladder work.
**Apple Pickers (50)** required from 7 September for about 4 weeks. Includes ladder work.
To work variable hours from Monday to Friday. Camping available on site.
*Applications* to the above address.

**BADSEY FIELDS NRS LTD:** Badsey Fields Lane, Badsey, Evesham, Worcestershire WR11 5EX (☎01386-830944; fax 01386-833668).

**General Horticultural Workers (10+)** Wages at Agricultural Wages Board rates. To work a 40 hour week or as arranged. To work from June onwards.
*Applications* to P. Campagna, Director, at the above address.

**T. W. & H. R. BRIGDEN LTD:** Pullens Farm, Ridgeway Cross, Near Malvern, Worcestershire WR13 5JN (☎01886-880232; fax 01886-880814).
**Field Supervisors (4)** required to work with foreign students, picking strawberries and raspberries. Wages paid at hourly rates for approx. 8 hours a day, 6 days per week (weather permitting). Must have fluent English, a full clean driving licence and work permit if necessary. Accommodation is available. Min. age 21.
**Accommodation Manager** to supervise foreign student workforce.
Period of work from early June to mid/end August, staying for full period of time if possible. Accommodation available. Must have full clean driving licence; min. age 21. Applicants must speak fluent English and possess a work permit if necessary.
*Applications* at any time to Mrs Brigden at the above address. Interview necessary.

**BRIAR POOL FARM:** Cledford Lane, Middlewich, Cheshire CW10 OJS (☎01606-737670; fax 01270-528241; e-mail Rachel@riwilliamson.freeserve.co.uk)
**Seasonal Marquee Erectors** to put up and dismantle tents during season May to October; there is a possibility of starting work in June, July, August or September according to applicants' availability. Pay at least National Minimum Wage, but is related to performance at erecting and dismantling. Must be able, fit and strong. Driving licence an advantage.
*Apply* to Andrew Willis or Rachel Williamson.

**S.H.M. BROOMFIELD & SON:** Elmbridge Fruit Farm, Addis Lane, Cutnall Green, Droitwich, Worcs WR9 0ND (☎01299-851592; fax 01905-621633). Award-winning family farm growing apples, pears, plums, cherries and raspberries. Established for over 90 years.
**Fruit Pickers (15)** Wages £4.50-£8 per hour. To work 5 or 6 days per week. Minimum period of work 2 weeks between 10 June 10 and 20 October. No experience or qualifications are necessary as full training is given on site. Min. age 17. Foreign applicants with work permits welcome; ability to speak basic English would be helpful. Room/mobile home accommodation available for £3 per night; camping places available for £1.50 per night.
*Applications* from May 25 to Colin Broomfield, Partner, at the above address.

**H.J. AND S.J. FORTNAM:** Puckmoor, Fosbury Fruit Farm, Putley, Ledbury, Herefordshire HR8 2QR (☎01531-670613). A farm growing apples, pears and plums. Beautiful countryside but near to amenities.
**Fruit Pickers (10).** Wages according to Agricultural Wages Board rates. To work September 1st to October. Previous picking experience useful. Campsite available with showers and toilets.
Overseas applicants entitled to work in the UK considered. Interview not necessary. *Applications* from June to Mrs F. Fortnam.

**C. FRANCIS:** Paddock House, Bear lane, Pinchbeck, Spalding, Lincolnshire PE11 3XA (☎01775-723953; e-mail cecilfrancis@aol.com). A small family company in the fens close to Peterborough. All strawberries are grown in large polytunnels and on a table top system, so pickers stay dry and do not need to bend down.

**Soft Fruit Pickers(20).** To work approx. 8 hours a day, 5 days per week. Staff needed from 1 June to 1 October. Min. period of work 4 weeks. Accommodation provided for weekly charge of £30 (hostel). Showers, cooking and sporting facilities included. Min. age 18. Overseas applicants with work permits welcome.
*Applications* from 1 April to the Office Manager at the above address.

**C.M. & G.W. GOACHER LTD:** Green Acres, Wood Lane, N. Whatley, Retford, Notts. DN22 9NG (☎01427-880341; fax 01427-880341)
**Fruit Pickers/Packers** Wages at Agricultural Wages Board stipulated rate. To work from 8am-3pm, with some extra work available; some weekend work possible. Period of work from mid June to mid July. Limited accommodation may be possible with sufficient notice, but these jobs will mainly be of interest to locally based applicants. Applicants must be fit and have common sense.
*Applications* to Mrs Judith Goacher, Company Secretary, at the above address, giving background info. and reference contacts.

**HARGREAVES PLANTS LTD:** Cowpers Gate, Long Sutton, Lincs PE12 9BS (☎01406-366300; fax 01406-366321; e-mail sales@hargreavesplants.co.uk; www.hargreavesplants.co.uk).
**Plant Nursery Workers.** A wide range of work is available from April-September, at both good piecework rates and hourly pay. Mobile home accommodation is available on a campsite which is noted for its friendly atmosphere. Student and foreign applicants are particularly welcome.
*Applications* by both post and e-mail are welcomed.

**HAYGROVE FRUIT:** Redbank, Ledbury, Herefordshire HR8 2JL (☎01531-633659; fax 01531-635969; e-mail fruit@haygrove.co.uk). Large soft fruit farm with long season.
**Field Assistants, Supervisors, Irrigation/Plastic Tunnel Construction Team, Drivers.** Earnings £200-£300 per week. To work 6 days per week. Mobile home accommodation available from £25 per week.
*E-mail* the above address for more information from February. Non EEA nationals must arrange work permits before applying. Cannot arrange work permits for you.

**S & P HODSON-WALKER:** Coulter Lane Farm, Coulter Lane, Burntwood, Staffordshire WS7 9EU (tel/fax 01543-674871). Fruit farm supplying top quality restaurants, supermarkets and farmers' markets.
**Farm Shop Staff (2/3).** Minimum wage. To work 5-6 days per week.
**Fruit pickers (10)** to pick strawberries, raspberries etc. Piecework rates. To work 5-6 days per week.
Minimum period of work for all positions 1 month. Positions available beginning June-end August. Accommodation available for pickers, for approx. £25 per week. Foreign applicants welcome; fluent English not necessary, though some is helpful. Minimum age 18.
*Applications* should be made from May to Shirley Walker at the above address. Interview required.

**MR & MRS JOHN LEWIS:** Yearsett Court Farm, Linley Green, Whitbourne, Worcestershire WR6 5RQ (☎01886-884782; fax 01886-884351). Located 25 miles south of Birmingham, the farm provides fruit for major supermarket and wholesalers.

**Strawberry Pickers (20-25).** Paid by weight picked. To work 6am-1pm, 6 days a week.
**Packhouse Staff (5).** To work approx 8 hours per day, 6 days a week.
Accommodation is available in self-catering caravans at a cost of £10 per week. Workers required from 1 June to 15 July for periods from one day or up to 6 weeks as desired. No experience necessary as training is given. Must be over 18 and fit. Students must produce student cards and university documents.
*Applications* from February to Mrs J. Lewis at the above address.

**LITTLE PETERSTOW ORCHARDS:** Peterstow, Near Ross on Wye, Herefordshire HR9 6LG (tel/fax 01989-730270).
**Fruit Pickers (4)** needed from June 6th-July 16th and September 10th-October 5th. Payment at hourly rates of at least £3.75 per hour or at piecework rates with which an average picker will earn £3.75 per hour but £6.00 per hour is possible. To work approximately 6 hours per day, 6 days per week weather permitting. Showers, cooking, tv, clothes washing, table tennis etc. provided in a separate block on a caravan/camp site. Minimum age 18.
*Applications* to Richard J. Wheeler, Owner/Partner, at the above address.

**MAN OF ROSS LTD:** Glewstone, Ross-on-Wye, Herefordshire HR9 6AU (☎01989-562853; fax 01989-563877). Situated in the Wye Valley, the farm supplies mainly to supermarkets.
**Fruit Harvesters (30)** to pick cherries, plums, apples and pears. Piecework rates. Hours according to crop needs, approx. 6-8 hours a day, 5-6 days a week. Min. period of work 1 month between July and September (July is a quiet month). Min. age 18 years. Overseas applicants welcome, provided they have the necessary work permits.
*Applications* from January to Karen Jackson at the above address.

**MANOR FARM:** Church Lane, Chilcote, Near Swadlincote, Derby DE12 8DL
**Strawberry Pickers** required to pick late May onwards. Wages are available on a piece rate system. Working hours starting 6.30/7.00am preferred. Campsite available at a weekly charge, washing machines, showers and toilets on site. Note that no cooking facilities are available: workers must provide their own. Min. period of work one day. Non EU applicants must have work permits. Applicants must be serious workers, no time wasters.
*Applications* to the above address f.a.o. Mrs Nicola Busby. Must apply in writing with a s.a.e. or IRC or no reply will be sent.

**THE MARQUEE COMPANY:** 1 Eldon Way, Crick Motorway Industrial Estate, Crick, Northants NN6 7SL (☎01788-822922 or 07784-263072; fax 01788-823333; e-mail sk@the-marquee-company.com).
**Marquee Erectors** for a well-established and fast growing company supplying modern aluminium frame structures. Work involves installing marquees and associated equipment at stately homes, sports grounds, corporate venues, race tracks in the Midlands and throughout the UK from May to October inclusive. Overseas applicants from Australia, New Zealand and South Africa especially welcome.
Pay at least National Minimum Wage. Overnight allowance of £50 per night when working away from base. Must be prepared to find own accommodation near Northampton, Rugby or Leicester. Applicants have to be physically fit and able to work long hours with enthusiasm and able to learn quickly.
*Contact* Glen Cartwright, Installations Manager.

**MONARCH MARQUEES:** 1 Hollis Road, Grantham, Lincs NG31 7QH (☎01476-576788; fax 01476-594954; e-mail sales@monarchmarquees.com). Erect marquees throughout the East Midlands.
**Marquee Erectors (3-4).** Wages £200 per week plus overtime. To work 40 hours per week plus overtime. Positions available from May to September. No accommodation available. Applicants must be physically fit as heavy lifting is involved. Foreign applicants with permission to work in the UK and good spoken English considered.
*Applications* should be made to H A Taylor at the above address from April onwards.

**PENNOXSTONE COURT:** Kings Caple, Hereford HR1 4TX (☎01432-840289). A busy fruit farm with a multi-national atmosphere situated in a beautiful part of England.
**Strawberry Pickers (35)** from mid-May to end September.
**Raspberry Pickers (10)** for month of July.
Wages on average £25-£35 per day, based on piecework rates. To work 6 days per week. Accommodation is limited. Some caravan accommodation may be available, though plenty of camping accommodation is available with full facilities. Trips arranged to places of interest on days off. Applicants should be able to fit in with cheerful, friendly atmosphere. Min. age 18. Overseas applicants welcome.
*Applications* for all pickers to be submitted, between April and first week in July and enclosing s.a.e. or IRC, to Mr N. J. Cockburn at the above address.

**ROBERT THOMAS FARMS:** Haywood Oaks, Blidworth, Notts NG21 0PE (☎01623-792239; fax 01623-792268; e-mail office@haywoodoaks.com).
**Vegetable Pickers (12).** Wages £4.20 per hour for 39 hours per week; lots of overtime available. No experience required.
**Tractor Drivers (3).** Basic wage of £6.20 per hour plus overtime. 39 hours per week with lots of overtime available. Full clean driving licence and previous tractor experience essential.
All positions available from 1st July 2003. *Applications* to the above address.

**SIDDINGTON FARM:** Leadington, Ledbury, Herefordshire HR8 2LN (☎01531-632664; fax 01531-632232).
**Strawberry Pickers.** Piecework rates. To work 7am-2pm, Sunday to Friday inclusive. Period of work from first week in June for approx. 8 weeks. Campsite provided for those bringing their own camping and cooking equipment. Kitchen, TV room, toilets and showers are provided. No fruit picking experience necessary. Friendly working atmosphere. Overseas applicants eligible to work in the UK welcome.
*Applications* to Mrs Houlbrooke at the above address.

**STANLEY & PICKFORD:** Rectory Farm, Stanton St John, Oxford OX33 1HF (☎01865-351214; mobile 07976-302404; fax 01865-351679; e-mail s.and.p@farmline.com; www.rectoryfarmpyo.co.uk). Runs a pick-your-own, and are suppliers of potatoes, strawberries, raspberries and other fruits.
**Fruit Pickers (30)** to pick mainly strawberries and raspberries. Wages at piece work rates. Period of work approx. June 5-August 5th. If the weather is suitable there is picking every day; hours of work are informal, but pickers can expect to work in the mornings and part of the afternoon. Accommodation is available on the farm in mobile homes and caravans with cooking facilities, communal room, showers etc. Previous experience would be an advantage.The farm employs field trainers to help staff pick correctly and efficiently.

*Contact* Mr R.O. Stanley, Partner, at the above address for a full information pack giving information on the work available, rates of pay, accommodation, training, accommodation etc.

**SNOWDEN'S MARQUEES:** 2nd Drove Eastern Industry, Fengate, Peterborough, PE1 5XA (☎01733-294613/4; fax 01733-345672; e-mail owen@snowdens.co.uk). Snowdens Marquees is a subsidiary of the Owen Brown Group, a leading marquee hirer in the show and hospitality market.
**Marquee Erectors required. Applicants must be over the age of 18, physically fit and able to work an average of 10 hours a day six days a week (extra hours are available) from 1 April – 30 September 2003. Wages, dependent on hours worked, average £250 per week. Successful applicants may visit some prestigious sporting locations, e.g. Ascot, Newmarket and Silverstone, etc.**
**Foreign applicants with all relevant work permits and acceptable level of spoken English are welcome. Please note however that accommodation is only provided when working away on site.**
**Applications should be made from 1 March 2003 to either Owen Brown or Paul Smith at the above address.**

**STOCKS FARM:** Suckley, Worcestershire WR6 5EH (☎01886-884202; fax 01886-884110). The farm is set in an area of outstanding natural beauty within reach of Worcester, Hereford and Malvern. It supplies supermarkets with fruit and breweries with hops.
**Harvest Workers** for harvesting hops by machine and fruit picking. Wages at usual agricultural rates. Work available from June to October. Self catering accommodation available. Applicants should like working in the countryside.
*Applications* to Mr R. M. Capper, Stocks Farm, at the above address.

**WITHERS FRUIT FARM:** Wellington Heath, Ledbury, Herefordshire HR8 1NF (tel/fax 01531-635504; e-mail withersfruitfarm@farmline.co.uk). A large soft fruit farm and apple grower in a beautiful setting with a large accommodation block.
**Casual Farm Workers (10)** for various jobs including driving, supervising and picking. Wages either £4 per hour or piecework; to work 6 days per week. Accommodation available. Min. period of work 4 weeks between 1st March and 31st October.
**Strawberry Pickers (10)** Wages per hour or piecework rates; to work 6 days per week. Picking in the mornings and weeding, planting and irrigation in the afternoons.
**Supervisors (4)** Wages £4.50 per hour; to work 6 days per week. Must be strong and be able to use own initiative.
Accommodation is available in shared caravans at a charge of £20 per week. Minimum period of work 1 month between June and September. Overseas applicants with work permits welcome.
*Applications* from January onwards to the above address.

# Sport

**AVALON TREKKING:** 40 Waverley Gardens, Etching Hill, Rugeley, Staffordshire WS15 2YE (tel/fax 01889-575646). Operating throughout the UK aiding groups of walkers along long distance foot paths.
**Walking Guides/Drivers.** Wages £80-£100 per week plus free board and accommodation. To work a 6 day week. Staff required from April to November;

minimum period of work 1 week. Applicants must be over 25 years old with experience of walking/guiding, and able to drive a minibus.
*Applications* from February to the above address.

**CITY LEISURE:** Oxford City Council, Third Floor, St Aldate's Chambers, Oxford OX1 1DS (☎01865-252181; fax 01865-252783; e-mail tstevens@oxford.gov.uk). City leisure manage 9 sports and leisure centres for Oxford City Council including swimming pools, an ice rink, sports halls, etc.
**Lifeguards/General Recreation Assistants (20+).** Wages from £5.14 per hour, with enhancements for shifts, night and weekend work. To work various hours. Min. period of work of 6 weeks. Positions are available from May to August. 16+, desirable to hold a lifesaving qualification. Spoken English required. Accommodation not available.
*Applications* should be made from March onwards to Tim Stevens. Interview necessary.

**JAMES GIVEN RACING LTD:** Mount House Stables, Long Lane, Willoughton, Gainsborough DN21 5SQ.
**Stable Staff** for duties including riding out, mucking out and all yard duties; will be able to take horses racing. Wages above National Minimum rates, with accommodation provided. To work from 7.30am-1.30pm and from 4.30-6pm, with overtime available. To work until September or by arrangement. Applicants must have previous experience of riding racehorses.
*Applications* to Lucy Coney, Secretary, at the above address.

**NORTHFIELD FARM:** Flash, nr Buxton, Derbyshire SK17 0SW (☎01298-22543; fax 01298-27849; e-mail northfield@btinternet.com). BHS approved riding centre and working farm, situated in a small village. There is a post office and a pub 100 yards away. 30 horses are used, including an Andalusian stallion at stud, a few breeding mares and young stock.
**Trek Leaders (2).** Approx. minimum pay £90-£100 per week plus free B & L. To work 8am-5pm, 5½ days per week. Work available from April to September/October; min. work period July-August, preferably June also. Applicants must be competent riders, good with people and preferably car drivers; Riding and Road Safety Test and First Aid qualification also preferred. Must also be prepared to help out on the farm when needed.
*Applications* between March and May only (no applications before March) to Mrs E. Andrews, Northfield Farm, at the above address. Interview required.

**NORTH KESTEVEN SPORTS CENTRE:** Moor Lane, North Hykeham, Lincoln LN6 9AX (☎01522-883311; fax 01522-883355).
**Part-Time Lifeguards** required during all vacations. Must have RLSS Pool Lifeguard (NPLQ), with spinal qualifications. Previous experience preferred. Approx. £4.39 per hour, with uniform provided. To work variable hours between 6.45am and 11pm including bank holidays.
*Application forms* available from the centre.

**PEAK DISTRICT HANG GLIDING CENTRE:** York House, Ladderedge, Leek, North Staffordshire ST13 7AQ (☎07000-426445; e-mail Mike@peakhangglidi ng.co.uk). The longet established hang gliding school; based in the Peak District National Park.
**Hang Gliding Instructor(s) (1/2)** Wages £80 per day. Hours by arrangement. To

work from July to September. Must be experienced.
**Telesales Assistant/Secretary.** Wages and period of work by arrangement. Must have a good telephone manner.
*Applications* to Mike Orr at the above address.

**WATERWORLD:** Festival Way, Festival Park, Etruria, Stoke-on-Trent, ST1 5PU (☎01782-205747; fax 01782-201815; www.waterworld.co.uk).
**Lifeguards** required for holiday periods. Wages dependant on age. Applicants must be over 16 and hold RLSS National Pool Lifeguard qualification.
For details please *contact* the Personnel Manager at the above address.

**WOODLANDS STABLES:** Woodlands Lane, Market Rasen, Lincolnshire LN8 5RE (☎07971-940087). Stables with 25 horses in training for flat and jump races.
**Stable Hands (2)** to ride and take care of horses and for general stable work. Wages from £125-£200 per week depending on experience. To work 7am-4pm with 3 hours for lunch. Min. period of work of 3 months. Positions are available all year. Applicants should preferably weigh under 10 stone, not smoke, ride well and live in. Accommodation cost is £10 per week. Foreign applicants welcome.
*Applications* should be made as soon as possible to Mr M. Chapman at the above address. Interview necessary.

**WOODSIDE FARM:** Hopwas Hill, nr Tamworth, Staffordshire, B78 3AR (☎01827-62901; fax 01827-68361).
**Stable Staff** required to muck out and bed down race horses, working from 7.30am-5.30pm with 1/2 hour for breakfast and 1½-2 hour lunch breaks. No age limit but applicants should have a pleasant attitude and if capable of riding race horses weigh under 60 kilos(9 stone 7 pounds).
**Farm Workers and Stud Workers** for stud work with thoroughbred horses. Work involves tractor driving, tending sheep, mucking out mares and foals, bringing in and putting out young stock. Hours of work 8am-5pm with 1/2 hour breakfast and 1 hour lunch breaks. Applicants must have a pleasant attitude, a basic knowledge of horses (or at least no fear of them) and be responsible with vehicles.
Wages for all positions at national minimum wage level plus help with finding accommodation. Work available at any time of year.
For *applications* contact Joy McMahon at the above address.

# Voluntary Work

## Children
**BIRMINGHAM PHAB CAMPS:** c/o M.S. Wallis, 2 Lenchs Green, Edgbaston, Birmingham B5 7PX (☎0121-440 5727).
Established in 1967, PHAB Camps is a charity run by volunteers, so administrative costs consume less than 1% of funds. 100 children take part each summer.
**Volunteers (17+)** to take groups of disabled children, or mixed groups of disabled and able-bodied children, aged 8-17 for one-week holidays between end of July and end of August. No pocket money, but board and lodging provided; volunteers will need to get to Birmingham to meet the coach. Must be able to work, play with, care for, and entertain the children; many children need feeding and changing, but

the holidays are fun. (Volunteers who are male, qualified nurses or able to drive mini-buses especially welcome). More information available at www.bhamphabcamps.org.uk.
*Applications* to Maxine Wallis, Chairman, at the above address.

**B.Y.V. ASSOCIATION LTD:** 4th Floor, Smithfield House, Digbeth, Birmingham B5 6BS (☎0121-622 2888; fax 0121-622 1114; www.byvadventurecamps.org.uk). Volunteers act as key-workers with 2 or 3 children during the week. Children are from disadvantaged backgrounds and greatly benefit from the positive contact.
**Volunteers (120 per year)** needed to accompany children on week-long summer breaks, either residential or camping, in Wales and the Midlands. No qualifications are necessary as training is available, but an interest and experience of work with children and young people is advantageous. All volunteers are police-checked. No wages are given, but all expenses on the camp are met. Camps take place in the school summer holidays; approx. July 21 to 24 August. Commitment is required 24 hours a day for the length of the camp. Birmingham and Midlands based volunteers are particularly encouraged to apply.
*Applications* from January to the BYV Volunteer Co-ordinator at the above address.

## Conservation and the Environment

**LINCOLNSHIRE WILDLIFE TRUST:** Gibraltar Point National Nature Reserve, The Field Centre, Gibraltar Road, Skegness PE24 4SU (☎01754-898079; fax 01754-762350; e-mail lincstrust@gibpoint.freeserve.co.uk; www.lincstrust.co.uk). Nature reserve with visitor centre.
**Volunteers (30-40)** to work in areas including site management, education and interpretation and running the visitor centre. No set period of work; some work for three months, others 1 day a week. Positions available all year round. No qualifications necessary. Involvement tailored to suit individual. Some funds may be available for individual formal training. No accommodation available.
**Residential Placement.** Training and involvement opportunity available to applicants seeking a career in nature conservation. Minimum period 3 months. Accommodation provided.
*Applications* should be made to Mr Kevin Wilson, Site Manager, at the above address. Foreign applicants welcome.

**ROYAL SOCIETY FOR THE PROTECTION OF BIRDS:** The Lodge, Sandy, Bedfordshire SG19 2DL (☎01767-680551; fax 01767 692365; e-mail volunteers@rspb.org.uk; www.rspb.org.uk). Nationally, the RSPB has over 9,000 volunteers.
**Volunteer Opportunities** available on over 100 reserves across the UK, at 13 regional/country offices and with over 100 youth and local groups throughout the UK.
**Residential Volunteers** taken on 31 reserves throughout England, Scotland and Wales.
Jobs/activities available include management of reserves, work with visitors, research, survey & monitoring, species protection, office/admin work. Specialist skills are always required. Volunteers can work as much or little as they wish, but must do a minimum of 1 week on the residential scheme; travel expenses to a maximum of 25 miles paid. Volunteers must be 18 or over and have a genuine interest in and enthusiasm for birds and wildlife. Foreign applicants welcome; a permit is not ordinarily necessary as this is unpaid work, but please check beforehand.

Further information can be found in the RSPB's free publication on volunteering, *You Can Do It*, available from the above address.
*Applications* should be made to Mrs Kate Tyler, Voluntary Wardening Scheme Co-ordinator, at the above address.

## Festivals and Special Events

**BIRMINGHAM FILM AND TV FESTIVAL:** 9 Margaret Street, Birmingham B3 3BS (☎0121-212 0777; fax 0121-212 0666).
The Birmingham Film and TV Festival is one of the UK's leading moving image festivals. It screens the best of international cinema and has developed specialisms in South Asian cinema and locally-produced work.
**Volunteer Festival Assistant, Technical Assistant, Press and Marketing Assistants and Runner (3/4).** All positions are unpaid, although reasonable travel expenses will be met. To work initially 3-5 days per week, then 6-7 days per week during the Festival build-up, and the Festival itself. Suggested min. period of work 2 months between July and September, with long term volunteers welcomed. No accommodation available.
Applicants should be studying or have studied a media orientated degree, or have some experience in film and TV. The posts involve long hours, so applicants should be enthusiastic and not afraid of working hard. However, the work is very rewarding, provides the opportunity to work and learn at the same time and gain good contacts for the future.
*Applications* from Feb/March to Ms Yen Yau, Deputy Director. Interview required.

**CHELTENHAM FESTIVAL OF LITERATURE:** Town Hall, Imperial Square, Cheltenham GL50 1QA (☎01242-263494; fax 01242-256457; e-mail adamp@cheltenham.gov.uk).
The Cheltenham Festival of Literature will be in its 54th year in 2003 and is the largest and most popular of its kind in Europe. There is a wide range of events including talks and lectures, poetry readings, novelists in conversation, creative writing workshops, exhibitions, discussions and a literary festival for children.
**Festival Volunteers (25)** to look after both the authors and the audience as well as helping with the setting up of events, front of house duties, looking after the office and assisting the sound crew. To work for 10 days from 10-19 October; the hours at the festival are fairly long, the festival day runs from 10.00am- midnight. Applicants should be graduates over 18, with have an interest in literature, arts administration or events management.
Volunteers are given free accommodation, food and drink. Free entry to all events is also provided. Overseas applicants are welcome but must have a very high standard of spoken and written English.
*Applications* should be sent to Adam Pushkin, Festival Officer, from June onwards to the above address.

## Fundraising and Office Work

**OXFAM:** 274 Banbury Road, Oxford OX2 7DZ (☎0845-3000 311/01865 311311; www.oxfam.org.uk/involved/placements).
Large registered charity working to overcome poverty and suffering.
Runs a **Volunteer Opportunities Scheme** from its Oxford headquarters. Volunteers are generally undergraduates or postgraduates. Some of the openings available

require particular skills or qualifications; all applicants must have basic office and computer skills. To work 3-5 days per week. Minimum period 3 months; opportunities available all year round.

Lunch and travel expenses are reimbursed. No accommodation is available. Suitably qualified foreign applicants with fluent English welcome. Training opportunities may be available with certain jobs.

*Applications* to and further details from Gareth Price-Jones at the above address.

# Heritage

**BERRINGTON HALL:** Near Leominster, Herefordshire HR6 0DW (☎01568 615721; e-mail yvonne.osborne@nationaltrust.org; www.nationaltrust.org.uk).
A National Trust Property. Provides the opportunity to mix with people from all walks of life with a common interest in conservation.
**Car Park Attendant.** To work Bank Holidays.
**Garden Help, Office Assistant, Shop Help and Events Co-Ordinator.**
**Volunteer Room Stewards** required every day from April to October.

These are volunteer posts which are available all year round. Min. age 18 years. No accommodation is available but travel costs are provided (up to 40 miles round trip). Volunteers who offer 40 hours of work receive a volunteer card entitling them to free entry to National Trust Properties in the UK and 10% discount in the shops. Overseas applicants welcome.

Anyone interested should *apply* to the House Steward at the above address.

**IRONBRIDGE GORGE MUSEUM TRUST:** The Wharfage, Ironbridge, Telford, Shropshire TF8 7AW (☎01952-583003; fax 01952-588016).
A World Heritage site.
**Volunteers** required for demonstrations of exhibits, site maintenance, street animation and wardrobe. The Trust is open Monday-Sunday 9.45am-5.15pm. Min. period of work 2 weeks. Volunteers required from April to October. Min. age 18. Must have good communication skills, be reliable and self motivated, and have excellent spoken English.

Some historical background is a plus, although training, costume, equipment and supervision are provided. Workers are given a luncheon voucher for a full day's volunteering, plus free entry to other I.G.M.T. sites. Museum insurance covers all volunteers. No accommodation available. Overseas applicants welcome providing their English is of a good standard.

An interview is not essential although it would help both parties to visit prior to placement. Other opportunities to volunteer are available at the Museum's other sites in the valley.

*Applications* year round to the Volunteer Co-ordinator, Blists Hill Victorian Town, at the above address.

**LUDLOW MUSEUM:** Ludlow Museum Resource Centre, Parkway, Ludlow, Shropshire SY8 2AG (☎01584-873852; fax 01854-872019; e-mail ludlow.museum@shropshire-cc.gov.uk).
The museum covers the geology and history of the area around Ludlow. It is a small place attracting mainly tourists visiting this beautiful region of Britain.
**Voluntary Museum Workers (2-3)** needed from June to August. To work either 9am-5pm Monday-Friday or part-time at least three days a week. Applicants should be interested in museums and need good spoken and written English.

Those interested in making *applications* should contact Ms K.J. Andrew, County Curator of Natural History, at Ludlow Museum Office.

**MUSEUM OF CANNOCK CHASE:** Cannock Chase Council, Valley Road, Hednesford, Cannock, Staffordshire WS12 5TD (☎01543-877666; fax 01543-428272; e-mail museum@cannockchasedc.gov.uk)
A small yet busy museum on an ex-colliery site telling the history of coal mining and domestic life in the local area.
**Volunteer Museum Attendants** are required to work variable hours 2-3 days per week including weekends. These positions are intended to offer unpaid work experience but there is the possibility of some paid hours if work becomes available. Staff are required from May/June to September. A variety of tasks will be involved including reception work, working with school and adult groups, tourist information, greeting the public and working in the museum stores and library.
Applicants should be at least 18 with a good basic education and preferably with some knowledge or interest in museums or history. Must have an interest in working with children, experience of public speaking, a good telephone manner, be willing to work with the public and be of smart appearance. Overseas applicants are welcome but must have a good standard of English.
*Applications* should be sent to Miss Lee Smith at the above address no later than April.

**WIRKSWORTH HERITAGE CENTRE:** Crown Yard, Wirksworth, Derbyshire DE4 4ET (☎01629-825225; e-mail heritage@crownyard.fsnet.co.uk). The 'Wirksworth Story' in a former silk mill offers a mock lead mine, information about local customs and social history. Family-friendly.
**General Museum Assistant.** Working hours to be arranged. Min. period of work of 1 month. Positions are available all year. Must be able to communicate confidently with the public and pro-active and enthusiastic and able to help with all aspects of running a small museum. No accommodation available.
*Applications* should be made to Mrs M. Vaughan at the above address. Interview necessary.

## Physically/Mentally Disabled

**LIFESTYLES INDEPENDENT LIVING PARTNERSHIP:** Worcestershire Lifestyles: Woodside Lodge, Lark Hill Road, Worcester WR5 2EF (☎01905-350686; fax 01905-350684; e-mail worcslifestyle@care4free.net). An independent charity established in 1991 to enable disabled people to exercise freedom of choice, extend their horizons, and make decisions about the lifestyle they wish to pursue.
**Volunteer Workers** are needed to enable people with a disability to lead as normal a life as possible in their own home. Duties can include intimate personal care, cooking, housework, shopping and sharing leisure interests. Full-time work in shifts can include weekends and sleeping over. Volunteers receive free accommodation in the counties of Herefordshire and Worcestershire, plus an allowance of £60.23 per week. Accommodation is shared with other volunteers, and all heating and lighting bills are paid by the social services.
Volunteer workers are required at all times of year. The normal minimum commitment expected is four months, but it may be possible to arrange placements during college vacations. Volunteers should be aged at least 18 and be honest, trustworthy, reliable and caring.
*Applications* should be sent to the Volunteer Recruiter at the above address.

**WORCESTERSHIRE LIFESTYLES:** Woodside Lodge, Lark Hill Road, Worcester WR5 2EF (☎01905-350686; fax 01905-350684; e-mail worcslifestyle @care4free.net).
An independent registered charity established in 1991 to assist people with disabilities to exercise freedom of choice, extend their horizons and make decisions about the lifestyle they wish to enjoy.
**Volunteer Workers** to act as the arms and legs of someone with a disability. Wages of £60.23 per week plus free accommodation are provided; to work 5 days a week, can include weekends and sleepovers. Staff are required for a minimum of 4 months all year round. Workers assist with personal care, household tasks and share leisure activities. Applicants should be over 18, honest, caring and adaptable. Training is provided. Overseas applicants with a good standard of English are welcome.
*Applications* at any time to Cora Jones at the above address.

# Vacation Traineeships & Internships

## Accountancy and Insurance

**NEWBY CASTLEMAN:** West Walk Building, 110 Regent Road, Leicester LE1 7LT (☎0116-254 9262; fax 0116-247 0021).
Chartered accountancy practice with 11 partners and 130 employees providing total financial service to small and medium sized enterprises.
The company offers **Vacancies For 2 Students** to experience working in a chartered accountant's practice. The work will involve assisting in accounts preparation and audit. Students at any level are invited to apply. Salary of £100 per week
Placements last for 8 weeks in the summer and are located in Leicester. No accommodation is provided.
*Applications* by 3rd March to M.D. Castleman, Partner.

## Business and Management

**THE BOOTS COMPANY:** Graduate Resourcing Department, D31 Building, Nottingham NG2 3AA (☎0115-959 4571; www.bootscareers.com).
An international organisation operating in retail, manufacturing and the marketing of leading consumer brands.
The Boots Company offers **Undergraduate Students Opportunities** available in a variety of areas including marketing, logistics, retail management, finance, personnel, engineering, telecommunications, manufacturing, technical, and information systems. Placements last for 8 weeks over the summer vacation and take place at the Head Office in Nottingham. Accommodation is provided.
*Applications* should be made via www.bootscareers.com.

**CAPITAL ONE:** Trent House, Station Street, Nottingham NG2 3HX (☎0115-843 6029; e-mail Siobhan.Carty@capitalone.com; www.capitalone.com).
International consultancy and finance corporation. Offices in the US, Canada, Europe, South Africa and the UK; 38 million customers worldwide.
**Trainee Business Analysts.** for 9-week placements starting end of June/beginning of July 2003 (exact dates to be confirmed). The role involves exposure to venture

capital, consulting, finance and general management business areas. Available to penultimate year students of engineering, economics, maths, sciences or similar. Applicants must have at least 26 UCAS points and a mathematical/science A-level. Located in Nottingham; wages to be confirmed. More information can be found on the website listed above.

*Applications* should be made online at www.gradsatcapitalone.co.uk. Interview required.

## The Law

**WRAGGE & CO:** 55 Colmore Row, Birmingham B3 2AS (☎ freephone 0800 096 9610; fax 0121-214 1099; e-mail gradmail@wragge.com; www.wragge.com/graduate).

Wragge & Co is a leading law firm providing a full range of quality legal services to clients in commerce, finance and industry. Wragge & Co enjoys a national reputation in areas such as corporate, dispute resolution, insurance litigation, property, employment, tax, information technology, EU/Competition, transport and utilities, project finance and banking. Wragge has also built 'Top five' reputations in selected niche areas such as construction, intellectual property and pensions.

**Easter and Summer Vacation Placements** are run at Wragge & Co. As part of our scheme, you will get the opportunity to experience different areas of the firm, attend client meetings and get involved in real files. There are also organised social events with our current trainees.

*Apply* on-line (paper application available on request) by 31 January 2003.

## Media

**VACATION WORK PUBLICATIONS:** 9 Park End Street, Oxford OX1 1HJ (☎ 01865-241978; fax 01865-790885; www.vacationwork.co.uk).

Since its establishment in 1967 Vacation Work has become widely recognised as a leading publisher of employment directories and travel guides for young people. It currently features over forty titles in its catalogue including *Summer Jobs in Britain*, *Work Your Way Around the World* and *Travellers' Survival Kit Australia and New Zealand*.

In 2003 the company will be looking for one or two people to work in an **Editorial Capacity** during the summer vacation. The work will involve assisting the editorial staff in the process of revising and up-dating the company's books. Duties are likely to include general secretarial and clerical work, organising mailings to featured organisations and editorial research and re-writing.

All candidates should be proficient at operating a word processor, and should be able to demonstrate an interest in or knowledge of the publishing business. Some writing or editorial experience is preferred. Applicants must be capable of working on their own initiative without direct supervision, although help and guidance will be given where necessary. They must be entitled to work in the UK and speak English as well as if it were their first language. The pay will be around £180 per week. Please note that no direct assistance can be given with finding accommodation.

*Applications* should be sent to Mr Charles James at the above address around Easter in order to arrange an interview.

# Science, Construction and Engineering

**CONOCO LTD:** Humber Refinery, South Killingholme, Immingham, North Lincs. DN40 3DW (☎01469-571571; fax 01469-555141).
Comoco Ltd. have positions for **3 Vacation Trainees** to work in their Chemical Engineering Department during the summer. Applicants should be university students in their penultimate year. The work involves trouble-shooting, de-bottlenecking, assisting with the day-to-day running of the plant to optimise throughput. Students receive £1,041 per month and help is given in finding accommodation.
*Applications* to R. Reed during November at the above address.

**GIFFORD AND PARTNERS:** Carlton House, Ringwood Road, Woodlands, Southampton SO40 7HT (☎023-8081 7500; fax 023-8081 7600).
Gifford and Partners is a firm of consulting engineers particularly interested in the design of building and highway structures and in marine works worldwide. Each summer the firm takes on **Students** to work in its regional office in Chester.
For further details see their entry in *The South* chapter.

**POWERGEN UK PLC:** Westwood Way, Westwood Business Park, Coventry CV4 8LG (☎0247-642 4723; fax 0247-642 5432; e-mail undergradplacements@pgen.com; www.powergenplc.com/jobs).
One of the largest private sector electricity generating companies in the world. They also offer telecom and internet services.
**Summer Vacation Placements** available in areas including **Business, IT, Engineering** and others to be confirmed. Wages to be arranged. Placements begin during June and run until the end of August. Applicants must be first or second year undergraduate students. The majority of placements are located in Coventry, although engineering placements tend to be in the company's various power stations. Powergen also offers undergraduate **Placements for sandwich-year students**, lasting 48 weeks and commencing in summer 2003. More information for all vacancies can be found on the website above.
*Applications*, comprising CV and covering letter, should be made to the above e-mail address. Before sending, applicants are advised to look at the company website, as they may begin to list a new address specifically for summer placements. Interview required.

**QINETIQ:** Knowledge and Information Systems Division (Mal) Recruitment Centre, D307, St Andrews Road, Malvern, Worcestershire WR14 3PS (☎01684-895642; fax 01684-894318).
Multi-disciplined teams are engaged in a broad spectrum of research, providing the principle focus for space research, satellite/land communications, imagery exploitations, parallel computing, software engineering, and command and control systems.
The Knowledge and Information Systems Division (Malvern) offers up to **20 Placements** for students over the summer vacation as well as placements for those undertaking sandwich course industrial placements. Trainees are employed on Research Science and technology-based projects at various locations throughout the UK.
The placements are open to undergraduates on Science or Engineering courses and last between 10 and 51 weeks. Competitive salaries offered.
Application forms are available at the above address. Early *applications* are recommended.

**SIEMENS COMMUNICATIONS LTD:** Siemens Communications Ltd, Technology Drive, Beeston, Nottingham, NG9 1LA (☎0115-9434925; Fax 0115-943 3078; e-mail opsjobs@siemenscomms.co.uk; siemenscomms.co.uk)
Siemens Communications Limited are a world class solutions provider employing 2,600 people and improving the business of their 40,000 customers. They currently have opportunities within various functions of the business for undergraduates seeking placement experience at the site in Nottingham.
One 3-month and one 12-month **Trainee Hardware Engineer** are needed for the Engineering Development Centre; the circuit design team wishes to appoint placement students with expertise in all aspects of digital design including microprocessor, memory and programmable logic design. One 3-month and one 12-month **Trainee Test Development Engineer** is needed for the Engineering Development Centre; Siemens are looking for enthusiastic undergraduates studying a technology related course such as software or electronic engineering. Three 3-month and three 12-month **Trainee Software Engineers** are needed for the Engineering Development Centre; the Applications Development Group is a software group producing applications associated with the core communications infrastructure. One 3-month and one 12-month **Trainee Manufacturing Engineers** are needed for the Manufacturing Facility: the manufacturing technical support team are skilled engineers providing a comprehensive support service to manufacturing, including provision of a Maintenance Team, Test Development Team and the Manufacturing Engineering Team.
For further details or to *apply*, please write enclosing your CV and stating which placement you are interested in to Mick Hooley, Personnel Manager, at the above address.

**PSA PEUGEOT CITROEN:** Ryton Manufacturing Division, Ryton-on-Dunsmore, Coventry CV8 3D2 (☎02476-886000; fax 02476-886064). Car manufacturer.
**Vacation Trainees (300)** to help fix components to the vehicles on the production line. Wages from £1,600 per month. A small number will be taken from the end of May and the greatest intake will be from middle June with a decrease in August. Work is located at the Ryton Manufacturing Plant, Ryton-on-Dunsmore, Coventry.
Experience of a production environment would be advantageous but not essential. Transport would be required as no public transport to the plant. Experience of shift work would be advantageous. All who apply would need to be aware that this would be a very busy production environment. Please call for more information. Minimum age 18 years old, should be in full-time education.
Contact Tracy McGhee, Personnel Assistant, for an *application form* on 02476-886199.

# The North

**Prospects for Work.**
While job vacancies in the tourist trade are scattered throughout the northern region, they are most abundant in the larger coastal resorts, the Yorkshire Dales and the Lake District.

The main resorts along the east coast are Bridlington, Filey, Whitby and Scarborough, one of Britain's most popular seaside destinations. Scarborough and Filey have a large number of seasonal vacancies, comparatively few of which have live-in accommodation. Further north lie South Shields, Whitley Bay and Berwick. Berwick has two large holiday centres run by British Holidays employing seasonal staff from April-October with some live-in work available. As well as hotels and restaurants, amusement arcades are another source of employment, particularly in Bridlington. Live-in jobs are comparatively rare. South of Scarborough along the coast are four major holiday centres run by Haven Leisure Ltd; Primrose Valley, Blue Dolphin, Cayton Bay and Reighton Sands. Job Centres advertise vacancies and seasonal vacancies appear in the

Scarborough Evening News six days a week (Thursday is the main day). Anyone interested in a seasonal position should contact Scarborough Job Centre. It is best to apply in January.

The principal tourist centre of the west coast is Blackpool, which has many vacancies for its many hotels, amusement arcades and fun parks. Recently aired plans to turn the town into Britain's answer to Las Vegas should, if they are implemented, increase these vacancies. In addition Blackpool has an especially long season; the end of the summer season is given a boost when the illuminations are turned on at the end of August; these remain an attraction until late November. The *Blackpool Evening Gazette* offers a mailing service on request and has a special 'Jobs Night' edition every Thursday. Few jobs offer live-in accommodation and accommodation can be difficult to find during the summer months.

Morecambe, Fleetwood, Southport, Thornton, Cleveleys and Lytham St Anne's, also in Lancashire, are popular tourist haunts too. Hexham in Northumberland has opened a new golf course recently. It is also worth contacting the local Golf Clubs directly.

There are lots of seasonal jobs in Northumberland at Haggerston Castle Holiday Park in Berwick and in hotel and catering from Amble to Berwick; Alnwick Jobcentre has a student register that matches people to seasonal vacancies.

In the main tourist centres in the Lake District – Windermere, Bowness-on-Windermere, Ambleside and Grasmere – jobs are available in holiday camps as well as hotels. Rural caravan sites in the area may also offer seasonal opportunities. Unfortunately, unless you are lucky renting a room in the Lake District it is likely to cost more than your weekly wage. The chances of saving much money are therefore minimal unless you are offered live-in accommodation or are able to camp. Hotels in the Lake District start advertising for staff about three weeks before Easter; wherever possible they will take on the same staff for the summer season too.

York and Harrogate are both on the tourist trail, and there is therefore a demand for extra hotel staff and shop staff. Your best chance of getting a job is to apply well in advance of the end of the student term. Attractions like the York Dungeons and Jorvik Viking Centre, and events such as the York Races may offer opportunities for two or three days' work. Similarly a wide range of short-term work is usually available in early July during the Great Yorkshire Show in Harrogate: jobs are advertised in the Jobcentre about a month beforehand. Three miles north of Ripon, the Lightwater Valley Theme Park takes on large numbers of seasonal staff which are also advertised in the Harrogate Jobcentre. In this area consult the *Yorkshire Evening Post* or *York Evening Press* for job advertisements.

Factory work provides a source of seasonal work in the North, with large factories recruiting extra people to work over the summer, mainly from June until September. They include Nestlé Rowntree and Terry Suchard in York and KP foods in Cleveland. Other factories to approach, either directly or through the local Jobcentre, are: Ben Shaws in Pontefract; Crystal Drinks Ltd in Featherstone; Unique Images in Bradford; and Glaxo Operations, Kerry Foods Ltd and Mono Containers in Durham. In the Durham area agencies such as Manpower usually recruit for this type of work.

The North has experienced rapid growth in call centre operations, notably at Doxford Park in Sunderland. Companies such as London Electricity, T-Mobil, Axiom, Littlewoods Home Shopping, Barclays and Subscription Services Ltd have relocated to this site. Other call centre operations throughout the region include Transco and BT call centre at North Tyneside, Abbey National at

Stockton and Orange Telecommunications at Darlington. These operations are known to employ students on a temporary basis, since their overall staff turnover is generally high. There is usually a training period and most applicants need good keyboard and customer service skills. Local job centres should be contacted for details.

Various local authorities, such as Gateshead, Greater Manchester, South Tyneside and Sunderland, may have work on playschemes or may need holiday cover in their many clerical departments. Large towns such as Leeds and Newcastle are the best places to try for retail jobs. The tourist trade in the Manchester area is currently booming following its 2002 hosting of the Commonwealth Games and the emergence of national attractions such as the Imperial War Museum North, Urbis and the Lowry arts centre. Other places recommended for general summer work are Alnwick, Bamburgh, Corbridge, Haydon Bridge, Hexham, Seahouses, Barnet Castle, Durham and Redcar.

City Councils and Local Authorities are worth contacting to find out about significant forthcoming events which may need extra staffing. Most local newspaper websites now have local job search facilities using *Fish4Jobs* – for example, try www.thisislancashire.co.uk; substitute the name of the county or town where you are hoping to find a job.

# Business and Industry

**ADAM EAGLE ASSOCIATES:** 6 Front Street, Hagg Bank, Wylam, Northumberland NE41 8JT (☎01661-853090; e-mail eagle@wylam75.freeserve.co.uk). A fundraising company which specialises in working with Wildlife Trusts.

**Membership Officers (45)** to work throughout Manchester, Teeside, Cheshire, Durham and Northumberland/Newcastle. Officers needed to represent the local Wildlife Trust, promoting it to the general public of the area. Some house-calling, distributing booklets to people who express an interest in wildlife conservation. Strictly no selling or persuasion, full training given.

Wages £4.00 per hour plus commission, average pay £120 per week. Work is part-time for 2-3 hours each weekday evening, starting at 5.45pm. Staff required between March and October for a minimum of 8 weeks. Must be aged 23 or over, presentable, mature manner and ideally have experience of dealing with the general public.

Information pack and information on *applications* from Adam Eagle at the above address.

**CONTRACT DATA RESEARCH LTD/CDR GROUP:** Eccles House, Eccles Lane, Hope, Hope Valley S33 6RW (☎01433-621282; fax 01433-621292; e-mail tony@cdrgroup.co.uk). A small company based in the heart of the Peak District, currently employing 14 staff. Hard work in a friendly and relaxed atmosphere.

**Data Processors (2-4).** Wages £4.31 per hour; to work 37½ per week. Staff are required for a minimum of 2 months between June and October. The job involves transferring information from paper records/plans to a computer database. No accommodation is available. Overseas applicants with a good understanding of English and the necessary qualifications are welcome. Please note that an interview is required.

*Applications* from May to Tony Witham at the above address.

**SUNNYHURST NURSERIES LTD:** Blackgate Lane, Tarleton, Preston, Lancs PR4 6UT (☎01772-812266; fax 01772-816420). Salad and vegetable plant

suppliers to commercial growers.
**Pallet Stackers (2).** Wages from £4.50 per hour. To work up to 40 hours per five day week. Minimum period of work one month. Positions are available from April to July. Applicants should have fork-lift truck driver's certificate. Fork-lift driving is necessary to assist the manual aspects of the work. Minimum age 21. No accommodation available. Foreign applicants with work permits and acceptable spoken English welcome.
*Applications* should be made from February to K. Marshall at the above address. Interview required.

**FIELD STUDIES COUNCIL:** Blencathra Centre, Threlkeld, Keswick, Cumbria CA12 4SG (☎01768-779601; fax 01768-779264; e-mail fsc.blencathra@ukonline.co.uk). An educational centre offering courses in geography, geology and ecology, providing accommodation for up to 70.
**Centre Assistants (2)** for general duties in the busy centre, with opportunities to observe and support the environmental education work. National Minimum Wage plus accommodation. To work 37½ hours, 5 days per week. Minimum period of work 7 months, April to October. Applicants must have A-Levels or equivalent. Suitably qualified foreign applicants authorised to work in the UK welcome. Fluent English essential.
*Applications* should be made from late February/early March to Mr Andy Simms at the above address. Interview required.

# Children

**ACORN ADVENTURES:** Acorn House, 22 Worcester Street, Stourbridge DY8 1AN. Multi-activity centres in the Lake District and North Wales. Acorn adventure are the leading provider of outdoor adventure camps for schools, youth groups and families, operating 9 activity centres in France, Italy, Spain and the UK.
**Instructors.** Must hold at least Instructor status with e.g. BCU or RYA, or have passed SPSA or MLTB assessment. Other nationally recognised coaching awards may be considered.
**Assistant Instructors.** Must be registered as training for the above award(s).
**Support Staff.** Maintenance and/or catering. No experience necessary.
**Fully Qualified Nurse.**
Please note that all staff must be available from April/May to September: full period only.
For further information or for *applications*, please contact the Recruitment Department for a full information pack on 01384-446057 or fax 01384-378866 or e-mail topstaff@acornadventure.co.uk.

**CHERUB NURSERIES & PRE-SCHOOLS LTD:** Cherub Childcare Centre, Lindsey Place, Arcon Drive, Anlaby Rd, Hull (☎01482-509598; fax 01482-576650). A well established company of 3 childrens' day nurseries in the Hull Area that has been in practice for 20 years.
**Nursery Nurses (2), Nursery Assistants (2).** To care for children 6 weeks to 8 years old, providing a high standard of care; a clean and hygienic nursery with safety is always the main priority. Basic wages. To work a maximum of 40 hours per week. Min. period of work of 4 weeks. Positions are available from June to September. Should be 18+ and NNEB B-tec qualified. Foreign applicants welcome. No Accommodation available.
*Applications* should be made to Paula Walton at the above address. Interview necessary.

**CITY LEISURE:** Minerva House, Pendlebury Road, Swinton, Salford, M27 4EQ (☏0161-7780378; 0161-7286145). City Leisure manages 11 facilities in Salford which provide playschemes throughout the summer holidays.
**Temporary Playscheme/Sports Workers** to provide quality care for children during the pay and play schemes. Wages £6.42 per hour; to work Monday to Friday, 10-30 hours per week during the school holidays. Staff are required from 21 July to 29 August for a minimum period of 6 weeks.Applicants must be over 18.
Experience of working with children is essential and a background in sporting activities is desirable. Overseas applicant are welcome but must be able to attend an interview in May/June.
*Applications* should be sent to Dawn Williams at the above address from May onwards. Interview necessary.

**HALTON PLAY COUNCIL LTD:** 10 Mersey Road, Runcorn, Cheshire WA7 1DF (☏01928-574087; fax 01928-567353).
**Play leaders (15)** £155 per week. 9am-5pm Mon-Fri.
**Play assistants (30)** £133 per week. 9am-5pm Mon-Fri.
**Volunteers (20)** £50 per week. 9.30am-4.30pm Mon-Fri.
All staff needed from 29 July to 16 August. *Applications* to A. Johnson, Manager, at the above address.

**KIDS AT HEART:** Low Moor Lane, Lingerfield, Knaresborough, N Yorks, HG5 9JN (☏01423-862192; 01423-860371; e-mail info@kidsatheart.co.uk)
**Play Worker** needed for the school holidays on a full or part-time basis to assist in preparation of activities and play programmes. Experience with children necessary.
**Nursery Nurse/Assistant** for June to September as holiday cover. Must have relevant experience.
Wages according to experience. *Applications* to Diane Pearson, Manager, at the above address.

**NST TRAVEL GROUP PLC:** Recruitment, Chiltern House, Bristol Avenue, Blackpool FY2 0FA (☏01253-530311; fax 01253-356955; e-mail info@nstjobs.co.uk; www.nstjobs.co.uk). An Outdoor Activity and ICT residential centre for children aged 9-13. NST Travel Group is Europe's leading educational tour operator.
**Activity/ICT Instructors (20)** To instruct a range of outdoor activities and ICT and to assist with the evening entertainment programme. While qualifications are valued they are not essential as full training will be given prior to working ith guests.
**Catering Assistants (5)** to assist the Catering Manager and be involved in all aspects of kitchen work. No previous experience required.
**Maintenance/Cleaning Assistants (4)** To assist the Maintenance manager. No previous experience required, but an interest in DIY useful.
Wages in line with the National Minimum Wage. Average working week 42 hours over 6 days. Minimum period of work 2 months. Staff required from January through to November. All positions are residential.
For more information and an *application form* please contact the above address.

**LAKESIDE YMCA NATIONAL CENTRE:** Ulverston, Cumbria LA12 8BD (☏08707-273927; fax 015395-30015). The camp is set in 400 acres of woodland on the shores of Lake Windermere in the Lake District National Park, and is one of the largest camps in Europe.
**Day Camp Leaders (30).** £35 per week plus travel expenses within Great Britain

and free B & L. To work 5½ days a week, 9am-5pm. Min. age 18 years. Min. period of work 8 weeks between early July and the end of August. Some experience of outdoor activities is advantageous and an interest in working with children necessary. The work involves leading groups of children aged 8-13 years in a wide range of activities, from environmental awareness to rock climbing.
*Application* forms available from January to May from Day Camp Director, Lakeside YMCA National Centre.

## Holiday Centres and Amusements

**ALLEN (PARKFOOT) LTD:** Howtown Road, Pooley Bridge, Penrith, Cumbria CA10 2NA (☎017684-86309; e-mail park.foot@talk21.com; www.parkfootulswater.co.uk). Family run caravan and camping park by Lake Ullswater. Set in magnificent scenery and perfect for outdoor activities.
**Bar Staff** to work 6pm to midnight. Min. age 18 years.
**Kitchen Assistants (4)** to help the head cook prepare meals, clear tables, operate the dishwasher and work the till. Hours 8am-2pm and 6-11pm.
**Cook/Chef** to prepare cooked breakfasts, lunches and evening meals. Hours 8am-2pm and 6-11pm.
**Adventure Supervisor (1)** to run a children's action club from the Park. Activities include archery, tennis, baseball, volleyball, football, arts (raft making and crafts) and pool tournaments. Hours 9am-5pm Monday to Friday during school holidays.
**Nanny/Mothers Helps (2)** each to look after two school age children and help with household duties. Live-in position. Must be able to drive.
**Secretary/Receptionist (1)** To work alternative early/evening shifts and shared weekends. Required from May-September. Must enjoy meeting people and have a pleasant telephone manner.
   Wages negotiable according to experience. Accommodation can be arranged in shared staff caravans. Period of work Easter, May Bank Holidays and from June to mid-September.
   *Applications* from Easter, enclosing colour photo, details of work experience and dates of availability, to Mrs B. Mowbray or Mrs F. Bell, Parkfoot Caravan Park.

**AMERICAN ADVENTURE THEME PARK:** Pit Lane, Ilkeston, Derby DE7 5SX (☎01773-531521; fax 01773-716140 www.americanadventure.co.uk). Theme park.
**Retail Staff (70).**
**Ride Operators (150).**
**Catering Assistants (120).**
Other job opportunities may be available; contact the park for details. Wages to be arranged. To work flexible hours. Foreign applicants with permission to work in the UK welcome; fluent English essential.
   Requests for further details and *applications* should be made at any time to the Personnel Department at the above address.

**FARSYDE STUD & RIDING CENTRE:** Robin Hood's Bay, Whitby, North Yorkshire YO22 4UG (☎01947-880249; fax 01947-880877; e-mail farsydestud@talk21.com). A family run stud farm with five holiday cottages. The centre is set in 70 acres of grassland in the North York Moors National Park, and a short walk from the beach.
**General Assistant** for support duties. £3 per hour for min. of 20 hours per week. Min. period of work 6 weeks between May/June and September/October.

Accommodation in house, cottage or caravan provided for £40 per week. Applicants must be competent riders, willing, self-motivated, cheerful, non-smokers, adaptable, able to relate well to children and adults, and also enjoy country life. Overseas applicants eligible to work in the UK and with basic English welcome.
*Applications* to Mrs A. Green, Owner/Manager, Farsyde Stud & Riding Centre.

**FRONTIERLAND WESTERN THEME PARK:** The Promenade, Morecambe, Lancashire LA4 4DG (☎01524-410024). Western-style theme park, comprising rides, arcades, a family bar and catering units.
**Ride Operators, Catering Staff (40)** Wages at the National Minimum rate. Hours flexible to suit the individual. Staff required between June and September. Minimum age 18. No accommodation available. Foreign applicants with permission to work in the UK welcome; fluent English essential.
*Applications* should be made from May to Mr S Riley at the above address. Interview required.

**LIGHTWATER VALLEY ATTRACTIONS LTD:** North Stanley, Ripon, North Yorkshire, HG4 3HT.
**Catering/Retail/Games/Attractions Assistants** needed between 26th May and 3rd September, for weekends in September and October and between 20th-28th October. Hours of work are on a 7 day rota working between 9.45am and 5-6pm, with wages according to age and the National Minimum Wage. All posts require applicants to be at least 16 years old.
*Applications* should be made in writing to Chris Steed, Training Manager.

**OASIS LAKELAND FOREST VILLAGE:** Temple Sowerby, Penrith, Cumbria CA10 2DW (☎01768-893004; fax 01768-893001; e-mail eleanor.tindall@centerp arcs.com). Set in the beautiful Lake District, Oasis leisure resort is now part of the CenterParcs group.
**Bar and Waiting staff, Kitchen Staff, Sports Attendants etc.** Wages a minimum of £4.61 per hour; to work 40 hours per week. Previous experience not essential. Staff are required for a minimum of 3 months. Permanent positions are available.
*Application forms* can be obtained by phoning the above number.

**PLEASURELAND LTD:** Pleasureland Amusement Park, Marine Drive, Southport PR8 1RX (☎01704-532717; fax 01704-537936; e-mail mail@pleasurelandltd.f reeserve.co.uk). An approved Investor in People and Positive Against Disability employer.
**Ride Operators (60).** Min. age 18.
**Cleaners For Grounds (4).** Minimum age 17 years.
**Toilet Cleaners (5).** Min. age 17 years.
**Car Park Attendants (6).** Min. age 18 years.
**Catering Assistants (40).** Min. age 17 years.
**Arcade Cashiers (6), Arcade Attendants (12).** Min. age 18.
**Supervisors and Team Leaders.**
Wages start at the National Minimum Wage and go up according to age and experience. National Vocational Qualification (level II) offered in Mechanical Ride Operations and customer service, with others pending. All staff to work 5 or 6 days per week. No experience necessary unless otherwise stated as full training will be provided. Minimum period of work one day between March and April. No accommodation available but local B & Bs cost approx. £15 per night. Overseas applicants with a good standard of English considered. Applicants should be able to

attend an interview.
All *applications* are handled by Southport Jobcentre (☎01704-306000; www.jobcentreplus.gov.uk).

**RIPLEY CARAVAN PARK:** Ripley, Harrogate, North Yorkshire HG3 3AU (☎01423-770050).
**Assistant Wardens (2)** for general duties, including gardening, and cleaning shower block and swimming pool. Wages specified on application. Period of work Easter to end of October. Positions suitable for a mature couple. Accommodation not provided, but can bring own tent/caravan.
Applicants must be able to attend an interview.
*Applications* from early 2003 to Mr P. House, at the above address.

**WENSLEYDALE CREAMERY VISITOR CENTRE:** Gayle Lane, Hawes, North Yorkshire DL8 3RN (☎01969-667664; fax 01969-667638).
**Visitor Centre Staff (up to 6).** From £4.60 per hour depending on age; 30-35 hours per week, five days a week. Needed from May-November to work in the five departments of the Visitor Centre. Age 18+. No accommodation available but help may be given in finding it.
*Apply* to Daniel Bradley, Catering Manager.

## Hotels and Catering

**THE BLUE BELL HOTEL:** Market Square, Belford, Northumberland NE70 7NE (☎01668-213543; fax 01668-213787; e-mail bluebel@globalnet.co.uk). A family run hotel with the youngest team of staff in a Three Star Hotel anywhere in Northumberland.
**Receptionists (2)** for telephone/reception duties. Wage by arrangement with variable tips. To work from 8am-4pm or 4-11pm, 5 days per week. Should ideally be aged 21.
**Waiting Staff (2)** Wages by arrangement plus good tips. To work from 7.30am-3pm or 6.30-11pm. Minimum age 18.
Accommodation provided. Period of work from April to November. Applicants for either position need commitment and dedication.
*Applications* to Paul Shirley, Partner, at the above address.

**BRACKENRIGG INN:** Watermillock, Penrith, CA11 0LP (☎01768-486206; e-mail enquiries@brackenrigginn.co.uk; www.brackenrigginn.co.uk). Rural lakeside hotel 5 miles from the nearest town.
**General Assistants.** Wages and hours by arrangement with 2 days off per week. Period of work from June to September. Min. age 18 years. Applicants must enjoy the countryside and be prepared to work hard. Training is provided so experience is not necessary. Overseas applicants welcome.
*Applications* to the Manager at the above address.

**BRATHAY HALL TRUST:** Ambleside, Cumbria LA22 0HP. A management training centre situated on the north west shore of Lake Windermere.
**General Assistants** needed for general duties such as washing-up, cleaning rooms, assisting chefs, bar work. Good pay and conditions, single room accommodation available if necessary. 42 hours a week with 2 days off per week. Staff needed all year round, min. period of work 3 months.Min. age 18 Applicants must be prepared to attend an informal interview if possible.

*Applications,* in writing, to the Housekeeper at the above address.

**BURNSIDE HOTEL:** Kendal Road, Bowness on Windermere, Cumbria LA23 3EP (fax 015394-43824; e-mail john@burnsidehotel.com).
**Restaurant Staff (1/2)** to help out in busy restaurant. Wages £160 p.w. To work 40-45 hours a week, 5 days per week.
*Applications* to Mr Whalley, Assistant Manager.

**CHADWICK HOTEL:** South Promenade, Lytham St. Annes, Lancashire FY8 1NP (☎01253-720061; fax 01253-714455; e-mail sales@thechadwickhotel.com).
**Restaurant Personnel (2).** Wages £150-£180 per week depending on age and experience. To work 45 hours per week. Min. period of work 8 weeks at any time of year. No accommodation is available.Overseas applicants are considered. Interview preferable but not necessary.
*Applications* to Mr. Corbett at any time.

**COPTHORNE HOTEL MANCHESTER:** Clippers Quay, Salford Quays, Manchester M5 2XP (☎0161-873 7321; fax 0161-873 7318; e-mail janet.marshall@mill-cop.com). 166 bedroomed hotel just outside Manchester boasting event facilities for 150, 2 restaurants, bars and a leisure club. Good transport to the city centre.
**Room attendants (2).** Wages £4.70 per hour. 16+. Physically strong with a good eye for detail.
**Food and Beverage Service Assistants (2).** Wages of £4.80 per hour. 18+. Experience in cash sales an advantage.
To work 37½ hours over 5 days including weekends and evenings (bar staff). Min. period of work of 4 months. Positions are available from June to October. Foreign applicants welcome. No accommodation available.
*Applications* should be made from May onwards to Janet Marshall at the above address. Interview necessary.

**DERWENTWATER HOTEL: Portinscale, Keswick CA12 5RE (☎017687-72538; fax 017687-71002). Diament Ltd. is an I.I.P. Company which won the International Environmental Award 1995 and Excellence Through People award; nominated employer of the year in May 2000. The hotel has 48 bedrooms/19 self-catering apartments and stands on the lake shore. Guests return to share the friendliness and enjoy the beautiful surroundings.**
**WAITING STAFF (2). From £144 per week. 5 days, 40 hours. Experience not essential.**
**BAR PERSON (1). From £144 per week. 5 days, 40 hours. Experience essential.**
**Staff required for a minimum of 6 months at any time of year. Accommodation available. Min. age 18. Overseas applicants with the ability to speak and understand English welcome.**
**Applications to the Personnel Department at the above address, enclosing a stamped addressed envelope.**

**THE FAMOUS SCHOONER HOTEL:** Northumberland Street, Alnmouth, Northumberland NE66 2RS (☎01665-830216; fax 01665-830287). The famous Schooner Hotel, a listed 17th Century Coach Inn is 100 yards from the beach and a golf course.
**General Assistants.** Wages negotiable. There is a high tipping potential. To work 40-45

hours per week. Live-in accommodation available. Min. work period 4 weeks between mid-June and mid-September. Overseas applicants with good English welcome.
*Applications* a.s.a.p. to the Manager, the Schooner Hotel.

**GEORGE WASHINGTON HOTEL:** Stone Cellar Road, High Usworth, Washington, District 12, Tyne and Wear NE37 1PH (☎0191-4029988; fax 0191-4151166). The hotel has 103 bedrooms, a restaurant and conference facilities for up to 200, a leisure club and an 18 hole golf course.
**Restaurant Waiting Staff, Bar Staff.** Wage negotiable. To work hours as required. Staff needed from July to December. Min. age 18. Previous experience required. No accommodation available.
*Applications* from May to Dawn Graham at the above address. Applicants must be available for interview.

**GLENRIDDING HOTEL:** Glenridding, Penrith, Cumbria CA11 0PB (☎017684-82228; fax 017684-82555; e-mail lynn@glenridding hotel.demon.co.uk). Lake District hotel. Suited to outdoor types. Surrounded by fells and Lakes.
**Food & Beverage Staff (2)** for general hotel work. Wages by arrangement with accommodation provided and a share of tips, plus a bonus of £65 per month worked on completion of contract. To work a 40 hour week on a 6 to 8 month contract. Period of work between March-September or April-October. Age 18-25
Candidates should *contact* John Dawes, Senior Manager, at the above address.

**M.B. & J. GOODWIN LTD:** Low Skirlington Caravan Park, Skipsea, nr Driffield, Humberside YO25 8SY (☎01262-468213/468466; fax 01262-468105).
**Bar Staff (2), Receptionist (1), Kitchen Staff (2), Entertainer (1)** to work on a holiday caravan site. Wages £180 per week. Normal hours, approx. 45 per week, including weekends and evenings. Period of work from June to September. Free accommodation provided in a caravan. Overseas applicants welcome.
*Applications* to M. B. & J. Goodwin Ltd.

**GRASMERE HOTEL:** Grasmere, nr Ambleside, Cumbria LA22 9TA (tel/fax 01539-435277; www.grasmerehotel.co.uk). A very busy 12-bedroom, award winning country house hotel.
**Assistant Cook (1).** £150 a week.
**General Assistant (1).** £150 a week. Duties include waiting, bar work, housekeeping, reception, office work and some kitchen work.
All staff work 40 hours, 5 days a week. Min. period of work 6 months, February to December. Live-in accommodation available for women only: own room with TV provided. Min. age 21. Preferably college trained or at least 1 year's experience. Overseas applicants with good knowledge of English welcome.
*Applications* to Mr P. Riley, Proprietor, at the Grasmere Hotel.

**HOLIDAY INN CARLISLE:** Parkhouse Road, Carlisle, Cumbria CA3 0HR (☎0870-4009 018; fax 01228-543178).
**Waiting Staff (6).** Mmust have previous experience of restaurant work and contact with customers.
**Bar Staff (4).** Must have previous experience of bar work.
**Porters (2)** for part-time work; must have previous experience of contact with customers.
**Chamber Staff (4).** Previous experience an advantage but enthusiasm is even more important.

**Grill Chef.** Must be qualified.
Rates of pay from £3.60-£4.75 per hour depending on age and experience. Limited accommodation available. Period of work June-August and October.
*Applications* to the Personnel Department at the above address.

**HOLMHEAD FARM GUESTHOUSE:** Hadrian's Wall, Greenhead via Brampton, Near Carlisle CA8 7HY (☎016977-47402). A bed and breakfast offering evening dinner parties situated on the Hadrian's Wall path with beautiful rural surroundings; positions therefore not suitable for socialites. Only 4 bedrooms to service and a clientele from all over the world, especially America.
**General Assistant (1)** required to help run a guest house. Wages £80 a week including B & L within a friendly home environment. Own mobile home with all facilities. To work up to 9 hours per day, 5 days a week with extra days off wherever possible. Period of work Easter to 1 November. Min. period of work June to end of August. Duties include helping prepare meals, washing up and cleaning rooms. Min. age 18. No experience required. Overseas applicants with spoken English and the correct documentation welcome (owner speaks Norwegian). Candidates should be available for interview, though if this is difficult references may suffice.
*Applications* from January to P. Staff, Proprietor, at the above address.

**LADY ANNE MIDDLETON'S HOTEL:** Skeldergate, York (☎01904-611570; fax 01904-613043). Independent 52 bedroom hotel located in the city centre, with own health and fitness club, conference and event rooms. Primarily catering for the leisure and small conference trade.
**Waiting Staff (2), Chamberpersons (2).** Up to £4.30 per hour. To work 39 hours per week. Min. period of work 3 months at any time of year. Accommodation is **not** available. Min. age 21. Overseas applicants welcome.
*Applications* at any time to Andy Clark at the above address. All applicants should be able to supply a current CV

**LEEMING HOUSE HOTEL:** Watermillock, Ullswater, nr Penrith, Cumbria CA11 0JJ (☎017684-86622; fax 017684-86443; www.macdonaldhotels.co.uk). Beautiful country house hotel set in own grounds with access onto the lake. Very good staff accommodation available within grounds.
**Waiting Staff (4).** Experience needed.
**Bar Staff/Porters (2).** Previous bar work experience required.
**Chamber Staff (4).**
Salary for all staff from £161.85 a week. To work 5 days a week with consecutive days off. Min. period of work 6 months. Accommodation available for £20 per week (some shared) plus all meals. Ages: 18-35 years. Overseas applicants eligible to work in the UK and with good English welcome.
*Applications* to the Personnel Manager, Leeming House Hotel.

**LINDEN HALL HOTEL:** Longhorsley, Morpeth, Northumberland NE65 8XF (☎01670-500000; fax 01670-500001; www.lindenhall.co.uk).
**Restaurant and Bar Staff/Silver Service Staff (5)** required for summer or weekend work. Staff will carry out general food and beverage service in two restaurants, bars and banqueting suites. Wages are £3.87-£4.10 per hour. Hours of work are flexible, up to 8 hours per shift, days and evenings. Candidates should be between 18-30 years old, have basic food and beverage experience and a smart, clean appearance. Must have own transport. Accommodation not available.
*Applications* should be made to the above address.

**LINDETH FELL HOTEL:** Bowness-on-Windermere, Cumbria LA23 3JP (☎015394-43286; e-mail kennedy@Lindethfell.co.uk; www.Lindethfell.co.uk). A country house hotel set in magnificent grounds on the hills above Lake Windermere, offering good views and excellent cooking in a friendly atmosphere.
**General Assistants (3).** £160 a week plus free B & L. To work 40 hours a week. Duties include helping in the dining room, bedrooms and kitchen. Work available all year. Applicants must be available for interview. Overseas applicants in early 20s and with good English welcome.
*Applications* from 1 January to P. A. Kennedy, Owner, at the above address.

**THE LODGE AT LEEMING BAR:** Bedale, North Yorkshire DL8 1DT (☎01677-423611; fax 01677-424507). Part of Leeming Service Area (A1/A684 Intersection).
**General Assistants (2).** To work 5 days a week. Must be hotel or catering students.
**Kitchen Assistants (3).** Split and straight shifts over 5 days. Must be catering students.
**Receptionist.**
**Senior Waiting Staff (2).** Wages plus tips. Split shifts, 5 days a week. Must be hotel or catering student with experience of silver service.
**Other Waiting Staff (3).** Wages plus tips. To work 5 days a week.
**Bar Staff (1).** Split shifts, 5 days a week. Must have previous bar and cash handling experience.
**Shop Assistants (2).** Straight shifts, 5 or 6 days a week.
**Cafe Assistants (6).** Straight and split shifts over 5 days.
**Cafe Assistants-Night Shift (2).** Straight shifts, 5 nights a week.
Wages to be arranged. Min. period of work 8 weeks between June and October. B & L available. Min. age 18.
*Applications* from April to Mr C. A. Les at the above address.

**MALLYAN SPOUT HOTEL:** Goathland, near Whitby, Yorkshire (☎01947-896486; e-mail mallyan@ukgateway.net). Hotel with predominantly young staff, in beautiful quiet countryside.
**Waiting Staff (2), Kitchen/Still Room Assistants (2), Chamber Staff.** From £140 a week plus free B & L. To work 40 hours/5 days per week. Work available all year for a minimum of 4-6 months, do not apply for less than 6 months. Intelligent workers preferred. Overseas applicants considered.
*Applications* with s.a.e. to Mrs Heslop, Mallyan Spout Hotel.

**NEWCASTLE HOLIDAY INN:** Great North Road, Seaton Burn, Newcastle-upon-Tyne NE13 6BP (☎0191-2019988; fax 0191-2368091). The hotel is situated on the outskirts of Newcastle, just off the A1/A19.
**Casual Room Attendants (6).** To work approx. 20 hours a week.
**Casual Events Waiting Staff (10), Bar Staff (2).** To work approx. 20-25 hours a week.
Wages by arrangement. Staff must be flexible and prepared to work shifts and late nights. Minimum period of work 2 months between June and September. No accommodation is available. Applicants must be over 16 (over 18 for Bar Staff positions) and have a good general education. Overseas applicants considered.
*Applications* from May to Human Resources Manager. Interview required.

**PATTERDALE HOTEL:** Patterdale, Lake Ullswater, near Penrith, Cumbria CA11 0NW (☎017684-82231; fax 017684-82440). A friendly family run, busy 57 bedroom Lake District hotel in beautiful surroundings.

**General Assistants.** Wages by arrangement.
Experience not necessary unless applying for Chef's position. Min. age 17. Free B & L provided. Opportunities for walking, climbing, etc. Min. period of work 6 months from March to December. Overseas applicants with good English welcome.
*Applications* from early 2002 to Choice House, 107 Dickson Road, Blackpool FY1 2ET, ☎01253-754211.

**QUEEN'S HOTEL:** Main Street, Keswick, Cumbria CA12 5JF (☎017687-73333). A 35-bedroom hotel in the heart of the Lake District.
**Chamber Staff (1), Waiting Staff (1), Bar Staff (2).** £210 per week gross; B & L available. To work 40 hours a week. Period of work between June and September. No qualifications or experience necessary. Overseas applicants with good English welcome.
*Applications* a.s.a.p. to Mr Peter Williams, Proprietor, The Queen's Hotel. Due to numbers only successful applicants will receive a reply.

**SHARROW BAY HOTEL:** Lake Ullswater, Penrith, Cumbria CA10 2LZ (☎017684-86301/86483; fax 017684-86349; e-mail enquiries@sharrowbay.com). Luxury hotel and Michelin starred restaurant set in a tranquil postion on the edge of Lake Ullswater.
**Stillroom Assistants.** Approx. £165 a week.
**General Assistants.** Min. £165 a week. To work in bedrooms.
Free B & L provided. All staff to work 50 hours/5 days a week. Preferred period of work 9 months from early March to end of November. Age: 17-30 years. Must have domestic interests and lots of common sense, and should enjoy living in the country and working as part of a team of perfectionists. References required.
*Applications* from January to the Manager, Sharrow Bay Hotel.

**ST LEONARD'S FARM PARK:** Chapel Lane, Esholt, Bradford BD17 7RB (tel/fax 01274-598795). A family farm open to the public.
**Snack Bar Assistant (2).** Food handling/preparation an advantage but training is given.
**General Farm Workers (2).** Experience of working with animals is an advantage.
**Shop Assistants (2).** Experience is not needed as training is given.
**Catering Assistants (2).** Important to like children.
For all positions wages are dependent on age and experience; to work weekends and school holidays a maximum of 6 hours per day, 3 days per week. Staff are required from April to September. Overseas applicants are welcome. No accommodation available.
*Applications* should be sent to Denise Wainhouse at the above address from March onwards.

**THE VENTURE CENTRE:** Maughold, Isle of Man IM7 1AW (☎01624-814240; fax 01624-815615; e-mail enquiries@adventure-centre.co.uk; www.adventure-centre.co.uk). Adventure training centre giving introductory instruction in outdoor activities to children aged 9-15 years.
**Catering and Domestic Staff.** Qualified or experienced cooks to cook, prepare and serve. Also to run the kitchen for groups of residential children (up to 60). Positions available from March to September.
*Applications* before March to Mr S. Read, Director, the Venture Centre.

**WILD BOAR HOTEL:** Crook, Near Windermere, Cumbria LA23 3NF (☎015394-45225; fax 015394-42498; e-mail wildboar@elh.co.uk). A small friendly hotel with a large proportion of live-in personnel, surrounded by beautiful countryside.
**General Assistant** to work in any area of the hotel, but mainly the restaurant, waiting, bar, portering or housekeeping (which involves serving teas/coffees, cleaning the lounges, setting and serving function rooms and other duties). Wages from £576 per month live-in (no deductions made from the figure for live-in).

Work is live-in in own bedroom with communal facilities, all food, with five days work out of seven. Period of work from May to the end of September/early October. The job involves dealing directly with guests so pleasant and outgoing personalities are essential. Common sense is more desirable than previous experience. The hotel is in the country on a road without public transport so applicants need either own transport or a liking of rural surroundings.

*Applications* to Wayne Bartholomew at the above address.

**YORK MARRIOT:** Tadcaster Road, York YO24 1QQ (☎01904-701000; fax 01904-702308). An IPP accredited hotel that has won awards for 5 Star employment practices. Set in idyllic surroundings, overlooking the racecourse with friendly and cheerful staff.
**Food and Beverage Associates (5)** to serve food and drink. Min. age 17 (18 for bar work). Bar and customer care experience essential. Must have good communication skills, smart presentation and be flexible. Expected to provide own black and whites. For waiting work need silver service experience and own black and whites.
**Chamber Staff (2).** Must have previous relevant experience. Uniform provided.

All staff to work 30-40 hours per week. Wages at least National Minimum. No accommodation provided. Min. period of work 12 weeks throughout the year. Overseas applicants welcome provided they have a good grasp of the English language.

*Applications* should consist of a CV and covering letter advising availability from March to the Personnel and Training Manager at the above address. All applicants must be available for interview.

# Language Schools

**MANCHESTER ACADEMY OF ENGLISH:** St Margaret's Chambers, 5 Newton Street, Manchester M1 1HL (☎0161-237-5619; fax 0161-237-9016; e-mail english@manacad.co.uk). City Centre English language school for international students, a member of ARELS, and British Council accredited.
**EFL Teachers (6-7).** Wages £275 per week to work Monday to Friday 9am-5pm; or £11-12 per hour for a 20 hour week. Minimum period of work of one month. Positions are available between 1 July and 31 August. Applicants should have a degree and an RSA or Trinity Certificate or Diploma; two years experience also required. Must be 22 or over.
**Summer Administrative Assistant (1-2)** Wages £220 per week to work 8:45am-5:30pm Monday to Friday. Applicant should be an undergraduate or gradate with excellent computer skills; must be aged 20 or over. Foreign language skills would be an advantage.

No accommodation for any position; foreign applicants with fluent English welcome.

*Applications* should be made from February onwards to Sandra Kaufman, Principal, at the above address. Interview required.

# Medical

**ANCHOR CARE ALTERNATIVES:** 24 Claughton Street, St Helens, Merseyside WA10 1RZ (☎01744-753135). Cares for the elderly and disabled in their own homes throughout the UK.
**Live-In Care Workers.** Wages from £5.78 per hour.
**Daily Care Workers.** Wages from £262.80 per week.
 Staff required all year round to care for mainly housebound people. Minimum period of work 1-3 months. Duties include personal care, cooking, housekeeping, laundry, shopping and companionship. Overseas applicants authorised to work in the UK welcome. Applicants must be friendly with a caring attitude.
 *Applications* 2-3 weeks before work is required to the Senior Area Manager at the above address.

**APEX NURSING & CARE SERVICES:** Emery House, 195 Fog Lane, Didsbury, Manchester, M20 6FT (☎0161-443 2091; fax 0161-443 4178).
**R.G.N. Qualified Nurses, Support Workers, Care Assistants** (as many as possible) to work in hospitals, nursing homes, people's own homes, support work, working with those with learning disabilities and mental health problems. Wages and possibility of accommodation to be discussed at interview. Required for all vacations and during term-time. Must have experience in the care field. Training may be possible for suitable applicants. Age 18+
 *Applications* to Front of House at the above address.

**APOLLO PERSONNEL SERVICES:** St Austins Chambers, St Austins Lane, Warrington, Cheshire WA1 1HG (☎01925-444332; fax 01925-657651; e-mail apollops@hotmail.com). Provides staff to numerous areas of the healthcare industry and can provide training where necessary.
**Care Worker(15).** Wages £5.00 per hour, to work 30 hours per week caring for elderly or disabled people in nursing homes or private residences. Positions available all year round; no minimum period of work. Applicants must be 18 or over. Foreign applicants with fluent English welcome. Training given; no accommodation available.
 *Applications* should be made at any time to Janet Kearns at the above address. Interview required.

**KINETIC NURSING SERVICES:** Unit 3, Clare Court, Rawmarsh Road, Rotherham S60 1RU (☎01709-839395; fax 01709-838331; www.kinetic-plc.co.uk).
**Carers.** Wages £5-£7 per hour; to work hours to suit. Applicants must have experience in caring and be over 18.
**Nurses (all grades).** Wages £11-£13 per hour; to work hours to suit.
 The work offered is usually in nursing homes or hospitals in Rotherham, Sheffield, Doncaster, Chesterfield and Barnsley. Travel expenses are paid. Staff are required all year round. Must speak perfect English.
 Applicants should *apply* as soon as possible to J. Clark at the above address. Interview necessary.

**NIGHTINGALES HOME CARE:** 343 Blackburn Road, Darwen BB3 OAB (☎01254-771574). An agency accredited to the social services.
**Community Carers (40)** for caring and cleaning in the homes of clients in the local community. Wages £4.50 per hour to work 8am to 10pm. Minimum period of work

1 month.
Applicants should hold NVQ1,2 or have 2 years experience in the care sector and must be mobile. Minimum age 18.
*Applications* should be sent to Linda or Joanne at the above address.

## Outdoor

**EVANS MARQUEE HIRE:** Butler Works, Wyresdale Road, Lancaster, Lancashire LA1 3JJ (☎01524-63090; fax 01524-69929; e-mail evans_marquee@hotmail.com). A small family run marquee hire company specialising in weddings and special events.
**Seasonal Marquee Erectors (20).** Wages £200 per week.
**Drivers (10).** Wages £220 per week; must be over 25.
To work 40+ hours per week; required from May to September. Applicants should be fit and healthy; work can at times be physically demanding and uncomfortable if the weather is poor. No accommodation available. Suitably qualified foreign applicants with work permits will be considered; fluent English not essential.
*Applications* should be made from April onwards to the above address. Interview required.

**NORTHERN MARQUEES:** Unit 5, Steps Lane Industrial Estate, Honley, Huddersfield HD7 2RA (01484-664958; fax 01484-666307).
**Marquee Erectors (3)** needed from June to September. Wages on application. Minimum age 18.
*Contact* Andrew Tinker, Owner, at the above address.

**E. OLDROYD AND SONS LTD:** Ashfield House, Main Street, Carlton, Wakefield, Yorkshire WF3 3RW (☎0113-282 2245; fax 0113-282 8775). Four generations of experience with fruit and vegetables: high media profile for rhubarb.
**Vegetable Harvesters (10)** to work with mobile packing units. Wages at agricultural wage rates. To work part or full-time, up to 8 hours per day; a 39 hour week. Min. period of work of 1 month; piece work rates also apply. Positions are available from January to March and May to September. Minimum age 19. No previous experience necessary as training will be given. Limited accommodation available. Foreign applicants welcome.
*Applications* enclosing a cv should be made from March onwards to Mrs J.Oldroyd Hulme at the above address. Interview possibly required.

**MILL NURSERIES LTD:** Ottringham Road, Keyingham, Hull, East Yorkshire (☎01964-623664; fax 01964-622986). This very modern tomato nursery uses intensive farming methods.
**Glasshouse Tomato Pickers (20).** Agriculturally based work, picking glasshouse grown tomatoes. Wages of £4.20-£4.90 per hour. To work 40-50 hours per week, Mondays to Saturdays. Minimum period of work is 4 months between March and November. Accommodation provided for £35 per week. No previous experience necessary.
*Applications* should be made from the beginning of February to Mr de Lang at the above address. No interview required. Foreign applicants with appropriate visa welcome.

**PANAMA SPORTS HORSES:** The Stables Cottage, Gisburn Park, Gisburn, Lancashire BB7 4HU (tel/fax 01200-445687; e-mail work@panamasporthorses.co.uk).
**Yard Staff (2)** to work all summer looking after horses, assisting at shows and

carrying out general yard work. Wages are negotiable depending on age and experience, accommodation available.
 For further details and for *applications*, contact Ailsa Richardson at the above address.

**WILLIAM LEITH & CO: Pier Road, Berwick upon Tweed, Northumberland TD15 1JB** (☎01289-307264; fax 01289-330517; www.supertents.co.uk).
**Marquee Erectors (10). Wages £450-£600 per week; to work 7 days a week, very long hours. Applicants must be over 18; driving licence an advantage.
 Applications to the above address.**

# Sport

**ALSTON TRAINING & ADVENTURE CENTRE:** Alston, Cumbria CA9 3DD (☎01434-381886; fax 01434-382725).
**Assistant Outdoor Activity Instructors.** Free B & L and training provided. Should have current driving licence. MLC or Canoe qualification useful. Domestic staff also required.
 For further details and *applications* contact Mr Dave Simpson, Head of Centre, at the above address.

**R.A. FAHEY:** Manor Farm, Butterwick, Malton, North Yorkshire YO17 6PS (☎01653-628001; fax 01653-628959). The following summer staff are needed for a racing yard.
**Stable Staff (1 or 2)** to care for and/or ride out racehorses. Five and a half days per week plus alternate weekends.
**Work Riders (1 or 2)** to work 7am-12.30pm, 3.30-5.30pm and Sat 7am-12.30pm. Payment at national minimum wage rates. Staff needed from May to September. Overtime available when travelling to race meetings. Some bonuses based on success of racehorses. Must have high standard of horsemanship skills. If riding, must be very capable and light weight. Age: 16+.
 *Applications* to J.H. Hardy, Secretary at the above address.

**KILNSEY PARK AND TROUT FARM:** Kilnsey, Near Skipton, North Yorks BD23 5HS (☎01756-752150 (days) and 01756-752320 (evenings); fax 01756-752224).
**General Assistant** to work in the fish farm, with tourist visitors, in the children's fishery etc. To work a five day week from 9am-5.30pm or later. Must like the public, including children, be able to handle fish, adaptable, have a friendly attitude and be happy to muck in.
**Pony Trekking Leader** to work a 5-6 day week in July and August. Should be a good experienced rider able to cope with and organise school groups.
 Wages for above positions depend on age and experience; no tips. Accommodation available. *Applications* to Mrs Vanessa Roberts, Partner/Manager at the above address.

**KRB THOROUGHBREDS LTD:** Spigot Lodge, Leyburn, North Yorkshire, DL8 4TL (☎01969-625088; fax 01969-625099; e-mail karl@karlburke.co.uk).
**Yard Hand(1).** Approx. wages £200 per week. To take care of racehorses.
**Grooms (2).** Wages negotiable according to experience. Work involves grooming and riding racehorses.
 Minimum period of work for both positions 3 months. Accommodation is available

at a charge of £50 per week. Suitably qualified foreign applicants with fluent English are welcome.

*Applications* should be made at any time to Kathryn Warnett, Secretary, at the above address. Interview required.

**NORTH HUMBERSIDE RIDING CENTRE:** Easington, Nr Hull HU12 OUA (☎01964-650250) A riding centre situated close to the sea.
**Stable Staff (1)** Wages £30 per week. To work 8 hours per day 6 days a week. Full board and tuition. Minimum period six weeks. The position involves general help with the running of riding holidays for adults and children aged 9-16. Minimum age 16. Overseas applicants are welcome.

*Applications* should be sent to Toni Biglin at the above address from January onwards.

**NORTH YORK MOORS ADVENTURE CENTRE:** Park House, Ingleby Cross, near Osmotherley, Northallerton, North Yorkshire DL6 3PE (☎01609-882571). Private outdoor centre, established for 20 years, set in a National Park, catering for small groups of up to 24 people.
**Instructors (2)** to instruct in rock climbing, canoeing, caving, orienteering and mountain biking. Also to help with day-to-day running of the activity centre, e.g. equipment repairs and building work.

Wages and hours by arrangement. B & L. available. Period of work March to end of September. English-speaking overseas applicants welcome. All candidates must be able to attend an interview.

*Applications* with s.a.e. from 1 February to Mr Ewen Bennett, North York Moors Adventure Centre.

**NORTHUMBRIA HORSE HOLIDAYS:** East Castle, Annfield Plain, Stanley, Co. Durham DH9 8PH (☎01207-230555/235354). A horse-riding centre that offers fully catered holidays for riders of all abilities.
**Post Trail Leaders (2).** From £164 a week. Outgoing, pleasant personality needed plus good horse-riding skills and knowledge.
**Riding Instructors (2).** From £200 a week. Must have British Horse Society Instructors Certificate, or equivalent foreign qualifications.
**Hotel Staff (2)** From £164 a week. To cook, clean, and do waiting and bar work. Must be able to work to a high standard.

B & L available. Period of work Easter to end of October. Min. work period 2 months. Overseas applicants with necessary qualifications, documentation and experience will be considered.

*Applications* a.s.a.p. to the above address.

**THE OUTDOOR TRUST:** Windy Gyle, Belford, Northumberland NE70 7QE (tel/ fax 01668-213289; e-mail trust@outdoor.demon.co.uk; www.outdoortrust.co.uk). Registered providing outdoor activities and development courses for a wide range of groups and individuals of all ages and abilities. Based in North Northumberland and Scotland.
**Senior Training Instructors (5).** Remuneration dependent on one or more of the following NGB awards: BCU, RYA, MLTB. Must hold a full clean driving licence and be willing to take responsibility for at least one area of the operation.
**Trainee and Voluntary Instructors (10).** Proficiency in at least one of the traditional outdoor activities required and an enthusiasm for helping with a variety of additional duties associated with residential outdoor centres. Trainees/volunteers

will receive full board and training with ample opportunities to develop skills and gain NGB awards.

Long hours, 6 days per week. Work is demanding but very rewarding. Min. period of work 2 months but longer term preferable. Discount on outdoor equipment possible.

*Applications* to recruiting at the above address.

**RAMBLERS HOLIDAYS LTD:** Hassness, Buttermere, Cockermouth, Cumbria, CA13 9XA (☎01768-770227). Walking centre situated on shore of Buttermere lake. Offer a 1 week walking holiday. Up to 22 guests, normally aged 40+.
**General Assistants (2)** needed immediately. To work 5½ days a week, split shifts. Wages to be negotiated. Applicants should have a pleasant personality and be able to work to a high standard.

Contact Ann Spalding, Manageress, for *applications* for these places.

**MRS G.S. REES:** Cross Farm Racing, Sollom, Tartleton, Preston, Lancs. PR4 6HR (☎01772-812780; fax 01772-812799). Small friendly yard situated in the Lancashire countryside, but near Southport and Preston.
**Stable Staff (2)** for racing stables. Wages of £176 p.w. plus overtime when going to race meetings. To work 40 hours p.w. Monday to Friday and Saturdays until 1pm, plus one weekend in three to be worked. Must have experience with horses and be a good rider. Weight should be under 9st 7lbs.

*Applications* to Mrs G.S. Rees at the above address.

**RIPON OUTDOOR SKILLS CENTRE:** 12 Littlethorpe Park, Ripon HG4 1UQ (tel/fax 01748-833614). Runs day courses and adventure holidays. Activities include abseiling, canoeing, rock climbing, mountain walking, caving, windsurfing and mountain biking.
**Instructors (2), Chief Instructor (1).** £350 per week. Hours specified on application. Must have relevant qualifications, including AALA, BCU, MIC, MLC, LRC, LCL, RYA, SPSA, First Aid and Life Saving. Accommodation is not provided. All applicants must be available for interview.

*Applications* to Mr J. M. Bull at the above address.

**ROOKIN HOUSE EQUESTRIAN & ACTIVITY CENTRE:** Troutbeck, Penrith, Cumbria CA11 0SS (☎017684-83561; fax017684-83276; e-mail deborah@rookin house.co.uk) Situated on a hill farm Rookin Housse is a multi activity centre offering quad biking, go-karting, archery as well as an equestrian centre with 38 horses offering trekking, hacking and lessons.
**Trek Leaders (2)** Wages from £150 per week, to work 40 hours per week. Applicants must be 18 or over, hold Riding and Road Safety qualifications and be able to ride well.
**Activity Instructor.** Wages from £150 per week, to work 40 hours per week. Applicants must be 18 or over and preferably hold GNAS for Archery Leader Award, First Aid Certificate and ATV Qualification. In house training can be provided if applicant does not hold the above.

For both positions work will involve taking clients on activities and the maintenance of equipment and surroundings. There is also a self catering unit which will require cleaning.

Accommodation is available at a charge of £20 per week. Overseas applicants are welcome but must have a work permit and speak good English. Staff are required from June to September and must work July and August.

*Applications* should be sent to Deborah Hogg at the above address from March.

**THE VENTURE CENTRE:** Maughold, Isle of Man IM7 1AW (☎01624-814240; fax 01624-815615; e-mail enquiries@adventure-centre.co.uk; www.adventure-centre.co.uk). Adventure training centre giving introductory instruction in outdoor activities to adults and children aged 9-90.
**Instructors (3).** Wage according to experience. Free B & L. Hours dependent on groups under instruction: 7-day week at times. Min. period of work 1 month between March and August.
Min. age 18 years. Essential training given to suitable candidates. At least one NGB Award helpful.
*Applications* before March to Mr S. Read, Director, The Venture Centre.

# Voluntary Work

## Archaeology

**ARBEIA ROMAN FORT:** Tyne & Wear Museums Service, Baring Street, South Shields, Tyne & Wear NE33 2BB (☎0191-454 4093; fax 0191-427 6862; e-mail liz.elliott@tyne-wear-museums.org.uk).
Part of the Tyne and Wear Museums service and within easy reach of Newcastle by metro. South Shields has good parks and beaches and is an ideal base from which to visit nearby cities or countryside.
**Volunteers (5 per week)** to excavate the site, record and process finds, draw the site and take photographs. To work from 8.45am-4.45pm, Monday-Friday. Volunteers are responsible for their own travel, board and other costs. Needed from June to 30 September. Min age 16; disabled people may find access to the site difficult.
*Applications* to Elizabeth Elliott, Office Manager, at the above address.

## Heritage

**LAKELAND ARTS TRUST:** Abbot Hall Art Gallery, Kendal, Cumbria LA9 5AL (☎01539-722464; fax 01539-722494).
An independent charity which runs a prize-winning and thriving art gallery and museums of social history, archaeology, and natural history in Kendal. Has just opened a prestigious arts and crafts house, Blackwell, overlooking Windemere.
**Volunteer Curatorial Assistants, Reception Staff, Event Helpers and Coffee Shop Staff** are required to work in Kendal Museum, Abbot Hall Art Gallery and the Museum of Lakeland Life and Industry. To work during July, August and September; there may be vacancies at other times. The work would suit both undergraduates and postgraduates hoping to gain museum experience.
The gallery also requires graduate or postgraduate students for **unpaid museum and gallery work experience.** To work 9.30am-5.30pm or part-time hours if living out. Interview if possible. Overseas students welcome, but working English is required.
*Applications* at any time to Cherrie Trelogan at the above address.

**LOSANG DRAGPA BUDDHIST CENTRE:** Dobroyd Castle, Pexwood Road, Todmorden, West Yorks OL14 7JJ (☎01706-812247; fax 01706-818901; e-mail info@losangdragpa.com; www.losangdragpa.com).
Losang Dragpa Centre is a Buddhist College and Meditation Centre based at Dobroyd

Castle in the heart of the Pennines. The Centre is a registered charity dedicated to serving the community by providing a place of inner peace for everyone regardless of spiritual inclination. **Volunteers** are welcome to join the resident community in various development projects, which include restoring Dobroyd Castle to its former glory. The Centre offers Buddhist teachings, meditations, accommodation and food in exchange for 35 hours work per week. Working visitors may stay for 1 week or 2 weeks (for international volunteers) during specific periods throughout the year.
Applicants must be at least 18 and able to speak a basic level of English. Interest in Buddhism is recommended. They particularly need help from those with specialised skills such as building, marketing, fundraising, decorating and landscaping. However, skills aren't essential as work can be found for any willing hands.

For more information or to *apply*, look at their website or contact reception at the above address.

**TOM LEONARD MINING MUSEUM:** Deepdale, Skinningrove, Saltburn, Cleveland TS13 4AP (☎01287-642877; fax 01287-642970; e-mail visits@ironstonemuseum.co.uk).
The Tom Leonard Mining Museum preserves and interprets the ironstone mining heritage of Cleveland and North Yorkshire. This is a unique, award-winning, small, independent museum run by volunteers on a day-to-day basis.
**Museum Guides (6+), Visitor Receptionists (2+), Collection Care (2+).** Expenses only are paid; no accommodation provided. Museum is open Mondays to Saturdays. Minimum period of work is four hours per week. Positions are available from July to October. Applicants should be interested in local history and heritage. Minimum age 16.

*Applications* can be made all year round to the Museum Manager at the above address. Interview preferred.

**WORDSWORTH TRUST:** Town End, Grasmere, Cumbria LA22 9SH (☎015394-35544; fax 015394-35748; e-mail c.kay@wordsworth.org.uk; www.wordsworth.org.uk).
A registered charity (no. 1066184) in the heart of the Lake District. Responsible for maintaining Dove Cottage, the Wordsworth Museum and the Wordsworth library. An internationally renowned literary centre with a unique collection, which offers accredited museum training.
**Volunteer Museum Assistants** needed around the year to guide visitors around Dove Cottage, the home of William Wordsworth, help in the shop and assist in the museum with tasks including providing reception and information services, cataloguing the collection and security. To work a 37½ hour, 5 day week on a 7 day rota; accommodation is available. Applicants must be aged 18 and over and have a high standard of spoken English. New Deal placements are available for those who are eligible.

*Applications* to Catherine Kay, Personnel Officer at the above address.

## Social and Community Schemes

**GREAT GEORGES COMMUNITY CULTURAL PROJECT: The Blackie, Great George Street, Liverpool L1 5EW (☎0151-709 5109; minicom/fax 0151-709 4822; staff@theblackie.org.uk).**
**Opportunities for anyone over 18 to try alternative education and the arts together with some sport, recreation and welfare in an inner-city context: including youth work, crafts and games; regular workshops with local**

youngsters; staging exhibitions and events; and projects from cookery to contemporary and African dance, from photography to fashion. Share cooking, cleaning, administration and some rebuilding work. Endless opportunities to learn and unlearn, to teach and to create. Wonderfully long hours. Stamina, a sense of humour and a sleeping bag required. Accommodation provided. Volunteers are expected to stay for at least 4 weeks and to contribute towards food costs. Volunteers are welcome throughout the year and particularly over the summer, winter and spring holiday periods. The Blackie has recently passed its 30th anniversary.
   For further *information* write to the Duty Office at the above address.

**MADHYAMAKA BUDDHIST CENTRE:** Kilnwick Percy Hall, Kilnwick Percy, York YO42 1UF (☎01759-304832; fax 01759-305962; e-mail info@madhyamaka.org; www.madhyamaka.org).
A large residential Buddhist college situated in a beautiful 40 acre historic estate. The centre offers a range of meditation classes and retreats suitable for all.
**Volunteers** (usually no more than 5 at any one time) for a variety of jobs including gardening, cleaning, cooking, painting, building and making repairs. Three vegetarian meals a day and dormitory accommodation are provided in return for work; free access is granted to a range of Buddhist meditation classes for those who are interested.
   Volunteers may stay for periods of up to one week every three months; they are expected to work for 35 hours a week, or 5 hours per day if staying for a shorter period. No particular qualifications or experience are required but applicants aged over 18 are preferred. Volunteers are asked to bring their own sleeping bag and work clothes.
   *Applications* should be sent to Working Holidays at the above address.

**MANJUSHRI MAHAYANA BUDDHIST CENTRE:** Conishead Priory, Ulverston, Cumbria LA12 9QQ (☎01229-584029; fax 01229-580080; e-mail info@manjushri.org.uk; www.manjushri.org.uk).
A residential Buddhist community with around 100 residents, founded in 1977 to provide a peaceful and inspiring environment where people can learn about the Buddhist way of life and practice meditation.
**Volunteers** needed for various duties including building, kitchen/garden help, and general household work/cleaning. B & L provided. Volunteers work 35 hours per week, Monday to Friday. Weekends free to explore and relax. Minimum period of work 1 week. Positions available all year round except January. Minimum age 16. Overseas applicants with reasonable English welcome. No smoking or drinking allowed on site. Volunteers are welcome to join in centre activities such as meditation classes and courses.
   *Applications* at any time to Terry Vallente, Working Visit Co-ordinator, at the above address.

# Vacation Traineeships & Internships

## Accountancy and Insurance

**COULSONS:** P.O. Box 17, 2 Belgrave Crescent, Scarborough, North Yorkshire YO11 1UD (☎01723-364141; fax 01723-376010; www.coulsons.co.uk).
Coulsons, a firm of chartered accountants, takes on **Trainees** to work in its Scarborough office, mainly during the summer vacation. Candidates would normally

be UK undergraduates intending to pursue chartered accountancy as a career. Vacation work would be offered only to students giving an undertaking to take up a training contract with Coulsons on the completion of their academic studies. Local candidates are at an advantage as accommodation is difficult to find.

For *further details* contact Mr P. B. Hodgson, Student Training Officer in April, at the above address. Please note that only those short-listed will be contacted.

## Science, Construction and Engineering

**BAE SYSTEMS (MARINE):** Waterside House, Barrow, Cumbria, LA14 1AF (☎01229-875833; fax 01229-875092).
Offers opportunities to approx. 20 students to undertake various projects within the Operations, Technical, Projects and Service departments. Applicants should be university students studying Electrical Engineering, Mechanical Engineering, Naval Architecture, Engineering with Management, Business or Manufacturing systems. Salary depends on year of study.
Placements occur in June-September in Glasgow or Barrow. No accommodation is provided. Overseas applicants are considered, but security clearance may be a problem.
*Applications* by March/April to Personnel.

**BOMBARDIER TRANSPORTATION:** Litchurch Lane, Derby DE24 8AD (☎01332-266083; www.bombardier.com).
The railway arm of DaimlerChrysler, Bombardier is a complete provider of railway systems. Has sites in Derby, Crewe, Wakefield, Ilford and East Ham.
**Vacation Placements** available throughout the company. Successful applicants will most likely be placed in Derby or Crewe since these are the largest operations. Wages and minimum qualifications vary depending on the work. Engineering and Production students are particularly sought, though requirements vary according to the business area. Further information can be obtained from the above address (brochure available from the phone number listed.
*Applications* should take the form of a covering letter and CV to the HR Officer, Graduate Recruitment at the above address; selected candidates will be invited to interview.

**FILTRONIC COMPONENTS LTD:** Airedale House, Royal London Industrial Estate, Acorn Park, Charlestown, Shipley, West Yorks BD17 7SW (☎01274-531602; fax 01274-531539).
Filtronic Components Ltd is an expanding company dealing in the research, development and manufacture of RF and microwave filters and sub-systems. It offers occasional **Summer Vacation Placements** in electronic design and development.
Those interested should *contact* Angela Dyer, Personnel Officer, at the above address.

**RELIANCE GEAR COMPANY LTD:** Rowley Mills, Penistone Road, Lepton, Huddersfield HD8 OLE (☎01484-601000; fax 01484-601001).
Reliance Gear is a design and manufacturing company which specialises in the production of precision electro-mechanical assemblies for use in servo-mechanisms and control applications. The company serves clients in the defence, aerospace, robotic and medical engineering industries.
The company usually offers **Work Experience** over the summer to two or three students who are about to enter their final year of study. Candidates should be motivated and keen to explore the engineering sector as a potential career field.

Training is offered through general experience gained in a number of the company's departments, including business sales, marketing, engineering, design, production control and quality control.

Wages are commensurate with the candidate's age, experience, qualifications and the job offered. Overseas applicants will be considered.

*Applications*, in early January and February, to A D Durie, Design Manager, at the above address.

**TEXTRON POWER TRANSMISSION:** Park Gear Works, Lockwood, Huddersfield, West Yorkshire HD4 5DD (☎01484-465500; fax 01484-465512; e-mail hr@davidbrown.textron.com; www.textronPT.com).

Textron Power Transmission is a manufacturing company, operating worldwide in the production of high quality gears and gear units. It has occasional **Summer Vacancies** for students, who will be employed in such areas as Manufacturing Engineering, Production Control, Manufacturing and General Site Services.

Applicants should be studying Mechanical Engineering and have an interest in engineering manufacturing processes and/or gearing. Suitably qualified overseas applicants will be considered.The salary is discussed at interview and no assistance with accommodation is given.

*Applications* should be made to Central Personnel Training Services, at the above address.

# Scotland

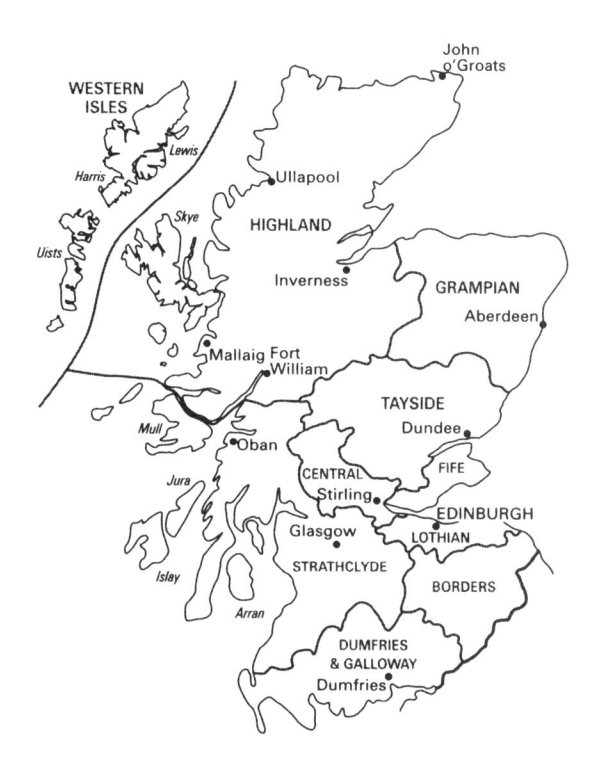

**Prospects for Work.**
The tourist industry in Scotland remains buoyant, particularly in the Highlands, Perthshire and the Islands, and has received huge boosts during the hot spells of recent summers. Since many hotels are in isolated areas, a considerable number of staff have to be recruited from outside. However, you will almost certainly be expected to work for the entire season, and should have the temperament to suit living in a remote place. The Jobcentre in Fort William is a good source for this type of work, as is the Jobcentre in Perth. The majority of hotels in rural Perthshire offer live-in accommodation, and frequently employ students over the summer. The Jobcentre in Inverness advertises vacancies as far afield as Ullapool, Gairloch and Lochcarron on the West coast and Aviemore, Kingussie and Grantown-on-Spey to the South as well as in the town itself. Due to the high level of local unemployment in less remote parts the only vacancies that remain

are usually for skilled or experienced staff. While in many areas employers routinely offer accommodation, Inverness is however an exception and few live-in jobs are available there.

Fruit picking jobs are particularly abundant in Perth and Tayside. The season usually lasts from the end of June until mid-September. In addition to the vacancies listed in this chapter, fruit-picking jobs are also advertised in the Jobcentre in Blairgowrie, but not in the Jobcentre in Perth which does however list other vacancies.

Edinburgh attracts a considerable number of tourists each year, particularly during the Festival in late August. As a result there is a wide range of jobs available particularly in hotels. The success and income of the festival is growing year on year and so the jobs it generates look set to stay and increase. With the introduction of a Scottish Parliament the need for hotel and catering staff in Edinburgh has increased further. If you speak a foreign language you could land yourself a job as a guide, and the District Council engages extra assistants and experienced gardeners to maintain the city gardens and flowers. There are always plenty of vacancies displayed in the Edinburgh Jobcentre. Note that accommodation is rarely provided with a job in Edinburgh, and can be difficult to find.

In the winter season, those seeking employment could try the skiing resorts of Aviemore, Aonach Mor and Glencoe Ski Centre. Again, a comprehensive search of jobs available in Scotland can be carried out at www.jobcentreplus.gov.uk and also at http://europa.eu.int/jobs/eures.

## Business and Industry

**DUNDEE INDUSTRIAL HERITAGE LTD:** Verdant Works, West Henderson's Wynd, Dundee DD1 5BT (☎01382-225282; fax 01382-221612; e-mail admin@dundeeheritage.sol.co.uk)
**Retail Staff(6)** Wages £4.10 per hour; to work flexible and variable hours over a 7 day period. Staff are required from June onwards.

Would be an advantage if applicants had previous retail experience and another language(s).

*Applications* should be sent to Rachel Dye at the above address.

**THE EDINBURGH SMOKED SALMON CO. LTD:** 1 Strathview, Dingwall Business Park, Dingwall, Ross-shire IV15 9XD (☎01349-860600; fax 01349-860606).
**Processing Workers (80)** required throughout the summer. Attractive rates of pay, plus attendance and production bonuses. Previous experience may attract a higher rate of pay. Assistance can be given in locating accommodation in Dingwall or Inverness, 12 miles from Dingwall. No qualifications are required.

*Applications* to the Personnel Officer at the above address.

## Children

**EAC LTD:** 59 George Street, Edinburgh EH2 2LQ (☎0131-477 7574; fax 0131-477 7571; e-mail: info@activitycamps.com).
**Activity Staff (100)** Average wage is £180 per week. To work a 5-day week of 37 hours. Positions available from the end of June to the end of August. All staff should be interested in sport, art and music. NGB qualification an advantage. RLSS very useful.

*Applications* to A.J. Fisher at the above address.

**PGL TRAVEL:** Alton Court, Penyard Lane (874), Ross-on-Wye, Herefordshire HR9 5GL (☎01989-767833; e-mail pglpeople@pgl.co.uk; www.pgl.co.uk/people). Over 50 staff needed to assist in the running of children's activity centres in Perthshire. Europe's largest provider of adventure holidays for children has offered outstanding training and work opportunities to seasonal staff for over 40 years.
**Experienced Activity Instructors** in canoeing, sailing, windsurfing, pony trekking, multi-activites, drama, arts and crafts and English language. Qualifications not essential as full training will be provided. Minimum age 18.
**Group Leaders** also needed to take responsibility for groups of children, helping then to get the most out of their holiday. Previous experience of working with children is essential. Minimum age 18.
 From £50-85 per week plus free B & L. Vacancies available for short or long periods between February and October.
 *Applications* can be made online, or request a form from the above address.

**MRS M.E. THOMSON:** Thomas Thomson (Blairgowrie), Bramblebank, Rattray, Blairgowrie PH10 7HY (☎01250-872062; fax 01250-872266; e-mail thomson@brambank.freeserve.co.uk.
**Mother's Help** to look after 3 children and a house, cooking etc., on a fruit farm from May/June-late August. Wages plus board, lodging and the use of a car; to work 6 days per week. Should be aged at least 22, a non-smoker and competent licensed drivers and have references; the job could suit a couple as other farm work is available for the partner.
 *Applications* to Mrs Melanie Thomson at the above address.

# Holiday Centres and Amusements

**ARDMAIR POINT CARAVAN SITE/BOAT CENTRE:** Ardmair Point, Ullapool, Ross-shire (☎01854-612054; fax 01854-612757; e-mail pete@ardmair.com; www.ardmair.com). Situated in a scenic area 3 miles north of the fishing village of Ullapool on a beach headland facing the Summer Isles
**Caravan Site Assistants (2).** Duties include reception/shop work, cleaning and grass-cutting. A large proportion of the work is out of doors and involves some tractor driving.
**Boat Centre Assistant (1)** for boat handling. Duties include renting out small boats and equipment, assisting with repair of fibreglass boats, and the servicing and repair of outboard engines.
**Easter Work.** Two people required for general pre-season work.
 Wages £5.00 per hour. To work 40 hours/6 days per week, with shifts covering 8am-8pm. Accommodation available. Min. age 18 years. All jobs best suited to people interested in water sports and/or outdoor pursuits. Overseas applicants with fluent English welcome.
 For further details and an *application* form send s.a.e. to the above address.

**WILLIAM GRANT & SONS:** The Glenfiddich Distillery, Dufftown, Banffshire, Scotland AB55 4DH (☎01340-820373; fax 01340-822083; e-mail david.mair@wgrant.com). Staff conduct tours of Glenfiddich Distillery in an educational but informal way. The distillery is fully operational. The work may particularly suit people interested in Scottish Culture or keen on improving their foreign language skills.

**Tour Guides** to conduct members of the public on tours of the distillery. £173 for 32½ hours per five-day week. No accommodation available but local B & B costs approx. £60-£70 per week including evening meal. Self catering accommodation can usually be found at £50-£60 per week. Min. age 18 years. Min. period of work end of June to end of August. Must be fluent in at least one foreign European language.

Experience with the general public desirable but not essential. Job requires a bright, cheery and very outgoing personality. Only applicants with fluent English considered. All applicants must be able to attend an interview at the distillery. Interviews are held before or during the Easter Vacation period.

*Applications* between January and March to Mr D.C. Mair at the above address in writing or by e-mail.

**LADY MACPHERSON:** 27 Archery Close, London W2 2BE (tel/fax 020-7262 8487).
**Holiday Helpers** required for a Scottish Highland home with children and animals. House is at 1,000 ft altitude and near the river Spey. Tennis court. Some indoor work and painting, general help on farm and in house. B & L provided, wages negotiable. Pest control/poisons licence and chainsaw licence helpful. Enthusiasm and willingness to play tennis and go trout-fishing with children preferred. Ample time for touring e.g. Loch Ness, weather rarely very warm. Two character references required.

*Applications* to the above address.

# Hotels and Catering

**ABERNETHY TRUST:** Ardeonaig, by Killin, Perthshire FK21 8SY (☎01567-820523; fax 01567-820955; e-mail AT@ardeonaig.org; www.ardeonaig.org). A residential outdoor centre.
**Housekeeping Staff (2), Catering Staff (2), General Estate Workers (2)** to work 5½ days a week as part of a residential Christian staff team. Wages £25 per week plus board and lodging. Staff required from June to September; minimum period of work 4 weeks. Minimum age 18. Christian commitment essential.

*Applications* from January to Philip Simpson, Centre Director, at the above address.

**ATHOLL ARMS HOTEL:** Bridgehead, Dunkeld, Perthshire PH8 0AQ (tel/fax 01350-727219). A 16-bedroomed hotel catering mainly for fishing parties and tourists, overlooking the River Tay in a conservation village.
**Kitchen Porters.** No experience required.
**Staff (3).** Some waiting, bar and kitchen experience.
Wages £4.20 per hour, accommodation available. Required to work 5½ days per week. Period of work April to October. Min. period of work 6 months. Minimum age 21. Applications from foreign nationals permitted to work in the UK who speak English to a conversational level welcomed.

*Applications* from January to Mr Cameron at the above address, interview necessary.

**AVIEMORE HIGHLANDS HOTEL:** Aviemore Mountain Resort, Inverness-shire PH22 1PJ (☎01479-810771; fax 01479-811473; e-mail sales@aviehighlands.dem on.co.uk). Situated in an all year round resort known for its superb environment and offering some of the best skiing in Scotland. A three-star hotel with over 100 bedrooms, a restaurant, lounge bar and the Illicit Still Bar (open to non-residents).

**General Assistants, Bar, Waiting, Housekeeping and Kitchen Staff.** Temporary live-in positions offered all year round. Weekly paid, MROP.
To *apply* send c.v to the above address.

**BALMORAL HOTEL:** 1 Princes Street, Edinburgh EH2 2EQ (☎0131-622 8891; fax 0131-558 1766; e-mail adinglwall@thebalmoralhotel.com). A 5 star hotel in and elegant Edwardian property in the centre of Edinburgh owned by Rocco Forte Hotels.
**Bar/Waiting Staff (6), Room Attendants (6).** Wages for all positions from £4.10- £4.50 per hour for a 39 hour week. To work 5-7 days per week. Min. period of work 4 months between April and October. No accommodation is available. Applicants should be 18+ and have at least 6 months experience. Overseas applicants with good English and work permit considered. Interview necessary.
*Applications* from March onwards to the Personnel Department at the above address.

**CALEDONIAN THISTLE HOTEL:** 10-14 Union Terrace, Aberdeen, Scotland AB10 1WE (☎01224-640233; fax 01224-641627). Part of the Thistle Hotel chain, the 77 bedroom Caledonian is situated in the heart of Aberdeen city centre.
**Food Service Staff (2)** for the cafe/bar or dining room. Wage £3.38 per hour (B & L included). To work split shifts for a 39 hour week. Min. period of work 3 months from April to October.
Staff should be at least 18 years old, and experience is preferred. Suitably qualified overseas applicants are welcome.
*Applications* to Mary Martin from January onwards.

**THE CEILIDH PLACE:** West Argyll Street, Ullapool, Ross & Cromarty, Scotland IV26 2TY (☎01854-612103; e-mail effie@ceilidh.demon.co.uk). A complex of buildings including a small hotel with 13 rooms, a bunk house, bar, coffee room, restaurant, bookshop, gallery and venue for music and drama.
**Cooks (3)** with natural skill and enthusiasm.
**Housestaff (2).** Must be fit.
**Waiting Staff(6).** Serving food and drink and clearing tables.
**Bar Staff (2).** Serving/stocking drinks and assisting with food service.
Wages paid monthly (less board and lodging allowance). Work available between May and October, min. period 3 months: no shorter period considered. Overseas applicants eligible to work in the UK and with necessary documentation welcome.
For further information and an *applications* form e-mail or write to the General Manager at the above address.

**CLACHAIG INN:** Glencoe, Argyll PH49 4HX (☎01855-811252; fax 01855- 811679; e-mail jobs@glencoescotland.com; www.glencoescotland.com). A busy, vibrant country inn set in the heart of Glencoe. Popular year-round with hillwalkers, climbers, mountain bikers, skiers and travellers. Specialists in real ale (award winning) with a significant food trade. A unique experience for customers and staff alike.
**General Assistants (15)** required throughout the year to help in all aspects of the business; bar work (serving both drinks and food), waiting on tables and helping out in the kitchen, housekeeping, renting and maintaining mountain bikes, and various odd jobs.
Previous experience is helpful, but a friendly outgoing personality and enthusiasm are more important. You must be clean and presentable, able to communicate well,

and be able to work well as part of a team. Accommodation and all meals may be provided. The minimum period of work is at least 3 months. Positions are available year round; those able to work over the New Year and Easter have priority when it comes to the summer months.

*Applications* (with a covering letter and detailed CV) should be sent to Guy Daynes at the above address approximately one month before you are available for work.

**CLIFTON HOUSE HOTEL:** Nairn, Nairnshire (☎01667-453119; e-mail macintyre@clifton-hotel.co.uk). A small hotel with a high ratio of staff to guests. A quiet location on the coast.
**Waiting Staff, House and Kitchen Assistants (6-7).** Wages and hours by arrangement. Min. work period 4 weeks between March and October. Needs careful, helpful and sensible staff as the hotel is also a house and the permanent staff have all been there for a long time. B & L provided, charge to be discussed. Experience preferable but not necessary. Common sense and versatility essential. Overseas applicants who speak French or English welcome.
*Applications* in writing or by e-mail to Mr J. Gordon Macintyre, Proprietor, Clifton House.

**DEE COOPER:** ☎01764-670071/679765; fax 01764-679728; e-mail dee@livein-jobs.demon.co.uk; www.livein-jobs.co.uk. Agent working with over 1000 hotels in Scotland. Free service.
**Live-in Hotel Staff.** Work can be found across Scotland. Wages and hours variable, all positions live-in. Foreign applicants with permission to work in the UK welcome.
For a list of relevant available jobs, *contact* Dee Cooper using the above details.

**CRAIGARD HOUSE HOTEL:** Boat of Garten, Inverness-shire (☎01479-831 206). Deluxe country house hotel.
**Chamber Staff/Waiting Staff (3).** Wages on application. Experience an advantage but not essential as training will be given. Min. age 18 years. Required to work until end of October. B & L provided for the right applicants. Overseas applicants with excellent English welcome. 5½ days per week.
Those with a good personality, willing to work hard and enjoy life in the Highlands should make *applications* to the above address.

**CRAW'S NEST HOTEL:** Bankwell Road, Anstruther, Fife KY10 3DA (☎01333-310691; fax 01333-312216; e-mail enquiries@crawsnesthotel.co.uk). Sandy and Eleanor own and manage this family hotel situated to the East of Fife, 9 miles south of St Andrews. It has 50 guest bedrooms, a large function suite, dining room and 2 bars.
**Kitchen Hands (2).** £195 per week plus end of season bonus. No experience necessary.
**Waiting Staff (3).** £195 per week. Some silver service experience would be useful, though is not essential.
All staff to work 5 days per week. Accommodation available and meals provided on duty. Good knowledge of English essential. Min. period of work 3-4 months between May and September.
*Applications* with photograph and s.a.e. to Mr A. Bowman at the above address.

**CRIEFF HYDRO LTD:** Ferntower Rd, Crieff, Perthshire PH7 3LQ (☎01764-

651612; fax 01764-651649; e-mail andrew.leaver@crieffhydro.com / lin.brammer @crieffhydro.com; www.crieffhydro.com). Crieff Hydro is a hotel and leisure resort set in 900 acres of central Perthshire countryside, approximately 20 miles north of Stirling. 216 rooms.
**Food and Beverage Service Assistants.** Wages rise from £3.70 to £4.20 per hour on completion of trial period. To work approx. 39 hours per week overtime available. Min. period of work is 6 months. Positions are available all year. Applicants should be 18+ and have a good level of spoken English; previous hospitality experience preferred. Overseas applicants welcome subject to valid work permits/visas and other travel documents. Accommodation and meals available for £28.50 per week; this does not include insurance or supplies (towels etc.).
*Applications* should be made to Andrew Leaver or Lin Brammer at the above address, or through their website. A phone interview is required.

**CRINAN HOTEL:** Crinan, nr Lochgilphead, Argyll PA31 8SR (☎01546-830261; fax 01546-830292; www.crinanhotel.com). Fishing village and sailing centre in a beautiful location.
**General Assistants** to work in all departments of the Hotel.
*Applications* from January to N.A. Ryan, Managing Director, at the above address, enclosing a recent full length photograph.

---

## THE CRINAN HOTEL - SCOTLAND

Crinan, by Lochgilphead, Argyll PA31 8SR
Fishing village and sailing centre in a beautiful location.

### GENERAL ASSISTANTS (ALL DEPARTMENTS)

Wages by arrangement plus tips, food and accommodation.
Period of work at least 10 weeks between April and October.

Send applications with photo (full length) to or telephone
Mr N.A. Ryan, Managing Director, The Crinan Hotel, Argyll, Scotland PA31 8SR.

Tel: 01546-830261 · Fax 01546-830292 · www.crinanhotel.com

---

**CROIT ANNA HOTEL:** Fort William, Inverness-shire PH33 6RR (☎01397-702268; fax 01397-704099; e-mail croitanna@compuserve.com; www.croitanna.co.uk). A 3 star family owned hotel, situated in the most scenic part of the Scottish Highlands.
**Housekeeping Staff (2), Waiting Staff (2)** Wages £4.20 per hour; to work 40-46 hours per week. Previous experience is helpful. Accommodation is available at a charge of £3.25 per day, deducted from pay. Staff required for a minimum of 3 months between 1st April and 15th November.
*Applications* from March to Paul Morgan at the above address.

**THE CROWNE PLAZA HOTEL EDINBURGH:** 80 High Street, The Royal Mile, Edinburgh EH1 1TH (☎0131-473 6514; fax 0131-557 9798; e-mail Humanresources@AllianceUK.com). A busy 4 star deluxe city centre hotel situated halfway between a castle and a palace, aiming to provide first class service for an international clientele.
**Waiting Staff (5).** Applicants must be over 18.

**Chamber Staff (5).** Applicants must be over 16.
Wages for all positions £4.30 per hour plus 20p end of season bonus. Min. period of work is 3 months. No experience necessary. No accommodation is available. Interview necessary (but could be conducted by telephone). Overseas applicants with valid work permits considered.
*Applications* from March to Human Resources Department.

**DALMUNZIE HOUSE HOTEL:** Glenshee, Perthshire PH10 7QG (☎01250-885 224; e-mail dalmunzie@aol.com). Country house hotel on 6,000-acre estate in a remote mountain situation.
**General Hotel Staff (6).** Wages and hours by arrangement according to type of job. B & L provided. To work 5 days a week. Period of work January to late October. Must be able to work the whole of September and for a minimum period of 2 months in total. Min. age 18 years. Overseas applicants with good English welcome.
*Applications* to Simon and Alexandra Winton, Proprietors, Dalmunzie House Hotel. Only an application enclosing s.a.e. will receive a reply.

**DUNDONNELL HOTEL:** Little Loch Broom, Near Ullapool, Ross-shire (☎01854-633234; fax 01854-633234; e-mail selbie@dundonnell.hotel.co.uk; www.sol.co.uk/d/dundonnellhotel). Busy family-run 24 bedroomed hotel just south of Ullapool in an area of outstanding mountain scenery. Location is remote but beautiful, and has no discos or shops. The following staff are needed to work in this 3 star quality establishment.
**Assistant Chef/Cook** (with experience).
**Dining Room Staff (3)** (one to take charge).
**General Assistants (3)** for kitchen and stillroom.
**Commis Chef/Cook, Bar Staff (2), Chamber Staff (2), Petrol Station Attendant.**
From £130 per 5½ day week, with higher rates for skilled and senior personnel. Free B & L in excellent accommodation (own room). Uniform provided. Min. period of work 12 weeks but longer period preferred. Most posts from Easter to October, with some from mid-May to end of September.
*Applications* with s.a.e. and photograph, including details of any previous work experience and dates of availability, to Mr and Mrs S.W. Florence, Dundonnell Hotel.

**DUISDALE HOTEL:** Sleat, Isle of Skye IV43 8QW (☎01471-833202; e-mail marie@duisdalehotel.demon.co.uk; www.duisdale.com). A country house hotel set in 35 acres of gardens and woodland.
**Kitchen Assistant (1).** Some cooking experience preferred.
**General Assistants (2).** Mainly room servicing and waiting; some barwork and reception work.
Wages by arrangement. Free B & L provided. Staff have each afternoon free as the hotel does not open for lunch. Min. period of work 2 months between April and October. Min. age 20. Previous experience preferred. Overseas applicants with fluent English accepted.
*Applications* to Mrs Campbell, Duisdale Hotel.

**EDINBURGH CITY TRAVEL INN:** 1 Morrison Link, Edinburgh EH3 8DN (☎0131-656 4344; fax 0131-228 9836). 'Travel Inn' is one of the the biggest and best budget hotel brands in the UK. City centre location, very busy during the summer months.

**Room Attendants (10).** To work for 5 days and approx. 40 hours per week.
**Food and Beverage Waiting Staff (10).** Full and part-time work available. Some experience is necessary.
Wages above National Minimum Wage. Min. period of work of 3 months. Positions are available from July to September. Foreign applicants are welcome but good English must be spoken and bank account and a National Insurance number required. No accommodation available.

*Applications* should be made from June onwards to Elaine Salton at the above address. Interview necessary.

**FREEDOM OF THE GLEN HOTELS:** Creag Dhu House, Onich, Near Fort William, Invernesshire, Scotland PH33 4RT (☎01855-821582; fax 01855-821463; e-mail jobs@freedomglen.co.uk; www.highlandjobs.com). Four distinctive hotels all in superb Lochside locations offering quality Highland hospitality. Staff can enjoy leisure facilites as well as living and working in the Scottish Highlands.
**Service Staff (45), Porters (5), Housekeeper (25), General Assistants (14), Receptionists (11)** Wages are £120-£160 per week. To work approx. 45 hours per week with a mixture of straight and split shifts. Min. period of work of 3 months. Positions are available from April to October. Full B & L available for all positions at a charge of £45 per week. Previous experience useful, but not essential. Foreign applicants with work permits and acceptable spoken English welcome.

*Applications* should be made from mid February onwards to Ruth Sime at the above address or completed on-line using www.highlandjobs.com.

**GEORGE INTERCONTINENTAL EDINBURGH:** 19-21 George Street, Edinburgh EH2 2PB (☎0131-225-1251; fax 0131-226-5644; e-mail sandra_mac kinnon@interconti.com). This 195 bedroom hotel is a 4 star de luxe establishment in the city centre. There is a fine dining room, a carvery restaurant, a clan bar and banqueting facilities.
**Hall Porter (1).** Applicants must possess a driving licence.
**Customer Service Agents (3)** for the restaurant.
**Customer Service Agents (5)** for banqueting operations.
**Room Attendents.**
For all positions: wages from £9,387 p.a. pro rata, working 40 hours per 5 day week (less considered for banquet work). Minimum age 18; minimum period of work is six months; positions are available between March/April and November/ December. Limited accomodation is available (£70 all-inclusive single room, £55 to share). Applicants should be interested in Personnel, enjoy working in a busy and friendly environment, and be able to provide a highly professional service. Foreign applicants with work permits and an ability to understand and speak English are welcome.

*Applications* should be made from February/March onwards to Sandra MacKinnon or Catherine MacFarlane at the above address. Interview required.

**GRAND ISLAND HOTEL:** Bride Road, Ramsey, Isle of Man IM8 3UN (☎01624-812455; fax 01624-815291). A beautiful Georgian hotel overlooking the Ramsey Bay, offering 2 restaurants, bars and leisure facilities.
**Day/Night Porters (2), Chef De Partie/Commis Chefs (3), Chamber Staff (3), Food/Beverage Staff (4), Receptionist, Trainee Managers (2).**
To work 40 hours per week. Details of wages, accommodation etc. on application. Live-in staff accommodation as part of the package at £20 a week. To work from April onwards. All applicants must be college trained.

*Applications* should be sent to The Deputy/Operations Manager, at the above address.

**THE GROG AND GRUEL:** Traditional Alehouse and Restaurant, 66 High Street, Fort William PH33 6AE (☎01397-705078; e-mail jobs@grogandgruel.co.uk; www.grogandgruel.co.uk). A traditional Alehouse situated in the town centre serving a selection of real ales and malt whiskies, with a family restaurant on the upper level, offering home-cooked dishes. Run by brothers Guy and Edward Daynes whose approach to business is informal and friendly – a blend of fun and hard work.
**General Assistants (5)** to help in bar and restaurant, and possibly in the kitchen. To work a 5 day week (occasionally 6 days) of typically 40 hours. Min. period of work 3 months.
  Accommodation cannot be provided, but is available locally. Staff should be at least 18 years old, but enthusiasm and a friendly, outgoing personality are more important than experience.
  For further details, or an *application form,* contact the General Manager at the above address.

**HILTON EDINBURGH AIRPORT HOTEL:** Edinburgh International Airport, Edinburgh EH28 8LL (☎0131-519 4425; fax 0131-519 4422; e-mail Personnel.manager@edinairport.stakis.co.uk). Recently built 150 bedroom hotel and leisure club within the boundaries of Edinburgh airport, popular with both tourists and business travellers.
**Room Assistants (4), Bistro Hosts (Breakfast and Bar) (8).** Wage for both positions £4.43 per hour. All staff to work 5 days out of 7 to make up 39 hours. No accommodation is available but meals on duty are provided. Min. period of work 3 months between March and December.
  Experience is preferred, although training can be given. Applicants must be over 18. Overseas applicants with a working knowledge of English considered. Interview necessary.
  *Applications* any time to the Personnel Department.

**HILTON EDINBURGH GROSVENOR HOTEL:** Grosvenor Street, Edinburgh EH12 5EF (☎0131-226 6001; fax 0131-220 2387; e-mail personnel.manager@edinburgh.stakis.co.uk).
**Room Assistants (10)** to work 8:30-4:30 for 39 hours a week.
**Breakfast Servers (6)** to work 6-11:30am for 5 days a week.
**Banqueting Hosts (15-20)** to work approx.15 hours a week.
  Wage for all positions minimum of £4.40 per hour. Training will be given. *Applications* to the above address.

**HILTON PLC:** Coylumbridge Hotel, Coylumbridge, Aviemore, Inverness-shire PH22 1QN (☎01479-813076; fax 01479-811706; e-mail hr_coylumbridge@hilton.coM). Hilton Aviemore operates 3 hotels and a family entertainment facility in the heart of the Scottish Highlands, whose attractions include golf, watersports and horse riding.
**Kitchen, Restaurant Waiting, Bar, & Housekeeping Staff** required. Salary £4.20 per hour. To work 39 hours over a 5-day week. Staff required from June to October. Min. period of work 12 weeks. Min. age 18. Experience preferred. Overseas applicants with basic English (communication level) welcome. Accommodation paid for out of wages at a rate of 67p per hour for 39 hours work.
  *Applications* from April/May to the Personnel Department at the above address.

**HOLIDAY INN EDINBURGH:** Corstorphine Road, Edinburgh EH12 6UA (☎0870-400 9026; fax 0131-334 9237). Edinburgh's largest hotel with 303 bedrooms, various restaurants, bar and leisure facilities.
**Waiting Staff, Housekeeping Assistants, Kitchen Porters.** Wages of £4.40 per hour for a 40 hour week completed over shifts; uniforms and meals when on duty also provided. Min. period of work of 3 months. Positions are available all year round. Full training provided. Minimum age 16. No previous experience necessary. Foreign applicants with work permits and acceptable spoken English welcome. No accommodation available.
*Applications* should be made to the Operations Manager at the above address. Interview required by phone if necessary.

**HUNTING TOWER HOTEL:** Crieff Road, Perth PH1 3JT (☎01738-583771; fax 01738-583777; e-mail michwlee@aol.com).
**Staff** for food and beverage service including breakfasts, lunches, dinners, weddings and functions. Wages by arrangement depending on experience plus tips; to live in or out. To work 5 days out of seven including weekends; period of work by arrangement. Applicants with experience of working in a four star country house hotel preferred.
*Applications* to Michael Lee or Graham Dewar at the above address.

**INVERSNAID PHOTOGRAPHY CENTRE:** Inversnaid Lodge, by Aberfoyle, Stirling FK8 3TU (☎01877-386254; e-mail linda@inversnaidphoto.com; www.inversnaidphoto.com). A residential photography workshop centre which hosts tutors of international repute in areas such as landscape, wildlife, and documentary. Situated on the shores of Loch Lomond, in an area of outstanding natural beauty 1½ hours from Glasgow.
**Domestic Helper (1)** for general cleaning duties and helping in the centre. Wages £125 per week with free B & L provided. To work 40 hours a week. Min. period of work 6 months between April and October. Min. age 20 and non-smoker. Cleaning and waiting experience preferable. Overseas applicants with good English will be considered.
*Applications* from February to Ms Linda Middleton at the above address. Interview preferred.

**LEDGOWAN LODGE HOTEL:** Achnasheen, Wester Ross, Highlands of Scotland IV22 2EJ (☎01445-720252; e-mail info@ledgowanlodge.co.uk; www.ledgowanlodge.co.uk). In an excellent hill walking area attracting clientele from all over the world. A good base for touring the highlands by car.
**Cocktail Bar, House, Pantry, Kitchen And Waiting Staff.** Average gross wage £250 per working 6-day week, depending on age and experience. Accommodation available in own room. To work approx. 50 hours a week with 1 day off. Min. period of work 8 weeks between Easter and October. Overseas applicants with fluent English considered.
Send *Applications* a.s.a.p., enclosing photograph, age and references if possible, to Mr G.T. Millard, Ledgowan Lodge Hotel.

**LOCH NESS LODGE HOTEL:** Drumnadrochit, Inverness-shire IV63 6TU (☎01456-450342; fax 01456-450429; e-mail donald@lochness-centre.com or info@Lochness-hotel.com). Highland lodge which dates back to 1740, near Loch Ness.
**All Positions in a Hotel (50).** Wages by arrangement with accommodation provided. Period of work from May to October. Applicants should be aged between 17 and 50;

previous experience not necessary.
*Applications* to Mrs Mary MacIntosh, Manager, at the above address.

**LOMOND WALKING HOLIDAYS:** 34C James St, Riverside, Stirling, Scotland FK8 1UG (tel/fax 01786-870456; e-mail paul@milligan.force9.co.uk). A family-operated company offering a full range of guided walking holidays throughout Scotland.
**Holiday Assistants;** duties will include driving, shopping and meal preparation. Wages are £200 per week plus meals and accommodation. To work 5-6 hours per day, 7 days a week. Min. period of work is 1 week. Positions are available from April to October. Applicants need to be over 24, have a full, clean driving licence (with category D, minibus entitlement), previous experience of driving vans, and the ability to cook for small groups in hostels.
*Applications* should be made to Paul Milligan at the above address from November onwards.

**MSL LEISURE:** Beachcomber, The Promenade, Leven, Fife KY8 4HY (☎01333-426820; fax 01333-429700; e-mail mmj@msl-leisure.co.uk). Leisure company incorporating amusements, childrens fun park and various food outlets.
**Café Assistants (3)** to cook, clean and possibly organise children's birthday parties. Wages by arrangement. To work 9.30am-9pm in 4/5 hour shifts. Min. period of work of 2 months. Positions are available from June to September. No accommodation available.
*Applications* should be made from March onwards to Mr Morris at the above address. Interview necessary.

**McTAVISH'S KITCHENS (OBAN) LTD:** McTavish's Kitchens, 8 Argyll Square, Oban PA34 4BA or McTavish's Kitchen, High Street, Fort William PH33 6AD (e-mail oban@mctavishs.com or fatwilliam@mctavishs.com). Restaurants in the beautiful West Highland towns of Oban and Fort William.
**Food Service, Self-Service Assistants, Kitchen Assistants, Cooks, Drinks Service And Cleaners.** There are a number of vacancies, particularly for students, between April and October and also late availability mid-August to end of September. Rate of pay not less than the legal minimum. Accommodation available. EU Nationals or evidence of permission to work in the UK.
*Applications* in writing with photograph and s.a.e., to the above address.

**MONESS HOUSE HOTEL AND COUNTRY CLUB:** Crieff Road, Aberfeldy, Perthshire PH15 2DY (☎01887-820446; fax 01887-820062). A private company offering holiday accommodation in a 12 bedroom hotel and 88 self catering cottages situated in 35 acres of grounds overlooking the picturesque town of Aberfeldy in the heart of Scotland.
**Bistro Staff (2), Restaurant Staff (2).** Wages from £4.25 per hour live-in. Must be over 18 and have food service experience. Bistro staff must have wine service experience.
All staff to work 39 hours a week. Min. period of work 10 weeks between April and October. Overseas applicants with good working English considered. Interview not necessary.
*Applications* from Feb/Mar to the General Manager.

**MORTON HOTELS LTD:** The Royal Golf Hotel, Dornoch, Sutherland, IV25 3LG, Scotland (☎01862-810283; fax 01862-810923).

**Breakfast Chef (1-2)** to work from 6am-2.30pm; duties consist of preparing breakfasts and lunches and for general kitchen preparation.
**Commis chefs** (1/2) to help kitchen with breakfasts, lunches and dinners. Wages in line with National Minimum Wage, with live in accommodation available for £20 per week. Period of work May-November.
*Applications* to the Personnel Manager at the above address.

**NEWTON LODGE:** Kylesku, Sutherland IV27 4HW (☎01971-502070; e-mail newtonlge@aol.com; www.smoothHound.co.uk/hotels/newton). A small hotel in the remote North West Highlands. Ideal place to save money for the summer.
**General Assistant** required for duties as required including dining room, kitchen help, bedroom work and general cleaning. Wage £130 per 6 day week, including room with shower and meals. Period of work mid May to mid September. Must have previous hotel experience. Non-smoker only.
*Applications* with photo and reference to Mrs Brauer.

**PRIORY HOTELS LTD:** The Square, Beauly, Inverness-shire IV4 7BX (☎01463-782309; fax 01463-782531; e-mail reservations@priory.hotel.com; www.priory.hotel.com). Small company operating hotels and restaurants in Inverness-shire.
**Kitchen Assistants (4), Front Of House Staff/General Assistants (6)** required to work in busy hotels in Beauly and Dalwhinnie. From £160, plus free B & L. 40 hours per week. Min. period of work 3 months but six month contract preferred. Smart appearance, good interpersonal skills and bags of common sense essential. Good fun with a bustling team of people. Overseas applicants with valid work permit welcome.
*Applications* any time to Blair Sinclair, General Manager, at the above address.

**QUALITY HOTEL CENTRAL:** 99 Gordon Street, Glasgow G1 3SF (☎0141-221 9680; fax 0141-226 3948; e-mail admin@gb627.u-net.com). A 222-bedroom Victorian railway hotel.
**Waiting Staff (1)** to work in hotel restaurant. Hours: 7am-10.30am, 11am-2.30pm and 5.30pm-10.30pm.
**Housekeeper/Room Attendant (1).** Working hours 8am-3pm and 5-8pm.
All staff receive £4.10 per hour if over 22 years and £3.50 if under. Period of work June to December.
Accommodation available for £22.75 per week.
*Applications* to Paul Catford, Regional Personnel Manager, at the above address.

**RAASAY OUTDOOR CENTRE:** Isle of Raasay, By Kyle, Ross-shire, Scotland IV40 8PB (☎01478-660266; fax 01478-660200; e-mail info@raasayoutdoorcentre.co.uk). An outdoor centre located on a remote and peaceful Hebridean Island. Sailing, windsurfing, kayaking and climbing offered to clients.
**Kitchen Manager (1).** Must have at least 6 years cooking and organisational experience. Wages negotiable depending on experience.
**Preparation Cooks (2).** Must have general cooking experience. Wages negotiable depending on experience.
**Kitchen Assistants (2).** To perform kitchen preparation and washing up duties. Must be motivated. Wages negotiable depending on experience.
**Cafe/Bar/Shop Assistants (3).** Must have experience and be organised and motivated. Wages negotiable depending on experience.
**Housekeeper (1).** Must have organisational and cleaning experience. Wages

negotiable depending on experience.
**Childminder (1).** Must have experience of looking after a three year old. Wages negotiable depending on experience.
**Office Person (1).** Must have worked in an office and have good computer skills, enjoy working with people and be organised.

All positions are for 44 hours work per week between March and October. Min. period of work 1 month. Board, accommodation and activities provided.

Overseas applicants must speak good English. Interview is necessary. *Applications* from March to Freya Rowe at the above address.

**ROSEDALE HOTEL:** Portree, Isle of Skye IV51 9DB (☎01478-613131; fax 01478-612531). A family-run hotel located on the harbourside in Portree, the administrative and commercial capital of the island and the adjoining mainland.
**Receptionist/Duty Manager (1).** Min. age 24. Must be educated to at least A level standard and be well presented, articulate and mature. Hotel background and training essential.
**Second Chef (1).** City and Guilds 706/1 and 706/2 required, plus two years' post-qualification experience. To assist AA rosette chef and be able to take charge in his absence preparing quality food with imagination and style.
**General Assistants (6).** To work a mixed rota in many departments but mainly restaurant and bar, with some housekeeping. Aged 21+. Should be well presented, articulate and interested in working with people. Hotel experience an advantage.

Wages specified on application. All staff work approx. 40-45 hours per week. Min. period of work early May to mid October. Priority given to those able to work the full or greater part of the season. An end of season share of gratuities is made upon completion of contract period. Non-smoking applicants only.

Write for an *application form* from mid-February to Mrs Rouse, Manager, at the above address.

**THE ROYAL HOUSEHOLD:** Buckingham Palace, London SW1A 1AA (☎020-7930 4832; fax 020-7360 7125).
**Assistants** for general cleaning/laundry duties of staff accommodation/bedding, and the occasional cleaning of more isolated buildings used for barbecues, at Balmoral Castle. Wages on application; accommodation is provided, as are meals during court visits. To work up to 35 hours per week on a rota. Must be able to work from mid July to mid October inclusive. Not suitable for students returning to college in September. Applicants should be aged between 18 and 50; no previous experience is necessary as training is given. All staff to be security screened before employment; this can take up to 2 months if candidates are from overseas. Valid work visa required prior to employment.

*Applications*, by April at the latest, to Miss Heather Colebrook, Chief Housekeeper, at the above address.

**ROYAL ZOOLOGICAL SOCIETY OF SCOTLAND:** Edinburgh Zoo Members House, 134 Corstorphine Road, Edinburgh EH12 6TS (☎0131-334 5001; fax 0131-334 7462). Edinburgh Zoo is Scotland's second most popular tourist attraction, with over half a million visitors a year viewing the world-famous animal collection.
**General Catering Assistants (40)** for work involving cash handling, customer service and general duties in a busy bistro style restaurant within the zoo. Wages £4.25 per hour.
**Waiting Assistants** to work in the highly rated members' restaurant and lounge. Wages of £4.25 per hour plus tips.

These wages may change depending on the timescale for implementation of minimum wage legislation. To work from 10am-6pm, 5 days a week. Period of work from May to October. Also to work around 4-8 hours overtime a week at 1½ times the usual rate. Experience of previous similar work preferred but not essential as full training is provided..
*Applications* to D Inverarity, Public Catering Manager, at the above address.

**RUFFLETS COUNTRY HOUSE HOTEL:** Strathkinness Low Road, St. Andrews KY16 9TX (☎01334-472594; fax 01334-478703; e-mail john@rufflets.co.uk; rufflets.co.uk ). A privately owned 22 bedroom upmarket hotel which holds two AA rosettes for food quality; young and friendly staff.
**Housekeeping Assistant (1), Restaurant Assistant (1), Lounge Service Assistant (1).** Wages range from £3.75 (under 21 years) to £4.25 per hour. All staff to work hours as required, 5 days out of 7. Accommodation is available at £3.50 per day. Min. period of work 6 months between 1st April and 30th November.
Experience is not essential, but all applicants must be over 18 years old. Foreign applicants fluent in English considered. Interview not always necessary.
*Applications* from January to John Angus.

**SCOTLAND'S HOTEL:** Bonnethill Road, Pitlochry, Perthshire, Scotland PH16 5BT (☎01796-472292; fax 01796-473284; stay@scotlands.co.uk). A 71 bedroom hotel with conference facilities, a leisure club, and an Italian restaurant, situated in an excellent location, just two hours away from Edinburgh, Glasgow, Aberdeen and Inverness.
**Bar Assistant.** £160 per week. Min. age 18 years. Split and straight shifts.
**Waiting Staff (2).** £160 per week. Silver service training or experience preferred. Split shifts.
**House Staff (2).** £160 per week. Cleaning or housekeeping experience preferred. Split and straight shifts.
All staff to work 8 hours per day, 5 days per week with no overtime. Accommodation available. Free meals on and off duty. Health and Leisure club restricted membership for all staff. Uniform provided and training will be given. Min. period of work 2 months between April and October. Overseas applicants with a good knowledge of English welcome. Where possible it is preferred that applicants are available for interview.
*Applications* from March to the Personnel Manager at the above address.

**STONEFIELD CASTLE GROUP:** Stonefield Castle Group, Castlehill, Howwood, Renfrewshire PA9 1DB (☎0150-570 4000; fax 0150-5703000). Stonefield Castle Group is a collection of hotels and other leisure businesses all located in the West of Scotland.
**Waiting Staff.** Full-time and part-time positions are available. To work at least 16 hours per week. Applicants should be at least 16 years old.
**Leisure Club Staff.** To work 40 hours per week. Applicants must be 18 or over, those who have pool lifeguard and first aid certificate are preferred.
**Housekeeping Staff.** To work at least 16 hours a week. Applicants must be at least 16.
Period of work from May to September. Minimum period of work 2 months. Wages £3.50-£5.00 per hour.
*Applications* from April to the Personnel and Training Manager at the above address.

**SWALLOW HOTEL:** 517 Paisley Road West, Glasgow GS1 1RW (☎0141-427

3146; fax 0141-4190 1602). 3 star, 117 bedroomed hotel near the city centre with leisure facilities, priding itself on excellent customer care and service.
**Restaurant Waiting Staff (10), House assistants (4).** Wages from £4.10 per hour, various hours. Min. period of work of 2 months. Positions are available from May to August. Any experience an advantage. Minimum age 16. No accommodation available.
*Applications* should be made from March onwards to Angela Bennett at the above address. Interview necessary.

**SUMMER ISLES HOTEL:** Achiltibuie by Ullapool, Ross-shire IV26 2YG (☎01854-622282; summerisleshotel@aol.com). Wonderful Highland location of hills, lochs and islands. A four star, family run hotel – a great opportunity to learn the business and save money.
**General Assistants** for waiting, bar, housekeeping and kitchen.
Wages min. £178 for 50 hours/6 days per week. End of season bonus. Free B & L provided. Experience preferred but training given. Applicants should be available for whole season, starting April/May. The jobs are suited to professional motivated people prepared to work hard and make the most of their free time by enjoying outdoor activities.
*Applications*, with s.a.e. and photograph, to Mr Mark Irvine, Summer Isles Hotel.

**THAINSTONE HOUSE HOTEL:** Inverurie, Aberdeenshire AB51 5NT (☎01467-621643; fax 01467-625084; e-mail thainstone.macdonald-hotel.co.uk). A four star country house hotel and leisure club, committed to training employees to a high level.
**Waiting Staff (4), Bartenders (2), Housemaids (2).** Wages by arrangement. All positions to work a 39 hour week. Min. period of work 3 months Between May and the end of September.
Board and accommodation is available for a 10p deduction from the hourly wage. There are no deductions for meal breaks, and staff may use the hotel leisure facilities. Experience is preferable, but training will be given. References are required.
*Applications* from April onwards to the Personnel Manager.

**M.F. WELLS (HOTELS) LTD.:** Gartocharn, Dumbartonshire G83 8RW (☎01389-713713; fax 01389-713721; e-mail recruitment@lochsandglens.com; www.lochandglens.com). A family run hotel and tour group with 5 hotels located in beautiful and remote areas of Scotland, and its own fleet of coaches.
**Kitchen Assistant, Dining Room Staff, Housekeeping Staff & Bar Staff** to work 40 hours a week. Both temporary and permanent positions available, as well as opportunity for career development. Wages in accordance with national minimum wage, accommodation available. Minimum period of work 12 weeks at any time of year; dates of work negotiable.
*Applications* at any time to the above address.

**WOODLEA HOTEL:** Moniaive, Dumfries-shire DG3 4EN (☎01848-200209).
**General Assistants (2).** £4.20 per hour live-out, for employees over 21 years. Tips in addition. To work variable hours. B & L may be available. Expected to help in all aspects of hotel including serving in the bar, toilet cleaning and kitchen and dining room work. Staff free to use swimming pool and other sports facilities when not in use by guests. Work available from Easter to end of October. Min. work period 3 months, preferably to the end of September.
*Applications* enclosing s.a.e., 2 references and dates of availability, to Mr Horley at the above address.

**THE WESTIN TURNBERRY RESORT:** Turnberry Hotel, Maidens Road, Turnberry, Ayrshire KA26 9LT (☎01655-331000; fax 01655-331879). A 5 star, luxury golf resort with 132 guest bedrooms and 89 golf lodge rooms over 800 acres on the coast of Scotland. The Resort is part of Starwood Hotels and Resorts Inc, the world's leading upscale hotel company.
**Commis Chef.** Wages £740 per month.
**Chef De Partie.** Wages £1,040 per month.
**Food and Beverage Waiting Assistant.** Wages £740 per month.
**Room Attendant.** Wages £728 per month.
**Guest Service Agent – Front Desk.** Wages £810 per month.
**Guest Service Agent – Concierge.** Wages £720 per month.
**Beauty Therapists.** Wages £835 per month.
**Golf Retail Assistants.** Wages £720 per month.
**Greenkeepers.** Wages £681 per month.
**Pool and Gym Attendant.** £835 per month.
 Accommodation is provided at a charge of £120 per month inclusive of resort transport and meals. All staff work 39 hours per week. Staff are required between April and June and finish in September or October. Applicants must be eligible to work in the European Union.
 *Applications* should be made in writing to Hamish Paterson, Human Resources Director at the above address or via e-mail to joane.dunabie@westin.com.

# Language Schools

**EDINBURGH SCHOOL OF ENGLISH:** 271 Canongate, The Royal Mile, Edinburgh EH8 8BQ (☎0131-557 9200; fax 0131-557 9192; e-mail english@edinburghschool.ac.uk). Founded in 1969, ESE is a year round school. Courses are directed by permanent staff, and have the back up of a permanent organisation. Arranges English language summer courses for school children (9-17 years) in Edinburgh and Strathallan.
**Activity Leaders** to be responsible for the smooth running of the afternoon, evening and weekend leisure programme. The job involves taking students on various cultural visits and organising and supervising sports. One leader is employed for every 10 students. Some leaders are required to live and supervise in halls of residence in addition to the above. Hours by arrangement. B & L available for a few applicants only. Courses are run between mid-June and early September, and also during April. Min. period of work 3 weeks.
 Applicants should be aged over 21, with a sound knowledge of one of the above locations. They should be enthusiastic and energetic, have good organisational abilities, get on well with teenagers and be interested in sports and cultural visits. Fluent English speakers only.
 *Applications* to The Principal at the above address.

**SCOT-ED COURSES:** 6 Blinkbonny Gardens, Edinburgh EH4 3HG (☎0131-332 1060; fax 0131-623 2154; e-mail scot-ed@blueyonder.co.uk). Summer school organisation that specialises in youth groups.
**EFL Teachers (4-6)** to teach mornings in the summer school and supervise group visits and sporting activities in the afternoon. Wages £200-250 per week. Minimum period of work 2 weeks between 23 June and mid August. Courses are in Edinburgh.
 *Applications* and CVs from 1st May by e-mail or to the address above.

## Medical

**INVALID SERVICES LTD:** 62 North Street, St. Andrews, Fife, KY16 9AH
(☎01334-472834; fax 01334-470602).
**Carers (many)** all dates. To provide care in clients' own homes. Age: 21+ and own transport helpful.
**Nurses (many)** May to September for nursing home shifts and in clients' own homes. Must have care and/or nursing qualifications.
**Domestics (many)** for Easter and Christmas vacations. Experience essential.
Accommodation not provided but arrangements can be made. Flexible hours. Pay from £5 per hour.
*Applications* to Joan Reid, Manager, at the above address.

## Outdoor

**AUCHRENNIE FARM:** Muirdrum, Carnoustie, Angus (☎01241-852800; e-mail j-gray@bigfoot.com). A 300-hectare farm whose main enterprise is strawberries, grown and packed on site.
**Strawberry Pickers (up to 200).** Piecework rates. To work 8 hours per day. Minimum period of work 2 months. Staff required from May to September. Minimum age 20. Foreign applicants with permission to work in the UK welcome. Good English an advantage. Accommodation is available at a charge of £20 per week (2002 figure).
*Applications* via e-mail or telephone from January/February 2003. Interview required.

**BALMORAL ESTATES:** Estates Office, Balmoral, Ballater, Aberdeenshire AB35 5TB (☎013397-42334; fax 013397-42271; www.balmoralestate.co.uk).
**Grouse Beaters (6)** to work from mid August to the end of September. Beaters receive £19.50 per day plus accommodation, dinner, bed, breakfast and packed lunch in exchange for working 8am-5pm. Applicants must be healthy and fit enough for a day's walking in the Scottish hills.
*Applications* to P.J. Ord at the above address.

**A.P. BARRIE & CO:** Colbeggie Farm, Coupar Angus, Perthshire, Scotland PH13 9HA (tel/fax 01828-628666; e-mail apbarrie@sol.co.uk). A specialist producer of soft fruit. Friendly atmosphere with many nationalities.
**Fruit Pickers, Packers And Supervisors.** Training will be provided. A large amount of picking is done under protection from rain, so full days in good crops are assured. Good piecework rates are offered for those willing to work hard. Must be willing to work long hours when required, but usually 8 hours a day for 5-6 days a week. Period of work April-October. All applicants must be on the farm by 10th July.
Accommodation either in caravans or bring your own tent. Hot showers, kitchen, dining room, recreational areas, games room and laundry area are provided. Entertainment such as Scottish dancing, discos, barbeques and football matches are arranged for the weekends. Bicycles can be borrowed to get to the nearest town, 1½ miles away. Applicants from outside the EU are welcome if they have valid work permits; the farm regrets that it cannot help obtain these.
*Applications* in writing to Mr Barrie or by e-mail, see above.

**MR S. CAMPBELL:** Cairntradlin, Kinellar, Aberdeenshire AB21 0SA (☎01224-790056; fax 01224-791581). A farm growing strawberries and raspberries for supermarkets and a local pick-your-own, situated 7 miles from Aberdeen.

**Strawberry/Raspberry Pickers (15).** Piece work rates paid daily. Picking as and when required, weather and crop conditions permitting; days off as arranged. Social evenings, e.g. barbecues and Scottish nights, arranged for student workers. Self-catering accommodation (7) provided in portacabins, with male and female dormitories, kitchen, toilets and showers. Camping area also available for those with equipment. Applicants must bring eating utensils, warm sleeping bags and warm clothing. Period of work 5 July until the end of August. Overseas applicants welcome.
   *Applications* to Mr S. Campbell at the above address. Enclose a stamped addressed envelope to ensure a reply.

**HAROLD CORRIGALL:** Leadketty Farm, Dunning, Perthshire PH2 0QP (☎01764-684532; fax 01764-684146; e-mail harold@leadketty.freeserve.co.uk). A small farm growing 20 acres of strawberries- 20 acres under tunnels and 3 acres of raspberries.
**Fruit Pickers (10).** Wages approx. £35-£55 per day; to work 7am-4pm per day, 6 days a week. Accommodation is available at a charge of £20 per week. Staff required for a minimum of 4 weeks between June and late August. Applicants must be 18 or over. The farm takes many European students with appropriate permits or authorisation. Good English speaking personnel required for **managerial posts** for approximately 3 months (June-August).
   *Applications* from February to Harold Corrigall at the above address.

**DRUMNADROCHIT BOARDING KENNELS & CATTERY:** Tor Nambreac, Bunloit Hill, Drumnadrochit, Inverness-shire IV63 6XG (☎01456-420250; e-mail drum.kennels@talk21.com).
**Boarding Kennel Assistant (1 or 2)** from June onwards to walk dogs, feed dogs and cats, clean kennels and cat chalets, answer telephone, deal with customers, take bookings and general maintenance. Hours and days by arrangement. Minimum wage paid. Accommodation in fully-equipped static caravan. Common sense, reliability and empathy with animals.
   *Applications* to Garry or Nina MacLeod at the above address.

**D.& B. GRANT:** Wester Essendy, Blairgowrie, Perthshire PH10 6RA (☎01250-884389; e-mail cmgrant99@yahoo.com).
**Fruit Pickers (50)** to pick strawberries and raspberries. Help also required to process fruit for freezing. Rates and shifts to be negotiated. To work 6 days a week. Period of work from July 10 to August 31. Caravan accommodation available.
   *Applications* to Colin M. Grant via e-mail or telephone.

**W. HENDERSON:** Seggat, Auchterless, Turriff, Aberdeenshire AB53 8DL (☎01888-511223; fax 01888-511434). Situated in the heart of the castle and distillery county of Aberdeenshire.
**Strawberry Pickers/Packers.** Piece work rates: around £20 per day but dependent on size of crop and weather. To work 7 hours per day, 6 days per week, but must be prepared to work variable hours. Period of work early July to mid August, min. 4 weeks. Self-catering accommodation available, for which there is a charge of £10 per week, but must bring own sleeping bag and eating utensils. Situated 1 mile from main road, with regular bus service between Aberdeen and Inverness.
   *Applications* from 30 January onwards to Mr W. Henderson, at the above address.

**LOWES FRUIT FARM:** Campend Farm, Dalkeith EH22 1RS (☏0131-220-0416; fax 0131-220- 0417; e-mail sharon@caledoniantrust.com) A busy seasonal fruit farm with a farm shop.
**Fruit Pickers (6)** Wages piece rate, to work from 8am-4pm.
**Shop Staff (2)** Wages piece rate, to work from 10am-6pm.
Staff are required from end of June to the end of August for a min. period of 6 weeks. Applicants must be over 18. Basic acommodation is available for £10 per week.
*Applications* should be made to Sharon at the above address from April.

**J & C McDIARMID:** Mains of Murthly, Aberfeldy, Perthshire PH15 2EA (tel/fax 01887-829899; e-mail dromcroy1@aol.com).
**Soft Fruit Pickers (about 20)** from 1 July to 30 August for picking and packing. £40 per day. Shower and toilet block available at campsite. Age: 18+.
*Applications* to Calum McDiarmid at the above address.

**PURVIS MARQUEES:** 4 East Mains, Ingliston Road, Edinburgh EH28 2NB (☏0131-335 3685; fax 0131-553 7655; e-mail sales@purvismarquees.co.uk).
**Marquee Erectors** wanted to work over the summer for around £4.80 per hour dependant on skills. The work involves erecting and dismantling marquees throughout the UK often working a 7 day week. Applicants should be quick to learn, impervious to the weather and have a sense of humour.
*Applications* to the above address.

**L.M. PORTER:** East Seaton, Arbroath, Angus, Scotland DD11 5SD (☏01241-870290; fax 01241-871220; e-mail susan@lmporter.co.uk). East Seaton is situated on the clifftops by Arbroath where conditions are ideal for growing fruit for Tescos, Sainsburys, Safeway and Asda.
**Strawberry/Raspberry Pack House Staff/Pickers (20)** for soft fruit picking, in July and August. Piece rate. Hours can vary with the weather conditions but otherwise average 8 hours a day. Youth hostel type accommodation and camp site facilities available. Applicants must be fit as work is hard but well rewarded.
*Applications* to Deborah Porter, Partner, at the above address.

# Sport

**CAIRNWELL MOUNTAIN SPORTS:** Gulabin Lodge, Spittal of Glenshee, Blairgowrie PH10 7QE (☏0870-4430 253; fax 0870-4430 253; e-mail info@cairnwellmountainsports.co.uk; www.cairnwellmountainsports.co.uk). A multi activity centre and hostel for 30-40 persons. In winter activities include ski school, snow board school and nordic skiing; in summer climbing, walking, hang gliding and adventures activities.
**Ski Instructors(2)** Wages £200 per week; to work 6 days per week. Required from January 5th to March 10th for a minimum of 5-10 weeks.
Must have a national qualification.
**Activity Instructors (2)** Wages £200 per week; to work 6 days per week. Required from April 16th to June 16th for a minimum of 4 weeks. Applicants must have a national qualification.
**Lodge Worker(1)** Wages £160 per week. Required from December to May 30th. No experience necessary.
Overseas applicants are welcome for the posts of lodge worker and ski instructor.Accommodation is available at a cost of £50 per week.
*Applications* should be sent to Gustav Fischnaller at the above address as soon as

possible. Interview and references are necessary.

**CALEDONIAN DISCOVERY LTD:** The Slipway, Corpach, Fort William PH33 7NB (☎01397-772167; fax 01397-772765; e-mail info@fingal-cruising.co.uk; www.fingal-cruising.co.uk). Organises activity holidays based on a barge cruising the Caledonian Canal/Loch Ness. The 12 guests take part in various outdoor activities at numerous stops along the way. Activities include sailing, canoeing, windsurfing, walking, and biking, with other specialist weeks available. The work is hard, but varied and great fun.
**Mate/Instructor (1).** £145-£220 per week net of living expenses and depending on experience. Experience and preferably qualifications in open canoeing and mountain walking required (windsurfing and sailing an advantage).
**Bosun (1).** £90 per week net of living expenses. Main duties: maintenance of boat, driving of safety boat, helping on deck. Training provided. Personal experience of outdoor sports an advantage. Must be keen to learn, with practical nature.
**Cook (1)** to prepare food for 18 people. £145-£200 per week net of living expenses. Must have experience in good cooking.
**Assistant Cook** (1 each week, part-time) to assist cook. To work their passage: no wage paid.

All full-time staff to work 6½ days a week and all crew live on board the barge. To work from mid April to mid October. Staff must be available for the whole season to qualify for a bonus with the exception of the assistant cook whose minimum period is one week. A two day recruitment event will be held in February or March.
*Applications* from December to Martin Balcombe at the above address.

**GALLOWAY SAILING CENTRE:** Shirmers Bridge, Loch Ken, Castle Douglas DG7 3NQ, South West Scotland (☎01644-420626; e-mail gsc@lochken.co.uk). A family owned centre in a glorious setting, which aims to give its visitors an enjoyable yet educational time in a safe and friendly atmosphere.
**Instructors: Dinghy (15), Windsurfers (5), Canoes (5).** Courses start at 10am and finish 5pm. Must be RYA qualified or have a similar level of competence. Overseas applicants with equivalent qualifications welcome.
**Cook/General Help (2).** No special qualifications needed but experience an advantage.
**Chalet Girl (1).** Must enjoy working with children.

Wages negotiable, hours variable. Applicants should be versatile, good with people and prepared to accept responsibility. Knowledge of DIY an advantage. Free B & L provided. Period of work from May to September, or peak season only.
*Applications* to Mr R. Hermon, Principal, at the above address.

**GLENCOE OUTDOOR CENTRE:** Glencoe, Argyll PA39 4HS (☎01855-811350). A residential holiday and outdoor activity training centre situated in the north west Highlands amongst the spectacular scenery of Glencoe.
**Domestic Assistants/Assistant Instuctor (4).** from £50 per week plus board and accommodation. To work 8 hours per day, 5 days per week: 3 out of 4 weeks domestic work (split shifts, afternoons free) and 1 out of 4 weeks assisting the team of instructors. Plenty of opportunity to take part in activities during free time. Min. period of work 2 months between January and end of July. Min. age 18. Applicants should be committed Christians willing to work hard as part of a Christian team.
*Applications* a.s.a.p. to Debbie Williams, Director, at the above address.

**HILTON PLC:** Hilton Coylumbridge Hotel, Coylumbridge, Aviemore, Inverness-shire PH22 1QN (☎01479-813076; fax 01479-811706; e-mail hr – coylumbridge@hilton.co

m). An excellent new accommodation facility with a good local benefits package.
**Leisure Staff.** National minimum wage for 39 hours work a week. Must have Lifeguard certificate and First Aid. Possible split shifts over a 5-day week. Min. age 18. Staff required from June to October. Min. period of work 12 weeks. Overseas applicants with basic English (communication level) welcome. Shared accommodation in staff hostel with basic facilities available for £27.30 per week. See Hilton plc for further jobs at the same hotel in the *Hotel and Catering* section.

*Applications* from April/May to the Personnel Department at the above address.

**LOCH INSH WATERSPORTS & SKIING CENTRE:** Insh Hall, Kincraig, Inverness-shire PH21 1NU (☎01540-651272; fax 01540-651208; e-mail office@lochinsh.com; www.lochinsh.com). Loch Insh Watersports and skiing centre nestled in the foothills of the Cairngom Mountains in the scenic Spey Valley. Lochside Restaurant and Watersports Centre. Snowskiing December to April. Bed and Breakfast ensuite accommodation and self catering log chalets on site.
**Watersports Instructors.** RYA and BCU qualified, or trainee instructor standard. To work 6 days a week.
**Skiing Instructors.** BASI-qualified, or trainee instructor standard. To work 6 days a week.
**Restaurant Staff.** To work a 5 or 6 day week. Experience preferred.
Wages variable. B & L provided at a charge of up to £45 a week. Free watersports and skiing for staff. Min. period of work 3 months, with work available all year round. Non-smokers only. Overseas applicants with good spoken English welcome.

*Applications* to Mr Clive Freshwater, at the above address.

**MONSTER ACTIVITIES:** South Laggan, by Spean Bridge, Inverness-shire PH34 4EA (☎01809-501 340 ext. Leisure; fax 01809-501 218; info@monsteractivities.com). A multi-activity centre catering for both family and group activities situated on the Caledonian Canal, on the shores of Loch Oich.
**Instructors (5)** to carry out various tasks including instruction in archery, windsurfing, sailing, rafting; duties also include equipment maintenance, client reception and staff training. Wages £150 per week. Hours of work vary. Applicants must have a first aid certificate, driving licence and a qualification relevant to the sport that they are teaching, e.g. Power Boat II or III, or Raft Guide Level 2 or 3.

*Applications* at any time after February to the Leisure Manager, at the above address.

**PERTH AND KINROSS LEISURE:** Company Headquarters, 2 High Street, Perth PH1 5PH (☎01738-477907; fax 01738-477910; e-mail DMGaffney@pkc.gov.uk). Provide leisure and community facilities throughout the Perth and Kinross area to promote development, health, fitness and wider leisure services.
**Relief Leisure Assistant (Wet Facilities).** Wages £5.29 per hour. RLSS pool lifeguard qualification needed.
**Relief Leisure Assistant (Dry Facilities).** Wages £5.29 per hour. First aid at work qualification needed.
**Sports Coaches** Wages from £5-£10 per hour. Appropriate coaching certificates needed.
Hours are variable. Positions are available at variable times throughout the year, especially holiday periods, weekends and evenings. No accommodation available. Foreign applicants welcome with appropriate work permit.

*Applications* should be made to Diane Gaffney, Administration Manager, by letter. Interview necessary.

**RAASAY OUTDOOR CENTRE:** Isle of Raasay, By Kyle, Ross-shire, IV40 8PB (☎01478-660266; fax 01478-660200; e-mail info@raasayoutdoorcentre.co.uk). An outdoor centre located on a remote and peaceful Hebridean Island. Sailing, windsurfing, kayaking and climbing offered to clients.
**Outdoor Activity Instructors (8).** To work 44 hours per week between March and October. Min. period of work 1 month. Must have first aid qualifications plus one of the following: Windsurfing RYA, Sailing RYA, Kayak BCU, Abseil and Climb, Walking S.P.S.A. Wages depend on responsibility and experience; board, accommodation and activities provided.
*Applications* to Freya Rowe from March at the above address. All applicants must speak good English. An interview is required.

# Voluntary Work

## Conservation and the Environment

**BTCV SCOTLAND:** Balallan House, 24 Allan Park, Stirling FK8 2QG (☎01786-479697; fax 01786-465359; e-mail scotland@btcv.org.uk).
BTCV Scotland is one of the UK's largest environmental conservation charities. It operates a network of local centres in, or close to, Scotland's 5 major cities.
**Volunteer Officers** required to assist in a varied range of projects e.g. community groups, recycling, environmental projects, administration and residential projects. Hours of work vary, expenses are paid to volunteers. Volunteer officers are required all year round for a minimum of 3-6 months. Training is provided in skills needed such as Health and Safety or First Aid. Suitable for New Deal placements. Those over 21 with a clean driving licence held for 2 years are particularly desirable.
*Applications* to Helen Paul at the above address.

**THISTLE CAMPS:** The National Trust for Scotland, 28 Charlotte Square, Edinburgh EH2 4ET (☎0131-243 9470; fax 0131-243 9593; e-mail conservationvolunteers@nts.org.uk; www.nts.org.uk).
The Charity protects and promotes Scotland's natural and cultural heritage. Thistle Camps are voluntary work projects organised by The National Trust for Scotland to help in the care and practical management of its countryside properties. Each year there are approx. 40 camps, running from March to October and lasting from one to three weeks. They are always of a **Practical Nature**, undertaking such tasks as mountain footpath improvement, habitat management, archaeology or working with crofting communities on Fair Isle (Britain's most remote inhabited island) and Iona. Volunteers must be aged over 16.
Camps are usually accommodated in a Trust basecamp or in similar hostel-type lodgings. All food is provided but volunteers are expected to help with the preparation of meals as well as general domestic tasks during the week. Participation in a camp costs from £45 (£30 for students etc), and volunteers must pay their own travel expenses to a central pick-up point. All volunteers must bring good waterproofs and sturdy footwear.
The programme for 2003 is available from January and *applications* should be made to the above address. Overseas applicants must apply by February to ensure a place.

**TREES FOR LIFE:** The Park, Findhorn Bay, Forres IV36 3TZ (☎01309-691292;

fax 01309-691155; e-mail trees@findhorn.org; www.treesforlife.org.uk).
Scottish charity dedicated to the restoration of the Caledonian Forest to a large, significant area of the Highlands of Scotland.
**Volunteers (300)** needed for a week at a time. To carry out practical restoration work including tree planting, fence removal, tree-felling, wetland restoration, tree nursery work, stock-fencing and seed collecting.

To work Saturday to Saturday inclusive (8 days). Volunteers may participate in more than one week. Required mid-March to beginning of June and beginning of September to end of October. All food, accommodation and transport from Inverness provided. Minimum age 18. Applicants must understand English and be reasonably fit, as work is physical. Foreign applicants welcome.

*Applications* should be sent to 'Trees For Life Work Week Booking' at the above address.

## Heritage

**STRATHSPEY RAILWAY CO. LTD.:** Aviemore Station, Dalfaber Road, Aviemore PH22 1PY (☎01479-810725; e-mail information@strathspeyrailway.co.uk).
Highland steam railway (not-for-profit organisation) which runs for 10 miles between Aviemore, Boat of Garten and Broomhill; tourist attraction with limited public services. Work is being done to extend the line to Grantown-on-Spey.
**Volunteer Guards, Ticket Inspectors And Booking Clerks.** Volunteers are also needed to help maintain the railway and its rolling stock and locomotives. Free but very basic accommodation in sleeping car at Boat of Garten station. Hostel for members who work at Aviemore £2.50 per night. Minimum age 16. Fitness needed for some jobs. Vacancies all year.

*Applications* to the above address.

## Physically/Mentally Disabled

**BEANNACHAR:** Banchory-Devenick, Aberdeen AB12 5YL. (☎01224-869138; e-mail beannachar@talk21.com; www.beannachar.co.uk).
Beannachar is one of the Camphill communities in which vulnerable children and adults can live, learn and work with others in healthy social relationships based on mutual care and respect.
Beannachar is a training community for teenagers and young adults with learning disabilities. **Volunteers** are needed for household, workshop, garden and farm duties during the summer, and also long-term volunteers at any time of year. Free B & L plus pocket money provided. To work long hours, 6 days a week. Min. age 19. Must have lots of enthusiasm and a positive attitude. Overseas applicants must speak fluent English. Min. work period 2 months between June and September, 1 year for long-term volunteers.

*Applications* at any time to Ms E.A. Phethean at the above address.

**SPEYSIDE TRUST:** Badaguish Outdoor Centre, Aviemore, Inverness-shire PH22 1QU (☎01479-861285; fax 01479-861258; e-mail info@Badaguish.org; www.badaguish.org).
The Centre specialises in outdoor recreation holidays for children and adults with learning or multiple disabilities. Clients enjoy various adventure activities and 24 hour respite care in a spectacular setting. Bagduish is 7 miles out of Aviemore in the Greenmore Forest Park; nearest shops are 2 miles away in Glenmore. Volunteers must enjoy the outdoors and take part in all activities offered.

**Volunteer Care Assistants** to work with people with Special Needs for 2 or more weeks from April to October. Volunteers are expected to work 10 hours a day with 2 days off a week. £30 pocket money per week plus B & L.
**Seasonal Care Assistant/ Instructor.** Paid post from April-October. Accommodation available at the Centre; residential work experience essential. 2 references required.
For more information and *applications* write to the above address.

**YOUNG DISABLED ON HOLIDAY:** Flat 4, 62 Stuart Park, Edinburgh EH12 8YE (☎0131-339 8866).
**Voluntary Workers** (as many as possible) required for holidays for disabled people in the U.K. and abroad for one week throughout the summer. Each volunteer needs to help a disabled person on a one-to-one basis. Workers are expected to make a minimum contribution towards accommodation, food and trips. Preferred age group 18-35, though anyone up to the age of 40 will be considered. No previous experience required, just patience. Overseas applicants welcome.
*Applications* to Alison Walker at the above address.

## Social and Community Schemes

**BRAENDAM FAMILY HOUSE:** Thornhill, Stirling FK8 3QH (☎01786-850259; fax 01786-850738; e-mail braendam@care4free.net).
**Volunteers** required throughout the year to work for a minimum of 6 months at a short stay family house for families experiencing disadvantage and poverty. £30 pocket money and full board provided in return for a 40 hour week within a 2 week rota (5 days off in 14 days); most accommodation is in a single room although it may be necessary to share. Tasks include direct support to families, participating in trips and outings, domestic chores, driving, organising children's activities and play and generally responding to the needs of families.
Volunteers are entitled to holidays, use of house car and bicycles for a small charge, and access to internet/e-mail, again for a small charge. Volunteers will also have the opportunity to explore Scotland on days off. Applicants must be over 18, be willing to work long days and to carry out domestic chores and maintain enthusiasm and energy for supporting families in need. A clean driving licence would be an advantage
*Applications* to Brian Guidery, Co-ordinator, at the above postal or e-mail address.

**EDINBURGH CYRENIANS:** Norton Park, 57 Albion Road, Edinburgh EH7 5QY (☎0131-475 2354; e-mail admin@cyrenians.org.uk; www.cyrenians.org.uk).
A professional and respected local charity, providing all kinds of practical help for homeless people since 1968. It is not a religious group and the only mission is to help homeless people.
The Cyrenian Trust runs two community houses (one in the city centre and another on an organic farm in West Lothian) that are primarily for young adults who are otherwise homeless, and who have experienced a variety of difficulties which they are seeking to overcome. Residential volunteers, of a similar age to residents, live alongside residents sharing the life and work of the community. Support and regular training is provided by non-residential staff. No experience needed.
Volunteers receive full B & L, weekly pocket money, holiday, leaving grants, and access to a time-off flat. Minimum commitment 6 months. Vacancies all year round. Overseas applicants with good working use of the English language welcome.
For further information and *application* form contact Volunteer Recruitment at the above address. Online applications are possible via website.

**IONA COMMUNITY:** The Iona Abbey, Isle of Iona, Argyll PA76 6SN (☎01681-700404; fax 01681-700460; e-mail ionacomm@iona.org.uk).
An ecumenical Christian Community sharing work, worship, meals and recreation with guests visiting the Macleod and Abbey centres on Iona, and Camas, the more basic outdoors centre on nearby Mull. Guests come and stay for a week to take part in the common life of work, worship and recreation.

Volunteers work in the kitchen, shop and office, help with driving, maintenance, housekeeping and with the children's and craft work activities programme.

**Volunteers** are needed for between 6 and 14 weeks between March and November. They receive full B & L, travelling expenses within the U.K. and pocket money of around £25 per week. They work 5½ days per week. Volunteers should be in sympathy with the Christian faith and the ideals of the Iona Community. Volunteers of 18+ are required. Overseas applicants with reasonable English welcome.

Recruitment begins in the autumn. For details and *applications* write to the Staff Co-ordinator, Iona Abbey, enclosing a stamped addressed envelope or International Reply Coupon.

# Vacation Traineeships & Internships

## Science, Construction and Engineering

**BAE SYSTEMS (MARINE):** Waterside House, Barrow, Cumbria, LA14 1AF (☎01229-875833; fax 01229-875092).
Offers opportunities to approx. 20 students to undertake various projects within the Operations, Technical, Projects and Service departments. Applicants should be university students studying Electrical Engineering, Mechanical Engineering, Naval Architecture, Engineering with Management, Business or Manufacturing systems. Salary depends on year of study.

Placements occur in June-September in Glasgow or Barrow. No accommodation is provided. Overseas applicants are considered, but security clearance may be a problem.

*Applications* by March/April to Personnel.

**CELTIC WELCOMES LTD:** Aston Cottage, Sorn Estate, Sorn, East Ayrshire KA5 6HR (☎01290-553347; fax 01290-553348; www.celticwelcomes.com). A tour wholesaler organising tours for group operators throughout the UK and Europe, specialising in Scotland, Ireland and Northern Europe.
**Administration & Marketing Support Assistants (2)** to assist with admin and any marketing in the company. Accommodation and living expenses covered. Hours by arrangement. Good spoken and written English essential. Other European languages (especially French and German) an advantage. Admin, business, marketing or computer skills also an advantage.

*Applications* should be made at any time to the above address. Interview required.

**HALCROW:** 16 Abercromby Place, Edinburgh EH3 6LB (☎0131-272 3300; fax 0131-272 3302; e-mail Beardl@halcrow.com; www.halcrow.com).
Traffic engineering and planning company.
**Trainee Placements (2-3).** Wages by arrangement. Variable hours; duration and timing of placement by arrangement.

Applicants must be at least 18, though graduates are preferred. Good numeracy, computer skills and English essential. Applicants should have or be studying towards a qualification in development planning, traffic engineering, economics, geography or similar. Suitably qualified foreign applicants with appropriate permits and fluent English welcome.

*Applications* should be made at any time to the above address. Interview required.

# Wales and Northern Ireland

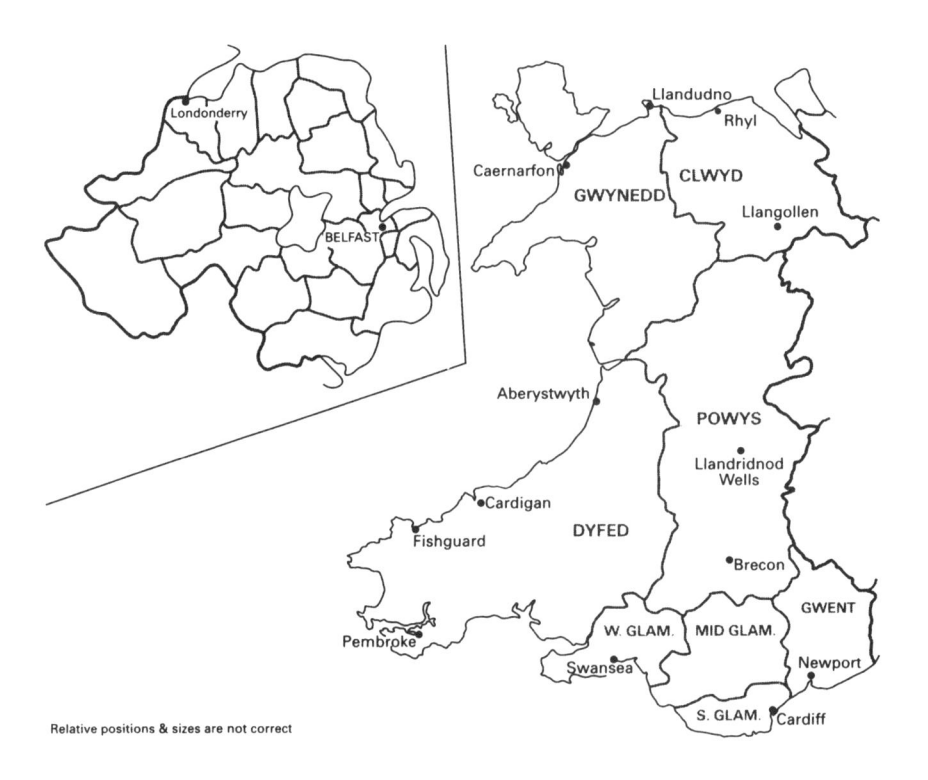

Relative positions & sizes are not correct

**Prospects for Work.**
*Wales.* Most of the seasonal jobs in Wales are to be found in hotels, restaurants and holiday centres. The towns offering the largest number of vacancies are Aberystwyth, Brecon, Cardiff, Llangollen, Llandudno, Newport, Porthcawl, Rhyl, Rogerstone, Swansea and Tenby. If you have some knowledge of riding, or are a good group leader, there are numerous riding schools and trekking centres in more remote locations; for those not local to Wales the advantage with this work is that accommodation will normally be provided. In the resort towns rented accommodation is limited and expensive.

Most Jobcentres, including those in Llandudno and Llangollen, advise jobhunters to contact them early. Local job ads appear in the *Brecon and Radnor Express*. The best paper for jobs around Llandudno is the *North Wales Weekly News* or the *Liverpool Daily Post*. Llandudno Jobcentre usually has a high number of vacancies for staff between April and September. In and around Llangollen, try the *Evening Leader* or the *Shropshire Star*. It is worth noting that there is very little chance of finding work with accommodation provided in the Llandudno area. In Tenby *The Tenby Observer* and *The Western Telegraph* are worth looking at while Swansea Jobcentre recommends the Thursday edition of *Western Mail* for jobs in the area.

Aberystwyth can offer a comparatively good supply of jobs – not only in pubs, hotels and restaurants, but at nearby holiday parks and caravan sites too. Rented accommodation in the town is limited since students from the local university take up most vacancies; this may be an advantage, however, in meaning short term lets are more available in summer. The local *Cambrian News* carries job advertisements.

In South Wales, Newport Leisure Services usually advertises vacancies for its playscheme in March or April each year. While Newport may not have the appeal of Llangollen or Brecon, it is one of the few towns in Wales to have plenty of rentable accommodation.

Call centres often recruit temporary staff, the main centres being in Cardiff and Swansea. Local Jobcentres have details of recruitment. Large manufacturing firms which may require temporary staff include Tetra Pak (who make cardboard milk and juice cartons) in Wrexham, the Driver and Vehicle Licensing Agency in Morriston, and R.F. Brookes in Rogerstone. Apply early to these firms and contact the necessary Jobcentre to establish whether or not application forms will be available.

The Royal Welsh Show in Builth Wells in mid July provides a number of jobs for a few weeks.

*Northern Ireland.* Over the last decade the economy of Northern Ireland has been the fastest growing of all the UK regions with unemployment rates now lower than some regions on the mainland, and strong economic growth. In and around Belfast most vacancies are in the retail, hotel and restaurant trade. Further afield hotel work is more plentiful in the lakeland areas of Co. Fermanagh and in seaside towns such as Portrush and Newcastle. Short term relief rangers are needed at the various country parks in Northern Ireland from April-May onwards, recruitment is through the local job markets. Students may register for seasonal work with private employment agencies or Employment and Training Jobcentres which are located throughout Northern Ireland. Holiday job vacancies for specific areas are usually advertised in local newspapers, job clubs and libraries.

# Business and Industry

**JOHN BROWNLEE:** Knockmakagan, Newtownbutler, Co. Fermanagh, Northern Ireland (☎028-6773 8277/028-6773 8275(home) or 07989-432131).
**Bottlers of Spring Water (2).** National minimum wage. Free accommodation at farm. Work available all year round. Overseas applicants welcome. *Applications* to Mr John Brownlee at the above address.

# Children

**ACORN ADVENTURE:** Acorn House, 22 Worcester Street, Stourbridge DY8 1AN (☎01384-446057; fax 01384-3788866; e-mail topstaff@acornadventure.co.uk.). Acorn Adventure is the leading provider of outdoor adventure camps for schools, youth groups and families. They operate 9 activity centres in France, Italy, Spain and the UK. Now approaching their 21$^{st}$ year of operation, their aim is the use the outdoors to provide

groups with 'an experience for life'.
**Instructors.** Must hold at least Instructor status with e.g. BCU or RYA, or have passed SPA or MLTB assessment. Other nationally recognised coaching awards may be considered.
**Assistant Instructors.** Must be registered as training for the above award(s).
**Support Staff.** Maintenance and/or catering. No experience necessary.
**Fully Qualified Nurse.**
 Please note that all staff must be available from April/May to September: full period only.
 *Applications* and requests for an information pack should be sent to the Recruitment Department at the above address.

**GRANGE TREKKING CENTRE:** The Grange, Capel-y-Ffin, Abergavenny, NP7 7NP (☎01873-890215; fax 01873-890157). Family-run guest house and trekking centre situated high in the Black Mountains, Wales. Remote area with breathtaking scenery; 8 miles to the nearest shops and no public transport.
**Nanny and Mothers' Help** required between April and November, wages by arrangement. Applicants should be 18+, duties include looking after 2 children aged three and four plus some cleaning, food preparation and waiting on tables.
 *Applications* to Jessica Grange at the above address.

## Holiday Centres and Amusements

**ANGLESEY MUSEUMS SERVICE:** c/o Anglesey Heritage Gallery, Rhosmeirch. Llangefni LL77 7TW (☎01248-724444).
**Seasonal Museums Attendants** to work in the museum shop, in ticketing and admissions, cleaning, security, guiding, customer care and stock control. Wages £4.30 per hour. To work from Easter until the end of September. All applicants must be available for the entire season. Min. age 18. Must speak Welsh fluently, and be a good communicator, organised and with an interest in museums and heritage.
 *Applications* to the Museums Officer at the above address before the end of February.

**ANGLESEY SEA ZOO:** Brynsiencyn, Anglesey LL6 6TQ (☎01248-430411; fax 01248-430213; e-mail fishandfun@seazoo.demon.co.uk). A family run public aquarium employing 30 staff and welcoming 100,000 visitors per year.
**General vacancies in catering and retailing** Wages £4.10-£5.95 per hour to work up to 39 hours per week. No accommodation is available. Staff required for a minimum of 2 months between March and October. Applicants should be over 16 and have relevant experience. A food hygiene certificate is desirable.
 Applicants should call or e-mail for further details and an application pack.
 *Applications* to Alison Lea-Wilson after January.

**BEAUMARIS GAOL AND COURT MUSEUM:** c/o Council Offices, Leisure Heritage Department, Llangefri, Anglesey LL77 7TW (☎01248-810921; fax 01248-750282). The gaol and court at Beaumaine is a specialist crime and punishment museum with a strong educational role.
**Seasonal Museum Attendants (5)** Duties include front of house work, reception, sales and customer care as well as operational maintenance and cleaning, care of the museum and guiding tourists around the museum. Wages £4.40 per hour; to work 30 hours per week from 10.15am-5.15pm on a 7 day rota. Applicants must be Welsh

speaking and available to work full-time from April 1st to September 30th.
*Applications* from early February to the above address. Interview necessary.

**GREENHILL YMCA NATIONAL CENTRE:** Donard Park, Newcastle, Co Down, Northern Ireland BT33 0GR (☎028-4372 3172; fax 028-4372 6009). Situated at the foot of the Mourne Mountains, overlooking the seaside town of Newcastle.
**Instructors (20).** To work up to 3 sessions per day. Experience or qualifications in one of the following is required: mountaineering, canoeing, orienteering, archery, environmental studies or working with young people on day camps. Min. age 18 but persons over age 20 preferred. Staff will be responsible for children and young people, so vetting references as to suitability in this area will be required.
**Drivers.** Must be over 25 years old, reliable, safe and experienced in driving minibuses and towing trailers. An up to date clean driving licence will be required.
**Domestic Hosts (5).** Must be hard-working, sociable and responsible.
**Cooks (3).** Basic cooking and catering qualifications necessary.
All staff are given expenses of £45 plus free B & L. Hours variable, 5 days a week in most cases. Min. period of work 6 weeks. Instructors and day camp staff must attend a staff training programme from 23 June to 30 June. The summer camp period is from 1 July to 28 August. Greenhill is a Christian Centre; applicants should therefore be supportive of its Christian ethos and promotion of the same. Applicants must speak fluent English and supply photocopies of relevant qualifications. One year Instructor posts (September-August) are also available for mature people who are active in the Christian faith.
*Applications* should be sent a.s.a.p. to the Volunteer Co-ordinator at the above address.

**HAFAN Y MOR HOLIDAY PARK:** Pwllheli, Gwynedd, North Wales LL52 6HX (☎01758-612112; fax 01766-810379; e-mail rhys.mann@bourne-leisure.com). Part of the Bourne Leisure Group. An all-action family holiday park on the picturesque Llyn Peninsula in the shadow of Snowdon.
**Staff** wanted for all leisure positions: Bar Staff, Catering, Staff, Chefs, Lifeguards, Sport & Leisure Staff, Retail Staff, Receptionists, Security Staff, Cleaners (400 in all). Needed from late March to early November. Wages in line with national minimum wage legislation, with increments according to age and experience. Uniform provided and attractive staff package.
With the exception of Lifeguards and chefs no qualifications are required, as full training will be given. Recognised qualifications can be gained in most positions. Live-in accommodation available to successful applicants aged over 18.
*Applications* to be sent to Personnel at the above address.

**PEMBROKESHIRE COAST NATIONAL PARK AUTHORITY:** Winch Lane, Haverfordwest, Pembrokeshire SA61 1PY (☎01473-764636; fax 01437-769045; e-mail PCNP@Pembrokeshirecoast.org.uk; www.pembrokeshirecoast.org.uk) A national park authority, responsible for building planning control, conservation and education regarding the environment within the national park.
**Visitor Centre Assistants (2) Site Guide Assistants (2)** to work from 2-5 days per week including week-ends. Applicants must be 18 or over with good communication skills and enjoy working with the public. It may be an advantage to have knowledge of the area.
**Coast Path Warden (1)** to work Monday to Friday. Applicants should have countryside skills. Main duty is maintenance of footpaths.
**Car Park Attendants (2)** working hours vary but will include weekends and holidays. Applicants should have good communication skills, experience of cash

handling and practical skills for machine maintenance.
**Summer Ranger Guide** working hours vary but will include weekends and holidays. Applicants should have up to degree level qualification in Tourism/Leisure or Environmental Studies.
For all positions the wage is £4.82+ per hour. Ability to speak Welsh is desirable for all jobs. Staff are required from March/April to September. No accommodation available. Information packs will be made available in 2003 and will also be available on the website.
*Applications* should be sent to Alison Wood at the above address during January and February.

**PRESTHAVEN SANDS HOLIDAY PARK:** Shore Road, Gronant, Prestatyn, Flintshire, LL19 9TT (☎01745-856471; fax 01745-855635).Part of the Bourne Leisure Group; an attractive all-action family holiday park near Prestatyn and Rhyl.
**Lifeguards, Pool Attendants, Bar Staff, Chefs, Receptionists, Retail Staff, Security Officers, Cleaners, Waiting Staff (250 in all):** Wages in line with National Minimum Wage, with increments according to age and experience. 39 hours of work a week including Public Holidays, daily hours vary according to job. 48 types of employment offered from April until late October.
Except for lifeguards no qualifications are necessary, as training will be given. No live in accommodation is available, therefore applicants must secure accommodation within the local area before applying.
*Applications* should be sent to Trevor Lewis, Administrator, Haven Leisure Ltd, at the above address.

**TRANS-WALES-TRAILS:** Pengenfford, Talgarth, Brecon, Powys LD3 0EU (☎01874-711398; fax 01874-711122; e-mail riding@transwales.co.uk www.transwales.co.uk). Based at a remote farm guesthouse in the Black Mountains of S.E. Wales: specialists in horse riding holidays for international adult visitors in the Brecon Beacons National Park. Ambient atmosphere, glorious countryside.
**General Domestic Assistants (2).** £120 per week. To work approx. 40 hours a week, with 1 day off which may be carried forward. Free horse riding, and free B & L. Age: 18-30 years. Duties include helping in the kitchen, bedmaking and cleaning. Assistants must be smart, responsible, of high moral standard and prepared to speak English clearly to foreign guests. Min. period of work 3 months between 1 April and 30 September. Overseas applicants with college-level English welcome.
*Applications* January to March to Mr and Mrs Paul and Celia Turner, Trans-Wales-Trails. Note: Only affirmative responses will be made.

# Hotels and Catering

**AMBASSADOR HOTEL:** Grand Promenade, Llandudno, North Wales LL30 2NR (☎01492-876886). A family run seafront hotel in the largest resort in Wales. Known for its unspoilt Victorian image, the hotel is close to Snowdonia National Park.
**Waiting Staff (2).** Wages by arrangement. Good conditions and hours. Free B & L. Must be over 17 years of age. Min. work period 2 months at any time of year.
*Applications* to Mr D.T. Williams, Proprietor, Ambassador Hotel.

**CAE-MOR:** The Promenade, Llandudno LL30 (☎01492-878101).
**Waiting staff (2)** for food service and customer care. Previous experience preferred, not essential. Hours to be arranged.
**Chamber staff (2)** to work 9.30am to 2.30pm approximately.

All from June to October. Pay at national minimum rate. *Applications* to Jacquie Marshall, Manager at the above address.

**CHIMNEY CORNER HOTEL:** 630 Antrim Road, Newtonabbey, Co. Antrim, N. Ireland BT36 4RH (☎028-9084 4925; fax 028-9084 4352; e-mail info@chimneycorner.co.uk).
**Waiting Staff (2), Commis Chef, Receptionist** required from 1st July. All posts work 40 hours per 5 day week, with the possibility of overtime, plus accommodation and meals on top of wages. Wages from National Minimum Wage (waiting staff may also get tips). The work is mainly restaurant work and overtime may be available at the hotel's night club. Training will be given for all posts; waiting staff should have a pleasant disposition, and applicants for receptionist should have good telephone skills and a basic knowledge of computers.
To apply *contact* Brenda Crawford, Manager at the hotel.

**CHRISTIAN MOUNTAIN CENTRE – PENSARN HARBOUR:** Pensarn Harbour, Llanbedr, Gwynedd LL45 2HS (tel/fax 01341-341646; e-mail office@cmcpensarn.org.uk).
**House Staff (4).** Wage and accommodation details on application. No qualifications necessary. To work 40 hours per week: min. period of work 3 weeks between March 1 and October 30. Applicants must speak English to a reasonable standard. The CMC is a Christian Centre and requires applicants who have a sympathy towards the faith.
*Apply* all year round to Mr R. Mayhew at the above address.

**CLARENCE HOTEL:** Gloddaeth Street, Llandudno LL30 2DD (☎01492-860193; fax 01492-860308).
**Waiting Staff (4)** to work from 7.30 to 10.30am and from 6 to 9.30pm. Some knowledge of food service and customer care preferred.
**Domestic staff (2)** to work 9.30am-2.30pm.
**Café Assistant (2)** to work 9am-5pm. Duties include food service, till and customer care. All required from June to October. Pay at national minimum rate. Minimum age 18.
*Applications* to Jacquie Marshall, Manager at the above address.

**COBDENS HOTEL:** Capel Curig, Snowdonia National Park, North Wales LL24 0EE (☎01690-720 243; fax 01690-720 354; e-mail info@cobdens.co.uk; www.cobdens.co.uk). Situated in the heart of Snowdonia, Cobdens is family owned and popular with climbers and walkers.
**Housekeeping/Bar/Waiting Staff (3).** Live-in with good rate per hour plus free food. To work 40 hours over five days per week. Experience preferred but personality more important.
**Kitchen Staff.** Must have a real interest in food.
Min. period of work 6 months preferred. Staff required all year round. Work is hard and to a high standard, but good fun. Overseas applicants with a reasonable standard of English welcome.
*Applications* any time to the General Manager at the above address.

**LAMPHEY COURT HOTEL:** Lamphey, Pembroke, Pembrokeshire SA71 5NT (☎01646-672273; fax 01646-672480). A four star country hotel and leisure centre set in a pleasant village near the coast. Under present owner for 20 years with a friendly team of 25 staff.
**General Assistants/Waiting Staff/Chamber Staff (2).** Wages £90-£160 a week.
**Breakfast Cook (1).** Wages £90-£160 a week.

**Gardener (1).** Wages £90-£160 a week.
All staff work 5 days a week. Min. work period 4 weeks, between Easter and the end of September. Some full-time positions are also available. B & L is available at £30 a week. Hotel experience helpful. Overseas applicants welcome.
*Applications* from February onwards to Mr or Mrs Lain, at The Court Hotel.

**THE FEATHERS ROYAL HOTEL:** Alban Square, Aberaeron, Cardiganshire, West Wales SA46 0AQ (☎01545-571750; fax 01545-571760; e-mail emma@feathers17.freeserve.co.uk). Originally an 18th century coaching inn, the Feathers Royal Hotel is now a modern well equipped hotel with a restaurant and conference facilities.
**General Assistants (4).** Live-in. Flexible hours and adequate free time. Must be energetic and adaptable. Min. age 18. Min. period of work the summer vacation. Overseas applicants with good working knowledge of English welcome.
*Applications* (with photograph) to Miss Emma Hunter, Feathers Royal Hotel or to emma@feathers17.freeserve.co.uk.

**FOELAS ARMS HOTEL:** Pentrefoelas, Betws-Y-Coed, Conwy, North Wales LL24 OHT (☎01960-770213; fax 01960-770150; e-mailfoelas-arms@btopenworld.com).
**Cook/Chef** needed. Wages by arrangement plus shared tips and accommodation. Period of work by arrangement. Minimum age 18 years.
*Applications* to Andrew Clutton, Landlord, at the above address.

**GRANGE GUEST HOUSE:** The Grange, Capel-y-ffin, Abergavenny, Gwent NP7 7NP (☎01873-890215). A small, informal family run centre situated in a very rural area, high in the beautiful Black Mountains, Wales. Remote area with breathtaking scenery; eight miles to the nearest shops and no public transport.
**Accommodation Worker/Assistant** to perform cleaning, waiting, taking 2 little girls aged 3 and 4 for a walk, gardening and customer care duties. Wages and hours negotiable, with free accommodation in a caravan with shower block. Min. period of work one month between Easter and October. Overseas applicants with good English welcome; preferable that candidates can visit for an interview, but not essential.
*Applications* should be directed to Jessica Griffiths from February onwards at the above address.

**LION HOTEL:** Y Maes, Criccieth, Gwynned LL52 0AA (☎01766-522460; fax 01766-523075). A busy 3 star hotel centrally situated in a seaside resort.
**General Assistants (Bar, Restaurant, Bedroom) (2).** £3.70 per hour depending on age. To work 39 hours a week over 6 days.
**Cook/Kitchen Assistant (1)** Wages £3.70-£4.25 per hour depending on age and experience. Clean accommodation is available, at a price to be negotiated. Min. period of work 4 months.
*Applications* from 1 March to Mrs S.A. Burnett, Manageress, at the above address.

**METROPOLE HOTEL:** Temple Street, LLandrindod Wells, Powys LD1 5DY (☎01597-823700; fax 01579-824828; e-mail info@metropole.co.uk; www.metropole.co.uk). Family owned and a member of the Best Western group, The Metropole is a 3-star Victorian style hotel with 122 bedrooms and extensive conference and banqueting facilities.
**Waiting Staff (6), Commis Chefs (4).** Wage at National Minimum Wage level. All

staff to work 5 days per week plus overtime if necessary. Min. period of work 4 months; staff required all year round. Accommodation available at a cost of £19.95 per week. Min. age 16 years. Overseas applicants welcome. All applicants must be available for interview.
*Applications* any time to Mr Nick Ireland, General Manager, at the above address.

**MIN-Y-DON HOTEL:** North Parade, Llandudno LL30 2LP (☎01492-876511; fax 01492-878169). Located on the north shore seafront, opposite the famous Victorian pier.
**Room Assistants (2), Hotel Assistants (2), Dining Room Assistants (2)** to work from June to October. Wages and hours by arrangement. Accommodation is available. Applicants should be under 21. Overseas applicants welcome.
*Applications* to the Manager at the above address.

**PORTH TOCYN HOTEL: Abersoch, Gwynedd LL53 7BU (☎01758-713303; fax 01758-713538; e-mail porthtocyn.hotel@virgin.net; www.porth-tocyn-hotel.co.uk). A country house hotel by the sea, filled with antiques. The house has been in the family for 50 years, and has been in the Good Food Guide for over 40 years.
GENERAL ASSISTANTS (10), ASSISTANT COOKS (4). Wages guaranteed above the National Minimum Wage. To work a 4½-day week in split shifts. Free B & L and use of tennis court and swimming pool. Intelligence and sense of humour required. Cooking experience useful but not essential. Min. period of work 6 weeks between March and November:**
Applications from those who are able to work over Easter and/or outside the summer university vacation period especially welcome. Travel expenses will be paid for those able to work for short stints over Easter and the spring bank holidays.
*Applications* with s.a.e. to Mrs Fletcher-Brewer, Porth Tocyn Hotel.

**ROYAL GATE HOUSE HOTEL:** North Beach, Tenby, Pembrokeshire SA70 7ET (☎01834-842255; fax 01834-842441; e-mail enquiries@royalgatehousehotel.co.uk). Family run hotel with superb views of Tenby harbour and Carmarthen bay.
**Waiting Staff (3).** To work 6 days a week. Shifts 7.30-10.30am and 6-10pm, plus some lunchtimes (noon-2pm). Min. age 18. Silver service experience preferred, but not essential.
**Chamber Staff (4).** To work 8am-1pm, 6 days a week. Min. age 18. Experience preferred.
**Bar Person (1).** To work shifts of 10.30am-3pm, and 6-11pm, 6 days a week. Also shifts of 11am-7pm and 7pm until closing in the residents' bar. Min. age 18. Experience essential.
Wages by arrangement. Some accommodation is available. Period of work March to November. *Applications* to Mr G.T.R. Fry at the above address.

**THE ST DAVID'S HOTEL AND SPA:** Havannah Street, Cardiff CF10 5SD (☎02920-313043; fax 02920-313075; e-mail ewarhurst@thestdavidshotel.com). The St David's Hotel and Spa, Wales' Premier five star hotel, is located at the waterfront of the Cardiff Bay development. One of Rocco Forte's Hotels, it offers excellent opportunities for staff development.
**Waiting Staff, Housekeeping Staff and Kitchen Staff.** Wages of £5.00 per hour.
**Spa Assistants** ; £4.50 per hour.
All to work five days per week. Fluent English essential.
*Applications* should be made to Elena Warhurst at the above address. Interview required for UK residents.

**TYN-Y-COED HOTEL:** Capel Curig, Betws-y-Coed LL24 0EE (✆01690-720331). A small friendly hotel in the centre of Snowdonia, which caters mainly for mountain users and tourists.
**General Assistants (4).** £120 per week for approx. 40 hours a week. To work 5 days per week on split shifts. Full board accommodation is included. Min. age 18.
*Applications* to G.F. Wainwright, Tyn-y-Coed Hotel.

## Language Schools

**ENGLISH STUDY CENTRE:** 19-21 Uplands Crescent, Swansea, West Glamorgan SA2 0NX (✆01792-464103; fax 01792-472303).
**EFL Teachers (3-4)** to teach adults or junior groups. £11-£12.50 per hour, 15 to 30 hours per week. Min. period of work three weeks between the beginning of June and the end of August. No accommodation provided. Must be graduates with TEFL qualifications and/or experience and able to speak English to the level of a native speaker.
*Applications* from March to Esther Richards, Principal, at the above address. Interview if possible.

**UNIVERSITY OF WALES ABERYSTWYTH:** Language and Learning Centre, Llandinam Building, Penglais Campus, Aberystwyth SY23 3DB (✆01970-622545; fax 01970-622546; e-mail: language+learning@aber.ac.uk). Attractive working environment in a secure seaside location between the coast of Cardigan Bay and the Cambrian Mountains. The centre offers courses to language learners and language teachers in a warm and welcoming academic environment.
**EFL Teachers(6-10).** £350 per week. 20 hours teaching per week, plus 16 hours social duties per month and 12 hours administration per month. Min. period of work one month between mid July and early September. B & L available. Applicants must speak English to the standard of someone who speaks it as a first language. First degree, TEFL qualifications and 3 years experience required. Interview necessary.
*Applications* from January 1 to Rex Berridge, Director, at the above address.

## Medical

**A & D NURSING AGENCY:** 1c Moorcroft Mews, High Street, Saltney, Flintshire CH4 8SH (✆01244-679111; fax 01244-677913; e-mail aandd.nursingagency@virgin.net).
**Qualified RGN, RMN and SEN Nurses** needed to cover for the sickness, holiday and maternity leave of permanent staff in various establishments including nursing homes, hospitals and industry. Wages £13.00-£19.00 per hour.
**Health Care Assistants** for care duties. Wages £5.10-£7.00 per hour.
Staff required at any time of year. Applicants should be aged between 18 and 65.
*Applications* to Debra Lee Mahon, Proprietor, at the above address.

**EVERYCARE:** 28 Carlisle Street, Splott, Cardiff CF2 2DS (✆02920-455300)
**Care Assistants** needed for ongoing positions. Wages of £4.50-£9.60 per hour, working hours to suit. Applicants must be over 18, with full driving licence, own transport and telephone.
*Applications* to the Care Manager, at the above address.

## Outdoor

**JOHN BROWNLEE:** Knockmakagan, Newtownbutler, Co. Fermanagh, Northern Ireland (✆028-6773 8277/028-6773 8275(home) or 07909-432131).

**Fruit Pickers (4-6).** Wages at piece work rates. Free accommodation at farm. Period of work September and October. Overseas applicants welcome.
*Applications* to Mr John Brownlee at the above address.

**DAVISON CANNERS LTD:** 107 Summerisland Road, Portadown, Co.Armagh, Northern Ireland BT62 1SJ (☎028-3885 1661; fax 028-3885 2288; info@davisonfreshfood.demon.co.uk). Harvests and processes fruit for retail, catering and bakery markets, mainly in the UK and Ireland.
**Fruit Pickers.** Wages at piece work rates. To work five to six days a week for approximately six weeks from September until the end of October. Accommodation is available.
*Applications* to Mr Ronnie Davison at the above address.

**NORTH DOWN MARQUEES LTD:** 39 Ballynathnett Road, Carryduff, County Down, Northern Ireland BT8 8DL (☎028-9081 5535; fax 028-9081 2344; e-mail northdown.marquees@virgin.net). One of the largest marquee companies in Ireland, established 20 years ago, always busy.
**Marquee Erectors (10).** Wages negotiable. Physically demanding work and hours can be long; applicants must be able to work under pressure and take responsibility. Positions are available from June to October. Foreign applicants welcome. No accommodation available.
*Applications* should be made from April onwards to the above address. Interview necessary, may be by telephone.

# Sport

**ARTHOG OUTDOOR EDUCATION CENTRE:** Arthog, Gwynned LL39 1BX (☎01341-250455; www.arthog.co.uk). A Local Education Authority run centre situated below mountains, about 1km from the sea. Fully staffed by 7 professional instructors, it takes up to 90 clients.
**Outdoor Instructors.** Activities include mountaineering, canoeing, sailing, walking etc. Wages according to qualifications. RYA, ML, or BCU qualifications useful, teaching certificate a bonus. Interested applicants without qualifications may be taken on, but on a voluntary basis. Work equivalent to 5 days a week, but long hours. Free board and accommodation provided. Overseas applicants considered.
*Applications* to Head Office at the above address.

**CANTREF TREKKING CENTRE:** Brecon, Powys LD3 8LR (☎01874-665223). Situated in the Brecon Beacon mountain range. Lots of riding involved and contact with a variety of people of all ages and from many countries.
**Pony Trekking Guides (2).** Wages on application. B & L available. Hours according to length of treks, with possibility of overtime. To work 6 days a week. Min. age 18. Pony Club B or BHS Stage 1, also Riding & Road Safety qualifications essential. Must be experienced rider and able to get along well with people. Period of work 1 June or 1 July to 1 September. Applicants must be prepared to work the specified length of time. Interview essential.
*Applications*, enclosing s.a.e., from March to M. Evans, Cantref Pony Trekking Centre.

**CHRISTIAN MOUNTAIN CENTRE:** Pensarn Harbour, Llanbedr, Gwynedd LL45 2HS (☎01341-341646; e-mail office@cmcpensarn.org.uk). A 50 bedded outdoor pursuits centre set in a tidal estuary within the Snowdonia National Park.

**Helpers.** £25-£70 per week plus full board and accommodation. To work 40 hours per week: min. period of work 3 months between March 1 and October 30. Overseas students with a high standard of English welcome. The CMC is a Christian Centre and requires applicants who have a Christian faith.

*Applications* can be made all year round to Mr M. Downey at the above address.

**CLYNE FARM CENTRE:** Westport Avenue, Mayals, Swansea SA3 5AR (☎ 01792-403333; fax 01792-403339; e-mail info@clynefarm.com; www.clynefarm.com). A converted farm complex on the Gower Peninsula with spectacular views. It offers a range of activities and accommodation from camping to self-catering cottages.
**Activity and Horse Riding Instructors.** Wages negotiable. To work 40 hours a week. Min. period of work 4 weeks from June to September. Accommodation may be available, charge to be negotiated. Min. age 18. Overseas applicants with good spoken English and eligible to work in the UK welcome. All applicants must be available for interview.
*Applications* from January to the Manager at the above address.

**GRANGE TREKKING CENTRE:** The Grange, Capel-y-ffin, Abergavenny, Gwent NP7 7NP (☎ 01873-890215). A small, informal family run centre situated in a very rural area, high in the beautiful Black Mountains, Wales. Remote area with breathtaking scenery; eight miles to the nearest shops and no public transport.
**Trek Leader and Assistant Leader** for a variety of work including mucking out, trek leading, tack cleaning, maintenance and dealing with customers. Some training available. Salary and hours negotiable. Free accommodation in caravan with shower block. Must be over 18 years old; first aid qualifications preferable. Also the possibility of looking after two little girls, aged 3 and 4, for a few hours a day.
    Min. period of work 1 month between Easter and October. Overseas applicants with good English welcome. Preferable that candidates can attend an interview but not essential.
    *Applications* from February onwards to Jessica Griffiths at the above address.

**HIGH TREK SNOWDONIA:** Tal y Waen, Deiniolen, Caernarvon, Gwynedd LL55 3NA (tel/fax 01286-871232; e-mail high.trek@virgin.net; www.hightrek.co.uk). A small company which offers guided walking holidays in Snowdonia.
**Trek Assistant (1).** £60 a week with free B & L. To work 5 days a week including some evenings. Duties include help with driving, group leading, domestic chores, etc. Applicants should be over 21, have a full driving licence, mountain leadership training and First Aid certificate. Must be very fit and have a strong interest in the outdoors and countryside. Should also have a flexible nature and be able to do anything from paper work to portering loads. Overseas applicants who fulfil these criteria will be considered.
    Min. period of work 6 weeks between Easter and October. Priority is given to those able to work the whole season. Applicants must be available for interview.
    *Applications* should be sent as early as possible to Mrs Mandy Whitehead, at the above address.

**LAKELAND CANOE CENTRE:** Castle Island, Enniskillin, Northern Ireland BT74 5HH (☎ 028-6632 4250; fax 028-6632 3319). An outdoor activity centre with activities including canoeing, sailing and mountain biking.
**Assistant Instructor (2), Kitchen Helper (1), Cleaner (1).** Minimum period of work 3 weeks from March to October. Free B & L. Minimum age 18. Applicants

must be interested in young people.
*Applications* from February, enclosing a photo, to Gary Mitten, Director, at the above address.

**MOUNTAIN VENTURES LTD:** Bryn Du, Ty Du Road, Llanberis, Gwynedd LL55 4HD (☎01286-870556; fax 01286-870454; e-mail bryn-du@lineone.net). Outdoor pursuit centre and water sports and activity centre. Provides residential packages for groups, including kayak and canoe paddling, rock climbing, abseiling and mountain walking from centres in the Snowdonia National Park.
**Instructors** needed: Mountain Ventures offers work opportunities as instructors to people who have appropriate qualifications and experience. There are also opportunities for summer assistant staff to take on work of a general nature, helping instructors and domestic staff in exchange for accommodation, food, some payment and the opportunity for some training in Snowdonia National Park during June and July, together with a group of other young people.
*Applications* to the above address.

**PGL TRAVEL:** Alton Court, Penyard Lane (874), Ross-on-Wye, Herefordshire HR9 5GL (☎01989-767833; e-mail pglpeople@pgl.co.uk; e-mail pglpeople@pgl.co.uk; www.pgl.co.uk/people). PGL Travel provides adventure holidays and courses for children. PGL has 25 activity centres located in the UK, France and Spain. Each year 2,500 people are needed to help run these adventure centres.
**Experienced Activity Instructors** in canoeing, sailing, windsurfing, pony trekking, multi-activites, drama, arts and crafts and English language. Qualifications not essential as full training will be provided. Minimum age 18.
**Group Leaders** also needed to take responsibility for groups of children, helping then to get the most out of their holiday. Previous experience of working with children is essential. Minimum age 18.
From £50-85 per week plus free B & L. Vacancies available for short or long periods between February and October.
*Applications* can be made online, or request a form from the above address.

**RHIWIAU RIDING CENTRE:** Llanfairfechan, North Wales LL33 OEH (☎01248-680094; fax 01248-681143; e-mail rhiwiau@aol.com; www.rhiwiau.co.uk.). Residential riding holiday cenre in Snowdonia National Park, catering for adults, families and unaccompanied children.
**Instructor/Ride Leader** to work from 8am-5.30pm, 5 days per week. Wages of £100 per week with full board provided. Must be aged over 18 and have either a BHS Preliminary Teaching or BET qualification.
**Assistants** to give general help in the house and organise evening activities. Wages £75 per week plus full board. To work from 8.15-10.15am, 12.30-1.30pm and 6-9.30pm, 6 days per week.
Period of work from June to September.
*Applications* to Ruth Hill, Proprietor, at the above address.

**SHARE HOLIDAY VILLAGE:** Smiths Strand, Lisnaskea, Co. Fermanagh, BT92 OEQ (☎028-6772 2122; fax 028-6772 1893; e-mail katie@sharevillage.org; www.sharevillage.org). The largest activity centre in Northern Ireland. A charity dedicated to providing opportunities for able bodied and disabled people to take part in a wide range of activities together. A team of 25-30 paid staff and volunteers works with families, individuals and groups of all ages.
**Outdoor Activity Instructors (6)** to work 5 days plus one night a week. Applicants

must be aged over 18 and have one of the following qualifications; RYA dinghy sailing instruction; BCU canoe or kayak instructor plus current first aid certificate; or RYA powerboat handling level II.
**Social Programme Activity Leaders (2)** to plan and run a programme of social activities including arts, drama, singing, storytelling, folk dancing etc. To work 5 days a week. Must love working with people and have plenty of different skills in arts, drama and dance.

Wages £50-£120 per week depending on qualifications plus meals and accommodation. To work from early May to the end of September/early October.

*Applications* to Katie Furley, Volunteer Co-ordinator, at the above address.

**SNOWDONIA RIDING STABLES:** Waunfawr, Caernarfon LL55 4PQ (☎01286-650342; e-mail riding@snowdonia2000.fsnet.co.uk) A trekking centre/riding school with approximately 50 horses including dressage/event horses, young stock and liveries.
**Trek Leaders (2)** Work includes care of horses, yard work, trek leading and light maintenance work. Wages on application: to work approximately 40 hours per week. Applicants must be over 18 with good riding ability. Staff are required from mid July to mid September. Overseas *Applications* are welcome. Accommodation is available in self catering caravans free of charge.

*Applications* should be sent to Mrs R. Thomas at the above address from Spring onwards.

**TAL Y FOEL RIDING CENTRE:** Dwyran, Anglesey LL61 6LQ (☎01248-430377).A friendly BHS approved centre on the shores of the Menai Straits. Facilities include indoor and outdoor menage, cross country training course, four miles of grass tracks, liveries, lessons and treks. Best Small Tourism Business in Wales 1998.
**Yard Staff/Ride Leaders (4).** £75 per week plus free accommodation in a caravan. To work from June to August; min. period of work 8 weeks. Must be qualified in riding and stable management. Overseas applicants who are available to attend an interview welcome.

*Applications* from January to Dr Judy Hutchings at the above address.

**TYN-MORFA RIDING CENTRE:** Rhosneigr, Anglesey LL64 5QX (☎01407-810072). The Riding Centre is situated on the West Coast of Anglesey at Rhosneigr within minutes of Anglesey's finest beaches. It is one of North Wales' oldest riding establishments, with beach riding a speciality.
**Trek Leaders Or Assistants (2)** to escort rides on the beach. Wages negotiable, according to age and experience. Hours: 8am-5pm, 6 days per week. Free B & L in caravan. Applicants should be aged 18+, be able to ride well and be responsible enough to take charge of rides. Season begins mid-May.

*Applications* from 1 April to Mr C.P. Carnall, Tyn-Morfa Riding Centre.

# Voluntary Work

## Conservation and the Environment

**CONSERVATION VOLUNTEERS NORTHERN IRELAND:** 159 Ravenhill Road, Belfast, Northern Ireland BT6 0BP (☎02890-645169; fax 02890-644409;

e-mail CVNI@btcv.org.uk).
Conservation Volunteers Northern Ireland is part of the BTCV, which involves over 70,000 volunteers each year in environmental projects throughout Northern Ireland, England, Wales and Scotland, making it the largest practical conservation charity in the country.
**Volunteers** to participate in practical conservation work throughout Northern Ireland. This includes community development work and use of practical skills etc. A number of week-long Working Holidays and Weekend Breaks are organised throughout the year or for those who wish to become Volunteer Officers, a commitment of at least six months is requested; types of positions available are: weekday officer, education officer, publicity officer, local groups officer, tree nursery officer and residentials officer.
To work 6 hours a day. No experience is necessary. Minimum age 18. Board and accommodation provided for Working Holiday volunteers at a cost of £66-£99 a week; limited amount of free accommodation for volunteer officers.
*Applications* for Working Holidays to Maddy Kelly, and for volunteers and Volunteer Officers to Lynn McCready, at the above address, at any time of the year.

**THE WILDLIFE TRUST OF SOUTH AND WEST WALES:** The Welsh Wildlife Centre, Cilgerran, Cardigan, SA43 2TB (☎01239-621212; fax 01239-613211; e-mail wildlife@wtww.co.uk).
The fourth largest wildlife trust in the UK, covering over 100 nature reserves. Concerned with educating people about the Welsh environment, and its protection and potential.
**Voluntary Assistant Wardens** are required for work on our nature reserves, including Skomer Island, a National Nature Reserve off the Welsh coast. Work can involve meeting visitors, census work, general reserve maintenance and wildlife recording, etc. Volunteers can work on a variety of reserves for periods from one week to three months. Island volunteers will work for a full week (7 days) or a maximum of 2 weeks between Easter and October 31. Self-catering accommodation is available free of charge. Min. age 16, and volunteers should have an interest in natural history. Overseas applicants welcome.
*Applications* should be sent to The Volunteers Co-ordinator at the above address.

# Heritage

**FFESTINIOG RAILWAY COMPANY:** Harbour Station, Porthmadog, Gwynedd, North Wales LL49 9NF (☎01766-516035; fax 01766-516035; e-mail tricia.doyle@festrail.co.uk; www.festrail.co.uk).
**Hundreds of volunteers** are needed throughout the year to help in the operation and maintenance of a 150-year old narrow gauge railway between Porthmadog and Blaenau Ffestiniog. The work done by individual volunteers depends on their skills, many of which are built up over a period of regular commitment to the railway which provides on-the-job training. The railway is divided into various diverse departments, and so jobs range from selling tickets and souvenirs to the 'elite' task of driving the engines.
Railway enthusiasts and non-enthusiasts of any nationality may apply provided they speak a good standard of English. Minimum age 16 years. Limited self-catering accommodation is provided for regular volunteers, for which a small charge is made; food is extra. Camping space and a list of local accommodation is also available.
*Further information* may be obtained from the Volunteers Resource Manager,

Ffestiniog Railway Company.
**WELSHPOOL AND LLANFAIR RAILWAY:** The Station, Pool Road, Llanfair, Caereinon, Welshpool, Powys SY21 OSF (☏01938-810441; fax 01938-810861).
Volunteer operated steam railway in mid-Wales offering working holidays in a leisurely atmosphere. Travels through the beautiful mid-Wales countryside in the delightful Banwy Valley. **Volunteer Maintenance Staff** (up to 10 at any time) for varied duties including the clearing of vegetation at any time of year. No pocket money paid, but accommodation available at cheap rates. Should be over 16, fit, healthy and enthusiastic.
*Applications* to the above address.

## Physically/Mentally Disabled

**SHARE HOLIDAY VILLAGE:** Smith's Strand, Linaskea, Co. Fermanagh, Ireland BT9 0EQ (☏028677-22122; fax 028677-21893; e-mail katie@sharevillage.org; www.sharevillage.org).
A residential outdoor activity centre for the disbled and the able bodied. Located on the shores of Upper Lough Erne activities such as day trips, barge trips, evening social events and a wide range of outdoor and art activities.
Share Holiday Village is looking for volunteers to work as **Carer Companions** to elderly and disabled guests who come on respite care holidays in the summer months. There are also limited places for volunteer outdoor pursuit instructors with relevant recognised qualifications e.g. RYA, BCU and First Aid Instructor Level. Approximately 200 volunteers are required for a minimum stay of 7 days from May until September. Shared accommodation and all meals are provided as are necessary travel expenses within Northern Ireland. Min. age 18.
*Applications* to the Volunteer Co-ordinator at the above address.

## Workcamps

**UNA Exchange:** Welsh Centre for International Affairs, Temple of Peace, Cathays Park, Cardiff, South Glamorgan CF10 3AP (☏029-2022 3088; e-mail info@unaexchange.org; www.unaexchange.org).
**Volunteers** required for international voluntary projects in Wales for social, manual, playscheme and environment projects. Usually 6-8 hours work per day, 5 days per week. Must pay own travel costs but free B & L provided. Min. age 18, no qualifications required. Period of work varies according to project but usually 2-4 weeks. Camps arranged all year round. Registration fee from £50. The UNA Exchange workcamps are primarily for overseas volunteers, though there are a few places for UK workers on some camps. Volunteers resident outside the UK must apply through the workcamp organisation in their own country. (British volunteers are also sent to projects overseas: registration fee from £90.)
Project leaders are also required. They are trained over one weekend in April, pay no fee and have travel expenses reimbursed.
*Applications* from March to the above address enclosing a s.a.e.

# Au Pair Home Help & Paying Guest Agencies

**Prospects for Work.**
Finding a job as a mother's help or au pair in Britain is comparatively and increasingly easy and is ideally suited to overseas visitors eager to improve their English. Families taking home helps are most common in London and the South-East, but mothers returning to work have brought a steady increase in demand nationwide. The majority prefer a commitment of six months to a year, but others require help for just two or three months over the summer.

The work may involve little more than light housework, playing with the children and some simple cooking. The pay, hours and training of au pairs in Britain can vary since the job is seen more as an opportunity to learn English and experience another culture than actual employment. So, while a few work longer hours, others are given great freedom, the use of the car and *Cordon Bleu* meals. Most enjoy something between the two and find working with a family to be a positive experience.

Hours vary according to the position: au pairs work 25-30 hours per week, *au pair plus* more than that, and *demi pairs* should expect to work about 3 hours per day. Mother's helps tend to work longer hours still, and are therefore usually UK nationals (see below). While the earning potential of qualified nannies has seen a dramatic rise recently, with the weekly salary of some as high as £350 with lucrative perks, au pairs should still expect to receive pocket money of around £45 or so per week. Mother's helps and au pairs plus can expect in the region of £60-£150. Free board and lodging is included. Qualifications are rarely required (except for nannies), but babysitting experience is always useful.

Changes to the law six years ago now permit the employment of males in what has been a traditionally female trade. Undeniably, au pairs remain predominately female, however the growing number of progressive agencies taking male au pairs find that increasingly more and more families are willing to try one and are in general pleased with their decision. Kingston College in Surrey recently began accepting male students on their National Nursery Examination Board nanny training course for the first time ever. Some agencies estimate that male au pairs account for up to 30% of the placements they make.

Many agencies specialise in the recruitment of home helps, and it is important to contact several in order to compare terms. Some may charge for their services, so check beforehand. You will be asked to fill out a questionnaire and should then receive a contract laying down working conditions, hours, pay, etc. Insist on being given more choice if you are not satisfied with the family allotted to you.

*Immigration:* nationals of the EU and of European Economic Area Countries are free to take employment in the United Kingdom including taking up 'au pair' placements.

Nationals of any of the following countries are also permitted to work as au pairs in the UK: Andorra, Bosnia-Herzegovina, Croatia, Cyprus, Czech Republic, The Faroes, Greenland, Hungary, Macedonia, Malta, Monaco, San Marino, Slovak

Republic, Slovenia, Switzerland and Turkey. Nationals of Bosnia-Herzegovina, Croatia, Macedonia, the Slovak Republic and Turkey must obtain a visa before travelling to the United Kingdom. Visa application forms (form IM2A) can be got from the applicant's nearest UK Overseas Mission with a visa section, or at www.ukvisas.gov.uk. Some au pair agencies only deal with EEA nationals.

The Home Office lays down certain regulations regarding au pairs; they must be single and without dependents; aged 17-27; should help in the home for a maximum of 5 hours per day, with 2 free days per week; receive full board, a reasonable allowance (normally up to £45 per week) and sufficient time to attend language classes.

The au pair should produce, on arrival, a valid passport and a letter of invitation from the host family giving full details of the family and household, the duties they will be expected to undertake, the allowance they will receive and the amount of free time they will have for study and recreation.

**3 TO 4 AGENCY:** Drift Hall, Bressingham, Diss, Norfolk IP22 2BB (☎01379-687324; fax 01379-687433; e-mail naomi@3to4-agency.co.uk; www.3to4agency.co.uk). Established since 1990, placing au pairs and nannies throughout the UK and in most of Europe.
**Au Pairs, Au Pairs Plus, Mother's Helps, Nannies.** Wages from £45 per week for au pairs and £55 for au pairs plus. The National Minimum Wage applies to mother's helps/nannies. Minimum stay 1 month. Agency offers comprehensive support, including accommodation in the event of a contract breaking down.

Applicants must be aged 17-27. Childcare/driving experience useful for au pairs; childcare experience necessary for mother's helps/nannies. Language not a problem.

*Applications* with references should be sent made to Naomi Rawlings, Director, at the above address.

**AAAU PAIRS UK LTD** 11 Roy Road, Northwood, Middlesex HA6 1EQ (☎01923-450714; fax 01923-833555; e-mail AAAUPAIRS@aol.com). Established since 2000, offering UK-wide placements.
**Au Pairs, Mother's Helps, Nannies and Housekeepers (up to 150).** Wages minimum £50 per week. To work 25 hours a week. Minimum stay 3 months for summer placements. Applicants must be able to provide references that can be checked – those already in the UK can sometimes be placed within one or two days. The agency tries to match applicants to families with similar interests.

*Applications* and enquiries to Mrs Savi Cockeram, Director, at the above address.

**ABBEY AU PAIRS AND NANNIES:** 8 Boulnois Avenue, Parkstone, Poole, Dorset BH14 9NX (☎01202-732922; fax 01202-466098; e-mail abbey.aupairs@virgin.net). Established in 1988, the agency places mainly girls with families around Bournemouth and Poole. Coffee mornings and language courses are arranged for au pairs.
**Au Pair Placements:** normal housework and childcare duties. Wages £45 per week for a 25 hour week, free accommodation. Min. period of work 2 months. Positions are available all year round.

*Applications* should be made at any time to Mrs Ursula Foyle at the above address.

**ACROBAT AUPAIRS AGENCY:** 31 Ella Grove, Knutsford, Cheshire

WA16 8UT (☏01565-651883; e-mail enquiries@acrobataupairs.com; www.acrobataupairs.com). Specialist au pairs agency with opportunities to work with families in Britain and learn languages at a local college or university.
**Demi Pairs (20)** for a maximum of 2-3 hours per day plus babysitting usually 2 evenings a week. Two days will be completely free for own leisure time. Own room and meals provided plus £15 pocket money a week.
**Au Pairs (70)** for up to 5 hours per day with 2 days off per week. Own room and meals provided plus £45 per week. Also opportunity to have English classes.
**Au Pair Plus (40)** for 30-35 hours per week plus babysitting 2-3 evenings a week. Two days free each week. Room and meals provided free of charge plus £60 a week salary. Can attend English classes.
**Nannies (20)** for 8-9 hours a day. Must have NNEB qualification or similar. Salary £120-£250 per week.
 All positions open for girls and boys aged17/18-27 years old. Vacancies range from 1 month to 2 years. Au Pair Plus for EC Nationals only and Nannies minimum age 18 years old.
 *Applications* welcome from all EC Nationals and Andorra, Bosnia-Herzegovina, Croatia, Cyprus, Czech Republic, Faroe Islands, Greenland, Hungary, Liechtenstein, Macedonia, Malta, Monaco, San Marino, Slovak Republic, Slovenia, Switzerland and Turkey.

**ACADEMY AU PAIR AGENCY:** 42 Milsted Road, Rainham, Kent, ME8 6SU (tel/fax 01634-310808; e-mail academy4aupairs@hotmail.com; www.academyagency.co.uk).Established for ll years and full members of REC. Staff are friendly, knowledgeable, and always available to assist in enquiries.
**Au Pairs.** £45 for 25 hours work per week. Must be aged between 18 and 27 with some babysitting experience. Non smokers and drivers preferred. *Applications* and enquiries to the above address.
**Au Pairs Plus.** £50-£60 for a min. of 30 hours work per week. Conditions as above.
**Mothers Helps.** Starting at £150 per week for a 40/45 hour week, must be experienced in sole charge childcare. Must be able to produce a current CV and references.
**Nannies.** Min. of £200 for 40/45 hours work per week. Qualifications required, such as BTECH, NNEB, NAMCW. CV and references required.
 Placements are throughout the UK from Edinburgh to the south coast of England. Work is available from mid June/early July to the beginning/mid September; min. period of work 2 months. Accommodation available at no extra charge. Overseas applicants welcome. An interview is not necessary for the au pair positions, but may be necessary for those wishing to work as nannies.
 *Applications* should be made enclosing an International Reply Coupon before the 1st of March to J Bosworth at the above address.

**ACE AU PAIRS:** 27 Chickerell Road, Park North, Swindon, Wiltshire SN3 2RQ (tel/fax 01793 430091; e-mail info@aceaupairs.co.uk; www.aceaupairs.co.uk). In business since 1999.
**Au pairs (150).** Wages minimum £45 per week (£50 in London). Some 6-week placements available, otherwise minimum stay is 2-3 months in the summer. Applicants must have proven childcare experience, and be aged 17-27. All nationalities eligible to work in the UK welcome. Male applicants usually provide police check.
 *Applications* with a minimum of 2 childcare references to V. Huntley, Proprietor.

Telephone interviews required with both agency and interested family.

**ANDERSON AU PAIRS & NANNIES:** 88 High Street, Hythe, Kent CT21 5AJ (☎01303-260971; fax 01303-230276; e-mail andersonau pairs@clan-anderson.f reeserve.co.uk; www.childcare-europe.com). In business since 1996. Member of IAPA.
**Au Pairs, Mother's Helps, Nannies** for placements in the UK. Also places people in the rest of Europe and America. Wages/pocket money from £45-70 per week for au pairs, more for nannies and mother's helps. Minimum stay 3-12 months. Summer placements can be made through partner agencies.
Applicants must be aged 17-27, have good childcare experience and some English. The agency offers a full advice service and 24-hour emergency number.
*Applications* should be made to Sarah Anderson, Director, at the above address.

**A-ONE AU PAIRS AND NANNIES:** Suite 216, The Commercial Centre, Picket Piece, Andover, Hampshire SP11 6RU (☎01264-332500; fax 01264-362050; e-mail info@aupairsetc.co.uk; www.aupairsetc.co.uk). This IAPA registered agency places au pairs and home helps; see website for details.
**Au Pairs/Au Pairs Plus** required for light housework and childcare 5 days per week. Wages from £45 per week for au pairs, from £60 for Au Pair Plus. Min. period of work of 2 months. Positions are available from June to September. Applicants should be 17-27 years old. Foreign applicants with acceptable spoken English welcome.
*Applications* should be made from March onwards to Mrs Hopwood, Proprietor, at the above address.

**ARNECLIFFE AU PAIR AGENCY:** Bwthyn Bach, Wilsill, Pateley Bridge, North Yorkshire HG3 5EB (☎01423-712709; fax 01423-712709; e-mail arnecliffeaupai rs@hotmail.com). A small, family-run service, aiming to provide personal support before and during a placement.
**Au Pairs** needed for various families in the UK and abroad. Pocket money of £45 per week, free board and accommodation with families in exchange for light housework/childcare. To work 15 hours a week. Min. period of work of 1 week. Positions are available all year. Applicants should be 17+ and preferably have childcare experience.
*Applications* should be made at any time to Jayne Humphreys at the above address.

**ARROW AU PAIR SERVICES:** Arrow House, 29 Mill Lane, Broom, Warwickshire B50 4HS (☎01789-491508; fax 01789-491200; e-mail info@arrowaupairs.co.uk; www.arrowaupairs.co.uk). In business since 2001, placing au pairs in England only.
**Au Pairs.** Wages from £45 per week. Minimum stay 2 months. Must be aged 17-27 and have permission to work in the UK. Childcare experience and some English ability necessary.
*Applications* via website or by phone to Michelle Parker, Owner. Telephone interview required.

**AU PAIR CONNECTIONS:** 39 Tamarisk Road, Hedge End, Hampshire SO30 4TN (☎01489-780438; fax 01489-692656; e-mail aupairconnect@aol.com; www.aupair-connections.co.uk). An Au Pair agency operating in Southern England; some of the loveliest locations in the UK. Good monitoring and recommended by

Au Pairs and families alike.
**Au Pairs/Mothers Helps (300).** £45 per week for au pairs and a minimum of £60 for au pairs plus. To work 25 hours per week or more. Period of work mid June-mid September; min. period of work six weeks. Must have a minimum of two years childcare experience and be at least 18. Accommodation available free of charge.
*Applications* from January to mid June to Denise Blighe at the above address. Note that all applicants must enclose either an IRC or a s.a.e.

**THE AU PAIR PROJECT:** 27 Oakfield Road, Clifton, Bristol BS8 2AT (☎0117-9744 779; fax 0117-9077 181; e-mail info@languageproject.co.uk). This is an agency which also has a language school and has long experience of working with foreign students. They arrange for au pairs to live and work in English families and can place around 50 suitably independent people in the Bristol/Bath area.
**Au Pairs (25)** To look after children and do some domestic work. Wages of £40-50 per week, full board and accommodation. To work 25 hours a week. Min. period of work of 4 months. Positions are available all year. Preferably aged 18-26 (those over 20 preferred), with good English and some previous experience helping with children.
*Applications* should be made at least 1 month before employment to Jon Wright at the above address.

**A22 AUPAIRS:** The Old Smithy, Fitzhead, Taunton, TA4 3JP (☎01823-401070; fax 01823-401071; e-mail enquiries@a22aupairs.com).
**Au Pairs (50)** required in June, to work 25 hours per week looking after children and carrying out light housework. Pocket money of £45 per week plus accommodation. Applicants should be aged between 17 and 27.
*Applications* should be made to Rebecca Haworth-Wood at the above address.

**AU PAIRS BY AVALON:** 7 Highway, Edgcumbe Park, Crowthorne, Berkshire RG45 6HE (tel/fax 01344-778246; e-mail enquiries@aupairs byavalon.com; www.aupairsbyavalon.com). In business since 1954. Incorporates Au Pairs of Surrey, European Au Pairs and Linden Bureau. Member of IAPA and REC.
**Au pairs (100+)** for families in the UK. Offers short term summer placements, minimum stay 8 weeks. Also has longer placements, minimum 6 months. Applicants must be aged 18-27; foreign applicants with permission to work in the UK welcome.
Write or e-mail Mrs Wendy Gibbings or Mr Gordon Gibbings by the end of May for information and an *application form.*

**BELAF STUDY HOLIDAYS:** Banner Lodge, Cherhill, Calne, Wiltshire SN11 8XR (☎01249-812551; fax 01249-821533; e-mail belaf@aol.com). Since 1975 BELAF has been organising holiday placements for European students in carefully selected families in Southern England, London and the surrounding regions, Wiltshire, Dorset, Hampshire, Gloucestershire and Somerset.
**Au Pairs (200).** £40-£60 per week plus accommodation. To work 25 hours per week from mid June to late August. Min. period of work 6 weeks. Min. age 18; all applicants must speak reasonably good English. Overseas applicants welcome.
**Work Placements (40).** 4-8 weeks throughout the year – in hotel, restaurant, tourism, engineering, schools. Minimum age 17 years.
*Applications* from January-May to Carole Browne at the above address.

**BUNTERS AU PAIR AND NANNY AGENCY:** The Old Malt House, 6 Church Street, Pattishall, Towcester, Northants NN12 8NB (☎01327-831144; fax 01327-

831155; e-mail office@aupairsnannies.com; www.aupairsnannies.com).
**Au Pairs.** Min. £45 for 25 hours and 2 evenings work over 5 days per week. Board and lodging included. Applicants should have some childcare experience such as babysitting. Must be aged between 18-27. Staff required from May to September, min. period of work 8 weeks. Overseas applicants with some knowledge of English and valid working visas welcome.
*Apply* before May to Mrs Caroline Jones at the above address.

**EDGWARE AND SOLIHULL AU PAIR & NANNY AGENCY:** PO Box 147, Radlett WD7 8WX (☎01923-289737; fax 01923-289739; e-mail info@the-aupair-shop.com; www.the-aupair-shop.com). Edgware and Solihull agencies have been established separately since 1963 and have now amalgamated.
Places **Au Pair** girls and boys throughout Great Britain and Ireland. Au Pairs live with the host family as a family member and have their own bedroom and full B & L, plus an amount of pocket money each week (approx. £50-£65). Pocket money is paid weekly in arrears. Period of work 6 months-2 years. Applicants must have permission to work in the UK.
For *further details* consult the above website or write to Amanda Pampel at the above address.

**EURO PAIR AGENCY:** 28 Derwent Avenue, Pinner, Middlesex HA5 4QJ (☎020-8421 2100; fax 020-8428 6416; e-mail europair@btinternet.com; www.euro-pair.co.uk). The agency supplies French speaking au pairs to British families in Great Britain and English speaking au pairs to French families in France. It takes great care in the selection of posts available and has a back-up service if things do not work out.
**Au Pairs (50+).** Wages of £60 for 5 hours work a day, five days a week, with free board and accommodation. Min. period of work of 12 weeks. Positions are available all year. Applicants should be 18+, childcare experience and driving licence helpful.
*Applications* should be made at any time to Mrs C. Burt at the above address. Telephone interview required.

**EUROYOUTH LTD:** 301 Westborough Road, Westcliff, Southend-on-Sea, Essex SS0 9PT (☎01702-341434; fax 01702-330104). Established in 1961, Euroyouth places Au Pairs, Paying Guests and School Groups, with or without language and sports courses. Au Pairs are placed throughout Britain, other positions are only for the Southend area.
**Au Pair** positions, all parts of the UK. Min. length of stay 3-6 months. Throughout the year.
**Paying Guest/Home Stays** in selected host families throughout the year in Southend, and Essex and some parts of London suburbs. Min. period of stay is 2 weeks. Sports courses are an optional extra. English language courses available in British Council recommended colleges in London for au pairs and paying guests throughout the year. All host families are personally known to the agency and every home inspected before bookings are made.
*Write* enclosing IRC/s.a.e. for details to Euroyouth, at the above address.

**GENEVIEVE BROWNE AU PAIRS:** Banner Lodge, Cherhill, Calne, Wiltshire SN11 8XR (☎01249-812551; fax 01249-821533; e-mail belaf@aol.com).
**Au Pairs.** Wages from £45-£50 for 25 hours work per week with board and accommodation. Usual au pair duties including housework and childcare. Min.

period of work of 4 weeks. Positions are available all year. Minimum age 18.
*Applications* should be made at any time to Carole Browne at the above address.

**JOLAINE AU PAIR & DOMESTIC AGENCY:** 18 Escot Way, Barnet, Hertfordshire EN5 3AN (☎020-8449 1334; fax 020-8449 9183; e-mail aupair@jolaine.prestel.co.uk; www.jolaine.com). Jolaine Agency has been successfully placing applicants in the UK and abroad since 1975 and operates a follow-up system to ensure that all applicants are happy with their stay.
Arranges **Au Pair/Plus and Mother's Help** positions in the UK throughout the year. Min. stay 6 months, max. 2 years. Payment is from £140 per week for a mother's help and £50-£70 for an au pair/plus. Also arranges Paying Guest family stays in the London suburbs throughout the year, from £85 per week. Accommodation available for individuals or groups of any size. Visits, excursions, activities and classes arranged on request.
For further information and *applications* forms write anytime enclosing s.a.e. or IRC to the above address.

**LARAH AU PAIRS:** 1 Paxton Gardens, Woodham, Woking, Surrey GU21 5TR (☎01932-341704; fax 01932-341764).
**Summer Au Pairs** wanted from June to September. Minimum stay 2 months. Approx. £50 pocket money for 25 hours per week. Approx. 5 hour day, 5 day week, but must be flexible. Must have childcare experience. Age limit 18-27 with at least basic English. Must have references.
*Applications* to the above address.

**LUCY LOCKETTS & VANESSA BANCROFT AGENCY:** 400 Beacon Road, Wibsey, Bradford, West Yorkshire BD6 3DJ (tel/fax 01274-402822; e-mail lucylocketts@blueyonder.co.uk; www.lucylocketts.com). In business since 1984.
**Au Pairs** for work around the UK. Pocket money £40+ per week. Childcare experience essential. Drivers and non-smokers preferred.
**Hotel Staff** from £140 per week.
Summer placements available, also longer stays (minimum 6 months). Interviews given where possible; placement takes about 2 weeks to organise after all paperwork has been received and checked.
*Apply* by May for summer placements to Lucy Holland, Owner, at the above address.

**MONDIAL AU PAIR AGENCY:** The Old Barn, Shoreham Lane, Halstead, Sevenoaks, Kent TN14 7BV (☎01959-533664; fax 01959-533504; e-mail mondialaupairs@aol.com; www.mondialaupairs.co.uk). Proprietor, Mrs Alison Freethy. The agency celebrated its 50th anniversary in 1999. It prides itself in matching applicants to families.
**Applicants** are placed mainly in London, Kent, Sussex and Surrey.
*Applications* should be made to the above address.

**MONDIAL PAYING GUESTS:** Four Wents Farmhouse, Goudhurst, Cranbrook, Kent TN17 2QD (☎01580-714714; fax 01580-720202; e-mail sales@mondialtravel.co.uk).
**Paying guest** stays arranged with families in south east London and the Weald of Kent for groups of students/individuals. For further details *contact* Mrs S.F. Roeder at the above address.

**MORTON AND DAIS:** The Stores Cottage, Warings Green Road, Solihull, West Midlands BN4 6BT (☎0121-7332433; fax 0121-2404411; e-mail nannies@waveri der.co.uk). A leading Nanny agency. Morton and Dais places UK nannies (including some men) in the UK and overseas. Minimum stay of 6-12 months, and summer nannies start in May. Nannies must be 18-28 and have experience of childcare. Nannies must have two or three childcare references and two character references. For both positions applicants should be medically fit. Personal interviews are required for Nannies. Wages are £70-£100 per week plus full board and accommodation.

Applicants should send a s.a.e. for an application form or telephone for more information.

**MUM'S ARMY LTD:** The Torrs, Torrs Close, Redditch B97 4JR (☎01527-402266; fax 01527-403990; e-mail marion@mumsarmy.u-net.com; www.mumsarmy.u-net.com)
**Summer Au Pairs.** £45 a week plus full board. To work minimum 25 hours a week. Duties include childcare, household duties and some cooking. Applicants should have common sense and some experience of looking after children. Non-smokers preferred. Driving would be helpful. Period of work June to end of September. Min. period of preferably 3 months.

For *application forms* write to the above address early.

**NORFOLK CARE SEARCH AGENCY:** 19 London Road, Downham Market, Norfolk PE38 9BJ (☎01366-384448; fax 01366-385226; e-mail viviennepartner@hotmail.com). Most work is based in the East Anglia region, and offers competitive salaries and good conditions for live-in staff. Country minded applicants are particularly welcome.
**Childrens' Nannies And Mothers' Helps.** £150-£200 a week plus full B & L. To work an 8-10 hour day. Positions available all year. Min. age 18. Staff must be based in the UK and have appropriate work permits.

Enquiries and *applications* to the above address.

**QUICK AU PAIR & NANNY AGENCY** 22 The Ridings, Norwich NR4 6UJ (☎0845-345 5945; fax 01603-455144; e-mail info@quickaupair.co.uk). Agency covering the whole of the UK and Republic of Ireland. A very caring, fast and efficient au pair placement service.
**Summer Au Pairs (30).** Wages from £45-£50 per week, free board and accommodation. To work 25 hours a week doing light housework and childcare duties with the possibility of overtime in the school holidays. Min. period of work of 2 months. Positions are available from mid-June to mid-September. Applicants should be 17+, have childcare experience and an ability to help with light housework. Foreign applicants welcome.

*Applications* should be made from March onwards via post or e-mail to Bryan Levy at the above. An application form is required, along with 2 character references, 2 childcare references, a 'Dear Host' letter, 2 (smiling) photos and a letter from the family doctor.

**RICHMOND & TWICKENHAM AU PAIRS:** The Old Parsonage, Main Street, Barton Under Needwood, Staffordshire DE13 8AA (☎01283-716611; fax 01283-712299; www.aupairsnationwide.co.uk). An established agency running since 1992, run by Vicki, who has been a Nanny/Au Pair. The agency places mainly French, Spanish and Danish girls, and all girls are given a second chance.
**Au Pairs (500 Per Year).** £45 per week plus accommodation. To work at least 25

hours per week all year round; min. period of work 2 months in the summer. Must have childcare experience, and be happy and confident with a good command of the English language.
Duties involve childcare, ironing, washing up and 2 nights babysitting a week. Applicants must be aged between 17-27. Overseas applicants welcome; interview is not necessary. Most au pairs are placed in south west London.
Applicants are requested to fill in *applications* forms available on the company Website, as above.

**ROWAN NANNIES:** The Rowans, Hollybush Close, Potten End, Berkhamsted, Hertfordshire (☎01442-876848; fax 01442-870865; e-mail rowannannies@hotmail.com). Agency established since 1991.
**Nannies and Au Pairs** for summer placements in the UK. Minimum stay the summer for these placements; 6 months for longer term placements. Foreign applicants with permission to work in the UK welcome.
*Applications* should be made to Lesley Samson, Owner. Personal interview not required, but application processing will take 2-3 weeks.

**SAPPHIRE AU PAIR/NANY AGENCY:** 4 Brookmans Avenue, Brookmans Park, Hatfield, Hertfordshire AL9 7QJ (tel/fax 01707-652187; e-mail sapphireaupairs@aol.com). Agency in operation since 1987, placing au pairs mainly in the UK but occasionally in Europe.
**Au Pairs, Mother's Helps, Nannies and Housekeepers.** Wages/pocket money £45 per week for au pairs, £80 for mother's helps and £150+ for nannies. Summer stays of 3-4 months available. Minimum age 19. Must have a fair or good knowledge of English. Driving licence an advantage. Foreign applicants with permission to work in the UK all welcome.
*Applications* should be made to Mrs Sapphire Ford at the above address. Interviews required where possible.

**SUPERSTUDY UK:** 1-3 Manor Parade, Sheepcote Road, Harrow HA1 2JN (☎020-8861 5322; fax 020-8861 5169; e-mail superstudy@btinternet.com; www.superstudy.com). An English language school based in Harrow, North West London. Open all year for work and study programmes and general English courses.
**Work And Study Students.** Students spend 15 hours per week as an au pair for their host family and 15 hours per week studying at the language school. They pay only for the language course and receive free board and lodgings in return for the au pair work. Work involves general housework and perhaps entertaining children. Students are required all year round, especially in July and August, for a minimum period of 8 weeks. EU and EEA nationals aged 19-29 with a reasonable standard of English should apply.
*Applications* at any time to the above address.

**UNIVERSAL AUNTS LTD:** PO Box 304, London SW4 0NN (☎020-7738 8937). Established in 1921.
**House Keepers, Nannies, Mothers' Helps,** etc. required, in both residential and non-residential positions. Must be available to sign on with the agency for min. of 2 months. Please note the agency does not place au pairs.
*Applications* at any time to Universal Aunts Ltd.

# USEFUL PUBLICATIONS

**GET 2003:** Hobsons PLC, Bateman Street, Cambridge CB2 1LZ (☎01223-273300; www.hobsons.com).
A careers guide for students that lists major employers; intended mainly for those choosing a career, but also a useful resource for those looking for vacation traineeships and internships. Normally distributed free to students, otherwise may be available for reference in careers departments or obtained from the above address. The website is a useful resource and offers other student career-related publications – click on the 'bookshop' link.

**ISCO PUBLICATIONS:** 12A Princess Way, Camberley, Surrey GU15 3SP (☎01276-21188; fax 01276-691833; e-mail info@isco.org.uk).
ISCO publishes the book *Opportunities in the 'Gap' Year* which is aimed at school leavers taking a year off before going into higher education. It gives details of paid and voluntary work, inside and outside the UK, as well as study opportunities. It also includes sections on the armed forces, expeditions and outdoor work. The booklet is available from ISCO or Amazonfor £5.95 plus £1 for postage within the UK.

**JOB MAGAZINE:** Jobs Subs, University of London Careers Service, 49-51 Gordon Square, London WC1H 0PN (www.careers.lon.ac.uk).
A weekly graduate careers magazine for London featuring part-time and vacation work as well as full-time graduate positions. A subscription costs £16 for twelve weeks (£25 in Europe and £31 other international destinations), including complimentary issues of Prospects today; to subscribe send cheques payable to the University of London to the above address, call 020-7554 4530 or e-mail job.ads@careers.lon.ac.uk.

**LIFETIME CAREERS PUBLISHING:** 7 Ascot Court, White Horse Business Park, Trowbridge, Wiltshire BA14 0XA (☎01225-716023).
Publishes *A Year Off... A Year On?* in association with the University and Colleges Admissions Service (UCAS). This is a guide to employment, voluntary work and working holidays for gap year students and anyone considering taking a break during their education or career. It provides information, addresses, and ideas plus a variety of accounts of personal experiences. The book is priced £8.99 (ISBN 0902876016).

**RECRUITMENT UK:** 24a Bristol Gardens, London W9 2JQ (☎020-7266 4947; fax 020-7289 6562; e-mail recruitmentuk@recruitment uk.net; www.recruitmentuk.net).
A quarterly magazine aimed primarily at Australians and New Zealanders looking for work in the UK,where it is primarily distributed, but it is also available free from the above address.

**TNT MAGAZINE:** 14-15 Childs Place, Earls Court, London SW5 9RX (☎020-7373 3377). A magazine available free in London from dispensers around tube stations that is packed with job advertisements; it is principally aimed at working travellers from Australia and New Zealand, but could be useful to any job-seeker.

**VACATION WORK PUBLICATIONS:** 9 Park End Street, Oxford OX1 1HJ (☎01865-241978; fax 01865-790885; www.vacationwork.co.uk). Publishes or

distributes the following titles in the UK.
*2003 May Supplement to Summer Jobs*(£6.00). Requirements for summer staff from employers in Britain and Abroad which arrive too late for inclusion in *Summer Jobs in Britain* or *Summer Jobs Abroad* are published in this booklet.
*Working in Tourism – The UK, Europe & Beyond* (£11.95). A comprehensive guide to short and long-term work in the tourist industry.
*Work Your Way Around The World* (£12.95). Contains invaluable information on ways to find temporary work worldwide, both in advance and when abroad.
*Teaching English Abroad* (£12.95). Covers both short and long term opportunities for teaching English in Britain and abroad for both qualified and untrained teachers.
*Working with the Environment* (£11.95). A guide to the enormous range of possibilities for short and long term work with the environment, both in Britain and around the world.
*The International Directory of Voluntary Work* (£11.95). A comprehensive guide to worldwide residential and non-residential voluntary work.

# ANY COMMENTS?

We have made every effort to make this book as useful and accurate as possible for you. We would appreciate any comments that you may have concerning the employers listed.

*Name:*

*Address:*


*Name of employer:*

*Entry on page:*

*Comments:*









*Have you come across any other employers who might merit inclusion in the book? (A free copy of a Vacation Work title of your choice will be sent to anyone who sends in the name and address of an employer subsequently included in the Directory.)*

**Please send this sheet to:
Andrew James or David Woodworth, Vacation Work,
9 Park End Street, Oxford OX1 1HJ, U.K.**

# Vacation Work publish:

|  | Paperback | Hardback |
|---|---|---|
| Summer Jobs Abroad | £9.99 | £15.95 |
| Summer Jobs in Britain | £9.99 | £15.95 |
| Supplement to Summer Jobs in Britain and Abroad *published in May* | £6.00 | – |
| Work Your Way Around the World | £12.95 | – |
| Taking a Gap Year | £11.95 | – |
| Taking a Career Break | £11.95 | – |
| Working in Tourism – The UK, Europe & Beyond | £11.95 | – |
| Kibbutz Volunteer | £10.99 | – |
| Working on Cruise Ships | £10.99 | – |
| Teaching English Abroad | £12.95 | – |
| The Au Pair & Nanny's Guide to Working Abroad | £12.95 | – |
| The Good Cook's Guide to Working Worldwide | £11.95 | – |
| Working in Ski Resorts – Europe & North America | £10.99 | – |
| Working with Animals – The UK, Europe & Worldwide | £11.95 | – |
| Live & Work Abroad - a Guide for Modern Nomads | £11.95 | – |
| Working with the Environment | £11.95 | – |
| The Directory of Jobs & Careers Abroad | £12.95 | – |
| The International Directory of Voluntary Work | £11.95 | – |
| Live & Work in Australia & New Zealand | £10.99 | – |
| Live & Work in Belgium, The Netherlands & Luxembourg | £10.99 | – |
| Live & Work in France | £10.99 | – |
| Live & Work in Germany | £10.99 | – |
| Live & Work in Italy | £10.99 | – |
| Live & Work in Japan | £10.99 | – |
| Live & Work in Russia & Eastern Europe | £10.99 | – |
| Live & Work in Saudi & the Gulf | £10.99 | – |
| Live & Work in Scandinavia | £10.99 | – |
| Live & Work in Scotland | £10.99 | – |
| Live & Work in Spain & Portugal | £10.99 | – |
| Live & Work in the USA & Canada | £10.99 | – |
| Drive USA | £10.99 | – |
| Hand Made in Britain - The Visitors Guide | £10.99 | – |
| Scottish Islands - The Western Isles | £12.95 | – |
| Scottish Islands - Orkney & Shetland | £11.95 | – |
| The Panamericana: On the Road through Mexico and Central America | £12.95 | – |
| Travellers Survival Kit: Australia & New Zealand | £11.95 | – |
| Travellers Survival Kit: Cuba | £10.99 | – |
| Travellers Survival Kit: Lebanon | £10.99 | – |
| Travellers Survival Kit: Madagascar, Mayotte & Comoros | £10.99 | – |
| Travellers Survival Kit: Mauritius, Seychelles & Réunion | £10.99 | – |
| Travellers Survival Kit: Mozambique | £10.99 | – |
| Travellers Survival Kit: Oman & the Arabian Gulf | £11.95 | – |
| Travellers Survival Kit: South America | £15.95 | – |
| Travellers Survival Kit: Sri Lanka | £10.99 | – |

### Distributors of:

|  |  |  |
|---|---|---|
| Summer Jobs in the USA | £14.99 | – |
| Internships (On-the-Job Training Opportunities in the USA) | £19.99 | – |
| How to Become a US Citizen | £11.95 | – |
| World Volunteers | £10.99 | – |
| Green Volunteers | £10.99 | – |
| Archaeo-Volunteers | £10.99 | – |

*Plus 27 titles from Peterson's, the leading American academic publisher, on college education and careers in the USA. Separate catalogue available on request.*

★ **Vacation Work Publications, 9 Park End Street, Oxford OX1 1HJ** ★
**Tel 01865–241978   Fax 01865–790885**

---

**Visit us online for more information on our unrivalled range of titles for work, travel and gap years, readers' feedback and regular updates:**

# www.vacationwork.co.uk